Outer Space

Problems of Law and Policy

About the Book and Authors

This book examines the international and domestic American legal problems associated with activity in outer space from a strong policy perspective, with particular attention given to problems associated with space commercialization and with military activities in outer space. *Outer Space: Problems of Law and Policy* is indispensable as a casebook, reference, and self-teaching tool for students, practitioners, academics, and members of the aerospace industry.

Glenn H. Reynolds, a graduate of Yale Law School, is an attorney with the Washington, D.C., office of Dewey, Ballantine, Bushby, Palmer and Wood. Beginning in the fall of 1989, Reynolds will be associate professor of law at the University of Tennessee. **Robert P. Merges,** also a graduate of Yale Law School, is associate professor of law, Boston University Law School.

Outer Space

Problems of Law and Policy

Glenn H. Reynolds
and Robert P. Merges

Westview Press
BOULDER, SAN FRANCISCO, & LONDON

Copyright © 1989 by Westview Press, Inc.

Published in 1989 in the United States of America by Westview Press, Inc., 5500 Central Avenue, Boulder, Colorado 80301, and in the United Kingdom by Westview Press, Inc., 13 Brunswick Centre, London WC1N 1AF, England

Library of Congress Cataloging-in-Publication Data
Reynolds, Glenn H.
    Outer space : problems of law and policy / Glenn H. Reynolds and
Robert P. Merges.
        p. cm.
    Bibliography: p.
    Includes index.
    ISBN 0-8133-7622-X
    1. Space law—Cases. I. Merges, Robert P. II. Title.
JX5810.R49 1989
341.4'7—dc19   88-31667
                                                                                  CIP

Printed and bound in the United States of America

The paper used in this publication meets the requirements of the American National Standard for Permanence of Paper for Printed Library Materials Z39.48-1984.

10   9   8   7   6   5   4   3   2   1

Contents

Preface and Acknowledgments   xiii
Introduction   xv

1 Some History and Background   1

SPACE HISTORY—*THE BRICK MOON*
AND ALL THAT, 1

  W. McDougall, . . . the Heavens
    and the Earth [The A-4], 3
  W. McDougall, . . . the Heavens
    and the Earth [Early Space Law], 5
  Some Observations, 10
  Further Reading, 11

THE SPACE ENVIRONMENT, 11

  Where Does Space Begin? 11
  What's It Like Up There? 12
  Meteoroids and Micrometeoroids, 13
  Vacuum and Microgravity, 13
  Getting There and Staying There, 14
  Rockets and Propulsion, 16
  When You Are There: What People
    Do in Space, 18
    Byerly, The Commercial/Industrial Uses of Space, 18
    Power Stations in the Sky, 20
  Further Reading, 23

2 The International Law of Outer Space: Basic Principles   25

  Introduction, 25
  The Roots of Space Law, 27
  Air and Sea Law: Rules Governing
    Overflight and Territorial Waters, 28
    DeSaussure, Maritime and Space Law, 28
    I. White, Decision-Making for Space, 36
    Center for Research of Air and Space Law,
      Space Activities and Emerging International Law, 38
  Notes, 42

UN Efforts and Aspirations, 43
McDougal & Lipson, Perspectives for a Law of Outer Space, 43
Notes, 46

3 Early Treaties Governing Activity in Outer Space   49

Jessup & Taubenfeld, The United Nations *Ad Hoc*
  Committee on the Peaceful Uses of Outer Space, 50
The Limited Test Ban Treaty, 52
Multilateral Treaty Banning Nuclear Weapon Tests, 53
Note, 55
  Matte, The Treaty Banning Nuclear Weapons Tests
    in the Atmosphere, in Outer Space and Under Water, 55
Note, 61
The Outer Space Treaty of 1967, 62
Multilateral Treaty on Principles Governing the Activities of States, 63
Note, 68
  Dembling & Arons, The Evolution of the Outer Space
    Treaty [Outer Space Treaty of 1967], 69
Note, 77
Sovereignty, Property Rights, and Space Resources, 77
  Christol, Article 2 of the 1967 Principles Treaty Revisited, 78
Notes, 82
Arms Control Provisions, 83
  Orr, The Treaty on Outer Space, 83
Note, 88
  Gorove, Arms Control Provisions in the Outer Space Treaty, 89
Notes, 93

4 Development and Defense: Treaties of the 1970s   95

The ABM Treaty, 96
Background, 97
  Treaty Between the United States of America
    and the Union of Soviet Socialist Republics [ABM Treaty], 97
Note, 98
The ABM "Reinterpretation," 98
Notes, 100
The Moon Treaty, 102
  Agreement on Activities of States on the Moon
    and Other Celestial Bodies, 102
  Nash, Contemporary Practice of the United States
    Relating to International Law, 110
Note, 115
  Spitz, Note, SPACE LAW—Agreement Governing the Activities
    of States on the Moon and Other Celestial Bodies, 115
Notes, 116
  Galloway, Issues in Implementing the Agreement Governing
    the Activities of States on the Moon and Other Celestial Bodies, 117
Note, 118

Walsh, Controversial Issues Under Article XI
of the Moon Treaty, 119
Notes, 120
Reynolds & Merges, The Role of Commercial Development, 121
Organizational Structures for Carrying
Out the Moon Treaty, 121
Galloway, Issues in Implementing the Agreement
Governing the Activities of States on the Moon
and Other Celestial Bodies, 122
Notes, 123
Christol, Alternative Models for a Future International
Space Organization, 124
Notes, 126
Goedhuis, Some Recent Trends in the Interpretation
and the Implementation of the Rules
of International Space Law, 127
Notes, 131
Dupuy, The Notion of the Common Heritage
of Mankind Applied to the Seabed, 132
Note, 133
Hufford, Ideological Rigidity vs. Political Reality, 133
Notes, 134
Developed World and Third World Views
on Space Development, 135
Finch & Moore, the 1979 Moon Treaty Encourages
Space Development, 136
Notes, 139
Dula, Free Enterprise and the Proposed Moon Treaty, 139
Notes, 144
Webber, Extraterrestrial Law on the Final Frontier, 145
Notes, 149
Rao, Common Heritage of Mankind and the Moon Treaty, 150
Notes, 152
A Note on the New International Economic Order, 152
Notes, 154
A Note on Common Property Resources
and Efficient Allocation, 155
Wihlborg & Wijkman, Outer Space Resources
in Efficient and Equitable Use, 159
Notes, 165

5 Other Treaties, Agreements, and Issues 167

The Liability Convention, 167
Cohen, Cosmos 954 and the International Law
of Satellite Accidents, 168
Notes, 175
Space Remote Sensing, 178
Logsdon & Monk, Remote Sensing from Space, 178
Notes, 185

Hamilton DeSaussure, Remote Sensing, 185
Principles Relating to Remote Sensing of the Earth from Space, 191
Rescue and Return of Astronauts, 194
Registration of Spacecraft, 195
Space Environmental Matters, 195

6 **Space Communications** 199

Space and International Telecommunications, 200
U.S. Regulation of Space Communications, 204
Office of Commercial Space Policy, U.S. Department
of Commerce, Space Commerce, 204
Note, 206
Senior Interagency Group on International
Communication and Information Policy, A White
Paper on New International Satellite Systems, 206
Notes, 217
Department of State [Legal Memorandum], 219
Notes, 225
Direct Satellite Broadcasting, 226

7 **Space-Related International Trade Issues** 229

Economics of Space Industries, 230
Reynolds & Merges, Toward an Industrial Policy for Outer Space, 231
Before the Office of the United States Trade Representative
Chairwoman, Section 301 Committee [Transpace Petition], 232
Note, 234
Determination Under Section 301 of the Trade Act of 1974, 235
Notes, 236
Glenn Reynolds & John Ragosta, International Trade in
Launch Services, 237
Note, 238
Export Controls and Trade in Space-Related
Goods and Services, 238
McFadden, Snyder & Schoettler, The Structure
of Export Licensing, 241
Notes, 244

8 **The Law of Private Commercial
Activities in Outer Space** 247

Jurisdiction, 248
Office of Technology Assessment, Space Stations and the Law, 248
Notes, 254
Tort Law, 258
Office of Technology Assessment, Space Stations and the Law, 258
Note on Liability: Approaches and Standards, 264
42 U.S.C. § 2458b. Insurance and Indemnification, 267
Comments on Proposed Regulations Governing Third-Party Liability
Insurance for Commercial Space Launch Activities, 268

Liability for Damage to Cargo, 270
The *Challenger* Disaster, 272
Contracts Relating to Outer Space, 273
  Contract for Launch Services, 274
Notes, 277
Sample Launch Agreement, 278
  Based on Agreement Between the United States of America
    Represented by the National Aeronautics and Space
    Administration and Satellite Business Systems for Launch
    and Associated Services, 278
Notes, 280
Intellectual Property, 282
  U.S. House of Representatives, 99th Cong., 2d Sess.,
    Rept. 99–788, 283
  H.R. 2725, 99th Congress, 1st Session, 286
Protecting Trade Secrets in Space, 289
  Reynolds, Book Review, 289
Administrative Law: Regulation and Deregulation
  of Space Activities, 290
  Commercial Space Launch Act of 1984, 290
Notes, 294
  Rules and Regulations, Department of Transportation, 295
The Land Remote Sensing Commercialization Act, 299
  Land Remote Sensing Commercialization Act of 1984, 299
Remote Sensing Regulations, 301
  Civilian Remote Sensing Licensing Regulations, 302
Criticisms of Remote Sensing Regulations, 303
  Merges & Reynolds, News Media Satellites
    and the First Amendment, 303
Note, 304
Extraterrestrial Contamination, 304

9 Some Issues of the Future   307

Governance of Space Societies, 307
  Space Settlements and the Law: Address of Justice
    William J. Brennan, Jr., 307
  Ragosta & Reynolds, In Search of Governing Principles, 309
  Declaration of First Principles for the Governance of Outer
    Space Societies, 310
  Remarks of William J. Brennan, Jr., Associate Justice,
    Supreme Court of the United States, 314
Notes, 316
Contact with Extraterrestrials, 317

10 Conclusion   325

Reynolds, Structuring Development in Outer Space, 326

Credits   331
Index   337

Preface and Acknowledgments

Writing a book has been compared to giving birth; the comparison is apt, except that few books are gestated in as short a time as nine months, and more people generally provide assistance in the conception and bringing to term of books than of children. The initial impetus toward this book came from a review of the two seminal works in space law, Andrew Haley's *Space Law and Government,* and Myres McDougal, Harold Lasswell, and Ivan Vlasic's *Law and Public Order in Space,* both of which were published in 1963. Despite all that has changed since then, those books remain in many ways the cornerstones of the field, and it is unlikely that anyone will match their breadth and depth for some time.

For all their many virtues, however, those books are not really suitable for use as teaching tools. The very depth of their coverage, and the broad range of the topics addressed, means that much must be passed over lightly or skipped entirely, and the passage of time has resulted in many changes— such as the adoption of the Outer Space Treaty of 1967 and the development of a commercial space launch industry—that render them incomplete or obsolete in places. Given that more and more law schools are teaching space law, the time seemed right for a volume in casebook-format that would be of use in law schools and as an entry point into the field for interested practitioners, scholars, and policymakers.

In developing our approach to this subject, we circulated a number of outlines to attorneys, scholars, government officials, and members of the industry. Among those who commented at some length (mostly favorably, and always constructively) were Dennis Ahearn, Walter Boyne, Robert Brumley, Richard DalBello, Arthur Dula, Nathan Goldman, Jefferson Hofgard, Neil Hosenball, Diana Josephson, John Logsdon, W. Michael Reisman, George Robinson, Courtney Stadd, and Jason Steptoe. In addition, we circulated draft chapters for review, and many individuals provided valuable input there as well. Among them were Walter Boyne, Heidi Ebel, Albert Halprin, John Ragosta, Gerald Rosberg, James Schoettler, and Josephine Stein. Among other individuals who provided helpful advice and equally helpful encouragement, were Joseph Califano, Lori Garver, Maria Hylton, Harold Edgar, Clark McFadden, Gueta Mezzetti, Peter Schuck, Douglas Weinstein, and, most especially, our excellent and long-suffering editor at Westview Press, Kellie Masterson, and her two able assistants, Mary Beth Nierengarten and Ellen Williams. Valuable research and organizational assistance was provided by several future lawyers of note: Rene

Augustine of Vanderbilt Law School, Cheryl Hesse of U.Va., Nina Nichols of Harvard, Laura Plessala of Georgetown, and Jamie Saltman of N.Y.U. and by the energetic and talented library staff at Dewey, Ballantine, Bushby, Palmer & Wood, Washington, D.C. We must also thank Dr. Charles Reynolds for being kind enough to make the palatial quarters of his so-called "cabin" on Norris Lake in the mountains of Tennessee available for extensive interruption-free drafting sessions. Neither he nor any of the other individuals named here is responsible for any errors that slipped through.

For reasons that immediately become apparent once one begins writing, the acknowledgments in virtually every book bestow enormous praise on the hapless typist responsible for the manuscript. In the case of this work, the misfortune was divided among the various and talented members of the word processing staff at Dewey, Ballantine, Bushby, Palmer & Wood. For their first-rate work, we too extend enormous (and well deserved) praise; if law professors got such high-quality support, the law reviews would all be twice as thick, which may be the reason why they don't.

A Note on Style

Since this book is organized as a casebook, it contains a considerable quantity of excerpted material. Except in the case of obvious typographical errors (which we have taken the liberty of correcting in a few cases), all excerpted material retains its original punctuation and emphasis. We have omitted footnotes, inserting especially important citations in brackets in the text. In general, however, we have tried to keep the number of citations manageable: This book is meant to be used in the classroom, not as a reference manual, and we have striven to guide readers to primary sources rather than provide a comprehensive bibliography ourselves. Those desiring all citations contained in excerpted material may, of course, refer to the originals. Excerpt titles are indicated in centered, bold-faced headings; excerpt ends are indicated by a centered ruler line. In light of the fact that this book will probably be used by nonlawyers, we have spelled out all names of journals, etc., in full, thus sparing the readers the arcana of bluebook abbreviations. In all other significant respects we have followed bluebook style to the best of our ability, though not all of the material excerpted does the same. We trust that the law review managing editors among our readers will forgive us.

Glenn H. Reynolds
Robert P. Merges

Introduction

To many, "space law" still belongs to the realm of science fiction. Yet many real-life lawyers work in the field already, and their numbers are growing rapidly. Their work cuts across the boundaries of traditional legal disciplines—from commercial law and contracts to international law and even torts—but is unified, like that of Admiralty lawyers, by the demands of an industry with unique problems. That industry is growing steadily and is placing new demands on its legal counsel (and on government officials responsible for regulating the area) every day. Furthermore, study of the problems faced (and created) by space industries and other uses of space helps to shed light on issues growing from high technology areas in general and is thus a useful part of an overall legal education.

In response, many law schools have begun teaching courses in space law, and many practitioners have had to educate themselves in an *ad hoc* manner. What has been lacking, though, is a comprehensive introduction to the subject. That is the purpose of this book.

The book is organized around the needs of the space industry and those who deal with it. As private companies become involved in providing launch services and in conducting research and manufacturing in outer space, and as governments band together for multinational space stations and other ventures, legal questions are raised that touch on virtually every subject in the law school curriculum, but in new settings. As a consequence, it is not enough for a lawyer in this industry to know just the traditional legal subjects; she must also know how to apply that knowledge to the special needs of the industry—although space contracts are still contracts, to be useful they must anticipate the kinds of problems that are likely to arise only in this industry. Those in the industry, meanwhile, will find it useful to familiarize themselves with the legal issues that are likely to be important to them.

In addition, it helps immeasurably to know something about the technical and scientific basis for the industry. One need not know how to design a rocket engine, or how to service a satellite. Nor does one need an exhaustive knowledge of the history behind the industry and the legal regime that has grown up around it. But to understand the problems the industry is likely to present, it will help to know something about the basics. For this reason, we provide a brief introduction to the history and technology behind the industry, as well as extensive references to the literature on those subjects.

Because government has traditionally played a major role in the shaping of the industry, lawyers and clients alike are likely to have to persuade policymakers to pay attention to their particular problems for some time. For that matter, law schools (both in the United States and, increasingly, in other countries) are key training grounds for future policymakers, meaning that those taking courses in this area may well be the space decision-makers of the future. For these reasons, we pay considerable attention to the policy issues involved, both in the context of individual areas of the law and more general discussions of various policy issues.

We also discuss a wide variety of international law issues. Many, like the jurisdictional provisions of the Outer Space Treaty, touch directly on the space industry. Others, like the ABM Treaty, do not. All, however, are an important part of space law and form part of the background against which events take place. And, of course, international law issues are of considerable importance to government lawyers and to policymakers.

Most legal texts are casebooks. That presents a problem in the aerospace field because there are so few cases. But the casebook format has many advantages, providing a variety of viewpoints and a sense of how legal rules are applied in courts. In addition, it presents the subject matter in discrete units, allowing the teacher more flexibility in organizing a course. With this in mind, we have emulated the casebook format by including excerpts from leading publications and from key legal sources such as treaties and statutes. However, in order to provide context and background, and to remedy gaps in the published literature, we provide a much greater than usual amount of original commentary and notes. Discussion points and study questions, along with references to additional reading, are also included. The result, we hope, is a book that will be useful both as a text in law school classes and as a tool for self-education by practitioners and interested people both within and outside the legal profession.

If the space industry is to develop as it should, there must be a body of law that supports its growth. That law is developing now, through the efforts of scholars and practitioners. It is our sincere hope, reflected in the pages of this book, that we can contribute to this process.

G.H.R.
R.P.M.

1

Some History and Background

This is a book about space law, not the history and technology of space exploration. But just as lawyers in other fields must know something (often a great deal) about their clients, lawyers serving the space industry must know something about the context in which they work. This brief introductory chapter provides an overview of how spaceflight (and space law) came to be a reality, of the key technical concepts needed to understand many important issues, and of the industry's directions in the future, along with a number of references for further reading. Readers are strongly encouraged to pursue those references, as what is set out here is the briefest synopsis (a "capsule version," if you will) of a rich and interesting literature.

SPACE HISTORY—*THE BRICK MOON* AND ALL THAT

The idea of space travel is not new—trips to the Moon and beyond have been the subject of fanciful tales for thousands of years. But not until the last century or so did people begin seriously examining the methods and implications of going into space. It is amazing, in retrospect, how much of the work of early pioneers has remained useful—even essential— to carrying out operations in space, and how clearly some of those early figures foresaw the problems and opportunities that would arise as human beings moved into outer space.

One of the first to do so, and in many ways the undisputed pioneer of space studies, was a Russian, Konstantin Tsiolkovsky. Tsiolkovsky's work, which started over a century ago, laid the foundation for many technological developments that followed, and anticipated much that still seems futuristic today. In 1883 he wrote of the problems likely to be encountered in zero gravity; in 1903 he published an essay entitled *Exploration of Cosmic Space with Reactive Devices* that outlined the principles of navigation in space. Throughout the rest of his life, he wrote and pondered not only the practical, but the philosophical aspects of outer space development.

Tsiolkovsky envisioned an era in which space exploration would lead to cities in space and, ultimately, to utopian societies throughout the solar system—a vision shared by many space supporters today. Because these societies would have access to unlimited solar energy and to all the resources of the solar system's planets and asteroids, Tsiolkovsky reasoned, they would be free from the scarcities that plague earthbound economies and hence free from social problems stemming from unequal distribution of wealth. When the Bolsheviks came to power in 1917, they found Tsiolkovsky's theories well-suited to their own professed belief that social injustices stemmed from unequal distribution of wealth—and found research into rockets a promising part of efforts (first by Lenin, then by Stalin) to build up the Soviet Union's technological base and armaments industry. Tsiolkovsky, previously an obscure schoolteacher, received a seat on the Soviet Academy, and his disciples (such as Sergei Korolev, F.A. Tsander, and Valentin Glushko) began serious work on rocketry, work that was to lead to a succession of firsts by the Soviet Union in the late 1950s and early 1960s.

Although Tsiolkovsky was the first to conduct serious study into problems of space flight, many others were soon doing the same—indeed, the American Edward Everett Hale had published a science fiction story about an artificial satellite used for navigation, entitled *The Brick Moon,* in the *Atlantic Monthly* as early as 1869. Serious work on the subject in the United States, however, began with Robert Goddard. Goddard published a paper in 1919 entitled *A Method of Reaching Extreme Altitudes* that described the prospects for reaching outer space using rockets. Although many skeptics (including the editors of the *New York Times*) subjected Goddard to ridicule for what were then thought of as far-fetched ideas (such as sending a probe to the Moon), he devoted his life to the perfection of liquid-fueled rockets and provided considerable inspiration and information to the German rocket pioneers who began organizing in the early 1920s. Goddard was the first to successfully launch a liquid-fueled rocket, and the first to demonstrate a working guidance system. Aside from Goddard, various groups of enthusiasts in the United States such as the American Rocket Society, the Cleveland Rocket Society, and the Yale Rocket Club did significant initial work in the development of rocket technology and in laying other important groundwork for later space exploration efforts.

In Britain, meanwhile, the Explosives Act of 1875 (which banned all private research in ordnance) proved a near-absolute barrier to actual experimentation, providing a concrete example of how bad or shortsighted law can frustrate space development. This did not stop British enthusiasts from contributing, however—it simply forced the British Interplanetary Society, including individuals like Phil Cleator and Arthur C. Clarke, to devote energies to long range studies, such as a famous 1939 plan for a Moon mission that served as the foundation for the actual Moon landing thirty years later.

Germany, too, had its pioneer in Hermann Oberth, who in 1923 published *Die Rakete zu den Planetenaumen* (The Rocket into Planetary Space). Oberth's book was far more ambitious than Goddard's work, discussing ways of putting human beings into space in the (relatively) near term and the problems (such as the need for space suits, the composition of space food, and the minutiae of operating space stations) that would have to be overcome. Oberth's book was followed in short order by a number of works by other German enthusiasts, most notably Walter Hohmann, whose 1925 work on celestial mechanics set out principles still relied on today and for whom the economical "Hohmann transfer orbit" used by interplanetary space probes is named.

The next twenty years were to see a flowering of German rocket science (unhampered by Explosives Laws) that began with small groups of dedicated individuals and culminated with the immense government-financed effort that produced the V-2 missile (designated the A-4 by its inventors). The V-2 was of dubious value as a weapon of war—each missile cost as much to build as a bomber, delivered a smaller load of explosives, and was destroyed at the end of a single mission—but it was the first really viable space booster.

W. McDougall, . . . the Heavens and the Earth: A Political History of the Space Age 43 (1985)

The A-4

In 1929 the Ordnance Ballistic Section of the German army assigned Walter Dornberger to develop a liquid fuel rocket of longer range than any existing gun, a sobering assignment, given that the Big Berthas of World War I fired projectiles sixty-five miles. Dornberger visited the "rocketport" of the amateur Verein fur Raumschiffahrt in Berlin, set young Wernher von Braun to work completing his doctorate, and together they recruited the Rocket Team. Just as in the Soviet Union, the rocketeers did not find state support—the state found them, and at a propitious moment. "The more time I have to think about it," wrote Willy Ley, "the more I have arrived at the conclusion that the VfR progressed as far as any club can progress. . . . Experimentation had reached a state where continuation would have been too expensive for any organization except a millionaires' club."

Von Braun and Dornberger chose for their lonely, spacious test site a sweep of sandy coast on the Usedom Peninsula beyond the mouth of the Peene River. But by the time Peenemunde opened in the fall of 1939, the Wehrmacht was rolling over Poland, and Hitler decided the big rockets would not be needed. Von Braun and Dornberger pressed on, with reduced budgets, toward a prototype of their majestic A-4, the first medium-range ballistic missile, standing 46.1 feet high. It was a single-stage rocket powered by LOX [liquid oxygen] and alcohol, developing a thrust of 56,000 pounds, a payload of 2,200 pounds, and a velocity of 3,500 miles per hour while inertially guided by gyroscopes and leveling pendulums to its target 200 miles distant. The first A-4 flight test finally took place in June 1942. It failed, and so did the next. But the third bird, in October, rose from the Baltic dunes in a stable and gentle arc fifty miles high until it passed out of sight en route to the impact area 119 miles downrange. Dornberger's team watched in exultation—like the Alamogordo physicists three years later, they attended in the delivery room as a new Power was born. But where the elemental blast of the atomic bomb rendered its makers diminished, apprehensive, in a sense imprisoned, the elegant, finned cylinder of the A-4 was a metaphor of liberation, defying gravity as it soared aloft with little hint—after the first moments—of the brute force it contained. An aspiring and creative thing, it had brushed the sleeves of space.

Although their work was financed by the military and led to the V-2, von Braun's team secretly dreamed of building rockets that would carry human beings into outer space. Unbeknownst to their superiors, the German rocket teams designed larger and more powerful rockets, winged spacecraft, and atmosphere-skipping rocket/ramjet space planes. With the end of World War Two, von Braun and virtually all of his key staff signed on to work for the United States, bringing their designs and the remaining stock of V-2s with them.

The immediate postwar period saw a brief flurry of interest in space activity. The exploits of the German rocket scientists were still fresh in everyone's mind, which lent credibility to plans that would have been thought outlandish in the prewar era. Arthur C. Clarke published a paper proposing the use of satellites placed in geosynchronous orbits (where they would remain in position above the same point on earth) as a means of relaying communications; shortly thereafter the RAND Corporation issued a prophetic report on the feasibility of using earth satellites for military purposes such as intelligence collection and weather observations.

But the postwar era was not fertile ground for rapid progress in the space field. America was occupied with satisfying the pent-up demand of its consumers, with helping Europe rebuild, and with countering the gradually-unfolding Soviet threat, while the European powers that had played an important role in prewar years were in no position to undertake any projects beyond recovering from devastation. The Soviet Union *was* working on development of large boosters as a counter to American air superiority, but results were not to come for some time and no one outside a select group of Soviet leaders and engineers knew what was going on.

Still, work on space boosters continued to progress slowly in the United States, and some American scholars, politicians, and diplomats began to take an interest in issues of space law. As the Soviet Union acquired the status of America's key adversary, interest in using satellites for reconnaissance grew. There were, however, serious concerns about the international law ramifications of satellite overflights, concerns that were sharpened considerably after the Soviet Union launched the world's first satellite, Sputnik. Some argued that such overflights would constitute violations of the sovereignty of the nations overflown, with injury being added to insult where the flights were for reconnaissance purposes. Much of U.S. strategy was influenced by these debates.

W. McDougall, . . . the Heavens and the Earth:
A Political History of the Space Age 185–189 (1985)

Few diplomatic issues seemed as urgent and loaded with implications for world peace as the law of outer space. Here were a new complex of frightening technologies *and* a virtually limitless medium, opened up simultaneously for human exploitation. And just as the voyages of the Age of Discovery stimulated inquiry into the law of the sea that advanced international law generally through the work of Hugo Grotius and others, so the launching of the Space Age inspired a burst of inquiry on the fundamental principles that ought to guide *all* the deeds of nation-states. The most beguiling legal problems were those tied to sovereignty: could nations claim space; divide it into zones according to some scientific, political, or technical principle; make it off-limits to weaponry; extend the cooperative framework of the IGY [International Geophysical Year]? What legislative and enforcement mechanisms were preferable for space law? What arrangements could be made for advance notice of launches, exchange of data, assessment of liability for damage caused by space vehicles? Who owned the moon or the electromagnetic spectrum? How could space boosters be distinguished from military missiles? Was space development best served by an international effort or by national programs operating under ground rules? A handful of visionaries tackled such puzzles even before Sputnik. John Cobb Cooper, air law expert and fellow of Princeton's Institute for Advanced Study, took up the question of sovereignty in a 1951 article, reviewing the history of air law from the Romans (who said land ownership extended *"usque ad coelum"*) to the great jurisprudential theorists of the seventeenth and eighteenth centuries (Samuel von Pufendorf limited sovereignty in the air to the ability for "effective control"), to the Chicago Convention of 1944 (which recognized complete and exclusive national sovereignty over air space). But how far up did air extend? Sounding rockets revealed that the atmosphere did not just stop, but gradually dissipated. Cooper opted for "effective control" (also the formula chosen by the 1885 Berlin Conference, which set rules for the colonization of Africa). "The territory of each state extends upward into space as far as the scientific progress of any state . . . permits such state to control it."

After Sputnik, numerous proposals were advanced for defining outer space. The so-called von Karman line set the boundary at the point at which a vehicle traveling seven kilometers a second loses aerodynamic lift and becomes a "spacecraft." Such an event would occur about fifty-three miles up. Cooper and common law (post–October 4, 1957) indicated that space simply stopped at that point below which an orbit could not be sustained. But such "lines" were a function of velocity and therefore of technology, and were in no way innate. Everyone knew where land ended and the ocean began, but now man had entered a realm that, in a real sense, did not exist except as a function of man's own tools. Any definition of outer space was a solipsism.

The critical variable in the definition of space was perceived military interest. The higher the boundary of national sovereignty, the greater the protection against unfriendly overflight, but the lesser the ability to ply the lower reaches of space for any purpose. It was guesswork in 1958 as to which would best suit American or Soviet interests. Similarly, whether a low limit was good or bad depended on the international regime that would obtain in space. If a rigid system of international control was instituted, then national freedom was best served by a high boundary. If a laissez-faire regime arose in space, then national freedom would be greatest by lowering "outer space" as close to the earth as possible: "Open Skies."

These ambiguities gave spacefaring nations no incentive to solve the riddle. State Department counsel Becker explained that the United States, while not recognizing any top limit to its airspace, conferred the right to ply space wherever it was. In short, the United States believed in "freedom of space," but reserved its position on what that freedom entailed or where it took effect. "Moreover," he continued, "there are very great risks in attempting to transmute a body of law based on one determined set of facts (e.g., air or sea law) into a body of law with respect to which the basic facts have not been determined." The State Department was "inclined to view with great reserve any such suggestions as that the principles of the law of space should be codified. . . ."

The principal concern of American policy was always the protection of spy satellites. But the right to launch satellites over the territory of other states was already established during the IGY. In this connection, George J. Feldman, counsel to the Senate Space Committee, declared that security considerations alone would preserve the principle of sovereign air space and work just as powerfully against a definition of where that air space ended. Satellites had already been launched without protest, implying that formal consent to satellite overflight was either unnecessary or implicitly given. "It is tempting to accept the first explanation—which would mean, for example, that President Eisenhower's Open Skies proposal is an accomplished fact. However, any such assumption would be premature and unjustified." Limited agreements on space might be made, but none should be sought "which are more comprehensive or explicit than our present knowledge warrants."

The same caution obtained in debate over sovereignty on heavenly bodies. As early as 1952 a UN lawyer, Oscar Schachter, asked "Who owns the universe?" and worried that we might someday read of colonial rivalries in space, of "lunar Washingtons and New Yorks, perhaps of King George mountains and Stalin craters." He suggested that space and celestial bodies belong, like the high seas, to all mankind. States should be allowed to develop settlements and mineral deposits, but in such a way as not to cause waste and destruction "against the general interest of mankind." The fear of a "scramble for colonies" in space, more rapacious even than the nineteenth century's scramble in Africa, also motivated space law theorists after Sputnik. But if space was not subject to sovereignty, what was its legal status? Was it *res nullius*—space as belonging to no one, but presumably subject to claims? Or *res communis omnium*—space as "the heritage of all mankind" with an implied right for all powers to regulate and reap the benefits of spaceflight? Or *res extra commercium*—with sovereignty and jurisdiction vested in the UN? The first threatened to stampede the powers, but the others implied an international control over national technology that the US and USSR alike were unlikely to accept.

Early discussion of such problems fell roughly into two categories, a fact acknowledged by leaders of the schools themselves, Andrew Haley and Myres McDougal. The former, an amateur rocketeer turned lawyer, counsel to the ARS [American Rocket Society] and president of the International Astronautical Federation, was the major exponent of the "natural law school." According to Haley, law rested on universal moral principles derived from the nature of man: moral precepts such as the Golden Rule that found expression in all great religions. Codified natural law theory arose, significantly, in response to problems posed by European discovery of the New World. But the law of nations, as the moral law of individuals writ large, did not constrain the states of early modern Europe, with unfortunate results. Now the world's governments again faced virgin territory. This time states must join in advance of the conquest of space to set standards and principles of conduct, and so avoid the old pattern of abuse and competition.

The "positivist school" of space law, associated with McDougal of Yale, argued that law emerged from patterns of common usage and could not be invented in advance of knowledge of the facts and emerging national interest. The difficulty in separating military and civilian activities rendered prohibition of the latter all but impossible, and space law in any case would always be a function, not a determinant, of international politics. High-blown principles and futile attempts to shackle the space powers would only make the principles appear ridiculous. Instead, the patterns of usage of space must be allowed to establish themselves before codification.

The two schools could aptly be termed the idealist and the realist. The most striking vindication of the realistic positivists was the fact that the secret NSC decisions had already rendered the space law debate academic. The reasons for the Superpowers' aloofness included the one offered in disparagement by the natural law idealists—that nations were obsessed by power and flouted the ethical imperatives embedded in every human being—*and* the one offered in sweet reason by the positivists—that it would be folly to make artificial rules for a vast area of human activity before the facts were known. Hence the USSR boycotted the Ad Hoc COPUOS [Committee On the Peaceful Uses of Outer Space] entirely, while the United States sharply circumscribed its agenda. The upshot was that discussion would proceed on such things as spacecraft registration and liability, sharing the radio spectrum and scientific data, but not on restrictions on the development and use of space technology by competing national states. Many space law theorists expressed their disgust with this narrow nationalism and hypocrisy, but the cries of "space for peace" and "space for all mankind" carried no further than if they had been shouted in the vacuum of space itself. The irony is that those enthusiastic about the human adventure in space should have been rejoicing. Competition was the engine of spaceflight. Had space exploration been truly internationalized or demilitarized, the Superpowers would have had little incentive to make huge investments for its realization. Space programs would have been stunted with malnutrition.

As the above passage demonstrates, the space law debate of the 1950s was of more than academic significance. Indeed, many believe that some elements of the United States government favored allowing the Soviet Union to launch the first satellite, as it did with Sputnik, on the ground that that would estop the Soviets from complaining about overflights by United States satellites. Whether or not that was the intention, it was certainly the effect—although there were a few *pro forma* complaints about intelligence satellites, the Soviet Union never seriously challenged the right of the United States to gather information that way.

That constituted a substantial victory for the American government: As an open society locked in cold-war struggle with a closed one, the United States found itself heavily dependent on the ability to gather information via technical means, of which aerial photography was the most significant. Originally, such information was gathered largely by high-altitude aircraft such as Canberra bombers and the U-2, but increasing Soviet proficiency at fighter interception and antiaircraft missile design made that risky. As a result, U.S. political and diplomatic strategy in the space arena throughout the ten years following the Sputnik launch centered around protecting the legality of satellite intelligence-gathering.

Through vigorous efforts in the UN's Committee on the Peaceful Uses of Outer Space (COPUOS), in the General Assembly and the Security Council, and in the negotiations and public posturing that led to the Outer Space Treaty, the United States championed a view of space as reserved for "peaceful" activities but open to military presences that did not violate this principle—i.e., reconnaissance satellites.

The Soviet Union, surprisingly to some, wound up going along. Perhaps this was because some farsighted Soviet officials realized that in the long run space surveillance was in their interest as well, or perhaps it was because the formulation that was chosen also did not outlaw ballistic missiles (which pass through space in flight), a technology in which the Soviets had invested much and demonstrated considerable competence.

Whatever the reason, this view was accepted and made part of the Outer Space Treaty; in fact, a few years later the Soviet Union wound up formally recognizing the legitimacy of satellite observation as part of the SALT I treaty, which bound the U.S. and the Soviet Union to refrain from interfering with each other's "national technical means of verification," a term that encompassed reconnaissance satellites. Other agreements in the post–Outer Space Treaty period, such as the ABM Treaty, the Accident Measures Agreement, etc. (see Chapters 4 and 5, *infra,* for more on these and other space agreements), followed this pattern, establishing outer space as a place in which military presences were permitted, but in which aggressive acts were not. This formulation, however, in large part reflected the technical capabilities of the two countries and their political and military needs; it remains to be seen whether it will survive coming changes in those factors.

Although the centerpiece of U.S. policy, however, issues of space militarization were not the only ones addressed in the negotiations leading up to the Outer Space Treaty (see Chapter 3). There was also a struggle over what limits existed to national sovereignty over outer space, the circumstances under which resources in space might be exploited, etc. This struggle was reflected in the Outer Space Treaty's statement that space should be used for the "common benefit of mankind," and "on the basis of equality," terms which were ultimately to prove insufficient to satisfy many "Third World" countries who feared that more developed nations would gain hegemony over outer space resources—or that exploitation of resources in outer space (such as metals and energy) would drive down market prices for their own exports. This led to an attempt to renegotiate matters in the form of the Moon Treaty (discussed in Chapter 4), which declared space resources part of the "Common Heritage of Mankind" and proposed an international regime for dividing up the profits from extracting them. U.S. ratification of that treaty was blocked by a coalition of industry and space activists, putting a damper (for some years at least) on international efforts at redistribution.

The aftermath of the Outer Space Treaty and related agreements saw a series of dramatic achievements in outer space. Unmanned probes visited most of the planets in the solar system (only tiny, distant Pluto being excepted). Manned missions first explored orbit (in American Mercury and Gemini missions and Soviet Vostok, Voskhod, and Soyuz missions), Americans landed on the Moon, the United States orbited Skylab, U.S. and Soviet spacecraft docked in orbit, the United States space shuttle flew, and the Soviets established first one, then a second, permanently manned space station in orbit.

Commercial activities in space had begun even before the Treaty, in the communications satellite field, and began spreading to include space manufacturing and research ventures, private launch services, and other efforts. Meanwhile, even more grandiose plans appeared on the drawing boards, plans for asteroid mining, solar power satellites, and space colonies. By the late 1980s the movement of people into space seemed unstoppable except by nuclear war or some similar calamity—for although individual nations might decide not to participate, the high level of overall involvement ensured that others would forge on regardless.

SOME OBSERVATIONS

It would be presumptuous to attempt to draw lessons, in the context of a space law text, regarding the future of humankind's expansion into outer space. However, the history of that expansion to date does hold some lessons for the space lawyer and for government and industry officials concerned with issues of space law.

One is that space technologies seem to grow faster than anyone, even among space enthusiasts, generally expects. When Arthur Clarke proposed the communications satellite it was openly pooh-poohed as science fiction—and even much later when INTELSAT, the international comunications satellite consortium, was formed many wondered why such systems would ever be necessary given the dozens of telephone circuits supported by existing transatlantic cables. Today, however, the communications satellite industry has revenues in the billions of dollars per year, and circuits are measured in the thousands and tens of thousands per satellite. And even Tsiolkovsky, who was so prophetic in many ways, did not see humanity venturing into space until the twenty-first century, an estimate that proved wildly pessimistic. Thus, in giving advice concerning larger issues it is important to keep an eye on the future, with the realization that the future may become the present more rapidly than anyone expects.

Another is that matters of national interest and security are more important in the space context than in many other areas, and that the law of outer space (in both the international and domestic contexts) tends to be driven by those interests rather than the other way around. Advice to clients—and plans by those clients and by governments—must take into account not only the "black letter" law where that is present, but the political circumstances involved. Prior to the late 1950s the "black letter" answer to the overflight question was that national sovereignty extended infinitely upward, but that answer was rapidly rendered obsolete by the changed circumstances of the Cold War and the Soviet Sputnik launch.

Lastly, it should be noted that the history of outer space is to a surprising degree the history of dedicated individuals and small groups manipulating larger powers in order to pursue their own goals, with Wernher von Braun's programs the paradigmatic (but far from the only) example. As outer space enterprises are integrated into everyday life, and as the entire field of space endeavors becomes larger and hence possessed of greater inertia, this may cease to be the case. However, it probably has not done so yet—the battle to block U.S. ratification of the Moon Treaty, for example, was spearheaded by what was then a small and new organization, the L5 Society (now the National Space Society), with great effect. The possibility that something like it may happen again should be kept in mind, and ways of dealing with such groups in crucial circumstances (for example, budget battles and future treaty negotiations and ratifications) should be explored. Otherwise space lawyers and their clients may find that someone else is making the rules by which they play.

FURTHER READING

W. Bainbridge, The Spaceflight Revolution: A Sociological Study (1976)
W. Burrows, Deep Black: Space Espionage and National Security (1986)
M. Collins, Liftoff (1988)
N. Daniloff, The Kremlin and the Cosmos (1972)
Dembling & Arons, The Evolution of the Outer Space Treaty, 33 Journal of Air Law & Commerce 419 (1967)
The Illustrated Encyclopedia of Space Technology (K. Gatland ed. 1984)
Goldman, The Moon Treaty: Reflections on the Proposed Moon Treaty, Space Law, and the Future, in People In Space (J. Katz ed. 1985)
T. McDonough, Space: The Next Twenty-Five Years (1987)
W. McDougall, . . . the Heavens and the Earth: A Political History of the Space Age (1985)
National Commission on Space, Pioneering the Space Frontier (1986)
Office of Technology Assessment, International Cooperation and Competition in Civilian Space Activities (1985)
Reynolds & Merges, The Role of Commercial Development in Preventing War in Outer Space, 25 Jurimetrics: Journal of Law, Science & Technology 130 (1985)
F. Winter, Prelude to the Space Age: The Rocket Societies: 1924–1940 (1983)

THE SPACE ENVIRONMENT

Space has changed in the years since the Second World War. Or, to be more precise, our understanding of space has changed. As Walter McDougall puts it, space is no longer the realm of dreams; it is now the realm of *Homo faber,* man (or, more properly, humanity) the tool-maker.

Since the peculiarities of space activity, including space commerce and space law, stem in large part from the special features of the space environment, it is important to understand something about that environment. Without such an understanding, it is simply impossible to appreciate the challenges that the space industry faces.

WHERE DOES SPACE BEGIN?

To a surprising extent, the answer to this question depends on who is asking it. As the excerpt from McDougall's book earlier in this chapter demonstrates, the question of where outer space begins is one of human definition, not practical delimitation. Below an altitude of approximately 69 miles, sustained orbit is practically impossible. Above an altitude of approximately 53–62 miles (the so-called von Karman line) aerodynamic lift is largely nonexistent. Yet X-15 aircraft flew higher than 62 miles, and satellites and other spacecraft pass through orbits lower than 69 miles—

and, once experiments with tethered satellites have borne fruit, may stay there for some time.

As you can see, there is no clear answer to the question of where space begins. But equally clearly, at some point above the earth, there exists an environment completely different from the one we have here. A sort of customary law has developed, discussed in following chapters, to the effect that any object in orbit is in space, and that seems enough to satisfy everyone for the time being. Whether that will remain so is unclear. *See generally* McDougal, The Emerging Customary Law of Space, 58 Northwestern University Law Review 618 (1963).

WHAT'S IT LIKE UP THERE?

Photos and movies taken in space give it a peaceful, surreal appearance. It looks like a place where the give and take of the atmosphere is replaced by a sort of perpetual stillness. But the appearance is deceptive.

In fact our atmosphere protects us from much of what is dangerous in space. First, there is a great deal of radiation. Visible light, X rays, infrared, radio and other forms of energy—collectively called electromagnetic radiation—are everywhere. This presents a danger, in terms of wear and tear on machinery and possible health effects on astronauts. (It also presents an opportunity, since many spacecraft are powered by these forces, both by generating electricity from sunlight using solar panels and—in the future—using light pressure from sunlight to propel spacecraft using "solar sails"). One of the primary problems caused by radiation is simple heat build-up: since the temperature of an unprotected object will rise rapidly on its sunlit side, special reflective and insulating materials have been developed to keep equipment (and people!) operational in space. In addition, this electromagnetic energy (when at frequencies other than those of infrared and visible light) can produce interference with communication, guidance and navigation equipment.

Second, subatomic particles from various sources shoot through space quite frequently. Many come from the sun; in fact, the flow of such particles from the sun is so steady it is referred to as the "solar wind." Fortunately for space travel, due to the small amount of mass and energy in these particles they do not normally pose a serious threat to activities in space.

A third source of potential trouble is radiation trapped in the earth's magnetic field—the Van Allen Radiation Belts. These are two bands of charged particles, one beginning at 250–750 miles up and ending at about 6,200 miles, and the other beginning at about 6,200 miles and extending to 37,000 to 52,000 miles. The composition of the two belts differs slightly, but flight trajectories for manned spacecraft must be designed carefully to avoid spending too much time within them. Unmanned craft, such as communications satellites, can and do operate within the belts, however; they can be designed to withstand the effects of the radiation for many years.

The high-speed solar protons emitted by a solar flare on the surface of the sun are probably the most dangerous of the radiation hazards to space flight. Flares themselves are the most spectacular disturbances seen on the sun. They appear as a sudden, large increase in light and radiation from a portion of the sun's atmosphere. Even on the earth, they can cause substantial problems—such as radio noise storms that interfere with communications. But from the point of view of the space traveller, the real danger caused by solar flares is the large number of high-energy solar protons they release into space. They can carry extremely high energies. As a consequence, they can cause the release of lethal doses of secondary radiation, such as gamma rays, when they collide with spacecraft. Until now this has never happened, largely because spacecraft can be shielded to protect against much of the radiation in this form. Nevertheless, solar flare radiation remains a real threat to human health in space.

METEOROIDS AND MICROMETEOROIDS

Space is also populated by larger particles, some with masses as large as several tons, called meteoroids. Most, however, are quite small, and are known as micrometeoroids. When a meteoroid enters the earth's atmosphere, it is called a meteor; remnants of meteors are often found on earth.

In space, micrometeoroids regularly strike satellites and other space vehicles. (In fact, some space scientists believe they are responsible for several otherwise inexplicable satellite malfunctions.) Over time, micrometeoroid impact can be expected to wear down the surface of satellites or space stations. This is especially important where sensitive materials, such as optical lenses or reflective coatings, must be exposed for the satellite or space station to do its job.

But even though micrometeoroid impact can be expected, the probability of impact with a devastatingly large meteoroid is quite low. Not all dangerous objects in space are of natural origin, however: as a result of accidental explosions and military antisatellite tests some orbits contain considerable quantities of artificial debris, a problem that is growing and may soon pose a real threat to many space activities. This issue is discussed further in Chapter 5.

VACUUM AND MICROGRAVITY

Two other features of the space environment are the relative absence of gases and other matter and the relative absence of gravitational pull—vacuum and microgravity, respectively.

Space is, by the standards of earth dwellers, quite empty. Yet space contains gases, albeit at concentrations that are tiny compared to the earth's atmosphere. This relative absence of gases is one of the features of the space environment that makes it attractive for manufacturing purposes. It is thought, for instance, that the space atmosphere will permit greater purity by reducing unwanted gases that are introduced in certain manufacturing processes on earth even when sophisticated vacuum pumps are used.

The other, more important, aspect of space for purposes of potential manufacturing applications is minimal gravity. The term "microgravity" is usually used to describe this characteristic of space. As this term implies, objects in space are affected by gravitational forces, which exist everywhere in the universe. The point is simply that these forces are less apparent within the frame of reference of an object in space than on the surface of a planet.

Space consequently is thought by some to hold great potential as a manufacturing site for the future. Advanced materials, for example, are often mentioned as possible products. On earth, alloys and other materials are susceptible to imperfections caused by tiny currents. These "convection currents," as materials scientists call them, result from the action of gravity during the cooling of alloys and other materials. Manufacturing in the microgravity environment of space can eliminate these imperfections.

Moreover, space may provide a more hospitable environment for growing intricate crystals, such as those used in semiconductor manufacture. It also allows the use of methods of separation (such as those used in McDonnell Douglas's Continuous Flow Electrophoresis experiment flown on board the Space Shuttle) that rely on forces too weak to be of much use under gravity. These are just a few examples of how scientists on earth plan to make use of the special environment of space; other ideas will no doubt appear as we gain more experience.

GETTING THERE AND STAYING THERE

The essential mathematics of rocket launches and earth orbits were worked out by astronomers in the seventeenth century, especially Johannes Kepler and Sir Isaac Newton. Of course, they probably had no expectation that their laws of celestial mechanics would have any application to practical engineering problems. But as it turns out the problems of determining how to get an object into space and how to keep it there are just two special cases of more general astronomical problems.

The key is that for the purpose of calculating orbits and trajectories a space vehicle is just another celestial body, whose motion is governed by the same laws that dictate the movement of the planets. To be sure, it is a tiny body relative to the earth. But the beauty of the astronomical laws of motion is that they apply regardless of the size of the object. (Until you reach sub-atomic sizes, anyway; much different forces operate at that level.)

Although many people believe the reason for weightlessness in space is that a spacecraft in orbit is "beyond gravity," that is not the case—in fact, the pull of gravity at the altitude of most orbiting spacecraft is not much less than it is on the surface of the earth. Nor is that a bad thing, since orbits themselves would not be possible if it were not for the pull of gravity. A spacecraft orbits not because it is beyond the influence of gravity but because the product of its forward velocity and the pull of gravity is such that it neither falls to earth nor goes sailing off into the void. Because of its forward velocity, a spacecraft in orbit is in a sort of neverending circular fall, in which the surface of the earth curves away as fast as the spacecraft approaches it. The greater the altitude, the smaller the forward velocity required to keep an object in orbit, and the more time required to complete an orbit. Thus, satellites at low orbits complete a circuit of the earth in ninety minutes, while those higher up may take twenty-four hours or longer.

Orbits taking exactly twenty-four hours for a circuit (which requires an altitude of approximately 22,400 miles) are called *geosynchronous* orbits, because the satellite completes a circuit in exactly the same time that the earth takes to revolve once; if the satellite's orbit is directly above the equator with no inclination (tilt), it will appear to remain precisely above the same spot at all times. That has many advantages, especially for communications satellites, as it means that antennas need not swivel to track the satellite but may remain pointed in the same direction constantly since the satellite appears motionless relative to the ground. Geosynchronous orbits are often called *Clarke* orbits after Arthur C. Clarke, who first proposed their use for communications satellites; they are also sometimes abbreviated as GEO, standing for GEosynchronous Orbit. Orbits of lower altitude than geosynchronous are often called Low Earth or Near Earth Orbits, and abbreviated LEO or NEO.

Orbits inclined at 90 degrees to the equator are known as *polar* orbits because they pass over both poles. They are useful for reconnaissance and resource sensing, since they ensure that the satellite will pass over the entire earth as it turns; such orbits can be timed so that every pass of the satellite over a particular point will occur at the same time of day, in which case they are known as *sun synchronous* orbits. These orbits are typically used by military photoreconnaissance satellites.

In addition, there are a number of locations in the earth-Moon system that have special qualities because of the interactions between the earth's and the Moon's gravitational fields. The best known of these are the Lagrangian points, named for Pierre Lagrange, the French mathematician who first calculated their existence. These are points of unusual orbital stability, so that if a satellite or other object is placed in them it will not tend to drift away under the perturbing gravitational influence of other planets. Because of this, these points have been proposed as ideal locations for space colonies—indeed, one space activist group, the L5 Society (now merged into the National Space Society), took its name from one of the points. On the other hand, the unique gravitational characteristics of these points have considerable military significance, which could make them unlikely candidates for peaceful colonies.

ROCKETS AND PROPULSION

To get a spacecraft into orbit in the first place requires a phenomenal amount of thrust. Enough force must be applied to overcome the craft's inertia, i.e., to get it moving, and then to overcome enough of the pull of gravity to place it in one of the orbits described above.

Rocket engines operate on the principle of Newton's Third Law, popularly stated as "For every action, there is an equal and opposite reaction." A highly combustible material is ignited in a small chamber; the explosive thrust generated by the combustion is directed out of a narrow exhaust nozzle. The unbalanced force within the rocket's thrust chamber resulting from the exhaust's exiting the nozzle causes an equal and opposite reaction—the rocket is hurled in the direction opposite the nozzle. Unlike other types of combustion engines (e.g., aircraft jet engines) rockets do not depend on atmospheric oxygen for combustion; instead, they carry their own source of oxygen, called the oxidizer, to support combustion. This is what allows them to burn in the vacuum of space.

There are two common types of rocket engines: solid and liquid fueled; the solid/liquid hybrid combines features of the two but is just beginning to enter common use. Liquid fueled engines have several advantages, most notably controllable thrust and restart capability, not present in solid fueled engines. Liquid fueled engines typically use liquid oxygen or nitric acid as an oxidizer, with kerosene or liquid hydrogen as the fuel. Solid propellants, on the other hand, are more stable, and easier to manufacture and store. They are also cheaper. Solid rockets contain powdered fuel and oxidizer cast in a plastic or glue-like compound. A third type of engine is a cross between the other two: the so-called solid/liquid hybrid engine, which uses solid fuel, but a liquid oxidizer. It combines an advantage of some liquid propellants, the ability to stop and re-start combustion, with several of the functional advantages of solid propellants. A number of other experimental engines have been proposed, but they have not yet been made operational.

There are a variety of other types of rocket engines that are not in general use but that may appear soon. One is the ion drive, in which electrical forces are used to expel small quantities of propellant at extremely high speeds; these engines produce low thrusts but can operate for long periods with low fuel consumption, making them suitable for interplanetary probes or other long distance applications. Another is the so-called ORION drive (named for the secret military project that developed it), which uses atomic explosives for propulsion. Although the idea struck many as absurd, a (non-nuclear) working model was tested in the late 1950s with excellent results. Because the Limited Test Ban Treaty (see discussion *infra* in Chapter 3) prohibits the detonation of nuclear explosives in the atmosphere or in outer space, partly for environmental reasons, ORION type drives are unlikely to be put to use any time soon. However, the concept has been validated, and the fact that such drives allow the acceleration of large payloads at low expense using proven technology may encourage some nation to explore the possibility of using Orion drives in the future.

Besides ORION drives, a number of other proposed launch systems are close enough to feasibility to warrant a brief mention. First is the Solar Sail, a simple concept that takes advantage of the small but measurable force exerted by photons emitted from the sun—or, in some conceptions, by giant lasers. These very large sails would be useful for moving cargoes around the solar system at low cost, or for cheaply and efficiently powering deep space probes. Second are laser launch systems, which work by directing a ground-based energy beam at a combustion chamber on the bottom of a rocket; the energy ignites the air in the combustion chamber and powers the rocket into orbit. The third launch system is the most unusual one: beanstalks. These would be essentially very long tethers, anchored on the earth and extending out into space beyond the geosynchronous orbit. The tethers would be launched using a conventional rocket; once in place, however, centrifugal or inertial force would keep them from falling back to earth. Solar power cells in space could then be used to supply the energy to lift objects up along the beanstalk and into orbit. While only at the conceptual stage of development, beanstalks offer an intriguing possibility for routine, cheap launches in the future. Other possibilities include "ram cannons," in which a projectile is fired through a barrel filled with gaseous propellant mixture, igniting the mixture like the centerbody of a ramjet engine. At this writing, experimental ram cannons have already reached 20% of the velocity needed to achieve orbit and could easily be scaled up to reach orbital velocities, although the enormous accelerations involved would limit them to cargo launches. In addition, the Air Force has been exploring the possibility of using anti-hydrogen as a propellant; antimatter hydrogen would be combined with ordinary hydrogen to produce highly efficient propulsion throughout the solar system. Only 35 milligrams of antimatter could propel a 120-ton aerospace plane carrying 30 tons of cargo to LEO at shuttle-like accelerations. Antimatter is being produced and stored at the time of this writing in very small quantities, and according to the Office of Technology Assessment could be produced and stored in the relatively near-term at costs of approximately $10 million per milligram. For more on these and other launch technologies see U.S. Congress Office of Technology Assessment, Launch Options for the Future (1988).

While these technologies are not yet operational, one or more of them will probably be developed in the future. This would likely have important political and economic consequences. The physics of beanstalks, for example, put a premium on equatorial launch bases. A number of equatorial nations have already declared sovereignty over the geosynchronous orbital slots above the equator (see the discussion of the Bogota Declaration in Chapter 4, *infra*), but these claims have been widely condemned and consistently ignored by spacefaring nations. Beanstalk technology would transform this conflict from a paper battle at the U.N. into a very real clash.

Likewise, cheaper launch capabilities would put space within reach of many more countries. This would in turn escalate the competition for scarce orbital slots, such as prime geosynchronous orbits for satellites. Moreover, since space capability has long been associated with military as well as civilian missions, cheap launches could make space a part of the military strategy of even small nations. Antimatter propulsion offers other possibilities: antimatter could conceivably be used in bombs of capacity equivalent to thermonuclear weapons. Such use is unlikely, though, as existing nuclear devices are cheaper and more reliable than antimatter devices are ever likely to be, and destructive enough to satisfy anyone.

WHEN YOU ARE THERE: WHAT PEOPLE DO IN SPACE

Satellites

Today, space is useful primarily because of the perspective it provides. Orbiting satellites, for example, make communication between distant points on earth much easier. Because of this, the satellite industry is the largest sector of commercial space activities today, as described in the following excerpt.

Byerly, The Commercial/Industrial Uses of Space, in Beyond Spaceship Earth: Environmental Ethics and the Solar System (E. Hargrove ed., 1986)

Communications satellites . . . are now big business. Their use began with NASA experiments using the satellite Echo I in 1960. NASA conducted ten successful development flights between then and 1974. . . .

[NASA's work spawned] a healthy industry. For example, the most recent figures show that about $2 billion worth of U.S.-produced satellite-communications ground systems were shipped in 1984, and service revenues for the seven U.S. common carriers were $555 million in 1984. In addition, the Communications Satellite Corporation (COMSAT) earned about $291 million in operating revenues in 1983 from communications to and from the United States. Currently, COMSAT has a monopoly on this internatonal service, but there are efforts by other companies to [launch satellites and] enter this field. Some 109 nations are members of the International Telecommunications Satellite Organization and seven nations have their own domestic communications satellites.

A significant issue facing the communications satellite industry is the emerging congestion of the geostationary arc. [See this section, *supra,* for description.] . . . This arc is becoming crowded, not because the satellites are near to bumping into one another but because of radio interference between adjacent satellites. There needs to be about a 2-degree angular spacing between satellites in order to avoid such radio interference.

* * *

Two additional large operational activities in space are . . . weather satellites and navigation satellites. Weather satellites—called metsats—have been operational since 1964. The United States normally has two of these in polar orbit and two in geostationary orbit. Those in polar orbit are [sun-synchronous, as defined above]. These satellites look down at the Earth to generate data on cloud cover, temperature, and water-vapor density and make a significant contribution to our ability to forecast the weather. The data that U.S. satellites generate is broadcast directly to the ground and anyone with the proper equipment can receive it. . . .

Navigation satellites can be used with relatively simple equipment to find one's position on the Earth to within about 100 meters horizontally and about 1,000 meters vertically (that is, in altitude). The first Navstar satellite—the name of the U.S. satellites—was launched in 1978, and several more will be launched until the government constellation is complete in [the late 1980s]. The total system . . . is called the Global Positioning System.

* * *

A [space technology] that has not really become fully operational [, but that has already given rise to a $10 million per year industry] is civilian remote sensing of the surface of the Earth. This technology can be used to generate data about the the Earth's surface, which in turn is used for mineral prospecting, for agricultural surveys and crop monitoring, for planning major construction projects such as pipelines, and for environmental monitoring and research. . . . It has recently been used for firefighting purposes: the infrared sensors on a U.S. satellite were used to locate hot-spots despite a very thick blanket of smoke that was preventing firefighters from knowing where to attack the fire. There is currently in planning a large research program called the International Geosphere/ Biosphere Program, which will attempt to study the Earth as a system in order to understand how our fundamental life-support system changes due both to natural and man-made causes. This program, when it gets underway, will undoubtedly use much data generated by remote sensing of the Earth from space.

Solar Power

The unending stream of energy from the Sun already serves as the power source for many spacecraft, especially space probes and satellites. But in an era of perceived energy scarcity on Earth, some have proposed tapping this vast resource for use here as well.

**Power Stations in the Sky, in The Illustrated Encyclopedia
of Space Technology 226–231 (K. Gatland ed., 1984)**

Can space technology help to solve the energy crisis? Specifically, is it
really practicable to think of tapping the "inexhaustible" energy of sunlight
in space and beaming it back to Earth?

*   *   *

In 1968 Dr. Peter E. Glaser of the Arthur D. Little Company proposed
the concept of satellite solar power stations [SSPS]. The idea depended on
the establishment of a huge array of solar cells to concentrate the maximum
amount of sunlight for the purpose of generating electricity by the process
known as photovoltaic conversion.

The energy thus generated would be transmitted to Earth in the form
of microwaves where it would be transformed back into electricity for use
in the national grid.

*   *   *

One of the major United States companies looking into the future of
solar energy is Boeing Aerospace, whose aim is to bring the concept closer
to engineering reality. They envisage a structure the size of a small city
producing twice the usable power generated by Grand Coulee, America's
largest hydroelectric dam. They calculate that it would take 45 of these
gigantic satellites to match the present total electrical generating power of
the United States. . . .

*   *   *

Critics of the SSPS wish to know more about possible environmental
effects of the microwave beams. Is it really true that there will be no
adverse [effects] on flora and fauna from a satellite power station that is
not so restricted in output as to be wholly uneconomic? Then again, would
not the microwave beams adversely affect the environment by heating up
the atmosphere?

*   *   *

All the same, the detailed studies so far carried out have shown that,
given the political will, [SSPS systems] could be developed in the foreseeable
future, certainly by the end of the century. There is obviously still much
work to do on such aspects as [transmission] frequencies least affected by
the weather, on minimizing spillover, on waste of the beam, on efficient
conversion techniques, and on proving beyond question that exposure of
living things to the beam is without risk.

Research and Development

To date, much of what has taken place in space must be characterized as basic research. Beginning with the early space probes, past the Apollo moon landings, and into the era of the Space Shuttle, space scientists collected data on the features of the space environment. Even now, a major initiative in space research is the Hubble Space Telescope, which will, when it is launched, be the first space-based astronomical instrument dedicated only to science.

Microgravity experiments on the Apollo, Skylab, and space shuttle missions produced the first results that suggested a more practical side to the space environment. These experiments showed some intriguing possibilities for manufacturing materials in space. As a result of these experiments, some observers believe that certain pharmaceuticals and composite materials will one day be made routinely in space. For today, however, it is only safe to say that the true potential of space as a manufacturing environment is as yet unknown. One of the primary reasons the U.S. Space Station is being built is to provide an environment to explore these possibilities.

Since research and development are critical to corporate survival, and since space has been identified as a likely site for these activities in the future, commercial concerns in the mid-1980s began to express some anxiety about the applicability of U.S. patent law to space activities. Since patents are one of the primary means of securing a return on R&D investment in the U.S., firms wanted to make sure they would be available for the fruits of research endeavors undertaken in space. Legislation which would deal with some of these problems by extending U.S. jurisdiction for patent purposes into space was introduced in several Congresses and has now passed. It is described *infra* in Chapter 8.

Space Colonies

To some, space is nothing less than the Final Frontier, or even the next logical step in human evolution. The idea of space colonies is not a new one—such colonies were proposed by the seminal Russian space writer Konstantin Tsiolkovsky in the early part of this century. More recently, however, the idea has begun to be treated seriously by a number of scholars.

In 1969, Princeton physicist Gerard K. O'Neill asked his students a question inspired by the Apollo moon landings of the same year: "Is a planetary surface the right place for an expanding technological civilization?" After considerable research and debate, the answer that he was given was "No." Instead, humanity would be better off in a number of self-supporting habitats, making use of solar energy and lunar and asteroidal materials. Further research, and consultation with such leading scientists as physicist Freeman Dyson, led to a design based on large cylinders of up to several miles in length, rotating to produce artificial gravity. The design called for the colonies to be located at Lagrangian points, where they would remain stable as a result of Earth-Moon-Sun gravitational interactions without additional stationkeeping assistance. One space activist group, the L5 society, took its name from one of the Lagrangian points as a statement of its support for the O'Neill concept and lobbied actively (and successfully, in the case of its effort to block ratification of the Moon Treaty) prior to merging with another group to become the National Space Society.

These initial designs have been refined a number of times, and will likely go through many changes before there is any substantial chance of their being implemented. In this, they may resemble the early British Interplanetary Society moon mission plans—better at anticipating the general nature of the problems encountered and their solutions than at diagramming the precise nature of future craft.

Yet such colonies are a distinct possibility over the long run, and would raise a variety of interesting legal questions. For example, the Outer Space Treaty and the Registration Convention provide for national jurisdiction and control over all space objects (see Chapters 3 and 5, *infra*), but the inhabitants of a space colony, sooner or later, are likely to object to a regime in which only earthside sovereignty is recognized. And, in the case of a U.S. colony, there would be interesting questions raised as to whether the Constitution would "follow the flag" in that context. Under the auspices of the Smithsonian Institution, a conference of leading academics and lawyers, including one Supreme Court Justice, has looked into these issues and drafted a "Declaration of First Principles" for the governance of space societies. Such issues are likely to receive further discussion in the future. *See* Chapter 9, *infra,* for a discussion of these questions.

Military Activities

Since before Sputnik, military use of outer space has been a major topic. In the first thirty years of the space age, the primary military use of space has been for communications and reconnaissance, one that most experts agree has exerted a stabilizing and beneficial effect on world affairs. Although there have been some efforts at developing techniques for denying enemies the ability to use space in this fashion—beginning with U.S. projects (named Bold Orion and SAINT) in the late 1950s and operational (or so it was claimed) systems on the part of both the United States and the Soviet Union in the 1960s and 1970s—it was not until the 1980s that serious prospects for more active military uses of outer space began to develop.

In principle, outer space may be used militarily in the same way that land, sea, and air are used: As a base for attacking the enemy, as a source of materials, as a vantage for observation, and as a means of rapid movement. Most proposals for future military uses of outer space, however, focus on antisatellite (ASAT) and ballistic missile defense (BMD) systems. Some of these pose legal problems—BMD systems based on nuclear weapons, for example, would violate the Outer Space Treaty (not to mention the more specific ABM Treaty), while the use of an antisatellite weapon to disable a satellite would undoubtedly constitute an aggressive act in contravention of the United Nations Charter. These topics are discussed *infra*, along with other topics growing out of the international law of outer space. For more on these topics see P. Stares, Space and National Security (1987); Reynolds, National Security on the High Frontier, 2 High Technology Law Journal 281 (1988).

Current military uses of space involve the use of three kinds of satellites: intelligence, communications, and early warning. Intelligence satellites are capable of taking photographs of dramatic resolution (reportedly, as good as a few inches), of monitoring communications (an activity known to the intelligence community as electronic intelligence or ELINT), and of producing all sorts of less dramatic but often important information concerning things like crop yields, rainfall, etc. Communications satellites allow central commanders to exercise control over far-flung forces to a degree that was not possible previously, and to receive real-time information about the progress of campaigns or about possible enemy action. Early warning satellites monitor enemy territory for missile launches, providing additional minutes of warning time that could prove crucial in a war—or, more importantly, deter a first strike to begin with.

In addition, meteorological satellites (metsats, in military jargon) provide data important for military operations and ICBM targeting adjustments. All of these, however, are what are known as "force multiplier" applications, meaning that their military role is one of amplifying the effect of other, more conventional, forces, not one of taking action on their own. Satellites capable of attacking targets on the ground are some time away, although eventually they could revolutionize land warfare, probably putting a premium on speed and concealment to a greater degree than any other type of weapon. For the coming decades, though, the key issues are likely to involve various objects in space and their relations with one another: ASAT weapons, and weapons capable of knocking out ICBMs during the space-flight phase of their trajectory. Those are likely to prove challenging enough.

FURTHER READING

The New Solar System (J. Beatty, B. O'Leary & A. Chaikin eds. 1982).

W. Burrows, Deep Black: Space Espionage and National Security (1986).

K. Gatland, The Illustrated Encyclopedia of Space Technology (1984).

Goldman, The Moon Treaty: Reflections on the Proposed Moon Treaty, Space Law, and the Future, in J. Katz, People In Space (1985).

T. McDonough, Space: The Next Twenty-Five Years (1987).

W. McDougall, . . . the Heavens and the Earth: A Political History of the Space Age (1985).

National Commission on Space, Pioneering the Space Frontier (1986).

Office of Technology Assessment, International Cooperation and Competition in Civilian Space Activities (1985).

Reynolds & Merges, The Role of Commercial Development in Preventing War in Outer Space, 25 Jurimetrics: Journal of Law, Science & Technology 130 (1985).

U.S. Air Force, Space Handbook (C. Cochran, D. Gorman, & J. Dumoulin eds. 1985).

F. Winter, Prelude to the Space Age: The Rocket Societies: 1924–1940 (1983).

2

The International Law
of Outer Space:
Basic Principles

INTRODUCTION

The activities of nations in outer space are governed by public international law. Although this is not a text in international law, it may be worthwhile to review some basic principles before going on to the specific rules applying to outer space. For more on these topics see Restatement (Third) of Foreign Relations Law, §§ 101–103 (1987).

International law may stem from several sources. *Treaties* are the most obvious—relevant treaties may be directly concerned with outer space (for example, the Outer Space Treaty of 1967) or may address outer space activity as part of more general subject matter (for example, the Limited Test Ban Treaty of 1963). But although treaties seem satisfyingly legalistic because they are signed, formal documents, they are not the only source of international law. *Custom* (the first, and still an important, source of international law) is another; by custom international law commentators mean general principles of international law not embodied in any treaty but observed, and considered binding, by civilized nations.

These are the authoritative sources of international law. In applying international law, courts, legal advisors, and other decisionmakers and counselors often rely on other sources as well. Frequently, writings by respected commentators are given great weight. And resolutions of the United Nations General Assembly, although not legally binding themselves, are often regarded as expressing a consensus view on the extent or nature of a rule.

One problem that many people, lawyers and non-lawyers alike, have with international law is that to them it does not seem like law at all because it lacks the sort of well-established enforcement mechanisms that domestic legal systems have. Violate the domestic law of a nation (say, by refusing to pay your taxes) and you will find yourself subject to all sorts of clearly defined penalties (like jail) meted out by officials and organizations whose responsibility it is to punish lawbreakers. The consequences of violating international law, on the other hand, are far less clear—

especially as the violators are likely to be sovereign nations, equipped with armies, air forces, etc., and hence hard to arrest. What punishments can be inflicted—via opinions of the World Court, resolutions of the United Nations General Assembly, or economic sanctions inflicted by the world community—are often of largely symbolic importance.

The enforcement problem has led some people to argue that there is no such thing as international law, and others to avoid the issue entirely by focusing on "black letter" legal issues while asserting that enforcement is a different problem altogether. Neither approach is helpful—nations in fact obey international law far more often than they violate it, and it is important to understand why they do so. On the other hand, nations will violate even well-established rules of international law when the stakes are high enough, and it is important to understand why they do that as well. For more on this topic see Reisman, Sanctions and Enforcement, in International Law Essays 381 (M. McDougal & W. M. Reisman eds. 1981). The discussion of those two issues could easily make up a book of its own, but following are a few observations that may be helpful in understanding why international law exists even in the absence of effective enforcement, and why and how problems will arise and nations will violate it from time to time.

1. *A system of international law is in the general interest of all nations.* While nations may (and inevitably do) disagree over specific rules, the global nature of modern business, the frequency of travel, and the tendency of problems of all kinds to extend across borders all require that governments deal with one another constantly. Without some framework for such dealings, enormous amounts of time would be wasted, and important problems would go unaddressed. Thus, it is in their interest for nations to agree on a set of rules that make cooperation easier and prevent the need for repetitive bargaining over ground rules and expected behavior. In some areas, such as public health, the framework for international cooperation has been quite successful. In other areas—where the benefits of cooperation are not as visible, or where the stakes or the incentives to cheat are higher—it has been less so. For a discussion of how mutual interests can lead to cooperation even in the absence of external enforcement mechanisms, or among adversaries, see R. Axelrod, The Evolution of Cooperation (1984). *See also* Kronman, Contract Law and the State of Nature, 1 Journal of Law Economics & Organization 5 (1985).

2. *Cooperation among nations is imperfect.* While it may be in the interest of nations to cooperate on many matters, the process for doing so involves human beings, who tend to make mistakes and act irrationally. Even where parties are acting rationally and in good faith, it is possible for both parties to an agreement to have different ideas about what was meant; in addition, no agreement can clearly address all possible situations that may arise. What is more, parties may find that it is necessary to address some topics ambiguously in order to accomplish an agreement on others.

The treaty mechanism attempts to deal with these problems by memorializing an agreement in concrete form in order to minimize confusion about what was agreed to; various rules of interpretation, etc. exist in order to deal (with varying degrees of success) with ambiguities and unforeseen situations in a way that is consistent with the intent of the parties. This set of rules, and the agreements to which they are applied, constitutes the most "legalistic" part of international law. The same sorts of problems arise with regard to customary law when it is confronted with new or unforeseen problems. In both contexts, the community of international legal scholars plays an unusually important role—because very few international legal disputes are ever decided by authoritative bodies, the consensus among scholars is often the closest thing to a judicial opinion that can be achieved. For an example of the interpretive process at work, see the Memorandum of the Department of State's Legal Adviser reproduced in Chapter 6.

Not all international legal problems stem from good faith disagreements, of course: there are also problems resulting from bad faith and dishonesty. With regard to these, matters of power and interest are of more importance than questions of law. However, nations that violate international law too often or too blatantly do pay a price in terms of isolation from the world community, reduced foreign trade and investment, etc. To avoid these consequences, nations that violate international law will almost always attempt to argue that their actions are in fact lawful; criticism of such arguments is an important role for international scholars, and (since such criticism can affect the way other nations respond to the violation) may in fact be regarded as part of the enforcement system of international law.

Generally, the guidelines on interpreting treaties resemble those used to interpret contracts, statutes, and other legal documents. Interpreters look to the language, the intent of the parties, and general rules of construction in interpreting international agreements. Naturally there is often room for dispute, and sometimes dispute where little room exists, as the discussion in Chapter 4 concerning the ABM Treaty demonstrates. *See generally* Restatement (Third) of Foreign Relations Law, §§ 111–113 (1987) (discussing treaty interpretation and related issues).

3. *Nations guard their own interests.* Any nation will violate the norms of international law when the stakes are high enough. How high the stakes have to be depends on the nation, the likely consequences of violation, etc. What is more, the absence of any authoritative decisionmaking body means that nations who wish to challenge a norm not embodied in a treaty must often violate it in order to do so. *See* Reisman, International Incidents: Introduction to a New Genre in the Study of International Law, 10 Yale Journal of International Law 1 (1984).

THE ROOTS OF SPACE LAW

The international law of outer space springs from several sources, most notably maritime law (represented in the fact that a nation's jurisdiction extends to any spacecraft under its flag), air law (which provides perspective on overflight issues and other related problems), and the legal aspirations embodied in the United Nations, which was still quite new when the Space Age began. To provide some of the flavor of those issues, a few excerpts from writings on each of these subjects follow. As you read them, you might keep these questions in mind: (1) How reasonable are analogies between the laws governing other fields, like aviation and shipping, and outer space law; and (2) What are some other ways of developing law that will respond to the practical needs of space industries and activities in a way that serves global needs?

AIR AND SEA LAW: RULES GOVERNING OVERFLIGHT AND TERRITORIAL WATERS

The principal sources of air and sea law are custom, embodied in the practice of nations over time; the 1944 Chicago Convention (governing air law); and the 1958 Convention on the High Seas (governing sea law). In addition, the Law of the Sea Treaty sets out a number of rules but cannot at this point be regarded as an authoritative source of sea law as many major sea powers, including the United States, have refused to ratify it. The Chicago Convention sets out rules on safety, training, certification and registration and declares the existence of national sovereignty over air space. The High Seas Convention does the same for the oceans, providing that national jurisdiction follows a vessel wherever it goes, delimiting the extent of territorial waters, and setting rules as to safety, etc. These topics are discussed further in Chapter 8.

DeSaussure, Maritime and Space Law, Comparisons and Contrasts (An Oceanic View of Space Transport), 9 Journal of Space Law 93 (1981)

Few realized, when the first Echo satellites were launched in the early sixties, the dramatic way in which communications satellites would fill the skies. Nor did they realize how crowded the geostationary orbit would become and how great the need would be for international regulation. The first satellite to operate in geostationary orbit was Syncom 2, which was launched in 1963. Between one hundred and ten and one hundred and twenty satellites now occupy that orbit. From one-quarter to one-half of them are functioning. A recent NASA study concluded that by the year 2000 there would be a tenfold increase in the international demand for communications satellite circuits.

The emergence of a transportation system in space, particularly a reusable system, will promote the same exponential growth in the carriage of cargo, and in human activity. How will it grow? Will it be by each nation regulating its own transport systems independently, by commonly agreed upon standards and practices, or by a new international agreement regulating space transportation?

The answer lies partially in the degree to which the most technologically advanced states believe it to their advantage to work out internationally accepted practices for their space operations. The U.S. will have the Space Shuttle, the USSR their Salyut-Soyuz-Progress system, and France has Ariane. The Soviets are reported to be planning a reusable spacecraft. China and Japan are trying to develop more sophisticated launch systems. The answer also lies in how much priority the U.N. Committee on Peaceful Uses of Outer Space (COPUOS) assigns to the formulation of an international regime for space transportation.

*   *   *

Whether a space transport regime takes shape through unilateral practice, concordant national rules, or multilateral treaty, the maritime and aviation regimes for international carriage are important references. Commerce at sea and in the air space has flourished by virtue of stable, internationally accepted rules, which regulate navigation. The purpose of this paper is to examine a few of the more important aspects of the maritime analogy for their applicability to space transport.

*   *   *

There has always been a need accurately to define aircraft and ships and to distinguish them from other objects which transit or occupy their respective spheres. A similar need will emerge to define those spacecraft used for transport and to distinguish them from other space objects.

The International Regulations for Preventing Collisions at Sea define vessels to include, "every description of water craft, including non-displacement craft and seaplanes, used or capable of being used *as a means of transportation* on water" (emphasis added). The INMARSAT Agreement defines the term *ship* as meaning "a vessel of any type operating in the marine environment (including inter alia) hydrofoil boats, air-cushion vehicles, submersibles, floating craft and platforms not permanently moored."

It seems that as space travel grows, we will need to establish a common definition of transport spacecraft or space vehicles. That is, spacecraft used primarily to carry goods or personnel from one place to another. It will also be necessary to distinguish them legally from other varieties of space objects. The key to defining the spacecraft for transport is navigability. Does it have the *primary* function of transportation? Is is designed basically for space flight rather than parking in a particular orbit? The fact that many satellites have internal rocket propulsion enabling ground controllers to reposition them in space does not endow them with navigability. Communications, remote sensing, weather, and reconnaissance satellites are not designed or intended for navigation in space. They carry only sufficient fuel to reach the desired orbit and perform their mission. INTELSAT satellites have been recently supplied just enough extra fuel to kick them out of the geostationary orbit at the end of their useful life. A true navigable craft however has enough fuel to traverse space and return to a particular place or orbit.

Navigate has been defined as steering or directing a ship or aircraft. Of all the space objects, it will be the spacecraft for the transport [of people and goods] that most nearly resembles ships and aircraft. How should they be described to differentiate them from other space objects? Webster's dictionary defines *spaceship* as "a rocket propelled vehicle for 'travel' in outer space." One might have preferred a definition which substituted the word *transport* for the word *travel.* It is broader. Transport clearly embraces cargo as well as human beings. If one adopts the test of navigability as described above, then a spaceship could be manned or unmanned. The U.S. Space Shuttle clearly qualifies as a spaceship. So, I submit, do the unmanned transport orbiters being developed by the Soviet Union, Japan, and the European Space Agency.

Once having defined the spacecraft for transport as a spaceship, its classification according to ownership and use becomes important. At sea, different rights and responsibilities flow from a ship's legal characterization. There are warships, other governmental vessels (with a subclassification depending on commercial or public use) and private merchant vessels. At the highest end of the scale is the warship. It enjoys complete sovereign immunity from foreign jurisdiction and has certain extraordinary rights on the high seas. Other governmental ships used for public purposes also have sovereign immunity, but not the special rights of warships. In most states, governmental ships used for private purposes no longer have immunity and, of course, neither do private merchant vessels. It has been necessary to classify vessels in order that all who use the high seas, or participate in maritime activity, understand the respective rights and duties of each type of vessel.

*   *   *

Should spaceships from the very outset be separately classified according to mission? In my view the answer is yes. Unlike other space objects, spaceships are instrumentalities of navigation. Those ships operated by the military for military purposes, like their counterparts at sea and in the airspace, need particular identification. Following along the lines of the Law of the Sea draft, military spaceships should be defined as those which are under military control and whose ground controller or space crew are subject to military discipline.

*   *   *

Without delving into the subject of maritime liens, it is apparent that to vest spaceships with the same quality of responsibility attributed to vessels could have dramatic implications. A spaceship, part of whose payload is carried under contract with a private corporation, which lands on foreign soil through intent or accident, might find itself the subject of an *in rem* proceeding brought by a foreign claimant. Nothing in the Liability Convention prevents judicial recourse by private claimants even where that Convention might apply.

As spaceship operations become routine and the options they afford for commercial venture more advanced, their legal status becomes a matter of great importance and so will the analogy to public and private vessels.

The Right of Passage

Defining and classifying spaceships is only the start. Greater activity in space means more launches, which could mean more launch sites, or, as they will certainly come to be known, spaceports. There are probably fewer than a dozen separate launch facilities in the world today. . . . Eight nations have expressed interest in establishing new international launch facilities. Five of these are equatorial states. Will there be, before the end of the century, an explosion in space transport to equal that generated by air transport in the last quarter of a century? It is certainly a distinct possibility.

The rapid proliferation of communications satellites may prove an interesting precedent. Technological advances and economies of increased spacecraft production will provide direct access to space for more and more states. This will require the greater traverse of foreign airspace.

Many writers have addressed the problem of innocent passage through airspace to the [realm of] outer space and have suggested the development of a rule comparable to the right of innocent passage for ships through territorial waters. I prefer the analogy to the landlocked state. That state has no access to the unique environment of the oceans except through the territory of another. It has no sea coast. In the same manner, states who develop the capability to launch vehicles in space may not be geographically positioned to do so without transiting foreign airspace. They too are landlocked. The Geneva Convention on the High Seas provides that landlocked states shall enjoy the right of free access to the sea and equal treatment in ports. A similar right is needed in space. It is at the outset of an active transport era that the greatest opportunity lies for the establishment of the principle of free transit to and from space. This right is less likely to emerge from the practice of states than by bilateral or multilateral agreement. Free transit through foreign air space would reduce the urgency to set forth a geometric border between air and outer space.

The Exercise of Exceptional Jurisdiction

The maneuverability of the spaceship will make it possible to approach and inspect alien satellites which are suspected of being a threat to the earth environment. It will be possible to remove the satellite to a high energy orbit, neutralize it, or control its return to earth. The Outer Space Treaty makes it clear, however, that the registry state retains jurisdiction and control over its space objects and undoubtedly this is meant to be exclusive. Any exercise of control over a foreign satellite would have to be on exceptional grounds.

The corollary to the principle of the freedom of the high seas is that all states normally have a duty not to interfere with foreign ships outside territorial waters. In a famous admiralty case a British Judge declared,

> In places where no local authority exists, where the subjects of all States meet upon a footing of entire equality and independence, no one State, or any of its subjects, has a right to assume or exercise authority over the subjects of another.

However, there is an exception to this principle of freedom of navigation. This exception involves the high seas right of approach. It is the right of any warship to approach a suspicious merchant vessel and verify her nationality and ensure she is not violating international law relating to fishing, submarine cable, and piracy, as well as misuse of the national flag. If the crew of the warship decides to board the suspect vessel, there is a heavy burden to substantiate the suspicion. Failure to do so makes the flag state liable for the loss, damage or delay to the merchant ship. Whether a similar exceptional right of approach will develop in space rests on the good will of spacefaring states. Both the fall to earth of the Soviet Cosmos 954, breaking up over an area of northwest Canada about the size of Austria, and the uncontrolled return to earth of parts of the eighty-five ton Skylab, illustrate the risks involved in deteriorating satellites.

*   *   *

Safety of Navigation

It might appear at present that space voyages will not require the type of uniform rules for navigation that govern at sea. Space is limitless, the public oceans are not. Sea transit will far exceed space transit for decades to come. The risk of actual collision between two manned craft in space is minimal when compared to shipwreck and collision. However, the near earth and geostationary orbits will be the most frequented areas of space and as noted above there is already overcrowding in the latter orbit. As fully reusable launch systems transport large payloads from earth to low orbit and return them, and as reusable space-based orbital vehicles develop to transfer men and equipment from low to high orbit and to land on celestial bodies, uniform rules will be required to govern landing, docking, staging and inter-orbital transfers. It is an inexorable certainty that a navigation code will become as necessary for space safety as it became for traffic safety in the air space and at sea.

International rules of navigation applicable to high seas navigation have been enacted by virtually all maritime states, and amendments are usually made simultaneously by international agreement. The International Regulations for Preventing Collisions at Sea of 1972 are a part of these rules.

They set forth measures to avoid collision, for maneuvering, towing, warning and distress signals. There have been a number of conferences between maritime states called for the purpose of standardizing rules for structural safety, fire and life saving equipment, and the use of radio and other navigational aids.

Whether an international space traffic code emerges through the concordant national legislation and regulation of the principal spacefaring nations, or through formal international agreement, it will become imperative to achieve uniform standards and practices. The Scientific and Technical Subcommittee working group on the use of nuclear power sources should be invited to consider the larger question of spaceship safety and to set forth suggested rules for uniform practices.

Status of Crew and Others

The Outer Space Treaty provides that all parties should regard astronauts as envoys of mankind. What special protection this affords, apart from providing all possible assistance in the event of accidents, distress, or emergency, is not clear. It is true they will not be treated as diplomatic envoys with governmental immunity. If they are forced down in foreign territory or on the high seas they will have a temporary diplomatic immunity until they are returned to their own country. To what further protection are they entitled?

Seamen have long been regarded as wards of the admiralty. They are endowed special protection not accorded fellow workers on land, except by statute. Two ancient rights which they have acquired through practice and usage are the rights to maintenance and cure, and to a seaworthy vessel. Whenever a seaman becomes disabled during a sea voyage through sickness or accident, he is entitled to the continuance of his wages until restored to health, and to all medical expenses. . . . The seaworthiness of the vessel is also an absolute requirement, and due diligence and care by the shipowner provides no exoneration for him if the court finds the vessel was not fit for whatever reason or cause. The concordant practice of maritime states has shaped a very strong maritime law in this regard.

Will states whose nationals sojourn into space develop a similar set of protective rules for all spacefarers? I think it likely. Land-based rules for employer liability are shaped around work done "in the course of employment" and "within the scope of authority." On-duty and off-duty status and whether the aggrieved employee was deviating from his normal route or performance become important considerations. In space, as at sea, the spacefarer should be comprehensively protected without regard to any of the legal considerations. Whether his travel into space is for only a few days, or for weeks or months, he has a high risk occupation and his duty period, like that of the sailor, is for twenty-four hours each day. Consider how appropriate to the future spaceman is the language used by Justice Rutledge in describing the sailor's life. He wrote:

. . . Unlike men employed in service on land, the seaman, when he finishes his day's work, is neither relieved of obligations to his employer nor wholly free to dispose of his leisure as he sees fit. Of necessity, during the voyage he must eat, drink, lodge and divert himself within the confines of the ship. In short, during the period of his tenure the vessel is not merely his place of employment; it is the framework of his existence. For that reason, among others, his employer's responsibility for maintenance and cure extends beyond injuries sustained because of, or while engaged in activities required by his employment.

Federated States such as the U.S. should exercise legislative and judicial jurisdiction only at the national level. In the United States, a Federal Wrongful Death statute for outer space is needed which would preempt state law. It might be useful to extend the Death on the High Seas Act to activities in space. The Federal Tort Claims Act should be amended to specifically cover acts in space and further revised to include claims based on strict liability for governmental conduct. As long duration voyages and habitation in space become a reality, the relatively short statute of limitations for judicial recourse needs to be extended. In admiralty, by constitutional grant, Federal jurisdiction is exclusive (with certain exceptions not relevant here). A uniform national space law is preferable to the hodgepodge of tort law applicable to aviation mishaps where state as well as Federal law is relevant. The working conditions of space crews and other personnel, minimum health standards for space flight, the provision for medical care and the extent of disciplinary authority of the mission and flight commanders must be defined only at the national and international levels.

On March 7, 1980, NASA promulgated rules on the authority of the shuttle commander in flight. Shuttle commanders have been given authority similar to that held by sea captains and aircraft commanders including the power to arrest and to use force if necessary to maintain law and order in orbit. The rules also establish a chain of command on board the shuttle in the event the commander or his copilot are incapacitated. The new rules recognize that the shuttle will carry non-NASA scientists, engineers and foreign researchers.

*   *   *

Salvage

Some years ago, Mr. Page, the President of the General Electric Missiles and Space Division, predicted there would be a million satellites in earth orbit in the 1990's. As time slips by, this prediction seems much too optimistic. There are approximately 4,500 space objects orbiting earth at the present, about one fourth of which are functioning. Although he may have miscalculated, the problems implicit in his prediction will be generated. The U.N. Secretariat's Report states it will "almost certainly" be necessary in time to sweep non-geostationary orbits planned for extremely large structures, such as those planned for in space construction of solar power satellites. It is also true that much of the artifacts brought into space will be salvageable. The Astronaut Agreement does not address the question of salvage. It does provide that, upon request, objects launched into space found outside the launching state shall be returned or held at that state's disposal. It also provides for the recoupment of expenses.

At sea, every recovery of lost or abandoned property, or property at peril, is subject to a salvage claim. Though limited to the value of the property saved, the award can be far in excess of expenses. This depends on the hazards involved, the value of the property at risk, the value of the property saved, and other considerations.

*   *   *

It is not too early for an appropriate body such as COPUOS to consider whether a salvage law for space will require an international agreement comparable, perhaps, to the Brussels Salvage Convention of 1910, or whether it can best develop through national law and practice.

Protection of the Environment

Already mentioned in connection with the need to control earth-threatening satellites such as unstable nuclear powered satellites is the need for a safety regime in space. However, the question of back and forward contamination in space is much broader than just the exercise of any right of removal of deleterious space objects. A special set of safety standards, uniformly adopted throughout the community of spacefaring states, is extremely desirable.

The Geneva High Seas Convention provides that every state shall draw up regulations to prevent pollution of the seas by the discharge of oil from ships and shall take measures to prevent pollution from the dumping of radio-active waste. . . . While it should be superficially attractive to transfer concepts being developed in this most vital area from the sea to space, it probably is not a useful analogy. First, because the law of the sea is itself in a state of confusion on this subject, and second, because the distinctive characteristics of the two environments call for entirely different approaches to the problem. Nevertheless, there must be a uniformity of approach, common standards and an international repository for the communication and exchange of all information on space contamination.

Conclusion

While the law of the sea does not represent an infallible guide to the developing law of space, space lawyers need some appreciation of maritime law. They need to become conversant with basic admiralty rules to vessel identification, navigation, management of ships, rights of seamen, the law of salvage, limitations of liability and governmental activity in sea commerce. It is with this perspective that they can compare the two environments, consider the relevance of maritime law, and select for adoption for space transport those legal principles which have proved beneficial to commerce on the oceans.

I. White, Decision-Making for Space: Law and Politics in Air, Sea and Outer Space 179 *et seq.* (1971)

Are Air, Sea, and Outer Space Legal Problems Comparable?

In Part II, selected international air and sea law rules were determined. The question now posed is this: Are the selected air and sea legal problems or problem areas and certain outer space legal problems comparable and are similar interests or preconditions perceived by national decision-makers in the three environments?

*   *   *

Access and Passage

Freedom of the high seas is a universally-recognized general principle of international law. Coastal and landlocked states alike have a right of freedom of access and use. Subject to certain limitations, there is also a right of innocent passage through territorial seas.

The aircraft of all states may fly freely over the high seas. However, innocent passage through territorial airspace is not a general right in international air law. Passage through territorial airspace must be authorized either by a contractual arrangement or by special permission. . . . National decision-makers seem to accept the principle of the freedom of the high seas primarily to protect or enhance an economic interest. Sharing the high seas for such uses as, for example, communications, transportation, or fishing is functional to both primarily exclusive and inclusive interests of a majority of states. Apparently the same finding applies in general to the airspace above the high seas.

It is clear, on the basis of the discussions of sovereignty and delimitation and resources in this chapter, that national decision-makers perceive an inclusive interest in outer space similar to that perceived in the high seas and the airspace over the high seas. A number of statements have been cited in which outer space, at least by implication, is characterized as a *res communis.* In fact, the [1967 Outer Space Treaty], and several of the General Assembly resolutions which it in effect supersedes, provide for free access and joint usage of outer space and celestial bodies.

*   *   *

Recognition of an inclusive interest in the right of access and usage came almost with the orbiting of the first satellites. . . . In 1958, Antonio Ambrosini, an Italian delegate in the First Committee, stated that in his opinion the lack of protest by overflown states amounted to a "tacit and unanimous agreement." The Yugoslavian delegate, Dobrivoje Vidic, in discussing freedom of movement in outer space, observed that:

> [B]y virtue of its very nature, and of the fact that penetration into it has been brought about by the common efforts and progress of the whole of mankind, no less so than by virtue of the fact that its abuse could be fatal to the whole world, outer space can only be regarded as *res communis.*

*   *   *

Costa Rica's Gonzalo Ortiz Martin stated the claim from the viewpoint of the small states: "If our small country had the economic and scientific means to shoot off satellites that might be placed in orbit, no one would dare to deny us the right to do so, as no one has denied the right to do so to those who have led the scientific race."

*   *   *

Apparently, the two fundamental reasons for insisting that ships and planes have a nationality and/or be registered are to assign responsibility and to afford protection. . . . [I]t was found that the state of nationality and registration is held responsible for enforcing, for example, safety standards and crew licensing requirements. Claims made concerning liability, nationality and registration, and safety are obviously interrelated. As there is no general enforcement agency, assigning responsibility to the flag state is likely to be the most effective means of enforcing what are essentially the protective rules concerning liability and safety. This same observation seems to apply to spacecraft.

*   *   *

The most important point, however, is that the types of injuries, damages, and losses being protected against are identically the same surface damages concerning which states have made claims and counterclaims in international air law. The only change seems to be the specific vehicle which is being protected against. That is, at its present state of development the spacecraft may warrant treatment as extrahazardous as, for example, did aircraft in the early days of aviation and so do nuclear ships now.

*   *   *

Safety is, of course, also a concern in spacecraft. Currently this is mainly a concern for surface damages which might result from spacecraft. However, there must increasingly be concern for personnel safety in manned vehicles, a point emphasized by the unfortunate tragedy in January 1967, involving the flight crew for the first Apollo flight.

Control over spacecraft is a primary concern in connection with surface damages. For example, the use of destruct devices gives launching states a degree of control over the hazards associated with launching a spacecraft. Another type of control is associated with both safety and interference, the ability to recover or destroy spacecraft which have completed their mission and simply clutter space. A more limited kind of control is the ability to free frequencies by "turning off" spacecraft when their mission is completed.

Concern for the safety of personnel in spacecraft has been limited since only highly specialized and well qualified crews have been permitted to man spacecraft. When and if spacecraft come to be used as common carriers, the concern will, of course, become more general and it might be expected that comprehensive rules comparable to those for air and sea common carriers will be agreed upon.

The problems of liability, nationality and registration, and safety, then, are quite comparable to the same problems in the air and sea environments. A smaller number of vehicles is currently involved in space and the hazards are generally greater. Otherwise the interests are basically if not identically the same and even the preliminary and tentative steps toward solution are comparable to those which have proved functional in the other two environments.

*   *   *

The problems of sovereignty and delimitation in air, sea, and outer space, while not identical, are reasonably comparable. And the fundamental interests which decision-makers perceive in relation to these problems appear to be identical. While particular air and sea rules are not directly applicable, the problems are comparable enough that knowing what the preconditions of rule acceptance are in air and sea law will be helpful in formulating acceptable rules for the space environment.

*   *   *

Of all problems or problem areas, liability, nationality and registration, and safety are most comparable in the three environments. Solutions to these kinds of problems are necessary and functional to peaceful and routine interaction in all environments. And while there are now far fewer spacecraft than ships and planes, and while the hazards from spacecraft are generally greater, the fundamental interests which decision-makers seek to protect and/or enhance are identical. In fact, the preliminary and tentative steps taken toward solving these problems are comparable to those which have proved successful in the air and sea environments.

Center for Research of Air and Space Law,
Space Activities and Emerging International Law
161 *et seq.* (N. Matte, Ed. 1984)

1. Early Aeronautical Law

a. The "Freedom of the Air" Doctrine

During the period from the time of the first manned aircraft to the conclusion of the Paris Convention of 1919, a number of differing opinions have been advanced as to the principles governing the status of the air-space. Theories range from the "freedom of the air," as advanced by the French jurist Fauchille, to the theory of "absolute sovereignty," which later became the generally accepted doctrine. Interposed was the notion of limited freedom of the air (above a territorial air zone) and a variety of compromise theories.

Of particular interest is the freedom theory advanced by Fauchille who argued that there were no presupposed sovereign rights over the air-space above a state.

*   *   *

Although this approach was widely accepted, state practice evolved towards the theory of sovereignty over air-space. The main reason for this was one of security. World War I and the growing use of aircraft for belligerent purposes showed that such a need did in fact exist. As a consequence, the theory of exclusive and complete sovereignty of the subjacent state over its air-space gained general acceptance.

b. *The Legal Status of Air-space*

In practice, a number of European states had implicitly recognized the theory of sovereignty over air-space before the First World War.

*   *   *

Various European states, such as France, the United Kingdom, Austria-Hungary and Germany passed national laws or regulations for the control of overflight over their territory.

*   *   *

In practice, therefore, the theory of freedom of the air had already been rejected before the First World War, not only for reasons of security, but also for reasons of safety, practicability, and doubtless also with a view to economic aspects of aviation.

c. *The Regulation of Commercial Activities*

States soon realized that the theory of sovereignty over air-space was of greater economic and commercial advantage than the theory of absolute freedom. In particular the granting of rights for landing could be made on a reciprocal basis or dependent on the grant of other favourable economic concessions. As a consequence, the Paris Convention of 1919 provided in Article XV that "every contracting State may make conditional on its prior authorization the establishment of international airways and the creation and operation of regular international air navigation routes with or without landing on its territory." Similarly, articles XXXVI and XXVIII of the Conventions provided that air commerce could only be carried out with the special permission of each state overflown. Thus, commercial freedom was excluded from the Paris Convention of 1919 and, at that early state of aviation, left to regulation by bilateral agreements between states. This approach for the carrying out of air commerce was confirmed in the Chicago Convention of 1944 and continues to apply today. The legal regime of air commerce is therefore predicated on the general acceptance of the theory of absolute and exclusive sovereignty over air-space.

2. The Air Space over the High Seas

a. The Chicago Convention and the Law of the Sea

According to Article 12 of the Chicago Convention, the rules applicable to flight over the high seas shall be those established according to the Convention. This provision refers to the rule-making power of the Council of the International Civil Aviation Organization (which is established by the Convention), with respect to the enactment of annexes to the Convention. The powers of the ICAO Council with respect to rule-making for the High Seas have been called "real international legislative powers."

*   *   *

b. The Legal Status of the Air-space Above the High Seas

It is generally recognized that the legal status of the air-space above the high seas is analogous to that of the high seas itself. The basic principle is that of *res omnium communis*. No state may exercise sovereign rights over any portion either of the high seas or of the air-space above. Furthermore, all states enjoy the freedom of use and navigation on and above the high seas.

*   *   *

c. The Regulation of Commercial Activities

The rule of freedom of air navigation above the high seas is applicable to both commercial and non-commercial services. As a consequence, the ICAO Council is empowered to make rules for the operation of both above the high seas.

*   *   *

3. The Relevance for the International Regulation of Space Activities

a. The Relevance of Analogies in General

The relevance of analogies taken from general international law in relation to the notions and concepts of space law has been the subject of much discussion. While it may be argued that such analogies have insufficient common ground to permit valid conclusions, it appears more meritorious to consider analogous notions and concepts as an auxiliary means of interpreting the legal status of outer space. The Outer Space Treaty has, after all, been drafted in the context of international legal instruments as well as general public international law. It must therefore be presumed that there is, in certain respects, a catena of notions which justifies a comparison between the concepts applicable to outer space with those of other environments.

b. Relevance for the Legal Status of Outer Space, the Moon and other Celestial Bodies

A number of notions and concepts of laws applicable to Antarctica, as contained in the Treaty of 1959, are of immediate relevance to the law of outer space. First, the freedom of scientific investigation provided for Antarctica served to inspire the negotiators and drafters of the Outer Space Treaty. By examining state conduct with regard to Antarctica in view of the Treaty and how it had been interpreted, this may assist in clarifying the exact meaning of the principle of freedom of use and exploration of outer space as established in the Outer Space Treaty. The freedom of exploration and use can be regarded as an extension of the earlier freedom established under the Antarctic Treaty. Similarly, the demilitarized status of Antarctica as provided under the Antarctic Treaty has clearly been the basis for the partly demilitarized status of outer space under the Outer Space Treaty and also for the totally demilitarized status of the moon and other celestial bodies under the Moon Treaty. Nevertheless, issues relating to claims of sovereignty regarding Antarctica have received quite different consideration and treatment as compared with outer space.

The concept developed in early aeronautical law regarding freedom of use has the greatest similarity with existing space law. However, if one considers the factors leading to the decline of the freedom of the air doctrine, the present status of outer space, the moon and other celestial bodies, may change when economic, military or other advantages induce states to lay claim on certain parts of outer space. A similar conclusion may be drawn from the evolution of freedoms in the law of the sea. As to the status of the air-space above the high seas, the freedom of use and of navigation may be compared with that prevailing presently in outer space. However, there is no single body responsible for regulating the freedom of use and navigation of outer space, as the International Civil Aviation Organization does for the air-space above the high seas. This may change, particularly if space transportation activities increase in the future to such an extent that regulation by an international body would become a necessity.

*   *   *

c. The Regulation of Commercial Activities

A comparison with the Antarctic Treaty and the legal status of Antarctica lends support to the conclusion that commercial activities in outer space are fully consistent with its legal status. This finding is corroborated by

Article VI of the Outer Space Treaty which countenances space activities in outer space under the supervision of state authorities. Commercial activities in outer space can thus be considered fully consistent with the freedom of use and exploration of outer space. A similar analogy can be drawn with the legal status of the air-space above the high seas, as well as with the status of air-space under the doctrine of the freedom of the air in early aeronautical law. The conduct of commercial activities was considered legal, whether carried out by commercial enterprises or by state bodies or other non-commercial entities. However, a major difference is that the Outer Space Treaty, as well as the Moon Treaty, contains express safeguards to ensure that commercial activities carried out by non-governmental entities are supervised to ensure that they act in accordance with both treaties.

NOTES

1. Nations on the high seas have in the past established temporary exclusion zones, barring vessels of other countries from particular areas of the ocean during military maneuvers. They have also established permanent zones of limited access on and over the high seas—for example, Air Defense Identification Zones stretching hundreds of miles beyond U.S. territorial waters, or exclusion zones around U.S. offshore radar installations (the so-called "Texas towers" facilities). *See, e.g.,* 14 C.F.R. §§ 99.1 *et seq.* (1988) (Air Defense Identification Zones). Might nations establish similar "keep out zones" around space facilities? Some have made such proposals: see Schwetje, Protecting Space Assets: A Legal Analysis of "Keep Out Zones," 15 Journal of Space Law 131 (1987). As you read the following chapters, with their discussion of treaty restrictions on military activity and treaty guarantees of equal access to space, you might consider whether such zones would be legal under international law, as well as whether they would contribute to stability or suspicion.

2. Spacecraft must expend considerable energy to make significant alterations in course—so much so that their ability to change path is very limited once they are in flight. In this respect they are very different from ships and aircraft. How might this affect notions of freedom of space, or the ability of nations to deny other nations access to some areas of space?

3. How much do astronauts really resemble seamen? While it is true that they must spend extended periods confined in their vessels, astronauts (unlike most seamen) are highly educated professionals who have chosen their careers in preference to many (often more lucrative) alternatives in order to have the opportunity to fly in space. This may change with time, of course, but until it does, proposals to model law governing the treatment of astronauts on that relating to seamen may be inappropriate in many respects. Seamen have traditionally received great protection from Admir-

alty courts because they have been presumed to be lacking in formal education (and hence easily bilked) while specialized in occupation (and hence unable to change jobs readily). *See* G. Gilmore & C. Black, The Law of Admiralty (2d ed. 1975) at 272 *et seq.*

4. While many specifics of the space environment differ from those of the air and sea environments, there are many similarities as well. One is that all three have very important potential for both military and economic uses; another is that many of their resources are not consumed by use— for example, ships do not "use up" the ocean by passing over it, and satellites do not "use up" outer space by passing through it. Of course, some unusual locations depart from this statement: some narrow straits impose limits on the ability of traffic to pass through them, while some orbits (chiefly the geosynchronous orbit) have limited capacity and no satisfactory substitutes. For a discussion of how rules regarding ocean navigation and fishing might provide models for an international regime governing space activity, see Reynolds & Merges, The Role of Commercial Development in Preventing War in Outer Space, 25 Jurimetrics: Journal of Law, Science, & Technology 130 (1985).

UN EFFORTS AND ASPIRATIONS

The 1967 Outer Space Treaty discussed in the next chapter did not appear all at once, but was the result of an evolutionary process in which the United Nations General Assembly, various scholars, and special negotiating committees took part. The following excerpt from an article by Myres McDougal and Leon Lipson, two Yale professors who were leading figures in the early evolution of space law, provides some perspective on the way in which that happened.

McDougal & Lipson, Perspectives for a Law of Outer Space, 52 American Journal of International Law 407 (1958)

The patterns of use of outer space will of course unfold in a context of conditions which even now, we suggest, can be identified as being certain to affect the law of space as it develops over the years. Some of these conditions are common to many areas of human conduct and interest; some are, in a measure, peculiar to the use of outer space. Those that are noted below are intended to be illustrative only.

One condition of first importance is the extraordinary interdependence of scientific, military, commercial, and other objectives that may be advanced by the same activities in space. Scientific observations on cosmic radiation may some day serve as a basis for the development of radiological warfare. A television relay station may be capable of use to interfere with communications instead of facilitating them. A reconnaissance satellite may be made to yield important economic benefits from services to meteorology. Geodetic observations made by celestial mechanicians may improve the accuracy of intercontinental ballistic missiles by making international maps more precise. For an orbiting satellite carrying a nuclear warhead, it is perhaps not easy to imagine an immediate commercial or scientific use that would not be served more efficiently by some other device, but it would be rash to say that no such use is possible.

By reason of this interdependence, it may be difficult to apply some well-known legal techniques—prohibition, conditional permission, allocation of responsibility for damage, regulation, and so on—on the basis of a supposed predominant category of use. If we want certain benefits we may have to accept certain risks. Especially in the preliminary exploratory stage (which may last for generations), we may have to stress those aspects of legal control that permit and encourage development, while doing our best to measure the size of the risk to which we are being exposed. This does not mean that we ought to reject the possibility of reaching, or at least talking about, an agreement to outlaw certain uses of outer space, for the marginal gains to be expected from those uses may not be worth their price; but it does imply that it will not be easy to define "peaceful purposes" or "scientific purposes" without risk of hampering activities that have multiple uses.

*   *   *

It is characteristic of the loose and primitive structure of the contemporary earth arena that many of the nation-state officials who will make the decisions are the same who will be making the claims. The difference in role may make a significant difference in self-image, in the length of the time range for the calculation of interest, and in recognition of need for reciprocity; but the objectives of their action as decision-makers will of course in measure overlap the objectives of their action as claimants. They will be, and they will take care to appear to be, concerned for the attainment of some modicum of security: the indefinite postponement of unacceptably destructive violence, the achievement of some stability of expectation as to modes of exercising effective power, the maintenance of public order against hostile or reckless or capricious threats. They will wish to conserve the potentially vast resources of space for the production of the largest net gain in all values, though their respective preferences for the distribution of the gain may be mutually incompatible. They will probably concur in demanding that as many of the uses of outer space as are capable of being shared without serious inconvenience be kept available for sharing. They will seek in various ways to adapt to their existing power objectives the potentialities opened up by the access to the new resource environment; the brave new worlds will not for some time suffice to redress or greatly distort the balance of the old.

*   *   *

A durable agreement by explicit international convention on anything like a code of law for outer space is not, in our opinion, something now to be expected or desired. One may indeed expect with rather more confidence a series of agreements, gradually arrived at, on particular subjects, such as the continuation of the International Geophysical Year; the exchange of certain types of information, such as tracking data and some signaling codes, beyond present levels; the use or abstention from use of certain radio frequencies; and the coordination of launching schedules. Particular projects, like the establishment of television or radio relay satellites, might (in addition to whatever economic or scientific merits they possess) serve to test the possibilities of broad international cooperation more fruitfully than conferences on "the law of space." Agreement might be reached—not necessarily by the execution of formal documents—to abstain from the pollution of space by shrapnel or other "junk," which might otherwise be thrown up in an attempt to impede the flight of hostile satellites or hostile communications; such agreement would probably depend on the assurance either that other means of averting the danger from the hostile activities were adequate or that the activities did not present a danger sufficiently great to justify the pollution.

The modes of reaching such agreements cannot now be charted with any precision. Some agreements may be explicit and formal; some may be simply a consensus achieved by the gradual accretion of custom from repeated instances of mutual toleration. Some may be bilateral, others trilateral or multilateral; some may be within the framework of the United Nations, others within some other existing organization or some machinery yet to be set up. Their details and sequence must, like much else in an indeterminate universe, depend on the order of experience in space as well as on the changing political context.

We recognize, however, that the order of that experience will in turn be affected by expectations which decision-making officials in the nation states possessing space capabilities entertain as to the space plans of others and by the reactions and attitudes of the earth community. In order to help allay anxieties about the possible weapons uses of space satellites and to help lay a foundation for closer cooperation in peaceful activities in space for common benefit—a cooperation from which an adequate and effective customary or conventional law might eventually emerge—the following suggestions might even now be considered by responsible officials:

(1) It was suggested in this JOURNAL early in 1957 that each state about to launch a satellite could register its intent to do so with an international agency, filing a flight plan and a description of certain characteristics of the satellite, such as load, weight, and size. This could be combined with willingness to submit to international inspection, to assure that the payload conforms to the description filed. This suggestion could be put into practice by any state, regardless of the agreement of any other state; but the decision to do so might well be affected by the communicated willingness of other launching states to agree to corresponding measures.

(2) Agreement might be reached to abstain from the launching of satellites fitted with nuclear or other explosive warheads. Such an agreement

probably would have to be contingent on the availability of effective pre-launching inspection of the type that is illustrated by the first proposal above. Whether it should or could be coupled with an agreement on the prohibition of the use of intercontinental ballistic missiles, and whether it should or could be considered as part of a possible general agreement on nuclear or universal disarmament, are matters of strategy, community and national, dependent upon the course of many variables.

(3) States possessing the capability of launching satellites might offer to launch certain types of satellites on behalf of, or even as trustee for, the United Nations. The launching state could retain responsibility for the launching operation, preserving control over the security of its rocketry; the United Nations would decide upon the purpose of the flight, determine the payload, design the instrumentation, and finance the construction of the satellite and its contents. The necessary United Nations decisions could be made by an arm of the United Nations, or authority to make them could be delegated to the launching state or conceivably to some other agent. The existence of such "trust satellites" would not necessarily preclude national satellites with similar or identical functions.

NOTES

1. Many of the suggestions made in this early article were ultimately embodied in later treaties—registration of spacecraft, for example, was provided for in the Outer Space Treaty and the Registration Convention, both discussed *infra,* while the Outer Space Treaty also bars the orbiting of nuclear weapons. The "trust satellite" concept never really came off (although the use of international organizations, such as INTELSAT, to administer some satellite functions bears some resemblance to the scheme envisioned by McDougal and Lipson); it survives, however, via repeated suggestions that the United Nations orbit its own reconnaissance satellites for the purpose of assisting in arms control verification and keeping an eye on potential trouble spots. So far the superpowers, who retain a monopoly on sophisticated satellite reconnaissance facilities, have resisted such efforts. That monopoly is eroding, however, and as the technology becomes cheaper and more readily available we are likely to see other nations, as well as private entities such as news networks and possibly even arms control groups, orbiting their own reconnaissance satellites. Perhaps once such enterprises are obviously imminent, the superpowers will be more friendly to the acquisition of such capabilities by the United Nations. Other potential concerns mentioned by McDougal and Lipson, such as pollution of the space environment by orbital debris, are of growing importance but have not yet been addressed. For more on these topics, see Chapter 5.

2. Shortly after the publication of the above article, the United Nations organized COPUOS, the Committee on the Peaceful Uses of Outer Space. That committee was until the mid-1970s the most important single source of international law relating to space activities. Since the mid-1970s, however, COPUOS has fallen victim to the increased factionalism of the United Nations, and its effectiveness has been diminished. For a discussion of the origins of COPUOS, see Jessup & Taubenfeld, The United Nations Ad Hoc Committee on the Peaceful Uses of Outer Space, 53 American Journal of International Law 877 (1959).

3

Early Treaties Governing Activity in Outer Space

The previous chapter outlined the basic principles of general international law governing activities in outer space. With this chapter we will begin to discuss the important early treaties providing more specific legal norms for nations' space activities: the Limited Test Ban Treaty of 1963 and the Outer Space Treaty of 1967. The process by which these were developed was a gradual one: the Limited Test Ban Treaty, which among other things prohibits nuclear explosions in outer space, was the result of discussions begun in the early 1950s, and of international pressure orchestrated by Nobel laureate Linus Pauling, who created worldwide concern regarding the hazards of nuclear fallout from atmospheric tests; the Outer Space Treaty developed as the result of a lengthy process of negotiation and refinement of language in the UN's Committee on the Peaceful Uses of Outer Space (COPUOS), the creation of which is described in the article by Jessup & Taubenfeld, *infra*. The negotiations leading up to the Outer Space Treaty are discussed at considerable length in Dembling & Arons, also *infra;* what becomes apparent from even a superficial reading of that piece is that one reason for the lengthy negotiation was that many of the nations involved lacked a clear sense of their interests—both future and contemporaneous—in any particular space regime. Most of the participants had only hazy ideas of what would come to pass in the space field, and how it would affect their own destinies, and even the United States and the Soviet Union seemed far more willing than usual to be persuaded by one another on most issues.

Paradoxically, this comparative lack of specifically self-serving goals may be one reason why the Outer Space Treaty is viewed with such respect— approaching reverence at times—by so many. Having been arrived at by nations operating behind an almost Rawlsian veil of ignorance, the Treaty can be said to represent a more general view of the interests of humanity instead of being merely a compromise among interested parties, shaped primarily by the balance of power. How close this perception is to the facts is another matter: the United States, at least, was quite concerned about maintaining its ability to operate intelligence–gathering satellites and hence was not unclear about its interests in that regard. Still, excepting such relatively narrow issues, it probably *is* the case that the participants in the processes leading up to the Outer Space Treaty took a broader and longer view than is typical in international negotiations, and that the Outer Space Treaty does gain in legitimacy as a result. Whether this circumstance can be duplicated in the future is unclear, but worth bearing in mind as a goal. This climate of reasonably objective, if not actually altruistic, debate can be contrasted with the much more self-interested debate over the Moon Treaty, described in the next chapter; the dismal results of the latter process speak for themselves.

The following excerpt from an article by Jessup & Taubenfeld describes the formation of the Committee on the Peaceful Uses of Outer Space. The COPUOS continues to be the United Nations' primary space-related body, although its influence has diminished along with that of the UN in general in recent years. As the article demonstrates, however, the key issues later dealt with in the Outer Space Treaty were identified early on.

Jessup & Taubenfeld, The United Nations *Ad Hoc* Committee on the Peaceful Uses of Outer Space, 53 American Journal of International Law 877 (1959)

After formal inaugural meetings, the Ad Hoc Committee formed a Technical and a Legal Committee. By mid-June these two Committees had completed their reports and the Secretariat had also prepared a Report on "the activities and resources of the United Nations, of its specialized agencies and of other international bodies related to the peaceful uses of outer space."

The members of the Technical Committee took as a basis working papers circulated by the United States and Italy on the scientific possibilities of use of outer space and on the activities and resources of the United Nations and the specialized agencies in the field of outer space. The Technical Committee also received oral comments from persons connected with such organizations as UNESCO, the World Meteorological Organization (WMO), the International Telecommunications Union (ITU) and the International Civil Aviation Organization (ICAO). There was general agreement that the exploration of space was "a task vast enough to enlist the talents of scientists of all nations." Just as there was no way to limit the definition of "atmosphere" for WMO's weather purposes, there was general agreement that outer space was scientifically indivisible. The usefulness of participation in space efforts by nations lacking launching capabilities, particularly through such voluntary cooperative scientific arrangements as the IGY's successor in this field, COSPAR (Committee on Space Research), was emphasized and the United States was complimented several times on its offers to permit scientists from other nations to design experiments to be carried out by U.S.-launched satellites. The stress was on cooperative efforts of the COSPAR type, though it was generally agreed that, when the research stage was passed, functioning intergovernmental arrangements of the WMO, ITU type were probably essential. The possibility of international launching sites was also raised.

The Technical Committee's report was approved by the *Ad Hoc* Committee on June 18, and became part of the report to the General Assembly. This report stressed that to make best use of all available talent and, in some cases, due to the costs involved, "space activities, scientific and technological . . . even more than . . . astronomy . . . inherently ignore national boundaries. Space activities must to a large extent be an effort of Planet Earth as a whole." The connection between military activities and space research with its hampering effect on exchange of information was also noted, but it was concluded that the development of space vehicles has reached the point in several countries where it was a question of engineering only, not of science.

*   *   *

The Legal Committee proceeded with the aid of working papers and drafts submitted by the United States and Mexico. Its report was also approved by the *Ad Hoc* Committee on June 18. The Committee observed that the provisions of the United Nations Charter and of the Statute of the International Court of Justice are, as a matter of principle, not limited in their operation to the confines of the Earth. It was agreed that not enough was now known about the actual and prospective uses of outer space to make a comprehensive code practicable or desirable, but that it was necessary to take "timely, constructive action and to make the law of space responsive to the facts of space."

> It was unanimously recognized that the principles and procedures developed . . . to govern the use of such areas as the air space and the sea deserved attentive study for possibly fruitful analogies . . . [though] outer space activities were distinguished by many specific factual conditions . . . that would render many of its legal problems unique.

Among legal problems susceptible of priority treatment, it was suggested, is the broad one of freedom of outer space for exploration and use. Here, the Legal Committee, in mentioning the flight of space vehicles "over" countries during the IGY, suggested that

> with this practice, there may have been initiated the recognition or establishment of a generally accepted rule to the effect that, in principle, outer space is, on conditions of equality, freely available for exploration and use by all in accordance with existing or future international law or agreements.

Other priority problems included by the Committee were liability for injury or damage caused by space vehicles, including the need for machinery to determine liability and ensure payment of compensation. Here, the Committee suggested the compulsory submission to the International Court of

Justice of disputes between states as to liability, and considered relevant ICAO experience with respect to the 1952 Convention on Damage Caused by Foreign Aircraft to Third Parties on the Surface. Allocation of radio frequencies, termination of transmissions, avoidance of interference between space vehicles and aircraft, identification and registration of vehicles through markings, call signs and orbit and transit characteristics, registration and co-ordination of launchings, and re-entry and landing problems were also considered of current importance.

Problems which may be ignored for the present, as either too remote from the point of view of technological development or because activities can be conducted without their resolution, were thought to include the determination of precise limits between airspace and outer space, the provision of regulations against contamination of outer space or from outer space, the promulgation of rules covering sovereignty, exploration, settlement and exploration of celestial bodies and rules for the avoidance of interference among space vehicles. As is obvious, the report avoids commitments on several problems which many feel are more imminent than the Committee is cautiously willing to acknowledge.

Thus, the Committee stressed at most a role of co-ordination or the promotion of co-operation for the United Nations, though the Swedish representative expressed fears that there might be an increasing gap between the great forward surge of space activities and the efforts of the United Nations to promote the use of space for the benefit of all mankind, unless immediate action was taken within the United Nations. Others, however, insisted on "modest proposals" to meet only the most pressing needs. The *Ad Hoc* Committee's caution is quite understandable in the political circumstances, since in any actual program for promoting the peaceful uses of outer space, the non-participation of the Soviet Union would rob the effort of much of its value. It was the obvious hope that if Soviet non-participation were due to any misunderstanding of the Committee's functions, that difficulty would be overcome. Of course, if, as a matter of national policy, the Soviet Union does not wish to co-operate in this effort, it will find pretexts for further refusals.

The Committee finished its work and approved its Report to the General Assembly on June 25, 1959.

THE LIMITED TEST BAN TREATY

Although a number of Resolutions by the United Nations General Assembly had previously called upon the space powers to refrain from military uses of outer space, the first legally binding document renouncing any such uses was the Limited Test Ban Treaty of 1963. That treaty, signed by the United States, the Soviet Union, and Great Britain (other nuclear powers, such as France and China, have not signed the treaty), forbids the explosion of nuclear devices in the oceans, the atmosphere, or in outer space. The text of the treaty itself follows; we will then discuss some of the issues raised by the treaty.

Multilateral Treaty Banning Nuclear Weapon Tests in the Atmosphere, in Outer Space and Under Water, 14 U.S.T. 1313, T.I.A.S. 5433

Done at Moscow August 5, 1963;
Ratification advised by the Senate of the United States of America September 24, 1963;
Ratified by the President of the United States of America October 7, 1963;
Ratifications of the Governments of the United States of America, the United Kingdom of Great Britain and Northern Ireland, and the Union of Soviet Socialist Republics deposited with the same Governments at Washington, London, and Moscow October 10, 1963;
Proclaimed by the President of the United States of America October 10, 1963;
Entered into force October 10, 1963.

The Governments of the United States of America, the United Kingdom of Great Britain and Northern Ireland, and the Union of Soviet Socialist Republics, hereinafter referred to as the "Original Parties,"

Proclaiming as their principal aim the speediest possible achievement of an agreement on general and complete disarmament under strict international control in accordance with the objectives of the United Nations which would put an end to the armaments race and eliminate the incentive to the production and testing of all kinds of weapons, including nuclear weapons,

Seeking to achieve the discontinuance of all test explosions of nuclear weapons for all time, determined to continue negotiations to this end, and desiring to put an end to the contamination of man's environment by radioactive substances,

Have agreed as follows:

Article I

1. Each of the Parties to this Treaty undertakes to prohibit, to prevent, and not to carry out any nuclear weapon test explosion, or any other nuclear explosion, at any place under its jurisdiction or control:

(a) in the atmosphere; beyond its limits, including outer space; or underwater, including territorial waters or high seas; or

(b) in any other environment if such explosion causes radioactive debris to be present outside the territorial limits of the State under whose jurisdiction or control such explosion is conducted. It is understood in this connection that the provisions of this subparagraph are without prejudice to the conclusion of a treaty resulting in the permanent banning of all nuclear test explosions, including all such explosions underground, the conclusion of which, as the Parties have stated in the Preamble to this Treaty, they seek to achieve.

2. Each of the Parties to this Treaty undertakes furthermore to refrain from causing, encouraging, or in any way participating in, the carrying out of any nuclear weapon test explosion, or any other nuclear explosion, anywhere which would take place in any of the environments described, or have the effect referred to, in paragraph 1 of this Article.

Article II

1. Any Party may propose amendments to this Treaty. The text of any proposed amendment shall be submitted to the Depositary Governments which shall circulate it to all Parties to this Treaty. Thereafter, if requested to do so by one-third or more of the Parties, the Depositary Governments shall convene a conference, to which they shall invite all the Parties, to consider such amendment.

2. Any amendment to this Treaty must be approved by a majority of the votes of all the Parties to this Treaty, including the votes of all of the Original Parties. The amendment shall enter into force for all Parties upon the deposit of instruments of ratification by a majority of all the Parties, including the instruments of ratification of all of the Original Parties.

Article III

1. This Treaty shall be open to all States for signature. Any State which does not sign this Treaty before its entry into force in accordance with paragraph 3 of this Article may accede to it at any time.

2. This Treaty shall be subject to ratification by signatory States, Instruments of ratification and instruments of access shall be deposited with the Governments of the Original Parties—the United States of America, the United Kingdom of Great Britain and Northern Ireland, and the Union of Soviet Socialist Republics—which are hereby designated the Depositary Governments.

3. This Treaty shall enter into force after its ratification by all the Original Parties and the deposit of their instruments of ratification.

4. For States whose instruments of ratification or accession are deposited subsequent to the entry into force of this Treaty, it shall enter into force on the date of the deposit of their instruments of ratification or accession.

5. The Depositary Governments shall promptly inform all signatory and acceding States of the date of each signature, the date of deposit of each instrument of ratification of and accession to this Treaty, the date of its entry into force, and the date of receipt of any requests for conferences or other notices.

6. This Treaty shall be registered by the Depositary Governments pursuant to Article 102 of the Charter of the United Nations.

Article IV

This Treaty shall be of unlimited duration.

Each Party shall in exercising its national sovereignty have the right to withdraw from the Treaty if it decides that extraordinary events, related to the subject matter of this Treaty, have jeopardized the supreme interests of its country. It shall give notice of such withdrawal to all other Parties to the Treaty three months in advance.

Article V

This Treaty, of which the English and Russian texts are equally authentic, shall be deposited in the archives of the Depositary Governments. Duly certified copies of this Treaty shall be transmitted by the Depositary Governments to the Governments of the signatory and acceding States.

DONE in triplicate at the city of Moscow the fifth day of August, one thousand nine hundred and sixty-three.

NOTE

The primary goal of the Limited Test Ban Treaty was not arms control, but the prevention of global nuclear contamination; even the provisions barring nuclear explosions in outer space were designed to protect against problems stemming from radiation and electromagnetic pulse—experiments with high-altitude nuclear explosions having caused damage to orbiting satellites and to electronic devices on the surface at great distances, as well as having created an artificial radiation belt that persisted for some years. The Test Ban Treaty can thus be viewed primarily as an environmental agreement rather than a military one, though it was, of course, of military importance.

Matte, The Treaty Banning Nuclear Weapons Tests in the Atmosphere, in Outer Space and Under Water (10 October 1963) and the Peaceful Uses of Outer Space, 9 Annals of Air & Space Law 391 (1984)

The atomic bombs which were dropped on two Japanese cities in 1945 may have ended the Second World War, but they left behind an awesome legacy which continues to haunt the "peace" that subsequently ensued. Two politically antagonistic powers, the U.S.A. and the U.S.S.R., which joined together to fight a common enemy (Hitler) for a limited purpose and short duration, continued their rivalry and mistrust of each other once the war had ended. The Soviet Union having gained veto power in, and permanent membership of, the U.N. Security Council, secured its long desired political parity with the West. However, American mastery over nuclear technology resulted in vast resources being invested by the U.S.S.R. in order to catch up. The intensity of its competition with the West was the cause of the U.S.S.R.'s rejection of the Baruch Plan of 1946 with respect to the prohibition of the manufacture of nuclear weapons and the internationalism of control of this new technology. There was undoubtedly a lack of mutual trust between the super powers and the plan, while it "seemed to be in conformity with the requirements of technical reality, . . . did not adequately reflect the conditions of political reality."

On August 29, 1949, the U.S.S.R. tested its first atomic bomb and thus entered the nuclear race. However, its efforts were not totally devoted to the development of nuclear technology but also to long-range rockets and jet propulsion in order to perfect the delivery system for its nuclear weapons. It was a refined version of the German V-2 rockets which helped the U.S.S.R. to launch Sputnik I on October 4, 1957. Every opportunity was taken to publicize, both at home and abroad, the U.S.S.R.'s superiority in the field of science and technology and in military capability. Up until the launch of Sputnik I, the U.S. had been the unrivaled world leader in technological achievements and military capabilities and, although assured that Sputnik I was of limited military significance, the U.S. President felt that something had to be done to follow the Soviet success. Civilian and military technological capabilities were thus geared to catch up with the Russians, especially after the launch failure of the Vanguard I satellite on December 6, 1957. Von Braun, with his army ballistic missile team, was given only three months by the then Secretary of Defense to convert a Redstone missile into a Jupiter C launcher, which finally brought the U.S. into the space age on January 31, 1958 when its first satellite, Explorer I, was launched.

*   *   *

Having acquired the necessary technology to build their first nuclear weapons, the U.S. and the U.S.S.R. continued the further development and testing of their nuclear arsenals. Between 1945 and 1958, the U.S. conducted 139 nuclear tests in the atmosphere and 18 under ground. The U.S.S.R. on the other hand conducted 55 similar tests, during the period between 1949 and 1958, all in the atmosphere. The extent of these tests caused serious concern not only with respect to the continued stockpiling of nuclear weapons but also about the adverse effects of radiation fall-out on the environment, as well as living beings. Already on December 3, 1955, the U.N. General Assembly had established the Scientific Committee on the Effects of Atomic Radiation, and at the London meeting of the Subcommittee on Disarmament the issue of banning nuclear tests dominated the discussions. However, while "the West argued that the establishment of a control system and the cessation of the production of fissionable materials for military purposes should precede any agreement to limit nuclear testing, the Soviets argued that a test ban was of such importance that it should be implemented immediately independent of any other disarmament measure and without control." France, which had not yet tested its nuclear weapons, did not share the views of the Western or Socialist powers and started to remove itself from the negotiations on disarmament, especially on the test ban issue. In 1958, the three nuclear powers—the U.S., the U.S.S.R., and the U.K.—convened a tripartite "Conference on the Discontinuation of Nuclear Weapons Tests" in Geneva. In 1962, the functions of the tripartite Conference were taken over by the U.N. Eighteen Nation Disarmament Committee's (ENDC's) "Subcommittee on a Treaty for the Discontinuation of Nuclear Weapons Tests." The U.N. Scientific Committee on the Effects of Atomic Radiation conducted studies and prepared two reports for submission to the General Assembly in 1958 and 1962. It concluded that nuclear tests might have serious adverse effects on the health of people exposed to nuclear radiation. In its 1962 report, the Committee emphasized that

> As there are no effective measures to prevent the occurrence of harmful effects of global radioactive contamination from nuclear explosions, the achievement of a final cessation of nuclear tests would benefit present and future generations of mankind.

However, the political realities of 1962 were such that "final cessation of nuclear tests" was not acceptable to the super powers. "Relations between the United States and the Soviet Union" as described by Barton and Weiler, "had been so dominated by cold war attitudes early in the era that comprehensive agreements would have been almost unthinkable."

President Kennedy was convinced that the space program should continue on the basis of strict competition with the U.S.S.R. since "he considered it essential to the national interest that the U.S. continue to develop the capabilities necessary for a full mastery of space and not pull back at a time when the U.S.S.R. was in the lead." The Cuban missile crisis obliged a more conciliatory attitude. The President was convinced that the only way to diffuse Cold War tensions was to develop areas of common interest with the U.S.S.R., "in a manner and scale that would involve meaningful movement towards a genuine rapprochement between the two countries." Specific areas of bilateral cooperation which were singled out under this policy of rapprochement and intensive negotiations with the U.S.S.R. resulted in

> (i) the 1962 Dryden Blagonravov agreement regarding scientific and research cooperation,

> (ii) the 1963 "Hot Line" Agreement with respect to the establishment of a direct communications link between Moscow and Washington,

> (iii) the 1963 bilateral understanding to support the U.N. General Assembly resolution on banning the placement of nuclear weapons in orbit around the Earth, and

> (iv) the tripartite 1963 Treaty Banning Nuclear Weapons Tests in the Atmosphere, in Outer Space, and under water.

It was the policy of selective rapprochement which contributed to U.S. acceptance of the partial nuclear test ban when, at the 1963 Moscow trilateral talks, all the "efforts to agree on a comprehensive treaty foundered on the inspection issue. The American negotiators knew that the Senate would not consent to a comprehensive test ban treaty that did not provide more on-site inspections on Soviet soil than the Soviets would accept."

The Soviet Union's willingness to conclude a treaty on nuclear test bans doubtlessly stemmed from its ability to monitor compliance with such a treaty; it had already developed surveillance satellites of such a degree of precision that it could match the U.S.A.'s technology in this field. There was also a desire to develop cordial relations with the West, in the pursuit of a policy of peaceful coexistence, given that relations with its communist ally, China, were rapidly deteriorating.

3. The Provisions of the 1963 Treaty

(a) Aim

The principal aim of the three original parties to the Treaty, i.e. the U.S.A., the U.S.S.R. and the U.K., in negotiating this Treaty was the speediest possible achievement of an agreement on general and complete disarmament which would put an end to the armament race and eliminate the incentive to the production and testing of all kinds of weapons, including nuclear weapons, at all times. To achieve this aim, they declared their determination to continue negotiations in this regard and expressed their desire to put an end to the contamination of man's environment by radioactive substances. To what extent this determination and desire have been executed shall be assessed later in this paper.

(b) Application

The Treaty has only five articles. Article I, which contains the main prohibition against nuclear tests, provides that

> Each of the Parties to this Treaty undertakes to prohibit, to prevent, and not to carry out any nuclear weapon test explosion or any other nuclear explosion, at any place under its jurisdiction or control:
>
> (a) in the atmosphere; beyond its limits, including outer space; or under water, including territorial waters or high seas; or
>
> (b) in any other environment if such explosion causes radioactive debris to be present outside the territorial limits of the state under whose jurisdiction or control such explosion is conducted.

A careful reading of this provision shows that nuclear explosions are prohibited in all environments except underground tests carried out within the territorial limits of the parties to the Treaty. Moreover, underground tests which could cause radioactive debris to be present outside the territorial limits of the concerned state party are also prohibited.

It is interesting to note that the drafters of the Treaty "avoided the doctrinal question where outer space begins since the prohibition runs within the atmosphere and beyond its limits." In other words, the 1963 Treaty considers both air and outer space as a single medium for the purposes of prohibition of nuclear tests. This view has long been advocated by the writer who considers it only logical to speak of an aerospace continuum governed by the norms and the rules of aerospace law, than to draw artificial boundaries between the air space, on the one hand, and outer space on the other. The 1963 Treaty is very clear on the areas to which it applies, in contrast to the 1967 Outer Space Treaty which is silent in this respect.

The prohibition contained in the 1963 Treaty seems to apply to all nuclear tests carried out in outer space, irrespective of the distance of their test sites from the Earth, since there is no outer limit of outer space. Similarly, such prohibition would apply to nuclear tests conducted on celestial bodies, since they form part of outer space and testing could result in contamination. This interpretation seems to be in line with the description given in article I of the Treaty of all environments in which nuclear tests are prohibited.

During the Treaty negotiations, prohibition of nuclear tests in the atmosphere and in outer space was readily accepted by the U.S.S.R. as well as the U.S. and the U.K. because monitoring was considered to be relatively easy and feasible. No provision was included with respect to verification of compliance with the Treaty. It was generally understood that each party could monitor the nuclear tests of the other parties by national means of verification.

During the U.S. Senate hearings on the 1963 Treaty, various senators expressed concern about the possibility of conducting nuclear tests in deep space and thus avoiding detection by monitoring devices. Robert S. McNamara, the then U.S. Secretary of Defense, in response to these concerns, stated that:

Multimegaton weapons development tests would have to be conducted more than 20 million miles from the earth—80 times as far away as the moon—if they were to have a good chance of escaping detection by a ground-based system. . . .

The United States on its own can deploy earth and solar satellite systems for detection of deep space nuclear explosions; . . .

While tests at extreme ranges are a technological possibility, they would involve years of preparation plus several months to a year of actual execution, and they could cost hundreds of millions of dollars per successful experiment.

He concluded that although "as a practical matter, illegal clandestine testing in deep space is not a reasonable proposition" one can properly protect against such testing.

The prohibition of explosions in the specified environments relates to "any . . . nuclear explosion." This phrase was inserted in article I to cover "peace-time nuclear explosions that are not weapons tests." Hence, nuclear explosions for peaceful purposes are also prohibited under the terms of article I. However, it is important to note that the prohibition applies to "nuclear" tests and not to those of a conventional, chemical or biological nature, or to high energy laser beam weapons etc. States parties must not only prohibit, prevent and not carry out nuclear tests but must also refrain from causing, encouraging, or in any way participating in, the carrying out of any of the prohibited tests. It was because of the broad nature of this undertaking that the U.S. refused to transport French personnel to the French Polynesian islands at a time when France was planning to conduct nuclear tests there. This would have been to encourage and participate in an indirect way in the conduct of the prohibited nuclear tests, and thus a violation of U.S. Treaty obligations.

*   *   *

4. Analysis and Assessment

The major advantage of the 1963 Treaty is the establishment of essentially favorable conditions for the peaceful use of outer space relatively free from the adverse effects of electromagnetic pulse (EMP) which can be created by a nuclear explosion in the atmosphere or in outer space. In space, the pulse is not dissipated by the atmosphere and the effect of a single two-megaton bomb exploded 50 km or higher above the earth could affect circuits in nearly all satellites in geostationary orbit, 36,000 km above the earth. New military satellites are being protected against EMP but commercial satellites are still very much threatened. Although commercial satellite systems can be reinforced against EMP, it may not be possible to keep them within cost-effective limits. Similarly, the Treaty has contributed to the world's relative freedom from radioactive contamination, since the major nuclear powers (the U.S.A., the U.S.S.R. and the U.K.) stopped high altitude nuclear testing after signature of the 1963 Treaty. Since it has been widely accepted and its provisions consistently respected, there is every reason to believe that this situation will continue to prevail in the future.

Nonetheless, it should not be forgotten that the Treaty was merely the outcome of selective rapprochement between the super powers, which alienated at least two other major powers, i.e. France and the Peoples Republic of China. They never became parties to the Treaty. While France considered it to be of only "limited practical importance," China "called the Treaty a 'big fraud to fool the people of the world' and accused the Soviets of 'selling out the communist camp.' The Treaty thus intensified the Sino-Soviet split." Both countries continued their altitude nuclear tests; between 1963 and 1982, France conducted 41 and China 22 such tests, and thus diminished the significance of the Treaty's prohibitions.

While the desire of the original parties "to put an end to the contamination of man's environment by radioactive substances" seems, to a limited extent, to have been fulfilled, their objective to "put an end to the armaments race" continues to be elusive. After signature of the 1963 Treaty, the U.S.S.R., the U.S.A. and the U.K. stopped nuclear tests in the atmosphere, but intensified and accelerated underground explosions. The nuclear stock-pile (not counting the increased destructive power) of the three original parties, according to the most conservative estimates, increased from 26,439 nuclear warheads in 1965 to 42,310 in 1982. According to Hussain, who undertook a thorough study of the impact of weapons test restrictions on arms control and disarmament,

> the hopes for the Partial Test Ban Treaty (PTBT) were that it should slow the technological progress and innovation of nuclear weapons by making tests more difficult and more costly to conduct. . . . It has not been particularly effective. Certainly, the PTBT has not slowed the rate of innovation of systems; on the contrary, most current technology has been derived from experimental underground nuclear test explosions following the Treaty's implementation.

Concern about the proliferation of nuclear weapons and the danger of nuclear war, resulted in adoption of the Treaty on the Non-Proliferation of Nuclear Weapons in 1968 (hereinafter referred to as the Non Proliferation Treaty). However, both Treaties have been ineffective in this respect. India, for example—a party to the 1963 Treaty—exploded underground its nuclear device in 1974 and other countries such as Israel, Pakistan, South Africa, South Korea, Brazil, Argentina, Taiwan, etc., in addition to France and China, have developed, and are developing their nuclear weapons' capability.

In retrospect, therefore, the expressed aims of the Treaty seem to have been nothing more than a political exercise to enhance and improve the image of the super powers. While the American President declared that the 1963 Treaty was "The first concrete result of 18 years of efforts by United States to impose limits on the nuclear arms race," it was clearly understood by the American government that the Treaty would "not reduce weapons in being or prevent their production" and moreover that "this Treaty is not in that direction—this treaty is not itself dealing with that problem."

NOTE

Aside from its obvious bars to nuclear explosions in outer space, the Test Ban Treaty would impose (among its signatories) a ban on nuclear fission as a means of space propulsion. As was mentioned in Chapter 1, the late 1950s and early 1960s saw considerable experimentation with ORION propulsion systems (so named because of the code name of the military project under which the experiments were conducted) that would use small atomic bombs as fuel. Those experiments were abandoned after the ratification of the Test Ban Treaty, whose plain ban on "any nuclear weapon test explosion *or any other nuclear explosion*" (emphasis added) in outer space does not admit of any loophole that would support nuclear explosive propulsion. For a short, clear history of the ORION project and how it was ended by the Treaty, *see* F. Dyson, Saturn by 1970, in Disturbing the Universe 107 (1979).

However, many nations with nuclear and space capabilities are not signatories to the Test Ban Treaty and would face no such impediment. As discussed *infra,* the Outer Space Treaty (to which many more nations are signatories) is not a bar to the use of nuclear explosives for propulsion so long as appropriate precautions against harm to other nations are observed. Although ORION technology is in some ways rather crude, its crudity may well be offset by its ability to deliver extremely powerful propulsion with relatively few new technical demands, allowing a new space power (such as a third world country not bound by the Test Ban Treaty) to perform impressive feats without developing the sophisticated technologies possessed by more experienced space powers.

Such uses by countries not signatories to the Test Ban Treaty might well lead to an amendment of the treaty to allow its signatories to do the same—or to pressure on nonsignatories to conform to its limits. This is a lesson worth bearing in mind with regard to arms control treaties in general: given the rapid spread of space technology, treaties binding only existing space powers—or worse yet, treaties binding only the United States and the Soviet Union—are likely to become obsolete, and may even become sources of conflict themselves. *See* the discussion regarding the ABM Treaty in Chapter 4, *infra,* for other examples of how overly narrow treaties may become subject to obsolescence.

THE OUTER SPACE TREATY OF 1967

Among all of the treaties relating to activity in outer space, the Outer Space Treaty of 1967 enjoys the broadest subscription and the highest regard. Although some of the regard for the Treaty may stem as much from sentiment as from any concrete benefits it provides—the Outer Space Treaty having been a triumph of consensus and forward-looking thought at a time when cold war tensions and narrow nationalism were the norm— the Outer Space Treaty does accomplish a great deal. It provides limits on military activities beyond earth, prevents the extension of terrestrial sovereignty to space or celestial bodies, and establishes a framework for the further development of law governing activity in outer space, serving as a precursor and underpinning to such essential documents as the Liability Convention, the Rescue and Return Agreement, and so on. On the other hand, the Treaty leaves many important questions unanswered.

Multilateral Treaty on Principles Governing the Activities of States in the Exploration and Use of Outer Space, Including the Moon and Other Celestial Bodies, 18 U.S.T. 2410; T.I.A.S. 6347

Done at Washington, London, and Moscow January 27, 1967;
Ratification advised by the Senate of the United States of America April 25, 1967;
Ratified by the President of the United States of America May 24, 1967;
Ratification of the United States of America deposited at Washington, London, and Moscow October 10, 1967;
Proclaimed by the President of the United States of America October 10, 1967;
Entered into force October 10, 1967.

The States Parties to this Treaty,

Inspired by the greater prospects opening up before mankind as a result of man's entry into outer space,

Recognizing the common interest of all mankind in the progress of the exploration and use of outer space for peaceful purposes,

Believing that the exploration and use of outer space should be carried on for the benefit of all peoples irrespective of the degree of their economic or scientific development,

Desiring to contribute to broad international cooperation in the scientific as well as the legal aspects of the exploration and use of outer space for peaceful purposes,

Believing that such cooperation will contribute to the development of mutual understanding and to the strengthening of friendly relations between States and peoples,

Recalling resolution 1962 (XVIII), entitled "Declaration of Legal Principles Governing the Activities of States in the Exploration and Use of Outer Space," which was adopted unanimously by the United Nations General Assembly on 13 December 1963,

Recalling resolution 1884 (XVIII), calling upon States to refrain from placing in orbit around the Earth any objects carrying nuclear weapons or any other kinds of weapons of mass destruction or from installing such weapons on celestial bodies, which was adopted unanimously by the United Nations General Assembly on 17 October 1963,

Taking account of United Nations General Assembly resolution 110(II) of 3 November 1947, which condemned propaganda designed or likely to provoke or encourage any threat to the peace, breach of the peace or act of aggression, and considering that the aforementioned resolution is applicable to outer space,

Convinced that a Treaty on Principles Governing the Activities of States in the Exploration and Use of Outer Space, including the Moon and Other Celestial Bodies, will further the Purposes and Principles of the Charter of the United Nations,

Have agreed on the following:

Article I

The exploration and use of outer space, including the moon and other celestial bodies, shall be carried out for the benefit and in the interests of all countries, irrespective of their degree of economic or scientific development, and shall be the province of all mankind.

Outer space, including the moon and other celestial bodies, shall be free for exploration and use by all States without discrimination of any kind, on a basis of equality and in accordance with International law, and there shall be free access to all areas of celestial bodies.

There shall be freedom of scientific investigation in outer space, including the moon and other celestial bodies, and States shall facilitate and encourage international co-operation in such investigation.

Article II

Outer space, including the moon and other celestial bodies, is not subject to national appropriation by claim of sovereignty, by means of use or occupation, or by any other means.

Article III

States Parties to the Treaty shall carry on activities in the exploration and use of outer space, including the moon and other celestial bodies, in accordance with international law, including the Charter of the United Nations, in the interest of maintaining international peace and security and promoting international cooperation and understanding.

Article IV

States Parties to the Treaty undertake not to place in orbit around the Earth any objects carrying nuclear weapons or any other kinds of weapons of mass destruction, install such weapons on celestial bodies, or station such weapons in outer space in any other manner.

The moon and other celestial bodies shall be used by the States Parties to the Treaty exclusively for peaceful purposes. The establishment of military bases, installations and fortifications, the testing of any type of weapons and the conduct of military maneuvers on celestial bodies shall be forbidden. The use of military personnel for scientific research or for any other peaceful purposes shall not be prohibited. The use of any equipment or facility necessary for peaceful exploration of the moon and other celestial bodies shall also not be prohibited.

Article V

States Parties to the Treaty shall regard astronauts as envoys of mankind in outer space and shall render to them all possible assistance in the event of accident, distress, or emergency landing on the territory of another State

Party or on the high seas. When astronauts make such a landing, they shall be safely and promptly returned to the State of registry of their space vehicle.

In carrying on activities in outer space and on celestial bodies, the astronauts of one State Party shall render all possible assistance to the astronauts of other States Parties.

States Parties to the Treaty shall immediately inform the other States Parties to the Treaty or the Secretary-General of the United Nations of any phenomena they discover in outer space, including the moon and other celestial bodies, which could constitute a danger to the life or health of astronauts.

Article VI

States Parties to the Treaty shall bear international responsibility for national activities in outer space, including the moon and other celestial bodies, whether such activities are carried on by governmental agencies or by non-governmental entities, and for assuring that national activities are carried out in conformity with the provisions set forth in the present Treaty. The activities of non-governmental entities in outer space, including the moon and other celestial bodies, shall require authorization and continuing supervision by the appropriate State Party to the Treaty. When activities are carried on in outer space, including the moon and other celestial bodies, by an international organization, responsibility for compliance with this Treaty shall be borne both by the International organization and by the States Parties to the Treaty participating in such organization.

Article VII

Each State Party to the Treaty that launches or procures the launching of an object into outer space, including the moon and other celestial bodies, and each State Party from whose territory or facility an object is launched, is internationally liable for damage to another State Party to the Treaty or to its natural or juridical persons by such object or its component parts on the Earth, in air space or in outer space, including the moon and other celestial bodies.

Article VIII

A State Party to the Treaty on whose registry an object launched into outer space is carried shall retain jurisdiction and control over such object, and over any personnel thereof, while in outer space or on a celestial body. Ownership of objects launched into outer space, including objects landed or constructed on a celestial body, and of their component parts, is not affected by their presence in outer space or on a celestial body or by their return to the Earth. Such objects or component parts found beyond the limits of the State Party to the Treaty on whose registry they are carried shall be returned to that State Party, which shall, upon request, furnish identifying data prior to their return.

Article IX

In the exploration and use of outer space, including the moon and other celestial bodies, States Parties to the Treaty shall be guided by the principle of cooperation and mutual assistance and shall conduct all their activities in outer space, including the moon and other celestial bodies, with due regard to the corresponding interests of all other States Parties to the Treaty. States Parties to the Treaty shall pursue studies of outer space, including the moon and other celestial bodies, and conduct exploration of them so as to avoid their harmful contamination and also adverse changes in the environment of the Earth resulting from the introduction of extra-terrestrial matter and, where necessary, shall adopt appropriate measures for this purpose. If a State Party to the Treaty has reason to believe that an activity or experiment planned by it or its nationals in outer space, including the moon and other celestial bodies, would cause potentially harmful interference with activities of other States Parties in the peaceful exploration and use of outer space, including the moon and other celestial bodies, it shall undertake appropriate international consultations before proceeding with any such activity or experiment. A State Party to the Treaty which has reason to believe that an activity or experiment planned by another State Party in outer space, including the moon and other celestial bodies, would cause potentially harmful interference with activities in the peaceful exploration and use of outer space, including the moon and other celestial bodies, may request consultation concerning the activity or ex-periment.

Article X

In order to promote international co-operation in the exploration and use of outer space, including the moon and other celestial bodies, in conformity with the purposes of this Treaty, the States Parties to the Treaty shall consider on a basis of equality any requests by other States Parties to the Treaty to be afforded an opportunity to observe the flight of space objects launched by those States.

The nature of such an opportunity for observation and the conditions under which it could be afforded shall be determined by agreement between the States concerned.

Article XI

In order to promote international co-operation in the peaceful explora-tion and use of outer space, States Parties to the Treaty conducting activities in outer space, including the moon and other celestial bodies, agree to inform the Secretary-General of the United Nations as well as the public and the international scientific community, to the greatest extent feasible and practicable, of the nature, conduct, locations and results of such activities. On receiving the said information, the Secretary-General of the United Nations should be prepared to disseminate it immediately and effectively.

Article XII

All stations, installations, equipment and space vehicles on the moon and other celestial bodies shall be open to representatives of other States Parties to the Treaty on a basis of reciprocity. Such representatives shall give reasonable advance notice of a projected visit, in order that appropriate consultations may be held and that maximum precautions may be taken to assure safety and to avoid interference with normal operations in the facility to be visited.

Article XIII

The provisions of this Treaty shall apply to the activities of States Parties to the Treaty in the exploration and use of outer space, including the moon and other celestial bodies, whether such activities are carried on by a single State Party to the Treaty or jointly with other States, including cases where they are carried on within the framework of international inter-governmental organizations.

Any practical questions arising in connection with activities carried on by international inter-governmental organizations in the exploration and use of outer space, including the moon and other celestial bodies, shall be resolved by the States Parties to the Treaty either with the appropriate international organization or with one or more States members of that international organization, which are Parties to the Treaty.

Article XIV

1. This Treaty shall be open to all States for signature. Any State which does not sign this Treaty before its entry into force in accordance with paragraph 3 of this article may accede to it at any time.

2. This Treaty shall be subject to ratification by signatory States. Instruments of ratification and instruments of accession shall be deposited with the Governments of the United States of America, the United Kingdom of Great Britain and Northern Ireland and the Union of Soviet Socialist Republics, which are hereby designated the Depositary Governments.

3. This Treaty shall enter into force upon the deposit of instruments of ratification by the five Governments including the Governments designated as Depositary Governments under this Treaty.

4. For States whose instruments of ratification of accession are deposited subsequent to the entry into force of this Treaty, it shall enter into force on the date of the deposit of their instruments of ratification.

5. The Depositary Governments shall promptly inform all signatory and acceding States of the date of each signature, the date of deposit of each

instrument of ratification of and accession to this Treaty, the date of its entry into force and other notices.

6. This Treaty shall be registered by the Depositary Government pursuant to Article 102 of the Charter of the United Nations.

Article XV

Any State Party to the Treaty may propose amendments to this Treaty. Amendments shall enter into force for each State Party to the Treaty accepting the amendments upon their acceptance by a majority of the States Parties to the Treaty and thereafter for each remaining State Party to the Treaty on the date of acceptance by it.

Article XVI

Any State Party to the Treaty may give notice of its withdrawal from the Treaty one year after its entry into force by written notification to the Depositary Governments. Such withdrawal shall take effect one year from the date of receipt of this notification.

Article XVII

This Treaty, of which the English, Russian, French, Spanish and Chinese texts are equally authentic, shall be deposited in the archives of the Depositary Governments. Duly certified copies of this Treaty shall be transmitted by the Depositary Governments to the Governments of the signatory and acceding States.

***

NOTE

In order to understand the Outer Space Treaty's provisions, and the high regard in which it is held, it is important to know something of the process by which it was developed. The Treaty grew gradually out of a series of conferences on outer space law and a number of General Assembly declarations stating general principles for international activity in outer space. This process is chronicled in the article by Dembling & Arons from which the following, rather lengthy, excerpt comes. The excerpt sets out some of the history prior to the negotiations of the Fifth Legal Subcommittee that led to the Treaty's final form, as well as the key happenings at the Legal Subcommittee during those negotiations. Together, these pieces of history provide considerable information regarding the positions of different parties and the contemporaneous understanding of drafters regarding the Outer Space Treaty's key provisions. Paul Dembling was General Counsel for NASA when the article was written; he is now a partner at the Washington, D.C., office of Schnader, Harrison, Segal & Lewis.

**Dembling & Arons, The Evolution of the Outer
Space Treaty, 33 Journal of Air Law & Commerce 419 (1967)**

An announcement was made on 8 December 1966, that agreement had been achieved among the members of the twenty-eight nation United Nations Outer Space Committee on the text of a treaty governing the activities of states in the exploration and use of outer space, the moon, and other celestial bodies. Approval of the Treaty was recommended unanimously by the Political Committee of the General Assembly on 17 December 1966. Two days later, the Treaty was endorsed by a unanimous vote of the General Assembly. Regardless of the total number of States which may sign and ratify the Treaty, a remarkable endeavor of great significance to international law and politics has reached fruition. Nations often in conflict with one another and adhering to widely divergent political philosophies have agreed on the first Treaty of general applicability governing activity in outer space.

The principles set forth in the Treaty had been advanced previously in the form of General Assembly resolutions, analogous international agreements, domestic legislation, statements by government officials, articles by scholars in the field and other expressions of views. However, agreement on the Treaty was primarily the product of the labors of the twenty-eight member Legal Subcommittee of the United Nations General Assembly's Committee on the Peaceful Uses of Outer Space during the Subcommittee's Fifth Session held in Geneva from 12 July to 4 August 1966, and in New York from 12 to 16 September 1966. The few issues requiring resolution subsequent to the conclusion of the Fifth Session were the subject of various bilateral negotiations and other discussions held during the Twenty-First Session of the General Assembly. Agreement was obtained on those issues shortly before the 8 December announcement that agreement on the Treaty as a whole had been reached.

*   *   *

Although the scope of the Treaty as eventually agreed upon includes both outer space and celestial bodies, an important aspect of the deliberations leading to agreement on the Treaty is the extent to which the nations and individuals involved were concerned, for the first time, with the formulation of realistic principles which might govern activity on celestial bodies in addition to, but as distinct from, outer space. This consideration of celestial bodies was based upon a body of thought and action that preceded the Fifth Session of the Legal Subcommittee. Even prior to 1960, a considerable amount of commentary existed on the question of "whether it is possible for a terrestrial nation-state to acquire sovereignty over all or part of a natural celestial body, and what would be required under existing law to make such a claim legally valid." Analogies were drawn to the manner in which nations had previously sought to exert legal claims to sovereignty over portions of the earth's surface, *e.g.,* through discovery, occupation, annexation and contiguity. Considerable discussion arose over the legal effect of the reported striking of the moon by an early Soviet satellite carrying the Soviet flag. However, the Soviet Union did not seek to exert any claim of sovereignty based upon this occurrence.

Although writers regarded the legal principles derived from exploration of the earth's surface as potentially applicable to exploration of celestial bodies, they did not consider such applicability to be desirable. The suggestion was made that "both public and private groups . . . work towards formulating standards and procedures that will guarantee access by all to these resources on equitable terms and prevent interference by one state with scientific programs of another. As early as 1959, the American Bar Association passed a resolution declaring that in the common interest of mankind . . . celestial bodies should not be subject to exclusive appropriation." A similar concern was evidenced at the official level. The United Nations Ad Hoc Committee on the Peaceful Uses of Outer Space, created by the General Assembly in 1959, took the position in its report that "some form of international administration over celestial bodies might be adopted." In an address before the General Assembly in September 1960, President Eisenhower proposed that:

1. We agree that celestial bodies are not subject to national appropriation by any claims of sovereignty.

2. We agree that the nations of the world shall not engage in warlike activities on these bodies.

3. We agree, subject to verification, that no nation will put into orbit or station in outer space weapons of mass destruction. All launchings of spacecraft shall be verified by the United Nations.

*   *   *

That a sense of urgency had developed concerning the need for an international agreement on the exploration of the moon and other celestial bodies was made clear in a statement by President Lyndon B. Johnson in May 1966. He emphasized the need to "take action now . . . to insure that explorations of the moon and other celestial bodies will be for peaceful purposes only" and "to be sure that our astronauts and those of other nations can freely conduct scientific investigations of the moon." The President suggested a treaty containing the following elements:

1. The moon and other celestial bodies should be free for exploration and use by all countries. No country should be permitted to advance a claim of sovereignty.

2. There should be freedom of scientific investigation, and all countries should cooperate in scientific activities relating to celestial bodies.

3. Studies should be made to avoid harmful contamination.

4. Astronauts of one country should give any necessary help to astronauts of another country.

5. No country should be permitted to station weapons of mass destruction on a celestial body. Weapons tests and military maneuvers should be forbidden.

Two days after the president made his statement, United States Ambassador to the United Nations Arthur J. Goldberg addressed a letter to Dr. Kurt Waldheim of Austria, the Chairman of the Committee on the Peaceful Uses of Outer Space, requesting an early convening of the Legal Subcommittee to consider the treaty proposed by President Johnson. . . .

C. No Weapons of Mass Destruction Shall Be Placed in Orbit or on Celestial Bodies, or Stationed in Outer Space in any Other Manner; Celestial Bodies Shall Be Used Exclusively for Peaceful Purposes

Article IV of the Treaty constitutes, as President Johnson stated, "the most important arms control development since the 1963 treaty banning nuclear testing in the atmosphere, in space and under water." Ambassador Goldberg explained to the Political Committee of the General Assembly that:

This article restricts military activities in two ways:

First, it contains an undertaking not to place in orbit around the earth, install on the moon or any other celestial body, or otherwise station in outer space nuclear or any other weapons of mass destruction.

Second, it limits the use of the moon and other celestial bodies exclusively to peaceful purposes and expressly prohibits their use for establishing military bases, installations or fortifications, testing weapons of any kind, or conducting military maneuvers.

Article IV is taken from Articles 8 and 9 of the United States draft. Both the United States and Soviet drafts reflect principles previously agreed upon in the Nuclear Test Ban Treaty, and the United Nations Resolution 1884 (XVIII), adopted by the General Assembly by acclamation on 17 October 1963. In addition, the last sentence of Article 9 of the United States draft, which provided for the use of military personnel, facilities, or equipment for peaceful purposes, is quite similar to Article I, Paragraph 2, of the Antarctic Treaty. Ambassador Goldberg explained to the Legal Subcommittee that:

As in the exploration of the Antarctic, man could not have penetrated outer space and survived in that hostile environment unless he had been able to draw upon the benefits of all research, civilian or military, involving both personnel and equipment. For any country engaging in space activity, military personnel, facilities and equipment played an indispensible role and would continue to be an essential part of future space programs.

Except for two differences of opinion, to be discussed below, agreement on the final text of Article IV was reached towards the conclusion of the Geneva portion of the Session on the basis of acceptance by the United States delegation of the language of the first sentence of Article IV of the Soviet draft, and acceptance by the Soviet delegation of the United States desire to include provision for the use of military personnel for peaceful purposes.

It is noteworthy that the prohibition contained in the first paragraph of Article IV applies to both outer space and celestial bodies, while the prohibition contained in the second paragraph of the article applies to celestial bodies only. Several of the delegations questioned the propriety of excluding outer space from the coverage of the second paragraph, the implication being that outer space may be used for nonpeaceful purposes. However, it is a well-known fact that both the United States and the Soviet Union have already launched satellites into outer space for military purposes, and examination of a ban on such satellites would have raised controversial issues presently within the purview of disarmament negotiations. The text of Article IV as agreed upon was conceded to be the most practical solution from the standpoint of expeditious conclusion of a treaty on outer space. As the Soviet delegate stated, "A number of questions would, of course, remain to be dealt with after the elaboration of the Treaty, particularly the use of outer space for exclusively peaceful purposes." In the interim, one might conclude that any military use of outer space must be restricted to nonaggressive purposes in view of Article III, which makes applicable international law including the Charter of the United Nations.

At the conclusion of the Geneva portion of the Session, two matters had not been resolved with respect to Article IV. The United States had previously revised and consolidated Articles 8 and 9 of its draft and tabled a single, two-paragraph article quite similar to Article IV of the Soviet draft. The second paragraph of the revised United States article read as follows:

> The moon and other celestial bodies shall be used exclusively for peaceful purposes. Establishment of military bases and fortifications, the testing of any type of weapons, and the conduct of military maneuvers shall be forbidden. The present Treaty does not prohibit the use of any types of personnel or equipment for scientific research or any other peaceful purpose.

The Soviet Union desired, however, to include the word "installations" between "military bases" and "fortifications," and to ban the use of "military equipment" on celestial bodies.

Concerning the use of the term "installations," the Soviet delegate did not articulate any reason for his delegation's insistence on the inclusion of that word, except for the possibility that the words "bases" and "fortifications," in Russian translation, do not adequately describe all of the possible structures that might be erected for military use on celestial bodies. The United States delegate argued that the term "installation" is too vague, possibly viewing "bases" and "fortifications" as terms connoting use of a facility for military purposes, while "installations" might be construed to apply to a facility used for peaceful purposes but constructed or inhabited by military personnel.

A more important point of disagreement was whether military equipment may be used on celestial bodies. Notwithstanding the analogy in Article I, Paragraph 2, of the Antarctic Treaty, the Soviet delegate argued that "if the use of military equipment in outer space was allowed, the essence of the treaty would be distorted and a loophole would be created for evading one of its most fundamental provisions." The United States position was that "Equipment used in outer space had, in many cases, been developed through military research; that was the case, in particular, with respect to the rockets carrying astronauts; that could not, however, be said to constitute a violation of the principle of the peaceful uses of outer space." The British delegate added that "The fact that a piece of equipment owed its origin to military development should not preclude its use for peaceful purposes foreseen by the Treaty and apparent to all as peaceful purposes."

As a reading of the second paragraph of Article IV indicates, the United States and its supporters eventually agreed to accept the use of the term "installations," while the Soviet Union and its supporters agreed to the inclusion of a provision which would not ban the use of military equipment on celestial bodies. Emphasis on the purpose for which a piece of military equipment is to be used on a celestial body, as stressed by the United States delegate, is reflected in the last sentence of Article IV. Thus, aside from the first paragraph of Article IV, the placement of a weapon or other item of military equipment of any description on a celestial body would appear to be prohibited unless it can be demonstrated that the item of military equipment will be devoted solely to the peaceful exploration or use of the celestial body. Agreement of the final text of Article IV was not reached until after the close of the New York portion of the Session in the course of compromising the few outstanding differences which stood at that time as a barrier to announcement of the agreement on the treaty.

**D. Assistance and Return of Astronauts
and Space Vehicles; Notification of Dangerous Phenomena
in Outer Space or on Celestial Bodies.**

Article V of the Treaty contains two distinct though related principles. The first two paragraphs set forth the principle of assistance to and return of astronauts, a subject which had been discussed in considerable detail during previous sessions of the Legal Subcommittee. The text of the first two paragraphs of the Article was taken almost verbatim from Article IX of the Soviet draft which restated Paragraph 9 of the *Declaration of Legal*

Principles. Although the principles of assistance and return are contained in Article 5 of the United States draft, the United States delegate acceded to the Soviet version subject to minor drafting changes. The third paragraph of Article V is derived from a proposal made by the United States during the Geneva portion of the Session as follows:

> A State conducting activities in outer space, including the moon and other celestial bodies, shall promptly notify the Secretary-General of the United Nations of any information relating to the physical safety of astronauts.

In the Working Group, this proposal was revised to require notification of either the other parties to the Treaty or the Secretary-General. It is noteworthy that the third paragraph of Article V constitutes a mandatory reporting obligation which the Soviet Union accepted. As discussed in connection with Article XI, the Soviet delegation rigorously adhered to its position that the reporting of activities in outer space and on celestial bodies generally should be only on a voluntary basis. As a result of the Soviet view, Article XI is ambiguous, as distinguished from the comparatively unequivocal obligation imposed on parties to the Treaty by the third paragraph of Article V.

The principles of assistance to astronauts in distress and their return to the launching State or other State of registry were already accepted by the members of the Legal Subcommittee as constituting humanitarian obligations.

*   *   *

E. Parties Shall Bear International Responsibility for National Activities in Outer Space.

Article VI of the Treaty assures that the parties cannot escape their international obligations under the treaty by virtue of the fact that activity in outer space or on celestial bodies is conducted through the medium of nongovernmental entities or international organizations. Perhaps the most important of the three sentences from the standpoint of domestic concern is the second, which states that the activities of nongovernmental entities in outer space and on celestial bodies shall require authorization and continuing supervision by the State concerned. The obvious example of activity covered by the second sentence is that of the Communications Satellite Corporation, a nongovernmental entity whose activities are authorized and regulated by United States federal agencies pursuant to federal statutes and regulations. However, while no one would doubt the need for governmental control over space activity at its present stage, the second sentence of Article VI would prohibit, as a matter of treaty obligation, strictly private, unregulated activity in outer space or on celestial bodies even at a time when such private activity becomes most common-place. Although the terms "authorization" and "continuing supervision" are open to different interpretations, it would appear that Article VI requires a certain minimum of licensing and enforced adherence to government-imposed regulations.

*   *   *

F. Parties to the Treaty That Launch or Procure the Launching of Objects into Outer Space Shall Be Liable for Damages.

Article VII concerning liability was also taken almost verbatim from an article of the Soviet draft, in this case Article VII. The Soviet draft was based on Paragraph 8 of the Declaration of Legal Principles. Although the United States draft contained no similar provision, the United States delegate readily agreed to the inclusion of Article VII of the Soviet draft, subject to minor drafting changes. The United States delegate, along with others, recognized that the Legal Subcommittee was in the process of drafting a detailed treaty on liability, but no objection was raised to the mere inclusion of an article stating the general principle in the present Treaty on outer space and celestial bodies. As the French delegate stated:

> The questions of liability and assistance were extremely complicated, and if any reference to them was included in the treaty under discussion, it should be very brief and simple and should merely establish the principle concerned. Any additional details might deal too rapidly with problems which had not yet been settled.

On this basis, agreement was reached shortly before the close of the Geneva portion of the Session on the inclusion of Article VII of the Soviet draft with minor modifications.

The subject of international liability for damage caused by space vehicles is indeed one involving a multitude of problems, discussed elsewhere by the authors in connection with the work of the Legal Subcommittee on the draft conventions on liability. Since Article VII of the Treaty is essentially a repetition of Paragraph 8 of the *Declaration of Legal Principles,* these problems were hardly touched upon during the Fifth Session in the course of discussion on liability. However, the Indian delegate questioned the meaning of the word "internationally," as used to modify "liable," and stated that the article would only be acceptable if "internationally" meant "absolutely." But other delegations noted that the concept of "absolute liability" was still being refined in discussions of the detailed draft treaties on liability and doubted the feasibility of embodying the concept of absolute liability in the text of Article VII. As the Australian delegate noted, "At earlier sessions the Subcommittee had found that absolute liability was necessarily subject to limitations and qualifications if justice was to be achieved."

*   *   *

G. Jurisdiction and Control over Personnel and Objects Are Not Affected by Their Presence in Outer Space or on Celestial Bodies.

Article VIII of the Treaty consists of three sentences, two of which state general rules concerning control and ownership of personnel and objects while in outer space and on celestial bodies. The third sentence imposes an obligation upon parties to the Treaty to return found objects to the party to the Treaty on whose registry they are carried. The State of registry is required to furnish identifying data if so requested. The third sentence, in providing for the return of space objects, can be regarded as a companion provision to Article V which provides for the assistance and return of astronauts. The return of space vehicles to the State of registry has been considered by the Legal Subcommittee in previous sessions as a part of a treaty that, if adopted, would regulate the assistance and return of astronauts.

Article VIII was taken from Article V of the Soviet draft which virtually repeated Paragraph 7 of the Declaration of Legal Principles. Article 7 of the United States draft was a similar provision but was concerned with control of persons and ownership of objects only on celestial bodies. Also, the United States version did not contain a provision for the return of objects. However, the United States delegate readily acceded to the Soviet version, applicable to both outer space and celestial bodies, subject to a few minor drafting changes. The most noticeable change was the substitution of the word "landed" for "delivered to" in the second sentence. Agreement on the final text of Article VIII was reached one week before the close of the Geneva portion of the Session, prior to the agreement on the final text of any other article.

*   *   *

I. Parties to the Treaty Shall Avoid Harmful Contamination of Outer Space, Celestial Bodies, and the Environment of Earth, and Shall Consult with Other Parties Regarding Potentially Harmful Experiments.

As stated by a leading proponent of the Treaty as an instrument of international cooperation, Article IX is "a provision which is designed to protect outer space and the celestial bodies from contamination and pollution and to protect the legitimate programs of States from undue interference."

Article IX was taken from Article VIII of the Soviet draft and Article 10 of the United States draft. The Soviet version was in turn a reiteration of Paragraph 6 of the Declaration of Legal Principles. Article IX of the Treaty closely follows the text of the Soviet version. However, the Soviet Union agreed to add specific language making the provision applicable to celestial bodies in addition to outer space, and agreed to add the provision of the United States draft prohibiting parties to the Treaty from conducting experiments which might cause adverse changes in the environment of earth.

*   *   *

The Japanese delegation proposed to add language which would have required parties planning potentially harmful experiments to report such planned experiments to the Secretary-General of the United Nations before undertaking them. The Soviet delegate, however, disapproved of this suggestion, stating that the essential information would be communicated more quickly to the other parties to the Treaty if the Secretary-General were not utilized as an intermediary. In addition, and more important, he regarded the Japanese suggestion to be in conflict with the position of the Soviet Union that the Secretary-General not play a role in the application of the Treaty by States. Although the Soviet delegate, after much debate, agreed to Article XI, which provides for the reporting of activities in outer space and celestial bodies to the Secretary-General, he drew sharp distinction between the mandatory consultations in advance of the event, under Article IX, and what he regarded as voluntary reporting after the event, under Article XI. . . . In view of the unequivocal refusal of the Soviet delegation to accept any provision requiring mandatory reporting to the Secretary-General, the Japanese proposal was dropped and agreement was reached on the text of Article IX, including the mandatory provisions for consultations on potentially harmful experiments, shortly before the close of the Geneva portion of the Session.

NOTE

As the above indicates, two key issues occupied the minds of the negotiators—the use of space and celestial bodies for military purposes, and the rights of nations to exercise sovereignty over space, celestial bodies, and the resources to be found therein. These issues were reexamined in more detail in the Moon Treaty (discussed in Chapter 4, *infra*). However, the rules set out in the Outer Space Treaty remain important, particularly as the Moon Treaty has not exactly found favor among the spacefaring nations.

SOVEREIGNTY, PROPERTY RIGHTS, AND SPACE RESOURCES

The rules against extension of sovereignty to outer space and celestial bodies resolved a good deal of confusion regarding such matters—prior to the Outer Space Treaty's entering into force, there had been considerable uncertainty regarding the ability of nations to claim sovereignty in space based on arriving at a particular place first, particularly after the Soviet

Union planted a flag on the Moon using an unmanned probe. After the Treaty, there remained a number of questions regarding what was meant by the no-sovereignty provisions, a question examined in the following excerpt from an article by Carl Christol. Essentially, the questions involve the classification of particular activities as inclusive (that is, those in which all nations are allowed to take part) or exclusive (those in which nations may exclude others). For pre-Treaty views on this subject, *see* M. McDougal, H. Lasswell & I. Vlasic, Law & Public Order in Space 749–871 (1963).

Christol, Article 2 of the 1967 Principles Treaty Revisited, 9 Annals of Air & Space Law 217 (1984)

With the constantly enlarging prospects for the exploration, use, and especially the exploitation of the space environment (outer space per se, the Moon, and other celestial bodies) and the resources of the environment, it is appropriate to reexamine the meaning of Article 2 of the 1967 Principles Treaty. This article provides that "Outer space, including the Moon and other celestial bodies, is not subject to national appropriation by claim of sovereignty, by means of use or occupation, or by any other means."

During the negotiations attending the drafting of the agreement, and in subsequent State practice, it has become clear that the space environment is perceived in international law as a *res communis,* that is to say, as an area available for inclusive uses, rather than for exclusive uses. However, pending the final drafting of Article 2, some doubts were expressed as to the prohibitory scope of the Article. Thus, in the early 1960's Jenks, on the basis of the language contained in Assembly Resolution 1721 A, which was the forerunner of Article 2, concluded that its prohibitions applied only to the "national appropriation of outer space or celestial bodies." He added: "The legal regime applicable to any of the natural resources which it may prove possible and profitable to exploit remains for consideration at a later stage in the light of fuller knowledge of what is practicable and probable."

An opposing view was put forward by Brooks. He took note of the fact that the draftsmen of the Principles Treaty, after having taken General Assembly Resolution 1721 A into account, had not limited the ban on appropriation only to territorial areas. In his view Article 2 constituted a ban on exclusive national rights to both the area and its resources. In his words: "Had the Space Treaty drafters intended only a territorial ban they would not have included 'means of use' or 'any other means' in amplifying the ban on national appropriation since . . . those terms do in fact move beyond mere territorial appropriation." In his view both States and international organizations were to be entitled to make use of the planetary resources as well as the area of outer space.

Following the final revision and adoption of Article 2 in the Principles Treaty its coverage was examined by Lachs. He concluded that the prohibition against national appropriation should be understood as including not only sovereign but also property rights. He submitted that "it should be read as covering both. 'Appropriation' in the wider sense is involved. States are thus barred from establishing proprietary links in regard to the new dimension."

This issue had been considered by the Legal Sub-Committee of the U.N. Committee on the Peaceful Uses of Outer Space (COPUOS) in 1966 when it was drafting the 1967 Principles Treaty. The Belgian representative stated on August 4, 1966, that notice had been taken of "the term 'non-appropriation' advanced by several delegations—apparently without contradiction—as covering both the establishment of sovereignty and the creation of titles to property in private law." The representative of France accepted this viewpoint on December 17, 1966, when he stated to the First Committee that a basic principle of the 1967 Principles Treaty was that there was a "prohibition of any claim to sovereignty or property rights in space." Lachs also called attention to the reasoning of Ortolan relating to the absence of property rights in the ocean: "La mer n'est pas susceptible de tomber dans la propriete des hommes parce que la mer ne peut etre possedee."

The *res communis* quality of the space environment and its natural resources has, with the increasing maturity of international space law, been reflected in international agreements and international practice. Such agreements, applicable to States and to international intergovernmental organizations, contain formal prohibitions against the assertion of national sovereignty over the space environment. They also negate national and international claims to exclusive property rights over the in-place resources of that environment. Thus, Article 11(3) of the Agreement Governing the Activities of States on the Moon and Other Celestial Bodies, approved unanimously by the UN General Assembly on December 5, 1979, provided that "Neither the surface nor the subsurface of the Moon, nor any part thereof or natural resources in place, shall become property of any State, international intergovernmental organization or non-governmental organization, national organization or non-governmental entity or of any natural person." In keeping with the *res communis* principle, allowance was made for the holding of property rights in natural resources which had been removed from their "in place" position on the surface of or from the subsurface of the Moon or other celestial bodies.

*   *   *

The relevant articles of the Treaty employ different terminology in adopting the *res communis* principle. Article 3 refers to the "activities" of States, which become parties to the agreement, in the exploration and use of the space environment. Article 6 makes reference to the outer space "activities" of non-governmental entities. Both Articles 6 and 13 authorize space "activities" by international organizations. Article 1, on the other hand, does not make specific reference to "activities," but does identify

States as having the right to engage in the free and equal exploration and use of the space environment, and as having the right to free access to all areas of celestial bodies.

From these provisions certain conclusions can be drawn. Presumably the additional right of free access to outer space, *per se,* exists, since, if this right were not present, the right of free access to the Moon and to other celestial bodies would be frustrated. It is generally accepted that mention of celestial bodies in the Treaty includes reference to the Moon. It is now considered to be the right of natural and juridical persons other than States, as well as States, to have the right of free and equal access to the space environment, *per se.* Moreover, the rights of such persons are extended to exploration, exploitation, and use. They may also engage, pursuant to Article 1, in scientific investigations, and pursuant to Article 4, in scientific research. These are all operational as distinguished from management activities.

It is, however, a fact that the Principles Treaty makes no explicit reference to the exploration, use, and exploitation of the resources of the environment. The agreement neither expressly authorizes nor prohibits, the exclusive acquisition of the resources of the area. Nonetheless, the general availability of such resources for inclusive exploration, exploitation, and use, by way of space-related "activities," can be supported on several grounds. First, as noted, the *res communis* principle measurably affected the thinking and the conclusions of the negotiators. Second, international practice has gone forward on the basis of the principle. Third, Article 2, through the acceptance of the principle of non-appropriation of the area—thereby rejecting the *res nullius* principle—ordained that the area was not "subject to national appropriation by claim of sovereignty, by means of use or occupation, or by any other means."

Thus, the conclusion may be drawn that States and other natural and juridical persons have the right of free and equal access to space environment, *per se.* Moreover, their rights are also extended to exploration, exploitation, and use. All of this is based on the fundamental proposition that Article 1 authorizes the exploration, exploitation and use of the area and the resources of the area provided such "activities" are carried out, as Article 1 specifies, "for the benefit and in the interests of all countries, irrespective of their degree of economic or scientific development, and shall be the province of all mankind."

*   *   *

The central issue presented by the foregoing prescriptions and examined here is whether the Principles Treaty in its entirety, as supplemented by subsequent international agreements, and by international practice, prevent juridical persons, other than States—and in particular international intergovernmental organizations—from claiming exclusive operational, as well as management, rights, which are denied to States. Being prevented from claiming sovereignty and exclusive property rights located in the space environment for themselves, it will be argued that States are also prohibited from granting quasi-sovereign and exclusive property rights over such areas and resources to those natural and juridical persons which are subject to national jurisdiction and which are created through international agreements.

It is clear that Article 2 prohibits national claims relating to the area of the space environment, and to the resources of that area, subject to the "not in place" terms of the 1979 Moon Treaty. This raises the question initially whether Article 2 can be construed to prevent the effective assertion by an international intergovernmental organization of exclusive rights—both operational, e.g., exploration, exploitation, and use, and governmental, e.g., prescription of rights and duties—to the area and its resources. The terms of Article 13 address themselves separately to the same question. Affecting the meaning to be accorded to these articles are the provisions of Articles 1 and 6. In short, does the Principles Treaty, particularly on the basis of the foregoing articles, impose the same constraints on international intergovernmental organizations respecting the space environment and its resources as are imposed on the States which are parties to the 1967 agreement?

With respect to Article 2, the inquiry will depend on the meaning to be accorded to the "by any other means" limitation. In assessing that limitation it must be kept in mind that, at the time the Principles Treaty was being drafted, the negotiators were focusing principally on the behavior and activities of the legal entities traditionally able to assert exclusive claims to areas and to resources, namely, States. But, in the negotiating history of Article 2 there is also a respectable view that the "by any other means" clause extends to the possible future claims of international intergovernmental organizations. Here the question is whether the "by any other means" provision denies to the signatories the power to grant to an international organization the power to make claims which States, acting on their own account and on behalf of their separate interests, may not assert. If this thesis can be maintained, such organizations would be subject to the same constraints as were specifically directed in Article 2 against States.

*   *   *

This thesis raises the potential applicability of a number of key legal concepts affecting authority over activities in the area and the resources of the area. The provisions of all of the space law treaties are relevant as are the 1969 Vienna Convention on the Law of Treaties, and the 1973 and 1982 ITU Conventions and accompanying Radio Regulations. Both international law generally, as well as the UN Charter, have relevance. The status and powers of international intergovernmental organizations, the utility of legal analogies, the terms of General Assembly resolutions between 1959 and 1967, the statements of negotiators, the views of commentators, the resolutions and reports of private groups of scholars, and such basic concepts as equity are applicable in achieving valid insights respecting the meaning to be accorded to Article 2. There is also the prospect of conflict between treaties and possibly the need to determine the respective powers of different international intergovernmental organizations. Aside from the critical legal issues there are also fundamental political issues which flow from the major differences between the advanced States and the developing States respecting their capabilities for engaging in the practical exploration, exploitation, and use of the space environment and its resources.

*   *   *

That the negotiators were successful in imposing limitations on purely national claims is not to be doubted. Further, it is clear that the negotiators were not laboring under the assumption that the Principles Treaty was a definitive statement of the emerging international law of outer space. Rather, they acknowledged without exception that they were at the threshold of the law, and that much of the book yet remained to be opened. Thus, from the perspective of scholarly analysis it is clear that excessive claims should not be made as to the meaning to be ascribed to the "by any other means" limitation of Article 2. While this is true, it would also not be appropriate to exclude from Article 2 any interdictory meaning that was considered relevant by the negotiators, and which constituted a meaningful part of the negotiating history of the Article and of the entire Treaty. In particular the terms of Article 2 must be viewed from the perspective of Article 1, which was designed to safeguard the interests of all mankind against exclusive claims and uses from whatever source or direction they might come.

NOTES

1. Christol makes two key points: that the restrictions of Article 2's no-sovereignty provision apply equally to international organizations and to states, and that those restrictions do not bar the exploitation of space resources, but merely the staking of exclusive claims to tracts of celestial bodies or space. This is a sensible reading based on the *res communis* principle: by way of analogy, the fact that the high seas are considered *res communis* does not prevent nations from fishing there, but only from excluding other nations from doing the same. In addition, this interpretation makes economic sense for a variety of reasons discussed in the context of the Moon Treaty in Chapter 4, *infra*.

2. As Christol mentions, some scholars writing in the wake of the Outer Space Treaty's ratification took the position that Article 2's no-sovereignty provisions bar *any* property rights in outer space resources. That position has lost its popularity over time, however, and is no longer held by many scholars. This particular debate has, at any rate, been overshadowed in the

1980s by the debate over language in the Moon Treaty dealing with resources, sovereignty, and the "common heritage of mankind" discussed in Chapter 4.

ARMS CONTROL PROVISIONS

The Outer Space Treaty contains a number of provisions limiting military activities in outer space. These provisions do not come close to banning all military activity, and there is some dispute concerning exactly what they do prohibit. Nonetheless, they place limits on military activity by prohibiting the emplacement of fortifications or military installations on the moon or other celestial bodies, or the orbiting of nuclear weapons or other weapons of mass destruction, and state generally that the moon and other celestial bodies are to be used exclusively for peaceful purposes. The use of outer space (as opposed to celestial bodies) for military purposes is intentionally subjected to fewer restrictions because ballistic missiles pass through space in flight and neither the United States nor the Soviet Union was willing to abandon its reliance on such missiles at the time the treaty was negotiated.

The following excerpts explore the meaning of these provisions, including what constitutes a nuclear weapon or other "weapon of mass destruction" and whether there is a distinction between "peaceful" and "nonmilitary" uses of outer space. As you read these, you should consider the following: Were the drafters of the Outer Space Treaty wise to use language susceptible of some ambiguity ("peaceful"; "other kinds of weapons of mass destruction") in order to maintain flexibility, or would they have been better off with more precise language of the sort used in the Test Ban Treaty? And, in light of what we know of the history of the negotiations leading up to the Treaty, which interpretations of these terms are more in accord with the Treaty's spirit?

Orr, The Treaty On Outer Space:
An Evaluation Of The Arms Control Provisions,
7 Columbia Journal of Transnational Law 259 (1968)

On October 10, 1967, the Treaty on Principles Governing the Activities of States in the Exploration and Use of Outer Space, Including the Moon and Other Celestial Bodies entered into force, and, hopefully, because of it "man's earthly conflicts will not be carried into outer space." The measures intended to restrict these conflicts are the arms control provisions of the Treaty, which President Johnson described as "the most important arms control development since the limited test ban treaty of 1963."

In his Letter of Transmittal to the Senate requesting its advice and consent to ratification, the President portrayed the Treaty as "enlarg[ing] the perimeters of peace by shrinking the arenas of potential conflict." He further saw in it a fundamental principle that "[n]o one may use outer space or celestial bodies to begin a war." Such statements as these could leave an overly optimistic impression of the extent to which military activities will be barred from outer space. While the Treaty surely can be considered "the basic charter for the future conquest and utilization of outer space," it does not guarantee that outer space will be free from the burden of man's conflicts. This conclusion follows from a careful reading of the text of the Treaty, especially the arms control provisions. Recent military developments also raise doubts about the effectiveness of the Treaty in limiting the military use of outer space. This comment will explore some of these developments in relation to the Treaty language.

*   *   *

The principal arms control provisions—found in Article IV of the Treaty—restrict military activities in two ways. First, the parties agree not to place in orbit around the earth, install on the moon or any other celestial body, or otherwise station in outer space, nuclear or any other weapons of mass destruction.

Second, the parties pledge that the moon and other celestial bodies shall be used exclusively for peaceful purposes and expressly forbid their use for the establishment of military bases, installations or fortifications, testing of any type of weapons, or conducting military maneuvers. However, this Article does permit the use of military personnel for scientific research or for any other peaceful purpose and the use of any equipment or facility necessary for the peaceful exploration of any celestial body.

The first restriction is based on United Nations Resolution 1884 (XVIII) commonly known as the "no bombs in orbit" resolution. This resolution welcomed expressions [of intent] by the United States and the Union of Soviet Socialist Republics "not to station in outer space any nuclear weapons or other kinds of weapons of mass destruction" and called upon all states "to refrain from placing in orbit around the earth any objects carrying nuclear weapons or any other kinds of weapons of mass destruction, installing such weapons on celestial bodies, or stationing such weapons in outer space in any other manner."

*   *   *

The language of the second restriction resulted from a compromise between similar language found in both the United States and the Soviet draft treaties. Much of the Treaty was taken verbatim from, or at least inspired by, a 1963 United Nations Resolution, entitled "Declaration of Legal Principles Governing the Activities of States in the Exploration and Use of Outer Space," [hereinafter referred to as the Declaration on Legal Principles]. Yet the measures designed to insure that the moon be used only for peaceful purposes were not specifically mentioned in that Declaration.

Additional Treaty provisions intended to assure compliance with the arms control objectives are in Articles I, II and XII. Article I guarantees "free access to all areas of celestial bodies." This follows the principle previously embodied in the Antarctic Treaty of 1959; namely, free access by all parties to installations of other parties.

Also operating against an arms race in space is the provision in Article II forbidding national appropriation of outer space or celestial bodies. Finally, Article XII provides that "[a]ll stations, installations, equipment and space vehicles on the moon and other celestial bodies shall be open to . . . other . . . Parties . . . on a basis of reciprocity." It should be emphasized that the "free access" provisions apply only to the moon and other celestial bodies and not to objects otherwise in outer space, i.e., a satellite in orbit around the earth.

The more general provisions of Articles I and III may also be relevant to an interpretation of the Treaty in the case of a particular space system. These provisions set out some of the basic principles which guided the draftsmen. It is primarily through the careful study of the Treaty language and history in light of actual and possible military space systems that the value of the arms control measures in limiting military activities in space can be determined.

*   *   *

Both the United States and the Soviet Union are using earth satellites for military reconnaissance. Such systems clearly do not fall within the specific arms control provisions of Article IV. Paragraph 1 of that Article is limited to "nuclear weapons or any other kinds of weapons of mass destruction" while the second paragraph applies only to "the moon and other celestial bodies." Under any interpretation of the Article, a reconnaissance satellite could not be a "weapon of mass destruction." It is arguable, however, that such satellites could be proscribed by the provision stipulating that "[t]he . . . *use of outer space* . . . shall be carried out *for the benefit and in the interest of all countries* . . ." (emphasis added). The meaning of this language is not clear as witnessed by the lengthy discussion it provoked in the Foreign Relations Committee hearings on the Treaty.

It was principally Senator Gore [Sr.] who questioned the breadth of this language, particularly as it related to reconnaissance satellites. He was concerned that this provision might be interpreted as prohibiting certain unspecified "uses" of outer space—not an unreasonable concern in light of its plain language. United States Ambassador to the United Nations, Arthur Goldberg, in addressing this point, stated that there was "no prohibition" in the language questioned. In explaining the admittedly broad language, the Ambassador included the following analysis:

> Article I, paragraph 1, is quite general in character. The specific obligations regarding exploration and use of outer space that the Treaty imposes are set forth in succeeding provisions.
> Where it was the intention of the Treaty drafters to provide specific legal obligations relating to benefits to be derived from space activity, this was clearly expressed.

The Ambassador was apparently saying that the language in question is too general to embody, or to be intended to embody, specific obligations. If this is so, then one wonders why the language was not placed in the preamble instead of the body.

Additional broad language which might be used to challenge the legality of reconnaissance satellites is found in Article III. There it is stated that "Parties . . . shall carry on activities in the . . . *use of outer space . . .* in the *interest of maintaining international peace* and security . . ." (emphasis added). The meaning of this provision is likewise unclear but it did not generate any lengthy discussion in the hearings. Many of the same questions raised with reference to the previous broad language are appropriate here.

The characterization presented, at least by the United States, styles satellite reconnaissance as "peace-keeping." It would therefore fall within the mandate of the language in question. Of course the validity of this characterization depends upon the role of reconnaissance in promoting or retarding the tensions which produce war. Admitting that space reconnaissance is a military use of space, the United States argues that its use is defensive which deters potential aggressive action and therefore maintains international peace.

The Soviet attitude toward reconnaissance from space has been quite different, at least prior to the adoption of the Declaration on Legal Principles. The Soviet draft of that Declaration contained a provision branding reconnaissance satellites "incompatible with the objectives of mankind in its conquest of outer space." Such a provision, however, was not included in either the Declaration or the Treaty. This omission speaks strongly for the conclusion that reconnaissance satellites are not prohibited under any intended interpretation of the Treaty.

*   *   *

Aerospace vehicles—vehicles which can function in both sensible atmosphere and the space environment—are an example of potential military systems which present problems of interpretation under the Treaty. One proven example of this combination airplane-spacecraft vehicle is the X–15. During flight at lower altitudes it operates partly on lift generated by passage through the air, but when it reaches top altitude of about 70 miles it depends solely on its rocket engine propulsion system to maintain it in flight.

Another aerospace vehicle—called the "Dyna-Soar"—was extensively designed by the United States but never actually flown. The project for its development was cancelled by the Department of Defense in December, 1963. A rocket would have lifted the vehicle to an altitude of about 100 miles (in the same way that a present-day manned spacecraft is fired into orbit around the earth) where it would have traveled much like a satellite. However, unlike a satellite, it would have dropped into that part of the atmosphere in which aerodynamic lift can be generated, and would have glided back to earth much like an airplane. In terms of today's aircraft this vehicle would have traveled great distances at high altitudes.

If it is assumed that both of the above vehicles could carry weapons of mass destruction, and laying aside the possibility of their being in orbit, the language most relevant to their status under the Treaty is "station such weapons in outer space in any other manner."

No attempt was made in the body of the Treaty to define "outer space" even though it appears in numerous provisions, including the title. There was little discussion of its meaning prior to the Treaty's adoption, but this does not mean that suggested definitions were unavailable. Numerous proposals have been made by both legal and technical writers although no general agreement can be found on any one definition. These proposals are valuable in revealing the problems facing any attempt at definition.

There was recognition by the United Nations that the problem of determining where air space ends and outer space begins would require its attention. In the General Assembly resolution adopting the Treaty, a study of the definition problem was requested. Responding to this request, the Committee on the Peaceful Uses of Outer Space recently held a number of sessions at which the problem was considered. While a definition has not been agreed upon, these sessions have produced enough discussion to justify analyzing the relevant considerations as judged by the Treaty's draftsmen.

The French were the first to advocate a study of the definition of outer space as it applied to the Treaty, and were the first to present their view of the issues involved. Central to their concern was that the Treaty affirmed renunciation by states of any sovereignty over outer space. Pointing out that states now retain sovereignty over congruent air space, they desired some delineation of where air space ends and outer space begins. In light of aerospace vehicles, this delineation seems even more desirable. Even if a nation's vehicle remained "over" its own territory, it might not be subject to that nation's jurisdiction and might even be in violation of the Treaty.

*   *   *

Even with an introduction this brief, one realizes the complexity of the problem of defining outer space. It is this complexity, coupled with the need for additional scientific data, that has led a number of countries to urge a cautious approach to the definition problem. Many feel that definition does not require priority attention. The one thing about the definition of outer space that can be said with certainty is that anything in orbit is generally accepted as being in outer space.

In determining how to treat aerospace vehicles under the Treaty, the word "station" and how it affects the interpretation of "such weapons in outer space" in Article IV could be relevant. No information pertinent to this admittedly subtle inquiry was found in the record of the draftsmen's discussions. "Station" seems to imply something more permanent than the passing through outer space which describes the flight of an aerospace vehicle. . . . The fact that ICBM's which simply pass through outer space are not considered violations of the Treaty supports an interpretation of "station" implying permanency.

*   *   *

The weapons prohibited "in orbit around the earth" and "station[ed] . . . in outer space" are "nuclear weapons or any other kinds of weapons of mass destruction." Usually given as examples of "other kinds of weapons of mass destruction" are bacteriological and chemical weapons. Conventional weapons are not included. Even the largest of the non-nuclear explosive weapons are not considered weapons of mass destruction. Any weapon developed in the future with the capacity to cause the extent of destruction or loss of human life which nuclear weapons can wreak would also be prohibited.

Even a term seemingly so clear as "nuclear weapon" is subject to conflicting interpretations when read in the context of a particular military system. One long range proposal for a defensive system against missiles includes a satellite using a focused beam of radiation from a nuclear reactor [i.e., an X-Ray laser] as an atomic heat ray to destroy an enemy missile. A similar system was studied by the United States but later abandoned as too expensive and unreliable. With the rapid advance of technology one cannot safely assume that it will not be revived.

A nuclear reactor used as the source of a radiation beam differs from the usual nuclear weapon in that it does not explode. While it is nuclear and a weapon, it is not necessarily therefore a weapon of mass destruction. Article IV could be read as prohibiting only nuclear weapons of mass destruction. Some support is found for this view in the Treaty language "nuclear weapons or any *other* kinds of weapons of mass destruction . . ." (emphasis added). It could be argued that the use of "other" implies that nuclear weapons were included only as an example of what the Treaty provision was actually intended to prohibit—weapons of mass destruction. This being true, then the status of a nuclear weapon under the Treaty should be decided on the basis of whether it can cause mass destruction.

In rejecting this argument, the Legal Adviser to the Secretary of State, Leonard C. Meeker, stated that "any nuclear weapon is forbidden in space . . . [e]ven a small one is considered . . . to be a weapon of mass destruction." His interpretation of the language would read "other" as assimilating nuclear weapons to weapons of mass destruction, and prohibiting both.

NOTE

Mr. Orr's piece provides a good survey of many of the issues as they appeared when the Outer Space Treaty was ratified. In many ways, little has changed—he describes the DynaSoar, which was never built, but the legal problems he describes in connection with the DynaSoar are just as applicable regarding the Space Shuttle or various aerospace plane designs now under consideration. Similarly, he describes the potential employment of space-based nuclear reactors to power X-Ray lasers for antimissile use. Although such designs are considered as impractical now as when he wrote, there has been considerable discussion of the use of X-Ray lasers powered instead by nuclear explosives. Unlike reactor-powered lasers, though, such devices would clearly violate the provisions of both the Test Ban and the Outer Space Treaty since they would involve both the placing of nuclear weapons in orbit and (when used) the detonation of nuclear weapons in orbit—although the test ban treaty forbids such detonations only in peacetime, a condition that would presumably have passed if antimissile systems were in use. Still, the Test Ban Treaty would forbid any in-space tests of such a system, leaving its reliability in doubt. In addition, of course, such a system (whether bomb- or reactor-powered) would face problems with the ABM Treaty, problems discussed in the following chapter.

As discussed earlier, however, some space powers could make use of nuclear explosives for space propulsion without violating any treaty obligations. The Limited Test Ban Treaty applies only to its signatories, a group that does not include a number of emerging space powers. The Test Ban Treaty forbids *any* nuclear explosion, whether peaceful or military, in outer space. The Outer Space Treaty forbids only the placing in orbit of "any objects carrying nuclear weapons or any other kinds of weapons of mass destruction" rather than prohibiting the use or orbiting of nuclear *explosives.* Nuclear explosives used for propulsion would not constitute "weapons" conceptually, since they are not intended to produce harm, and probably would for technical reasons be unsuited for destructive purposes. Thus, the Outer Space Treaty's arms control provisions would probably not bar the use of ORION type nuclear propulsion, at least for peaceful purposes. Users of such systems would, however, remain liable under Article VII for any damage caused by use of such a system, meaning that its use anywhere near the earth would be limited by dangers to other spacecraft and satellites from radiation and electromagnetic pulse.

**Gorove, Arms Control Provisions
in the Outer Space Treaty: A Scrutinizing Reappraisal,
3 Georgia Journal of International
and Comparative Law 114 (1973)**

Nuclear and Other Weapons of Mass Destruction

Paragraph one of article IV of the Treaty relates to nuclear weapons and any other kinds of weapons of mass destruction. The initial problem presented by the Treaty is the lack of a definition of what constitutes a "nuclear weapon" or a "weapon of mass destruction." It may be presumed that all arms which utilize atomic energy in accomplishing their intended purpose, irrespective of their size or destructive force, would be regarded as nuclear weapons. At the same time, it may also be assumed that conventional weapons do not come under the category of either nuclear weapons or any other weapons of mass destruction. While there is no indication in the Treaty as to how many people must be affected to constitute a weapon of mass destruction, a group of 20 to 30 people or less probably would not constitute such a mass. If on the other hand, bacteriological and chemical weapons were used, even against a small group, then these weapons would seem to fall under the category of weapons of mass destruction.

Second, the states parties to the Treaty undertake not to *install* nuclear and other weapons of mass destruction on celestial bodies or *station* them in outer space in any other manner. The drafters omitted any reference to the moon in this provision even though in other parts of the Treaty they have fairly consistently referred to the "moon and other celestial bodies." It is by no means clear, however, whether the omission of the word "moon" was intentional, or if the implication is correct that no restriction is placed on the installation of atomic weapons on the moon. One may surmise, however, from the frequently used phrase "moon and other celestial bodies" that the moon is to be regarded as a celestial body under the Treaty. Moreover, it would make little sense to permit installation of weapons of mass destruction on the moon while prohibiting such installation on other celestial bodies, when man's use of the latter looms in the more distant future.

Significant questions with respect to the interpretation of paragraph one of article IV relate to the meaning of the words "install" and "station." At what point does a weapon become installed? Is the mere presence of a weapon on a celestial body prohibited? Furthermore, what constitutes stationing in outer space? Is this identical with orbiting, or does it have a distinct meaning? Any definition of installation of a weapon should require something more than the mere presence of a weapon on a celestial body. On the other hand, station should be interpreted to include the placing of a weapon in a relatively fixed orbit in relation to the underlying celestial body, such that the speed of the orbiting object would coincide with the speed of rotation of the celestial body.

*   *   *

Use for "Peaceful" Purposes

The second paragraph of article IV states that the moon and other celestial bodies shall be used by the parties exclusively for peaceful purposes. Like paragraph one, this provision obligates only the states parties to the Treaty and is not declaratory of a more general obligation. It should also be noted that this provision makes no reference to outer space. This is not an accidental omission. Both paragraphs one and two of article IV express the underlying policy of prohibiting only certain uses of atomic and other weapons of mass destruction in outer space, yet not completely outlawing their use.

*   *   *

Another interesting problem that may have some practical relevance to the future application of paragraph two relates to the size of celestial bodies. How large must a celestial body be to be considered such a body? Would a meteorite or asteroid or a small moon of a celestial body constitute such a body under the terms of the Treaty? An example of the potential problems was indicated when not long ago scientists reported that it might become technically feasible for a future space expedition to steal one of the smaller size moons (5–10 miles in diameter) of Mars, to remove it from its Martian orbit and to place it in orbit around the earth, and thus effectively change the solar system. Would the removal of a celestial body from its natural position by human intervention change its characterization as a celestial body under the Treaty? A meteorite which lands on earth by natural forces and without human interference presumably loses its designation as a celestial body under the Treaty. But the same is probably not true with respect to the example of the Martian moon.

Paragraph two contains one of the most controversial provisions in the Outer Space Treaty. The meaning of "peaceful" has given rise to at least two major interpretations. Under one interpretation the word "peaceful" means nonmilitary, while under a second interpretation the term means nonaggressive.

There is a vast difference insofar as the outcome of these two different interpretations is concerned. Under the former interpretation no military activities could be conducted on the moon and other celestial bodies except those which are specifically permissible under the paragraph two language, *e.g.,* the use of military personnel for scientific research. Under the latter interpretation, activities nonaggressive in nature would be permissible, even if they are conducted by the military, with certain exceptions. These exceptions are those specifically forbidden by article IV, *e.g.,* the establishment of military bases, installations and fortifications, the testing of any types of weapons and the conduct of military maneuvers on celestial bodies. Those advocating this second position have referred to the Charter of the United Nations for their meaning of peaceful. The former position is supported by the Statute of the International Atomic Energy Agency which distinguishes peaceful from military uses of atomic energy.

In reality it would appear that the drafters of the Outer Space Treaty have not adopted either of the above interpretations. Two facts support a meaning of peaceful that is distinct from earlier usages. First, certain activities, such as scientific research or the use of any equipment and facility necessary for peaceful exploration are not prohibited, even if undertaken by the military. Second, certain other activities, such as the establishment of military bases, installations and fortifications, the testing of any type of weapons and the conduct of military maneuvers, are forbidden even if these activities are of a nonaggressive nature.

*   *   *

One possible standard is the relation of an activity to national security. Certain activities may not be as critical or significant as others. Therefore, it would be better to identify those activities which constitute minimal threats to national security and permit those regardless of the ultimate purpose for such activities or their conduct by military personnel. In this manner the whole bothersome issue of peaceful versus military or aggressive could be avoided for the most part, although questions of interpretation would still remain. For example, nation states may decide to permit photography of their underlying territories from outer space regardless of the ultimate purpose for the photographs. If this were to be done, the type of problem which might arise would relate only to the interpretation of the word "photography," which would appear to be much more easily identifiable than any ultimate use or hidden purpose.

*   *   *

It may also be of interest to point out that the use of any equipment or facility is permissible under paragraph two so long as such use is necessary for the peaceful exploration of the moon and other celestial bodies. Therefore, it would appear that military equipment or facilities could legitimately be used for such purpose. However, as pointed out, it may be argued that the word peaceful was not meant to imply nonmilitary.

A similar argument may be predicated on the language in paragraph two that allows the use of military personnel for scientific research or for any other peaceful purposes. Thus, scientific research is regarded by the drafters as an activity basically of a peaceful character. This is the connotation that may reasonably be drawn from the use of the phrase "for scientific research or for any other peaceful purposes." It may then be safe to assume that no scientific research is prohibited by the Treaty regardless of whether or not it is conducted by civilian or military personnel. There may be strong doubts about this assumption, but the express language does not place any restriction on the objective of the research. Thus, the object of the research, whether the advancement of science, military defense, or perhaps even outright aggression, would have no bearing on the lawfulness of any research activity under paragraph two. Admittedly, this construction may run contrary to the general spirit and other provisions of the Treaty, *i.e.,* that the exploration and use of outer space be carried out for the benefit and in the interests of all countries, and that the moon and other celestial bodies be used exclusively for peaceful purposes. However, the wording of the provision pertaining to the free use of military personnel for scientific research makes no mention of the moon or other celestial bodies or, for that matter, of outer space. Thus, one may assume that it was meant to apply generally. The drafters of the Treaty have indicated that scientific research should not be curtailed and realistically they have allowed the use of military personnel to further such research. It is reasonable to conclude that regardless of its objective or where it takes place, scientific research is favored by the Treaty terms.

NOTES

1. In his call for more precise definitions of terms, Gorove takes a different position than Orr, who generally seems more comfortable with flexible interpretations. There are arguments both ways: overly specific definitions may be rapidly rendered obsolete by technological or other change, while overly broad definitions may be so vague as to be meaningless. The Outer Space Treaty's reference to "nuclear weapons or any other kinds of weapons of mass destruction" seems a good compromise: it includes what the drafters were most immediately concerned with, the stationing of nuclear bombs in orbit, as well as possible new weapons, unforeseen by the drafters but posing similar threats to global security, that might arrive later.

2. Despite the concerns mentioned by both Orr and Gorove, the legality of satellite reconnaissance is no longer a major issue. Partly because the technology for such reconnaissance has become widespread and familiar, and partly because the benefits of such systems in promoting stability and in verifying arms control agreements are widely recognized, few nations now dispute the legality of such activities. The Soviet Union formerly opposed satellite surveillance, but has ceased to do so; in 1972 it signed the SALT I Treaty, 24 U.S.T. 3462, T.I.A.S. 7504 (expired), in which each party undertook not to interfere with the other's "national technical means" of verification, a term encompassing satellite reconnaissance (see Chapter 4). More recently, the United Nations COPUOS has drafted principles on remote sensing that underscore its legality in general. For more on the international legal status of remote sensing, see Chapter 5. There have also been some interesting developments in U.S. domestic law relating to private entities' use of satellite reconnaissance technology. *See* Merges & Reynolds, News Media Satellites and the First Amendment, 3 High Technology Law Journal 1 (1988), and Chapter 8, *infra.*

3. Many issues touched on by the Outer Space Treaty only briefly and in general, such as the treatment of liability or the duty to rescue and return astronauts, are addressed in more detail by later agreements—for example, the Liability Convention or the Rescue and Return Agreement. These "miscellaneous treaties," along with other issues, are discussed in Chapter 5.

4

Development and Defense: Treaties of the 1970s

With the early treaties discussed in Chapter 3, the international community established some basic principles to govern space. In the 1970s, attention was focused on more specific goals. That decade produced two important treaties that will have a significant impact on future activities in space: the Antiballistic Missile (ABM) Treaty of 1972, and the Agreement Governing the Activities of States on the Moon and Other Celestial Bodies of 1979, known as the Moon Treaty.

In this chapter we will keep to the chronological order established in Chapter 3 and consider the ABM Treaty first. Although this Treaty is far less comprehensive in its treatment of space activities, it is more important than the Moon Treaty in at least one respect: its signatories—the United States and the Soviet Union—are the major space powers, while neither these nations nor any other space power (save France) has yet signed the Moon Treaty. *See* Current Developments, The Moon Treaty, 79 American Journal of International Law 163 (1985).

In the second part of this chapter, we will explore the reasons for this. As we will see in the excerpts from Rene-Jean Dupuy and Eilene Galloway, both *infra,* the major controversy revolved around the provisions of Article XI, which declared that outer space and celestial bodies are "the common heritage of mankind." At issue was the future development regime that would govern the exploitation of the vast resources of outer space. A definitive review of those resources concluded that the moon alone contained huge amounts of raw materials for making "structural metals, silicon glass, and ceramic products." Staff of Comm. on Commerce, Science and Transportation, U.S. Senate, 96th Cong., 2d Sess., Agreement Governing Activities of States on the Moon and Other Celestial Bodies, Part 4 (1980) at 415. Although the meaning of the "common heritage" principle is shrouded in mystery, its origins in the ideologically divisive Law of the Sea Treaty guaranteed that its interpretation in the space context—where so many potentially important natural resources are at stake—would become politicized. While some observers from the developed countries believed the Moon Treaty would promote development, see the excerpt from Finch and Moore, *infra,* the consensus of this group, reflected in the excerpts from Dula and the Georgetown student note by Alan Duane Webber, *infra,* was that the vaguely communitarian "common heritage" principle would put a crimp on pioneering space development activities. In this view, the common heritage principle would lead to a centralized administrative structure requiring firms and governments to share their bounty with all the nations of the earth—thus standing as a major disincentive to high-risk development activities.

Representatives from the underdeveloped countries take a different view of the common heritage principle. As the excerpt from Rao, *infra,* shows, they saw the Moon Treaty as the first step in the essential process of bringing the underdeveloped world into parity with the wealthy nations. The Treaty in this view invites the establishment of an international regime to equitably distribute the proceeds from space resource development, on the theory that such resources belong to all mankind. In this sense, the Treaty is one of the first manifestations of the New International Economic Order, a proposed restructuring of the global economy based generally on principles of sharing and equitable development rather than "neo-colonialist exploitation." This new economic thinking is described in a brief note after the Rao excerpt.

Western legal commentators and economists remain unpersuaded of the merits of the principles underlying the New International Economic Order, however, as the excerpts from Webber and Dula, and the Note on Common Property Resources and Efficient Allocation, all *infra,* demonstrate. They believe instead that the best way to encourage development is to permit pioneering firms and governments to keep their profits. Without the lure of substantial profits—undiminished by the uncertainties of a scheme of international sharing—they argue that space development is too risky to be undertaken by any rational organization. Dula takes perhaps the extreme free-market view; others, notably Webber, and some of the economists cited in the Note, see some merit in an international regime for allocating development rights—so long as the profit-sharing component of the regime is kept separate from the system used to allocate development rights.

So we have some interesting issues awaiting us in this chapter. We turn first to the ABM Treaty, its background, and what it means for space activities.

THE ABM TREATY

The ABM Treaty severely limits the deployment, testing, and use of missile systems designed to intercept incoming strategic ballistic missiles. It is a bilateral treaty between the United States and the Soviet Union that took effect in 1972. Missiles, launchers, and ABM-related radars are prohibited or sharply limited under the Treaty, which applies to sea-, ground-, and space-based ABM systems (see Article V, reproduced below). There is one exception to the general prohibition of Article II: Article III permits each side to maintain one ABM system around its capital and another around a group of Inter-Continental Ballistic Missile (ICBM) silos of its choosing. Article IV also allows the U.S. and the Soviet Union to keep the development and testing operations they had at the time the Treaty was signed.

BACKGROUND

The ABM Treaty grew out of the Strategic Arms Limitation Talks (SALT I), which began in November of 1969. The basic philosophy behind the Treaty was simple. The recently developed ABM systems, with their potential to give one side protection against the other's missiles, might give one nuclear power the impression that it could launch an attack against the other without suffering significant damage itself. This was obviously a frightening scenario; importantly, it was just as dangerous whether or not it was true, so long as one side *believed* it had an advantage. The solution to this problem (and the related threat of a massive "spending race"), it was agreed, was a treaty limiting the deployment of these systems. Thus the ABM Treaty was born.

Only two of the Treaty's sixteen articles relate to space, Articles V and XII. They are set forth below.

Treaty Between the United States of America and the Union of Soviet Socialist Republics on the Limitation of Anti-Ballistic Missile Systems [The ABM Treaty], May 26, 1972, 23 U.S.T. 3435, T.I.A.S. No. 7503

Article V

1. Each Party [i.e., the United States and the Soviet Union] undertakes not to develop, test, or deploy ABM systems or components which are sea-based, air-based, space-based, or mobile land-based.

2. Each Party undertakes not to develop, test, or deploy ABM launchers for launching more than one ABM interceptor missile at a time from each launcher, nor to modify deployed launchers to provide them with such a capability, nor to develop, test, or deploy automatic or semi-automatic or other similar systems for rapid reload of ABM launchers.

*   *   *

Article XII

1. For the purpose of providing assurance of compliance with the provisions of this Treaty, each Party shall use national technical means of

verification at its disposal in a manner consistent with generally recognized principles of international law.

2. Each Party undertakes not to interfere with the national technical means of verification of the other Party operating in accordance with paragraph 1 of this Article.

3. Each Party undertakes not to use deliberate concealment measures which impede verification by national technical means of compliance with the provisions of this Treaty. This obligation shall not require changes in current construction, assembly, conversion or overhaul practices.

NOTE

There are two points worth mentioning about Article V. Paragraph 1 specifically refers to "space-based" ABM systems even though in 1972, when the Treaty was signed, no such systems were operational. Second, Paragraph 2, limiting the capacity of ABM missile launchers to one missile at a time, does not prevent a party from placing more than one non-missile projectile on a launcher. (This was one component in the controversial Reagan Administration "reinterpretation" of the ABM Treaty, discussed in the following section.)

Article XII is significant in that it represents the codification of the "open skies" principle. (The SALT I Agreement, another bilateral treaty adopted in 1971, also prohibited interference with the "national technical means of verification" of the other country; it has since expired. See Interim Agreement on Certain Measures with Respect to the Limitation of Strategic Offensive Arms, with Protocol (SALT I), 23 U.S.T. 3462, T.I.A.S. 7504 (effective Oct. 3, 1972; expired).) With this provision, space-based surveillance satellites not only became legal; they became an essential component of the international arms-control regime.

THE ABM "REINTERPRETATION"

From the time the ABM Treaty was signed until 1985, there seemed to be general agreement concerning its meaning. Both the Soviet Union and the United States conducted research into such futuristic alternative technologies as lasers and particle beams (research is not prohibited under the Treaty). At the same time, neither nation went ahead with either testing or deployment of mobile ABM systems or components, since both these activities are banned under Article V.

In 1985, however, the Reagan Administration needed to obtain legal clearance for the testing of "Star Wars"/Strategic Defense Initiative space-based defense components. The SDI concept, immediately dubbed "Star Wars" by the press when it was formally launched in 1983, called for the U.S. to embark on a massive research program to develop defensive systems that would render nuclear weapons (or at least those delivered via ICBMs) obsolete. Such a system, it was thought, could use satellites equipped with lasers or other high-energy beams to destroy incoming missiles, thus ensuring the safety of the United States. In short, the Star Wars proposal resurrected the dream of a "peace shield" over the country—a dream that would seem to have been surrendered in the ABM Treaty of 1972.

The Reagan Administration was not so quick to give up on the dream, however. Under a "broad interpretation" of the ABM Treaty, the Administration, headed by State Department Legal Adviser Abraham D. Sofaer, put forth an alternative interpretation. Just as the in-house counsel of a major corporation is unlikely to disappoint its Chief Executive Officer in the rendering of legal opinions, so the State Department's Legal Adviser did not disappoint the President by declaring his plans contrary to the Treaty. Not surprisingly, the new interpretation would have allowed the government to begin full-scale testing of space-based lasers and other advanced weapons; under the State Department's reading of the ABM Treaty, "Star Wars" could continue on schedule.

The structure of the reinterpretation is somewhat elaborate. Basically it revolves around Agreed Statement D, a controlling interpretive addendum to the Treaty that was agreed to by both parties. It reads as follows:

> In order to insure fulfillment of the obligation not to deploy ABM systems and their components except as provided in Article III of the Treaty [reproduced above], the Parties agree that in the event ABM systems based on other physical principles and including components capable of substituting for ABM interceptor missiles, ABM launchers, or ABM radars are created in the future, specific limitations on such systems and their components would be subject to discussion in accordance with Article XIII and agreement in accordance with Article XIV of the Treaty.

The Reagan Administration reinterpretation places great emphasis on one aspect of Statement D: it is the only provision in the Treaty that *explicitly* refers to technologies that might be developed in the future— "ABM systems based on other physical principles." Sofaer and other Reagan Administration officials drew one simple conclusion from this provision: Only this Statement, which concerns the two ABM systems permitted in Article III, applies to technologies that were not in existence when the Treaty was signed. Thus the remainder of the Treaty, under this view, has no bearing on the testing of new ABM technologies. (Note that even Sofaer *et al.* did not argue that ABM systems based on new technologies can be *deployed;* presumably, even they read the language of Statement D as requiring the Parties to confer on new developments prior to deployment.) The upshot: Star Wars/SDI testing does not violate the ABM Treaty.

There are a great many problems with the reinterpretation. Whether one looks to the plain language of the Treaty's text (in its *entirety*), the conduct of the Parties subsequent to signing the Treaty, the negotiating history, or the understandings of the ratifying bodies, it is difficult to escape the conclusion that the proposed reinterpretation of the Reagan Administration was wrong. The broad language of Article V(1) banned "ABM systems or components" as defined in Article II. Article II defines such systems by their *function* ("a system to counter strategic ballistic missiles") and states that such systems are those *"currently consisting of"* missiles, launchers, and radars (emphasis added). The only exception is set forth in Article III, which allows each side to keep two ABM systems in place. As is clear from its language and the accounts of the treaty negotiators, Statement D was meant to clarify this exception. (Notice that Statement D—the linchpin in the reinterpretation—begins with "In order to insure fulfillment of the obligation not to deploy ABM systems and their components except as provided in Article III of the Treaty. . . .")

The reinterpretation thus fails to pass the test of even minimum plausibility. Raymond L. Garthoff, one of the key U.S. officials who negotiated the Treaty, puts it this way:

In examining the text of a treaty, the most important facts are the effect of the language, intent of the parties, and purpose of the provisions. The interrelation and mutually reinforcing effect of the several provisions in its articles (and related agreed statements expanding on them) are also important. Judge Sofaer [as he prefers to be called] in effect turns the process of interpretation of the text on its head: instead of interpreting the terms of the treaty as a whole, he disaggregates and then reassembles them, often with great violence to the clear meaning of the language. Bending the parts to fit his preferred pattern, he constructs a kind of ABM Treaty Mod II, "Made in the USA," to suit the needs of a policy giving priority to the Reagan administration's SDI [i.e., Star Wars] program, rather than to the intent and purpose of the United States and the Soviet Union when together they concluded the ABM Treaty.

R. Garthoff, *Policy Versus the Law: The Reinterpretation of the ABM Treaty* 20 (1987).

NOTES

1. Prior to the dramatic reinterpretation of the ABM Treaty, military leaders and the Reagan Administration argued that the Star Wars program, or Strategic Defense Initiative (SDI), was not a violation of the Treaty because it was only in the research stage. As General James A. Abrahamson, Director of the Strategic Defense Initiative Organization, explained in Congressional testimony on the program, "[The ABM] agreement does permit research short of field testing of a prototype ABM system or breadboard model. Our research under the SDI program will be within those limits." Department of Defense Appropriations for 1986: Hearings Before the Subcomm. on Defense Appropriations of the House Comm. on Appropriations, 99th Cong., 1st Sess. 568–69 (1985).

2. Sofaer presented his views on the reinterpretation in an article in the Harvard Law Review. *See* Sofaer, The ABM Treaty and the Strategic Defense Initiative, 99 Harvard Law Review 1972 (1986).

3. Garthoff, in the book quoted from above, has recreated the negotiating history behind the "currently consisting of" language in Article II. Quoting from Memoranda of Conversations made at the time, he concludes:

> I argued that "the Soviet side, as well as the American, recognized that there could be *future* systems, and while the question of constraints on future systems would be settled elsewhere than in Article II, the correct way of indicating a valid connection between components and systems in Article II would be to include the word 'currently.'" Ginevsky [the chief Soviet nego-tiator] agreed to take up that proposal with his delegation, and the next day brought a new Soviet draft of Article II incorporating the language. . . . A fully agreed upon Article II was incorporated into the latest version of the Joint Draft Text of the treaty. . . .

R. Garthoff, *supra*, at 44.

4. A 1986 article has rehearsed in detail the Senate hearings leading up to ratification of the Treaty. The author concludes his analysis with the following statement:

> Considering the legislative history as a whole, the Reagan administration's permissive interpretation of the ABM Treaty appears to differ substantially from the consenting Senate of the Treaty. A fair reading of the Senate hearings strongly suggests two conclusions about the meaning of the ABM Treaty: first, when Article III, paragraph 1 of Article V and Agreed Statement D are read together, their import is that the development and testing of "Star Wars" technology in any basing mode other than a fixed, land-based mode is prohibited; and, second, that the deployment of such technology in even the fixed, land-based mode is prohibited under the Treaty.

Kennedy, Treaty Interpretation by the Executive Branch: The ABM Treaty and "Star Wars" Testing and Development, 80 American Journal of International Law 854, 866 (1986). *See also* A. Sherr, A Legal Analysis of the "New Interpretation" of the Anti-Ballistic Missile Treaty (1986); Chayes & Chayes, Testing and Development of "Exotic" Systems Under the ABM Treaty: The Great Reinterpretation Caper, 99 Harvard Law Review 1956 (1986).

5. Many members of Congress were so incensed at the proposed rein-terpretation that the Senate threatened to block ratification of another arms control treaty—the Intermediate Nuclear Forces (INF) Treaty of 1988—until the Reagan administration withdrew the ABM reinterpretation. *See* Norman, Showdown Nears on ABM Treaty, 238 Science 147, 149 (1988). In addition, because the ABM reinterpretation goes against the understand-ing of many Senators who ratified that treaty, some Senators demanded that they be given access to the entire negotiating record of any future treaties, to assure that detailed understandings of all provisions could be

embedded in the ratification proceedings, thus undercutting any future reinterpretation maneuvers. *Id.,* at 149. *See also* Norman, Senator Blasts Administration's Reinterpretation of ABM Treaty, 234 Science 1489 (1988).

THE MOON TREATY

Agreement on Activities of States on the Moon and Other Celestial Bodies (UN General Assembly Resolution 34/68)

The States parties to this Agreement,

Noting the achievements of states in the exploration and use of the moon and other celestial bodies,

Recognizing that the moon, as a natural satellite of the earth, has an important role to play in the exploration of outer space,

Determined to promote on the basis of equality the further development of co-operation among states in the exploration and use of the moon and other celestial bodies,

Desiring to prevent the moon from becoming an area of international conflict,

Bearing in mind the benefits which may be derived from the exploitation of the natural resources of the moon and other celestial bodies,

Recalling the [1967] Treaty on Principles governing the Activities of States in the Exploration and Use of Outer Space, including the Moon and Other Celestial Bodies, the Agreement on the Rescue of Astronauts, the Return of Astronauts and the Return of Objects launched into Outer Space, the Convention on International Liability for Damage caused by Space Objects, and the Convention on Registration of Objects launched into Outer Space,

Taking into account the need to define and develop the provisions of these international instruments in relation to the moon and other celestial bodies, having regard to further progress in the exploration and use of outer space,

Have agreed on the following:

Article 1

(1) The provisions of this Agreement relating to the moon shall also apply to other celestial bodies within the solar system, other than the earth, except in so far as specific legal norms enter into force with respect to any of these celestial bodies.

(2) For the purposes of this Agreement reference to the Moon shall include orbits around or other trajectories to or around it.

(3) This Agreement does not apply to extraterrestrial materials which reach the surface of the earth by natural means.

Article 2

All activities on the moon, including its exploration and use, shall be carried out in accordance with international law, in particular the Charter of the United Nations, and taking into account the Declaration of Principles of International Law concerning Friendly Relations and Co-operation among States in accordance with the charter of the United Nations, adopted by the General Assembly on Oct. 24, 1970, in the interests of maintaining international peace and security and promoting international co-operation and mutual understanding, and with due regard to the corresponding interests of all other states parties.

Article 3

(1) The moon shall be used by all states parties exclusively for peaceful purposes.

(2) Any threat or use of force or any other hostile act or threat of hostile act on the moon is prohibited. It is likewise prohibited to use the moon in order to commit any such act or to engage in any such threat in relation to the earth, the moon, spacecraft, the personnel of spacecraft or man-made space objects.

(3) States parties shall not place in orbit around or other trajectory to or around the moon objects carrying nuclear weapons or any other kinds of weapons of mass destruction or place or use such weapons on or in the moon.

(4) The establishment of military bases, installations and fortifications, the testing of any type of weapons and the conduct of military maneuvers on the moon shall be forbidden. The use of military personnel for scientific research or for any other peaceful purposes shall not be prohibited. The use of any equipment or facility necessary for peaceful exploration and use of the moon shall also not be prohibited.

Article 4

(1) The exploration and use of the moon shall be the province of all mankind and shall be carried out for the benefit and in the interests of all countries, irrespective of their degree of economic or scientific development. Due regard shall be paid to the interests of present and future generations as well as to the need to promote higher standards of living and conditions of economic and social progress and development in accordance with the Charter of the United Nations.

(2) States parties shall be guided by the principle of co-operation and mutual assistance in all their activities concerning the exploration and use of the moon. International co-operation in pursuance of this Agreement should be as wide as possible and may take place on a multilateral basis, on a bilateral basis or through international inter-governmental organizations.

Article 5

(1) States parties shall inform the Secretary-General of the United Nations as well as the public and the international scientific community, to the greatest extent feasible and practicable, of their activities concerned with the exploration and use of the moon. Information on the time, purposes, locations, orbital parameters and duration shall be given in respect of each mission to the moon as soon as possible after launching, while information on the results of each mission, including scientific results, shall be furnished upon completion of the mission. In the case of a mission lasting more than 60 days, information on conduct of the mission, including any scientific results, shall be given periodically at 30-day intervals. For missions lasting more than six months, only significant additions to such information need be reported thereafter.

(2) If a state party becomes aware that another state party plans to operate simultaneously in the same area of or in the same orbit around or trajectory to or around the moon, it shall promptly inform the other state of the timing of and plans for its own operations.

(3) In carrying out activities under this Agreement, states parties shall promptly inform the Secretary-General, as well as the public and the international scientific community, of any phenomena they discover in outer space, including the moon, which could endanger human life or health, as well as of any indication of organic life.

Article 6

(1) There shall be freedom of scientific investigation on the moon by all states parties without discrimination of any kind, on the basis of equality and in accordance with international law.

(2) In carrying out scientific investigations and in furtherance of the provisions of this Agreement, the states parties shall have the right to collect on and remove from the moon samples of its mineral and other substances. Such samples shall remain at the disposal of those states parties which caused them to be collected and may be used by them for scientific purposes. States parties shall have regard to the desirability of making a portion of such samples available to other interested state parties and the international scientific community for scientific investigation. States parties may in the course of scientific investigations also use mineral and other substances of the moon in quantities appropriate for the support of their missions.

(3) States parties agree on the desirability of exchanging scientific and other personnel on expeditions to or installations on the moon to the greatest extent feasible and practicable.

Article 7

(1) In exploring and using the moon, states parties shall take measures to prevent the disruption of the existing balance of its environment whether by introducing adverse changes in that environment, by its harmful con-

tamination through the introduction of extra-environmental matter or otherwise. States parties shall also take measures to avoid harmfully affecting the environment of the earth through the introduction of extraterrestrial matter or otherwise.

(2) States parties shall inform the Secretary-General of the United Nations of the measures being adopted by them in accordance with Paragraph 1 of this Article and shall also, to the maximum extent feasible, notify him in advance of all placements by them of radio-active materials on the moon and of the purposes of such placements.

(3) States parties shall report to other states parties and to the Secretary-General concerning areas of the moon having special scientific interest in order that, without prejudice to the rights of other states parties, consideration may be given to the designation of such areas as international scientific preserves for which special protective arrangements are to be agreed upon in consultation with the competent bodies of the United Nations.

Article 8

(1) States parties may pursue their activities in the exploration and use of the moon anywhere on or below its surface, subject to the provisions of this Agreement.

(2) For these purposes states parties may, in particular:

(a) Land their space objects on the moon and launch them from the moon;

(b) Place their personnel, space vehicles, equipment, facilities, stations and installations anywhere on or below the surface of the moon.

Personnel, space vehicles, equipment, facilities, stations and installations may move or be moved freely over or below the surface of the moon.

(3) Activities of states parties in accordance with Paragraphs 1 and 2 of this Article shall not interfere with the activities of other states parties on the moon. Where such interference may occur, the states parties concerned shall undertake consultations in accordance with Article 15, Paragraphs 2 and 3 of this Agreement.

Article 9

(1) States parties may establish manned and unmanned stations on the moon. A state party establishing a station shall use only that area which is required for the needs of the station and shall immediately inform the Secretary-General of the United Nations of the location and purposes of that station. Subsequently, at annual intervals that state shall likewise inform the Secretary-General whether the station continues in use and whether its purposes have changed.

(2) Stations shall be installed in such a manner that they do not impede the free access to all areas of the moon by personnel, vehicles and equipment of other states parties conducting activities on the moon in accordance with the provisions of this Agreement or of Article 1 of the Treaty on

Principles governing the Activities of States in the Exploration and Use of Outer Space, including the Moon and Other Celestial Bodies.

Article 10

(1) States parties shall adopt all practicable measures to safeguard the life and health of persons on the moon. For this purpose they shall regard any person on the moon as an astronaut within the meaning of Article V of the Treaty on Principles governing the Activities of States in the Exploration and Use of Outer Space, including the Moon and Other Celestial Bodies and as part of the personnel of a spacecraft within the meaning of the Agreement on the Rescue of Astronauts, the Return of Astronauts and the Return of Objects launched into Outer Space.

(2) States parties shall offer shelter in their stations, installations, vehicles and other facilities to persons in distress on the moon.

Article 11

(1) The moon and its natural resources are the common heritage of mankind, which finds its expression in the provisions of this Agreement, in particular in Paragraph 5 of this Article.

(2) The moon is not subject to national appropriation by any claim of sovereignty, by means of use or occupation, or by any other means.

(3) Neither the surface nor the subsurface of the moon, nor any part thereof or natural resources in place, shall become property of any state, international intergovernmental or non-governmental organization, national organization or non-governmental entity or of any natural person. The placement of personnel, space vehicles, equipment, facilities, stations and installations on or below the surface of the moon, including structures connected with its surface or subsurface, shall not create a right of ownership over the surface or the subsurface of the moon or any areas thereof. The foregoing provisions are without prejudice to the international regime referred to in Paragraph 5 of this Article.

(4) States parties have the right to exploration and use of the moon without discrimination of any kind, on the basis of equality and in accordance with international law and the provisions of this Agreement.

(5) States parties to this Agreement hereby undertake to establish an international regime, including appropriate procedures, to govern the exploitation of the natural resources of the moon as such exploitation is about to become feasible. This provision shall be implemented in accordance with Article 18 of this Agreement.

(6) In order to facilitate the establishment of the international regime referred to in Paragraph 5 of this Article, states parties shall inform the Secretary-General of the United Nations as well as the public and the international scientific community, to the greatest extent feasible and practicable, of any natural resources they may discover on the moon.

(7) The main purposes of the international regime to be established shall include;

(a) The orderly and safe development of the natural resources of the moon;

(b) The rational management of those resources;

(c) The expansion of opportunities in the use of those resources;

(d) An equitable sharing by all states parties in the benefits derived from those resources, whereby the interests and needs of the developing countries, as well as the efforts of those countries, which have contributed either directly or indirectly to the exploration of the moon, shall be given special consideration.

(8) All the activities with respect to the natural resources of the moon shall be carried out in a manner compatible with the purposes specified in paragraph 7 of this Article and the provisions of Article 6, Paragraph 2, of this Agreement.

Article 12

(1) States parties shall retain jurisdiction and control over their personnel, space vehicles, equipment, facilities, stations and installations on the moon. The ownership of space vehicles, equipment, facilities, stations and installations shall not be affected by their presence on the moon.

(2) Vehicles, installations and equipment or their component parts found in places other than their intended location shall be dealt with in accordance with Article 5 of the Agreement on the Rescue of Astronauts, the Return of Astronauts and the Return of Objects launched into Outer Space.

(3) In the event of an emergency involving a threat to human life, states parties may use the equipment, vehicles, installations, facilities, or supplies of other states parties on the moon. Prompt notification of such use shall be made to the Secretary-General of the United Nations or the state party concerned.

Article 13

A State party which learns of the crash-landing, forced landing or other unintended landing on the moon of a space object, or its component parts, that were not launched by it, shall promptly inform the launching state party and the Secretary-General of the United Nations.

Article 14

(1) States parties to this Agreement shall bear international responsibility for national activities on the moon, whether such activities are carried out by governmental agencies or by non-governmental entities, and for assuring that national activities are carried out in conformity with the provisions set forth in this Agreement. States parties shall ensure that non-governmental entities under their jurisdiction shall engage in activities on the moon only under the authority and continuing supervision of the appropriate state party.

(2) States parties recognize that detailed arrangements concerning liability for damage caused on the moon, in addition to the provisions of

the Treaty on Principles governing the Activities of States in the Exploration and Use of Outer Space, including the Moon and Other Celestial Bodies and the Convention on International Liability for Damage caused by Space Objects, may become necessary as a result of more extensive activities on the moon. Any such arrangements shall be elaborated in accordance with the procedure provided for in Article 18 of this Agreement.

Article 15

(1) Each state party may assure itself that the activities of other states parties in the exploration and use of the moon are compatible with the provisions of this Agreement. To this end, all space vehicles, equipment, facilities, stations and installations on the moon shall be open to other state parties. Such states parties shall give reasonable advance notice of a projected visit, in order that appropriate consultations may be held and that maximum precautions may be taken to assure safety and to avoid interference with normal operations in the facility to be visited. In pursuance of this Article, any state party may act on its own behalf or with the full or partial assistance of any other state party or through appropriate international procedures within the framework of the United Nations and in accordance with the Charter.

(2) A state party which has reason to believe that another state party is not fulfilling the obligations incumbent upon it pursuant to this Agreement or that another state party is interfering with the rights which the former state has under this Agreement may request consultations with that state party. A state party receiving such a request shall enter into such consultations without delay. Any other state party which requests to do so shall be entitled to take part in the consultations. Each state party participating in such consultations shall seek a mutually acceptable resolution of any controversy and shall bear in mind the rights and interests of all state parties. The Secretary-General of the United Nations shall be informed of the results of the consultations and shall transmit the information received to all states parties concerned.

(3) If the consultations do not lead to a mutually acceptable settlement which has due regard for the rights and interests of all states parties, the parties concerned shall take all measures to settle the dispute by other peaceful means of their choice appropriate to the circumstances and the nature of the dispute. If difficulties arise in connection with the opening of consultations, or if consultations do not lead to a mutually acceptable settlement, any state party may seek the assistance of the Secretary-General, without seeking the consent of any other state party concerned, in order to resolve the controversy. A state party which does not maintain diplomatic relations with another state party concerned shall participate in such consultations, as its choice, either itself or through another state party or the Secretary-General as intermediary.

Article 16

With the exception of Articles 17 to 21, references in this Agreement to states shall be deemed to apply to any international inter-governmental organization which conducts space activities if the organization declares its acceptance of the rights and obligations provided for in this Agreement and if a majority of the states members of the organization are states parties to this Agreement and to the [1967] Treaty of Principles governing the Activities of States in the Exploration and Use of Outer Space, including the Moon and Other Celestial Bodies. States members of any such organization which are states parties to this Agreement shall take all appropriate steps to ensure that the organization makes a declaration in accordance with the provisions of this Article.

Article 17

Any state party to this Agreement may propose amendments to the Agreement. Amendments shall enter into force for each state party to the Agreement accepting the amendments upon their acceptance by a majority of the states parties to the Agreement and thereafter for each remaining state party to the Agreement on the date of acceptance by it.

Article 18

Ten years after the entry into force of this Agreement, the question of the review of the Agreement shall be included in the provisional agenda of the General Assembly of the United Nations in order to consider, in the light of past application of the Agreement, whether it requires revision. However, at any time after the Agreement has been in force for five years, the Secretary-General of the United Nations, as depository, shall, at the request of one-third of the states parties to the Agreement and with the concurrence of the majority of the states parties, convene a conference of the states parties to review this agreement. A review conference shall also consider the question of the implementation of the provisions of Article 11, Paragraph 5, on the basis of the principle referred to in Paragraph 1 of that Article and taking into account in particular any relevant technological developments.

Article 19

(1) This Agreement shall be open for signature by all states at United Nations Headquarters in New York.

(2) This Agreement shall be subject to ratification by signatory states. Any state which does not sign this Agreement before its entry into force in accordance with Paragraph 3 of this Article may accede to it at any time. Instruments of ratification or accession shall be deposited with the Secretary-General of the United Nations.

(3) This Agreement shall enter into force on the 30th day following the date of deposit of the fifth instrument of ratification.

(4) For each state depositing its instrument of ratification or accession after the entry into force of this Agreement, it shall enter into force on the 30th day following the date of deposit of any such instrument.

(5) The Secretary-General shall promptly inform all signatory and acceding states of the date of each signature, the date of deposit of each instrument of ratification or accession to this Agreement, the date of its entry into force and other notices.

Article 20

Any state party to this Agreement may give notice of its withdrawal from the Agreement one year after its entry into force by written notification to the Secretary-General of the United Nations. Such withdrawal shall take effect one year from the date of receipt of this notification.

Article 21

The original of this Agreement, of which the Arabic, Chinese, English, French, Russian and Spanish texts are equally authentic, shall be deposited with the Secretary-General of the United Nations, who shall send certified copies thereof to all signatory and acceding states.

Nash, Contemporary Practice of the United States Relating to International Law, 74 American Journal of International Law 419, 421–426 (1980)

Moon Treaty

Senator Frank Church, chairman of the Senate Committee on Foreign Relations, and Senator Jacob K. Javits, ranking minority member of the committee, addressed a joint letter to Secretary of State Cyrus R. Vance on October 30, 1979, in which they expressed concern that several aspects of the (United Nations) Agreement Governing the Activities of States on the Moon and Other Celestial Bodies (Moon Treaty) could prove damaging to the national economic and security interests of the United States.

One source of concern was their view that the law of the sea negotiations had shown that the meaning attached to the concept, "common heritage of mankind," by many countries of the world was contrary to the economic interests of the United States and of other countries with free enterprise/free market economies. Another source of concern was their view that the treaty would result in a "de facto moratorium" on resource-related activities in outer space (through the commitment to negotiate a subsequent resource regime), which would not deter the Soviets from moving forward in resource development under the guise of scientific investigation because they would have "no fear of significant competition from the West, which must rely on its industry to provide commercial initiative."

Secretary Vance, in his replies to Senators Church and Javits on November 28, noted that on November 1, Ambassador Richard W. Petree had placed on record the U.S. interpretation of various treaty provisions, including those of concern to the Senators, during the debate on the resolution of the UN Special Political Committee commending the Moon Treaty and recommending that it be opened for signature. The United States had joined with 27 other countries, including the United Kingdom, the Federal Republic of Germany, France, Belgium, the Netherlands, Italy, Canada, Australia, and Japan, in sponsoring the resolution, which had been adopted by consensus on November 2. (The General Assembly approved the resolution on December 5, 1979.)

The Secretary clarified the legal significance of the U.S. actions to date in connection with the treaty, stating, in part:

Of course, our cosponsorship of the resolution and joining in consensus approval of the resolution does not entail legal obligations for the United States. Only ratification of the Treaty after the advice and consent of the Senate can impose binding obligations upon the United States. The Administration has not yet turned to questions relating to signature of the Treaty or its submission to the Senate. When we begin to consider such matters, we will give the most careful consideration to concerns which you and others have raised in regard to the Moon Treaty. I would, however, like to address myself to some of your points in a preliminary way.

In regard to the important matter of the exploitation of the natural resources of the moon and other celestial bodies, the Treaty contains no moratorium on exploitation and, in fact, has provisions designed to facilitate and encourage such exploitation. For example, Article XI(3) of the Moon Treaty makes clear that although the 1967 Outer Space Treaty provides that "Outer space, including the moon and other celestial bodies, is not subject to national appropriation by claim of sovereignty, by means of use or occupation, or by any other means," this "non-appropriation" principle applies to the natural resources of celestial bodies only when such resources are "in place." Thus, Article XI(3) would permit ownership to be exercised by States or private entities over those natural resources which have been removed from their "Place" on or below the surface of the moon or other celestial bodies. (Such removal is permitted by the article contained in the 1967 Outer Space Treaty which states, inter alia, that "Outer space, including the moon and other celestial bodies, shall be free for exploration and use by all States. . . .")

We also do not believe that the Treaty would benefit the Soviet Union to the disadvantage of the United States. While the Soviet Union first proposed a Moon Treaty, their draft text contained no detailed provisions concerning exploitation. It was, rather, characterized by the Soviets as a "navigation treaty." It was the United States which in 1972 first proposed detailed provisions concerning exploitation and the common heritage concept. (The 1967 Outer Space Treaty, which the United States has ratified with the Senate's advice and consent, already had provided that outer space was the "common province" of mankind and that "the exploration and use of outer space, including the moon and other celestial bodies, shall be carried out for the benefit and the interests of all countries, irrespective of their degree of economic or scientific development . . ." (Article I).) Until July of 1979, the Soviet Union maintained strong opposition to the common heritage concept, and it was essentially because of this opposition that the Treaty was not concluded several years ago. Likewise, the Soviets, as well as the United States, opposed the concept of a moratorium on exploitation of natural resources.

The statement of Ambassador Richard W. Petree, U.S. Deputy Representative to the Security Council, enclosed with the Secretary's letters, summarized important U.S. space activities during the year and U.S. views on issues before the UN Outer Space Committee. In regard to the Moon Treaty, Ambassador Petree stated, in part:

[T]he draft Moon Treaty . . . is, in its own right, a meaningful advance in the codification of international law dealing with outer space, containing obligations which are of both immediate and long-term application in regard to such matters as the safeguarding of human life on celestial bodies, the promotion of scientific investigation and the exchange of information relative to and derived from activities on celestial bodies, and the enhancement of opportunities and conditions for evaluation, research and exploitation of the natural resources of celestial bodies. We think it useful to address some of the especially significant provisions contained in the draft Moon Agreement, this "fifth star" in the constellation of outer space treaties.

*   *   *

The common heritage concept, which was initially suggested by Argentina, but formally proposed by the United States in 1972, is set forth in Article XI, paragraph 1, which makes clear that its meaning for purposes of the Moon Treaty is to be found within the Moon Treaty itself. Likewise, its meaning in the Moon Treaty is without prejudice to its use or meaning in any other treaty. Article XI also makes clear that the parties to the treaty undertake, as the exploitation of the natural resources of the celestial bodies other than the earth is about to become feasible, to enter into negotiations to establish a mutually acceptable international regime to govern the exploitation of those mineral and other substantive resources which may be found on the surface or subsurface of a celestial body. My Government will, when and if negotiations for such regime are called for under Articles XI and XVII, make a good faith effort to see that such negotiations are successfully concluded.

*   *   *

The draft treaty, as part of the compromise by many delegations, places no moratorium upon the exploitation of the natural resources on celestial bodies by States or their nationals, but does provide that any exploitation of the natural resources of celestial bodies be carried out in a manner compatible with the purposes specified in paragraph 7 of Article XI and the provisions of paragraph 2 of Article VI. We view the purposes set forth in paragraph 7 as providing both a framework and an incentive for exploitation of the natural resources of celestial bodies. They constitute a framework because even exploitation which is undertaken by a State Party to the Treaty or its nationals outside of the context of any such regime, either because the exploitation occurs before a regime is negotiated or because a particular State may not participate in the international regime once it is established, will have to be compatible with those purposes set forth in Article XI, paragraph 7, of the Moon Treaty.

In a letter of November 13, 1979, Senator Richard Stone, also a member of the Senate Committee on Foreign Relations, urged Secretary Vance to reevaluate the U.S. position on the draft moon treaty, which he described as having "extremely dangerous potentialities" because it appeared to decrease "the ability of the United States to advance in yet unexplored fields" and to "greatly inhibit the actions and desires of U.S. corporations in space, negate the notion of free enterprise, and . . . place the United States in a position subservient to the Soviet Union."

J. Brian Atwood, Assistant Secretary of State for Congressional Relations, replied to Senator Stone on behalf of the Secretary in a letter of January 2, 1980, as follows:

The provisions of the Moon Treaty must be considered in the context established by the 1967 Treaty on Principles Governing the Activities of States on the Exploration and Use of Outer Space, Including the Moon and Other Celestial Bodies (the "Outer Space Treaty") to which approximately 75 countries, including the United States, are parties. This Treaty received the advice and consent of the Senate without reservations.

*   *   *

The Moon Treaty places no limitations on the exploitation of celestial natural resources by any government or private entity beyond those already contained in the 1967 Outer Space Treaty except that the "activities with respect to the natural resources of the moon shall be carried out in a manner compatible with the purposes specified in paragraph 7." (See Article XI(8) and the environmental protections contained in Article VII).

*   *   *

In regard to the international regime dealt with in Article XI(5) of the Moon Treaty, neither the "common heritage of mankind" concept as embodied in the Moon Treaty nor any other provision of the Treaty compels any specific form of international arrangement for the regulation of the exploitation of moon or other celestial body resources. Neither the Treaty nor the "common heritage" concept entails any specific obligation on States in regard to the establishment of such a regime except the commitment to engage in good faith negotiations to establish a mutually acceptable international regime to govern the exploitation of natural resources on celestial bodies when exploitation of such natural resources is about to become feasible.

The Law of the Sea experience with the common heritage concept, while relevant, would in no way be controlling regarding the negotiations of any such future agreement. Article XI(1) of the Moon Treaty makes clear that the common heritage concept in the Moon Treaty finds its meaning totally within the text of the Moon Treaty itself. A future negotiation for the regime to govern [the] moon or other celestial body resources could, however, benefit from the Law of the Sea experience, just as it could benefit from the experience of such multinational cooperative ventures in outer space as INTELSAT, which organization is evidence that the criteria set forth in Article XI(7) of the Moon Treaty can be met by institutional arrangements quite different from those contemplated in the Law of the Sea negotiations on sea-bed mining.

*   *   *

We do not believe that the Moon Treaty language would inhibit commercial investment by non-government entities in the exploitation of celestial natural resources or the operation of the free enterprise system in outer space generally. The article of the Moon Treaty most relevant, Article X, makes clear that all States Parties to the Treaty have a significant interest in the possible future exploitation of the natural resources of the moon and other celestial bodies and that their views are to be given serious consideration at any future international conference which may attempt to establish an international regime specifically concerned with exploitation of celestial natural resources. Given the legal context established by the 1967 Outer Space Treaty, such an interest can be neither denied nor ignored.

It is important to note that efforts by some developing countries to have the Treaty provide for a moratorium on the exploitation of the natural resources of celestial bodies except under the auspices of an international regime were rejected. The Treaty contains no moratorium on exploitation and, in fact, has provisions designed to clarify certain important ambiguities in the 1967 Outer Space Treaty and to otherwise facilitate and encourage the exploitation of celestial natural resources. For example, Article XI(3) of the Moon Treaty makes clear that although the 1967 Outer Space Treaty provides that "Outer Space, including the moon and other celestial bodies, is not subject to national appropriation by claim of sovereignty, by means of use or occupation, or by any other means," this "non-appropriation" principle applies to the natural resources of celestial bodies only when such resources are "in place."

NOTE

This excerpt summarizes the position of those who negotiated and helped draft the Moon Treaty. The views of the State Department, which supported the Moon Treaty, are set out more fully in Staff of Senate Comm. on Commerce, Science & Transportation, 96th Cong., 2d Sess., Agreement Governing the Activities of States on the Moon and Other Celestial Bodies, Part 3, 316–318, 363–365 (Comm. Print 1980). Unfortunately for them, a host of other space interest groups mounted a storm of protest over the Treaty, culminating in the failure of the Senate to even vote on ratification. *See, e.g., id.,* at 318–326, 366–379 (summary of space group L–5 Society's Objections to Moon Treaty, and text of L–5 society point-by-point rebuttal of State Department memorandum). The issues that the negotiators thought were resolved in the Treaty's text in fact proved to be the downfall of the agreement, particularly the "common heritage" language in Article XI. In the excerpt that follows, a student Note written at the time the Treaty was being debated points out some of the problems with the Treaty.

Spitz, Note, SPACE LAW—Agreement Governing the Activities of States on the Moon and Other Celestial Bodies, 21 Harvard International Law Journal 579–584 (1980)

Most of the provisions of the Agreement have already been set forth in previous space accords. The 1967 Treaty on Principles Governing the Activities of States in the Exploration and Use of Outer Space, including the Moon and Other Celestial Bodies, which has seventy-six member states including the United States and the Soviet Union, set forth the principle that the moon and other celestial bodies shall be used exclusively for peaceful purposes.

* * *

The significant change in space law which the Agreement makes is the application of the "common heritage" principle to the natural resources of the moon. The [Outer Space] Treaty declared that the moon was not subject to national appropriation and that outer space was the "province of all mankind." However, neither it nor subsequent agreements have addressed the natural resources question. A commitment to "an equitable sharing" by all states in the moon's resources and the establishment of an international regime to achieve that purpose will have a significant effect on the exploitation of the solar system. The common heritage provisions of the Agreement, when viewed with similar themes raised in the Law of the Sea Conference and the discussions on Antarctica, points to a trend growing in acceptance in the international community. If it achieves broad acceptance, the Agreement could have great impact outside the area of space law.

However, a great potential limitation on the effectiveness of the Agreement is that it makes no provision for signatory states to compel the participation of other states. There is also no mechanism to protect the interests of member states against non-participants. Even though the Agreement may be adopted widely enough to have some force as customary international law, it will need the acceptance of those states capable of conducting space operations to be effective.

Though the Agreement should have no trouble winning acceptance by developing states, the support of the two current space powers is more problematic. The Soviet Union in particular opposes international control of the natural resources of space, and from the beginning of the discussion it opposed the application of any part of the Agreement to celestial bodies other than the moon. Soviet ratification of the Agreement, if it occurs at all, will be reluctant. The United States stance on the Agreement is less clear. Since the exploitation of the moon's natural resources has seemed far in the future, the State Department and the National Aeronautics and Space Administration have been supporting the drafting process since its inception. Recently however, the United States seems to have reconsidered its position.

This points up the basic dilemma of the Agreement. Without the common heritage provision, the Agreement is largely a reiteration of previous treaties. With them, it loses its appeal to the two space powers whose support it will probably need. The success of the Agreement may hinge on the willingness of the United States and the Soviet Union to accept the common heritage provisions.

NOTES

1. The Author of this Note states that "a great potential limitation on the effectiveness of the Agreement is that it makes no provision for signatory states to compel the participation of other states. There is also no mechanism to protect the interests of member states against non-participants." Was it a mistake for the drafters of the Treaty to assume that the central administrative organization called for in Article 2 would be joined by all countries? What problems could a single non-joiner cause for those who have joined? Is the "equitable distribution" provision enough of an incentive for developing countries to join?

2. The excerpt from an article by noted space lawyer Art Dula, reproduced *infra,* is an example of the writing that came out of the anti-treaty camp. A similar piece appeared in the magazine of the L–5 Society at the time of the Treaty debate. *See* A. Dula, "Free Enterprise and the Proposed Moon Treaty," L–5 News, October, 1979, at p. 1 cols. 1–3. See also Christol, The ABA and the Moon Treaty, 9 Journal of Space Law 77 (1981) (describing deliberations behind ABA's formal recommendations on Treaty).

3. As of this writing, the Soviet Union has yet to sign the Treaty. It has long taken the position that space resources should be freely exploitable by the nations that find and develop them. Did the fact that the U.S. refused to ratify the Treaty make it politically easier for the Soviet Union—which sometimes styles itself the friend of the developing world—to refrain from ratifying it itself? What would be the dynamics of a centralized international agency governing space resources having only one of the two major powers—the U.S. or the Soviet Union—as a member? Would it be economically feasible for one to join and not the other? Also, it is interesting to at least ponder the thought that the Soviet Union, the nation with the greatest practical experience in the area of centralized economic planning and control, may know all too well the pitfalls of such arrangements.

Absent adoption by the major space powers, the Moon Treaty is unlikely to play a major role in the future. Nevertheless, the failure of the major space powers to ratify the Treaty does not mean it is irrelevant. For one thing, as one of the first international documents to embody concepts identified with the New International Economic Order, it reflects important intellectual trends among the developing nations of the world. In addition, it should be recalled that the U.S.-Soviet domination of space capability is by no means a permanent affair; other nations—some of whom have already signed the Moon Treaty—are rapidly developing such a capability, as was shown in Chapter One. Thus the Moon Treaty is far from a dead letter on the international scene.

Galloway, Issues in Implementing the Agreement Governing the Activities of States on the Moon and Other Celestial Bodies, Proceedings of the Twenty-Third Colloquium on the Law of Outer Space, 1980, at 19-24

Article I, paragraph 1 of the Moon Agreement text provides that "the provisions of this Agreement relating to the Moon shall also apply to other celestial bodies within the solar system, other than the earth, except in so far as specific legal norms enter into force with respect to any of these celestial bodies." COPUOS related this principle to paragraph 1 of Article 11 which provides that "The moon and its natural resources are the common heritage of mankind, which finds its expression in the provisions of this Agreement, in particular in paragraph 5 of this article." Paragraph 5 of Article 11 provides for the establishment of an international regime when exploitation of the natural resources of the moon and other celestial bodies is "about to become feasible" but states that this provision must be implemented in accordance with article 18 of the Agreement. . . . The official COPUOS Understanding is as follows:

> The Committee agreed that by virtue of article I, paragraph 1, the principle contained in article XI, paragraph 1, would also apply to celestial bodies in

the solar system other than the Earth and to its natural resources. (Paragraph 62).

This is a significant interpretation regarding natural resources of celestial bodies, and it is part of the negotiating history, but its form—and the fact that this COPUOS understanding (as well as the other understandings) is usually omitted when the Moon Treaty text is distributed—raises the issue of the exact legal status of such an understanding. When the General Assembly voted on the treaty text, specific reference was made to the COPUOS understandings as paragraphs 62, 63, and 65, which could tend to strengthen the status of the understandings; nevertheless, this is an issue which can arise in the future to create problems, and when analysts first read these understandings and realize their importance, they wonder why these points are not included in the treaty text.

The delegates to the 1979 COPUOS session thought it was necessary to clarify article I, paragraph 2 which provides that "For the purposes of this Agreement references to the moon shall include orbits around or other trajectories to or around it." In response, COPUOS recorded this understanding:

> Following a suggestion for clarification of article I, paragraph 2, the committee agreed that the trajectories and orbits mentioned in article I, paragraph 2 do not include trajectories and orbits of space objects in Earth orbits only and trajectories of space objects between the Earth and such orbits. (Paragraph 63).

This means that trajectories to the Moon—and other celestial bodies—and orbits around the Moon are covered by the Agreement, but not covered are earth-orbiting spacecraft and trajectories from the earth to orbits around the earth.

NOTE

The Moon Treaty does not cover earth orbits or trajectories into earth orbit. In 1976, however, there was an attempt to make earth orbits subject to a "common heritage"–like regime. In the Bogota Resolution, a group of developing nations located near the equator on various continents declared that geosynchronous orbits overhead were subject to their sovereignty. The geosynchronous orbit issue is discussed in Chapter 8. Much of the common-resource discussion later in this chapter applies to that resource as well. It is safe to say that the Resolution has not met with widespread international acceptance.

Walsh, Controversial Issues
Under Article XI of the Moon Treaty,
5 Annals of Air & Space Law 489–498 (1981)

III. National Appropriation and Property Rights

Another issue in Article XI . . . is what its provisions regarding national appropriation and property rights entail. Paragraph two of this article provides that "the moon is not subject to national appropriation by any claim of sovereignty, by means of use or occupation, or by any other means." Consistent with this paragraph is the first sentence in paragraph three which states that:

Neither the surface nor the subsurface of the moon, nor any parts thereof or natural resources in place, shall become property of any State, international, intergovernmental or non-governmental entity or of any natural person.

These two provisions in Article XI appear to greatly limit the extent of an entity's activities on the moon and other celestial bodies, although definitions for appropriation and property are not given. The latter provision regarding property may, in fact, be of greater consequence because it applies not only to States, but to international, intergovernmental and non-governmental entities, and natural persons.

The prohibitions imposed by the two aforesaid provisions appear, however, to be negated by a subsequent provision in the article. A latter part of paragraph three states that:

The placement of personnel, space vehicles, equipment facilities, stations and installations on or below the surface of the moon, including structures connected with their surface or subsurface, shall not create a right of ownership over the surface or subsurface of the moon or any areas thereof.

Thus, even though national appropriation of the moon is prohibited, and even though the surface and the subsurface of the moon cannot become property of the various listed entities, numerous activities which are usually associated with appropriation and property rights are explicitly allowed.

*   *   *

IV. Exploitation of Natural Resources

Closely related to the issues regarding the common heritage of mankind, national appropriation and property rights is the issue of the exploitation of natural resources. The specific issue is whether Article XI of the Moon Treaty prohibits or limits the exploitation of natural resources on the moon and other celestial bodies. . . .

[I]t is clear that the treaty places no moratorium upon the exploitation of natural resources on the moon and other celestial bodies. . . .

NOTES

1. This article draws on some useful Congressional hearings on the Moon Treaty. *See* U.S. House Comm. on Science and Technology, Hearings Before the Subcomm. on Space Science and Applications on International Space Activities, 1979, 96th Cong., 1st Sess.

2. Walsh notes these seemingly paradoxical positions in the Treaty: it prohibits national appropriation of the moon and celestial bodies, and says that the surface and the subsurface of the moon cannot become property of the various listed entities, yet it also explicitly allows numerous activities which are usually associated with appropriation and property rights—e.g., "the placement of personnel, space vehicles, equipment facilities, stations and installations on or below the surface of the moon, including structures connected with their surface or subsurface." Can they be reconciled? Does the right to exploit always imply what we would consider full ownership? Consider the following quote from a noted space law authority:

> The CHM [Common Heritage of Mankind] principle does not impact upon preferences as to forms and means of economic organization and production. More specifically, the CHM principle cannot reasonably be considered to be in opposition to the free-enterprise system of economic relationships. Both the free-enterprise and socialist states will be able to live very comfortably within the CHM principle. This result is assured by the provision of Article II, par. 7(d) which prescribes that as much special consideration is to be accorded to those countries "which have contributed either directly or indirectly to the exploration of the Moon" as is to be given to the developing countries.

C. Christol, The Modern International Law of Outer Space 288 (1982).

Another attempt to find limitations on the Common Heritage principle in specific provisions of the Treaty was made by another space law commentator:

> The principle that "the ownership of space vehicles, equipment, facilities, stations and installations" shall not be affected by their presence on the Moon (Article 12(1)), suggests that ownership of mineral resources displaced on, or removed from, the Moon may be established under the internal law of the state involved.

J. Fawcett, Outer Space: New Challenges to Law and Policy 14 (1984).

3. Regarding the question in Note 2, consider these examples: (a) mining rights on government land (where the claimant is required to perform minimum developmental activities to maintain her claim); *see, e.g.,* Lindley,

A Treatise on the American Law Relating to Mines and Mineral Lands within the Public Land States and Territories (3d ed. 1914); and (b) the law of prescriptive easements, which allows one who repeatedly uses a right of way over another's land to obtain an equitable right to continue such use. *See generally* R. Powell, Real Property § 1026 (P. Rohan ed. 1977). Keep in mind that these are doctrines of Anglo-American law; they might not be persuasive to representatives from the developing world, where legal structures are often considerably different.

4. The example of ships at sea, described in the following excerpt, is also instructive. Note that this topic is also described in the discussion of Article II of the Outer Space Treaty in Chapter 3.

Reynolds & Merges, The Role of Commercial Development in Preventing War in Outer Space, 25 Jurimetrics: Journal of Law, Science & Technology 130, 143–44 (1985).

An obvious corollary to [any] discussion of incentives [for space development] is the necessity that enterprises have some assurance that their efforts to make use of space resources will not be subject to interference by other enterprises or by the military branches of states. Such assurance does not constitute a right to exclusive use of a resource, except in the narrowest sense (i.e., in the same sense that an oceangoing vessel's passage requires the exclusive use of the small patch of ocean which it occupies). Rather, it embodies the very basic right to be left alone. To some extent, of course, that right will be protected by whatever military forces the enterprise can claim protection from (its own, if the enterprise is a governmental one, or its government's, if the enterprise is a private one). Such protection may be enough—it is, after all, about all that is available to enforce the maritime order. [For a discussion of this topic see Reisman, Sanctions and Enforcement, in International Law Essays 381 (M. McDougal and W. M. Reisman eds., 1981).]

ORGANIZATIONAL STRUCTURES FOR CARRYING OUT THE MOON TREATY

In the excerpts that follow, we explore Articles 2 and 18 of the Moon Treaty. These provisions call for an international organization to supervise the exploitation of space resources. How would such an organization be structured? How would it be governed? How broad would its authority be? These are the questions we turn to next.

Although the Moon Treaty itself is unlikely to ever be ratified in the U.S., the issues it raises—especially those concerning possible organizational structures for a space resources agency—are quite worthy of study. This is so for several reasons. First, it is likely to serve as the basis for any future proposed agreements on space; it was, after all, many years in the making, and thus reflects a careful balancing of current international interests. Second, the "common heritage" concept, and especially the new developing-nation economic thinking on which it is based, is not likely to fade any time soon. These are ideas that western policymakers need to become familiar with—whether their goal is to oppose them or merely understand them. And third, as we will see in the Note on Common Property Resources and Efficient Allocation at the end of this chapter, even some western economists believe that an international organization will be required to allocate development rights over space resources. Consequently, it is important to carefully explore the alternative organizational forms a space resource allocation agency might assume. That is the goal of this section; we start with the second part of the Galloway article excerpted above.

Galloway, Issues in Implementing the Agreement Governing the Activities of States on the Moon and Other Celestial Bodies, Proceedings of the Twenty-Third Colloquium on the Law of Outer Space, 1980, at 19–24

5. Appropriate Body to Formulate an International Regime

According to Article 18 of the Moon Agreement, an international regime can be planned by States Parties any time after the treaty has been in force for five years, or as a result of action in ten years by the General Assembly. Under the first option, it is possible for a small group of States Parties to control planning for operations which affect "the common heritage of mankind." Under the second procedure provided in Article 18, it is possible that planning for operations of a technological space system would be assigned to the Legal Subcommittee of COPUOS. In any event, it will be many years before feasibility for exploiting natural resources can be established and thus we have time to consider additional approaches to this problem. The existing model which is apt to be most adaptable is that of INMARSAT which affords a realistic example of how to relate the attainment of general objectives to institutional arrangements. This task should not be regarded as primarily an issue for argument but as an opportunity for sober, objective analysis of the most effective technical means required for the smooth operation of a necessary function.

The method used thus far to formulate space law has been outstandingly successful as compared to the law of the sea. The law of the sea is being negotiated from a composite text which includes every conceivable problem, a method which naturally raises a maximum number of questions and takes much longer to achieve international agreement. In contrast, space law started from the charter 1967 Treaty on Outer Space and as different problems developed new treaties were formulated to meet specific situations. Space law was expanded to cover assistance to astronauts, their return and the return of space objects; liability for damage from space objects; and registration of space objects. Similarly, space law as developed by the International Telecommunication Union (ITU) is tailormade for space communications. The specific function of space communications is further provided for by INTELSAT and INTERSPUTNIK. Navigation has been improved by using satellites, and INMARSAT takes "into account that a very high proportion of world trade is dependent upon ships" and therefore provides "for the benefit of ships of all nations through the most advanced suitable space technology available, [and] for the most efficient and economic facilities possible consistent with the most efficient and equitable use of the radio spectrum and of satellite orbits."

In addition, space law has been formulated during the past 22 years in numerous bilateral and multilateral agreements on specific programs requiring the use of space technology.

The only conclusion that can be drawn is that extraordinary expertise has been demonstrated in handling specific functions which can be improved by the use of space science and technology and this has brought about a remarkable degree of international cooperation in the peaceful uses of outer space. This same ability can be used in working out viable operational and economic arrangements for the Moon and other celestial bodies, and if we are temporarily overcome by this task, it is only because we are trying to formulate space law many years, perhaps decades, in advance of the actual commitment of resources to the Moon and other celestial bodies.

NOTES

1. Many of the excerpts in this chapter refer to the negotiations concerning the United Nations Law of the Sea Treaty. This was an international agreement drawn up to govern the development of mineral resources in the deep seabed—primarily manganese nodules, given today's technology. See the excerpt from Hufford, *infra.*

2. Consider Galloway's point about the Moon Treaty trying to make law far in advance of the actuality of space resource development. How does this compare with the general approach taken in the Outer Space Treaty of 1967? Is the Moon Treaty more specific in its aims than the OST? Is this perhaps the reason it was more divisive—i.e., unlike in 1967, more than general principles were at stake? Consider also the following differences between the OST negotiations and those surrounding the Moon Treaty: (a) political developments in the U.N. since 1967, (b) more advanced technologies in the late 1970s as compared to the mid–1960s, and (c) an increase in the number of nations with space capabilities or the potential for developing them.

**Christol, Alternative Models for a Future
International Space Organization,
Proceedings of the Twenty-Fourth Colloquium
on the Law of Outer Space (1981), pp. 173–180**

It is becoming increasingly evident that an optimization of opportunities and benefits may require the establishment of a new body capable of dealing in a practical way with increasingly large-scale and complex operational activities. . . .

As a regime emerges for the Moon and its natural resources, attention will have to be given to the characteristics of the mandated organization. In assessing the role and the functions of that future body, including its powers and duties, it may become highly desirable to determine if it, over time, will be augmented by a number of other space-oriented organizations having special and discrete responsibilities. An alternative would be to consider the establishment of a broadly-based international space agency or organization having general and wide-ranging rights and duties.

*   *   *

The Special Issue of Voting

In the creation of international intergovernmental organizations the issue of voting rights has become a central issue. Two basic alternatives have been the bureaucratic model in which each member possesses one vote and the corporate model in which there can be weighted voting based either on the ownership of shares or on the amount of use. Votes may be allocated on the basis of regional interests as well as a very wide combination of other factors.

INTELSAT's voting procedures are particularly instructive. The Assembly, whose functions are more political than technical, makes recommendations to the Board of Governors respecting general policy and long-term objectives. Voting is on a one-State, one-vote basis. INTELSAT's Meeting of Signatories, composed of technicians, also operates on a one-State, one-vote basis. However, the Board of Governors, limited to about 20 representatives of States, operates on a weighted-voting formula. Under the terms of the agreement a signatory possesses an investment share corresponding to its percentage of use of the system when compared with the total amount of the use of the INTELSAT space segment. No State may possess more than 40% of the quota of votes with the United States being restricted to this percentage. INTELSAT has demonstrated that the bureaucratic organizational model can be joined effectively to a corporate organizational model in which ownership of shares or allocation of shares can be dependent on the extent of use with the heavier user being given voting rights in proportion to use. [For more on INTELSAT, see Chapter 6, *infra.*]

INMARSAT also allows for a hybrid voting process. Each of the parties possesses one vote in the Assembly. In the Council, however, 18 of the 22 members hold investment shares, while the remaining four do not have to meet this requirement. No representative may possess on behalf of one signatory more than 25% of the total voting participation in the organization. This is subject to an exception contained in Article 14(3)(b)(iv), which reads: "To the extent that the investment share of the Signatory is in excess of 25% offered for distribution in accordance with the procedure set forth in this paragraph, the voting of the representative of the Signatory may exceed 25 percent."

*   *   *

Another technical organization, the ITU, accords to each of its members a single vote in its periodic world administrative radio conferences.

No single model necessarily fits the needs of a future special or general international space organization. It would be expected that there would be a need for an accommodation of views among the space-resource States and those which are in the process of development.

*   *   *

Parties Subject to the Jurisdiction of a Space Tribunal

*   *   *

Existing international intergovernmental organizations have been granted the judicial power to resolve disputes arising among their members respecting their respective rights and duties pursuant to the terms of their several constitutions. Further, such organizations may, in specified circumstances, initiate legal actions before the tribunal of the institution in order to obtain a clarification of their own rights and duties.

It has already been recognized that international organizations dealing with space-environment activities need a judicial arm. For example, pursuant to the terms of the relevant INTELSAT agreements and annex, an arbitral tribunal can arrive at a binding decision both where member States and INTELSAT, per se, have presented justiciable issues. Where the decision is that rules and regulations of an organ of INTELSAT are invalid, the decision is binding on all of the members as well as the organization. Likewise, the terms of the 1973 ITU Convention made provision for a number of procedures for the resolution of disputes including arbitration. The members are bound by the terms of the decision.

The 1976 INMARSAT Convention also made provision for wide-ranging processes for dispute resolution including both arbitration and reference to the World Court. These processes contemplate disputes between members and also between members and the organization. If the holding confirms that the organization has exceeded its authority the ruling becomes binding on all the parties to the agreement.

*   *   *

Under Article 11, paragraph 5 of the Moon Treaty, it would be possible to establish a special dispute-resolving instrumentality to deal with the equitable distribution of Moon benefits. While not all space uses and activities may be equally amenable to dispute-resolving procedures, since contending claimants for equitable shares to the benefits derived from the exploitation of the Moon's natural resources will be seeking to obtain something that has previously been unavailable for distribution, they may be more inclined to support the process than in a situation where they might fear having to give up something already within their possession or control.

*   *   *

In terms of policy it would be possible to establish a Space Court as was suggested in 1962, or a separate and special International Spatial Tribunal as was suggested in 1976. Alternatively, a space tribunal might form a part of a more complete international organization where it optimally would have the same authority as has been assigned to the International Court of Justice.

*   *   *

It has been possible to devise in the ITU an international organization capable of dealing with the allocation and sharing of constantly renewing electronic spectra. . . . It should be no more difficult to formulate a governing body having the power to distribute on an equitable basis the benefits derived from the disposition of Moon minerals or other Moon resources.

NOTES

1. Christol says that nations may be less inclined to support an allocation scheme in a situation where "they might fear having to give up something already within their possession or control." How does this square with the point made in the introduction to the Outer Space Treaty in Chapter 3, that the OST was drafted before it was known how widespread space capabilities would become, and that the OST was therefore less concerned with national self-interest than it otherwise might be? Again, note the similarities to the Rawlsian "veil of ignorance," and its predecessor, Jean-Jacques Rousseau's "state of nature." *See* J. Rawls, A Theory of Justice 118–192 (1971) (Chapter 3, The Original Position). Note also the limitations of this concept in the space arena; the U.S. and Soviet Union are obviously

closer (at this point) to development of space resources than many other nations. They are thus less analogous to individuals in a hypothetical "original position," since this assumes complete ignorance over what attributes one will have when one leaves the original position.

2. For an assessment of the relationship of organizational structures to the purposes and goals of six international intergovernmental space organizations, four of which engage in communications activities, see the background paper on "Multilateral intergovernmental cooperation in Space Activities," U.N. Doc. A/CONF.101/BP/10, 10 January 1981. The study was made in connection with plans for the Second United Nations Conference on the Exploration and Peaceful Uses of Outer Space.

3. Christol concludes that INTELSAT might be the best model for an organization to govern space resources; it "has demonstrated that the bureaucratic organizational model can be joined effectively to a corporate organizational model in which ownership of shares or allocation of shares can be dependent on the extent of use with the heavier user being given voting rights in proportion to use." Compare this to the assessment of INTELSAT in the excerpt from Allen Duane Webber's article in the Georgetown Law Review, *infra. See also* Fleming, DuCharme, Jakhu & Longman, State Sovereignty and the Effective Management of a Shared Universal Resource: Observations Drawn from Examining Developments in the International Regulation of Radiocommunication, 10 Annals of Air & Space Law 327 (1985) (most workable systems to allocate rights over shared universal resource such as radio frequencies do not rely on claims of sovereignty, but instead on pragmatic allocation schemes). For more discussion on the optimal design for a central administrative agency, see the Note on Common Property Resources and Efficient Allocation at the end of this chapter.

4. The operating agreements for Inmarsat, Arabsat, Intelsat and Intersputnik are reproduced in United States Senate Committee on Commerce, Space and Transportation, Committee Print: Space Law—Selected Basic Documents, second edition, 95th Congress, Second Session (1978). *See also* Chapter 6, *infra,* for more on INTELSAT and the ITU.

Goedhuis, Some Recent Trends in the Interpretation and the Implementation of the Rules of International Space Law, 19 Columbia Journal of Transnational Law 213–233 (1981)

[S]ome States continue to assert that under the terms of the [Outer] Space Treaty the *whole* of outer space—like the seabed by virtue of the U.N. Resolution adopted on 17th December 1970—has been established as the common heritage of mankind.

Although the discussions in the Law of the Sea Conferences have shown that the import of this term is far from agreed upon, the following basic implications of this concept are generally recognized: first, that the area to which it applies cannot be appropriated; second, that it requires a system of management in which all countries share; third, that it requires an active sharing of benefits from the exploration of the resources between all countries; and fourth, that it requires the dedication of the area to exclusively peaceful purposes.

When one examines the content of the [Outer] Space Treaty, one notices that it satisfies *only one* of the abovementioned requirements. Art. II of the treaty provides that outer space, including the moon and other celestial bodies, is not subject to national appropriation. Whereas this article has prohibited the appropriation of *areas of* outer space it is silent on the appropriation of *resources.* Although a number of commentators have contended that the appropriation of resources by a State would violate the "benefit clause" contained in Art. I(1) [*see, e.g.,* the excerpt from Rao, *infra*], the great majority of States, including the two Space Powers, consider that *de lege lata* the appropriation of the natural resources of outer space, by analogy with the *present* rules underlying the freedom of the seas, merely forms part of the freedom of that space for exploration and use, a freedom which has been confirmed by the Treaty. Nothing has been said in the Treaty about the sharing or management of these resources. [Note: These issues are discussed in the section dealing with the Outer Space Treaty in Chapter 3.]

It should further be noted that the Treaty has not dedicated the use of the *whole* of outer space to exclusively peaceful purposes. The only exception is contained in Art. IV(2) which provides that the moon and other celestial bodies shall be used by all States Parties exclusively for peaceful purposes. . . .

On the basis of the above considerations, it seems clear that the contention that the Outer Space Treaty has established the *whole* of outer space as the common heritage of mankind is untenable.

*   *   *

Despite the fact that a number of States continued even during the last, 22nd, Session of the Committee, to voice their opposition to the adoption of the common heritage concept and stressed the need of a Moratorium, the text of a draft containing both the notion of common heritage and provisions implying the permissibility for States to start their operations on the moon before an international regime has been established, was finally unanimously accepted. As several of the deliberations on the Draft took place behind the scenes, one can only speculate on the reasons which prompted the opponents of these two principles to withdraw their objections. One may not be too wide off the mark if one suggests that the following factors led to the achievement of a consensus.

First, as was mentioned above, a great number of States vigorously criticized the lack of progress in the implementation of the rules of the Space Treaty. There appeared to be a strong feeling of the need to achieve a breakthrough on at least one of the issues which for many years had been discussed.

The second explanation may be sought in the influence of the two most powerful decision-makers in the field of space law, namely the United States and the Soviet Union, who apparently were in agreement both on the need to complete without further delay the Draft and on the provisions it should contain.

*   *   *

Among the problems which are likely to arise during the interim period, attention may be given to two of the most important issues. According to Art. IX of the Agreement, States Parties may establish manned and un-manned stations on the moon. What happens when the States which are capable of establishing such stations wish to erect such stations in the same area? Art. XV contains a number of provisions to be applied when disputes between States Parties arise. In paragraph 2 it has been laid down that a State Party which has reason to believe that another State Party is not fulfilling the obligations incumbent upon it pursuant to the Agreement or that another State Party is interfering with the rights which the former State has under the Agreement, may request consultations with that Party. Any other State Party which requires to do so shall be entitled to take part in the consultations. Paragraph 3 provides that if the consultations do not lead to a mutually acceptable settlement which has due regard for the rights and interests of all the States Parties, the parties concerned shall take all measures to settle the disputes by other peaceful means of their choice and appropriate to the circumstances and the nature of the dispute.

Experience in the field of international disputes in general has demon-strated the extent to which the reluctance of States to submit their disputes to adjudication or arbitration is due to the uncertainties regarding the content and the meaning of the legal rules to be applied. The Agreement contains in particular one provision the interpretation of which will give rise to wide and serious divergences. Art. II(1), reproducing a rule contained in Art. IV(2) of the [Outer] Space Treaty, provides that the moon shall be used by all States Parties exclusively for peaceful purposes. Since the conclusion of the Space Treaty, this provision has proved to be one of the most controversial ones laid down in the Treaty. On the meaning of the term "peaceful purposes" two fundamentally different interpretations came to the fore. Under one interpretation the term means *non-military* while under the other the term means *non-aggressive*. In this connection it should be noted that, notwithstanding the fact that more than half of all American and Soviet spacecraft at present orbiting the Earth serve military purposes, both countries describe *all* their space-missions as "peaceful." The unac-ceptable consequences of interpreting the term "peaceful" as "non-aggres-sive" have been set forth in an article published in 1968 by the present writer. [*See* Goedhuis, An Evaluation of the Leading Principles of the Treaty On Outer Space of 1967, 15 Netherlands International Law Review 24 (1968), at 24.]

*   *   *

One example may be given of the dissensions which would result from permitting the use of the moon for "non-aggressive" purposes. In doctrine it has been submitted that since defensive and *deterrent* capabilities serve the cause of peace, it is only when such devices are *intentionally* used for aggressive purposes that they lose their peaceful status. [*See* C. Christol, The International Law of Outer Space 268 (1966).] As all arms have deterrent capabilities, such an interpretation would enable States to claim that the deployment of any arms on the moon—except those carrying nuclear weapons or any other kind of weapons of mass destruction, which under the terms of Art. III(3) of the Agreement have been forbidden— would constitute a use of the moon for peaceful purposes.

*　　*　　*

Postscript

I [wish to] make a few observations on the political objections to the Treaty voiced by some members of Congress and leading aerospace companies.

The main object of this opposition was the concept of the moon and its natural resources being declared to be the common heritage of mankind, a concept of which the U.S. delegation in COPUOS was the main architect. It has been asserted that the acceptance of this theory would create "a system of international socialism" and "would foreclose the commercial uses of outer space by American enterprise." The submission that the Treaty would foreclose the commercial uses of outer space by American enterprise is based on a misinterpretation of Art. II of the Treaty, which— as mentioned above—permits the exploitation and use of the natural resources of the moon *before* an international regime governing the exploitation of these resources has been established. It further was noted that the purpose of the insertion in paragraph 3 of Art. II of the words "natural resources in place" (proposed by the American delegation in the COPUOS in 1973), was to allow for the existence of property rights over natural resources when removed from the places on the moon where they were obtained.

By the opponents of the present Moon regime it was further submitted that free enterprise institutions simply cannot make significant investments in space when there is the threat of suit over treaty terms of "ex post facto" appropriation of their investments by a nebulous future international regime. In this context attention should be drawn to paragraph 7 of Art. XI in which under (d) it has been laid down that in the *equitable* sharing by all States Parties in the benefits derived from the natural moon resources special consideration shall be given to the efforts of those countries which have contributed either directly or indirectly to the exploration of the moon. The provision that the sharing of the benefits should be "equitable" does obviously not mean that the sharing should be "equal."

Although, when, at some time in the future, efforts will be made to arrive at the intended international regime, considerable difficulties may arise in assessing the compensation of the efforts of the countries or companies which have been exploiting and using the natural moon resources in the period prior to the establishment of an international regime, there appears to be one crucial factor which should be able to allay the fears expressed regarding the appropriation of investments made. The United States, as one of the two major Space Powers, will have a decisive influence on the terms of the international regime to be established. It can hardly be assumed that the American negotiators would agree to any elimination of the profits earned through the taking of risks by those companies which started the exploitation and use of moon resources.

Although it should of course be admitted that in general disputes in the interpretation of any treaty of highly political content can never be avoided, the question may be asked whether, insofar as the Moon Treaty is concerned, the disputes which have arisen could not have been prevented if the final text of the Treaty had not been rushed through the United Nations in a great hurry before a consensus on the exact meaning and content of the concept of the moon and its natural resources being the common heritage of mankind had been achieved.

NOTES

1. Goedhuis notes that the Moon Treaty had reached somewhat of an impasse during U.N. negotiations. He gives two reasons why it was broken and progress was finally made: (a) the desire of all countries to enact some kind of Treaty expanding on the Outer Space Treaty; and (b) what he calls "the influence of the two most powerful decisionmakers in the field of space law, namely the United States and the Soviet Union, who apparently were in agreement both on the need to complete without further delay the Draft and on the provisions it should contain." Does this suggest that the · critics of the Treaty—whose main point is that the U.S. would come out a loser during negotiations to actually set up the administrative organization to govern space resources—might have underestimated the bargaining power of the U.S.? What does this tell you about the legitimacy of the point made by some commentators, that a key problem in the ratification process was the lack of communication between space industry and the diplomatic agencies that negotiated the Treaty? *See, e.g.,* Goldman, Reflections on the Proposed Moon Treaty, Space Law, and the Future, in People in Space: Policy Perspectives for a "Star Wars" Century (J.E. Katz ed. 1986).

2. A number of the preceding excerpts have referred to the United Nations Law of the Sea Treaty; this was the international document that introduced the phrase "common heritage of mankind." Owing to this fact, and to its importance as a precedent-setting agreement, we have included

an article by Hufford, *infra,* which describes the Law of the Sea Treaty and its background.

3. In a recent publication by Stephen Gorove, Studies In Space Law: Its Challenges And Prospects (1977), Gorove, discussing the problem arising in the interpretation of the term "peaceful purposes," suggests that "it would be better to identify those activities which constitute minimal threats to national security and permit those regardless of the ultimate purpose for such activities or their conduct by military personnel." *Id.* at 91. Regarding this proposal, the question is whether there is any chance of States agreeing on a definition of what constitutes a minimal threat to their national security.

Dupuy, The Notion of the Common Heritage
of Mankind Applied to the Seabed,
8 Annals of Air and Space Law 347–353 (1983)

The common heritage of mankind concept was solemnly established when it was applied to the deep seabed following presentation of the Pardo Doctrine at the United Nations and its embodiment in the Declaration of Principles by the XXVth General Assembly (1970). . . . The introduction of such a notion is intriguing for jurists, since, so far, reference to humanity has appeared only in the broadest sense in so-called humanitarian law, including not only the choice of armed conflicts but also "humanitarian intervention" or "crimes against humanity."

The reference to the notion of heritage has repeatedly raised the question whether humanity or mankind may be considered a "subject" of international law able to be endowed legally with a heritage. It was wondered in which form mankind could be embodied to be the holder of rights, and it was sometimes believed that the United Nations, an organization with a universal vocation, could act on behalf of mankind. Some observers contended that, in a strictly interstate system, the United Nations could not properly claim to represent peoples and individuals, while others responded that governments have this dual role and that, in the absence of a federal structure at the world level, there was no alternative but to consider the United Nations as being able to execute this function.

In the writer's view, this kind of debate is meaningless. Indeed, it neglects one basic question: what is meant by humankind? The answer seems easy: grouping human beings as a whole, mankind embraces all peoples in common ownership of a domain which is rich in resources. The concept of the common heritage thus appears as fundamentally harmonistic; but, in fact, such a view fails to take into account the contradiction and conflicts between States, and was denounced. It was said that the super powers proceeded to a "recovery of all concept." . . . From the outset, behind the reassuring veil of the common heritage, clashes occurred at the Third Conference on the Law of the Sea, and they will continue within the organs of the Authority. As soon as a transcendental notion is established, social forces strive to capture it. This is all the more evident in the case of the international seabed, since provision was made that it should be under an Authority endowed with powers which go beyond those of a State. However, the problem arose as to who would control the Authority: the technologically advanced countries, or the developing countries which claim numerical superiority and the democratic legitimacy this confers.

It should be mentioned here that the common heritage regime was defined by States—the legislators of international laws; and, naturally, governments are inclined to make decisions in terms of the immediate benefits to be derived.

It is remarkable that, despite the difficulty in perceiving the overall interests of mankind, States participating in the Conference were able to separate a notion based on a legal philosophy from singularly rich prospects. There will always be a risk of misappropriation or seizure, but the ideological pattern on which the concept rests will remain as a reference model. It is this aspect which the writer wishes to analyze.

To a great extent, it is a result of the efforts of the Third World. The basic philosophy of the concept is not only harmonistic, but also prospective and strategic. The notion of mankind has a twinfold meaning:

—it is interspatial, in that it regroups all contemporaries irrespective of the location of their establishment;

—its scope is intertemporal, because mankind includes not only today's people, but also future generations.

NOTE

The following excerpt, written by D. Brian Hufford, describes the Law of the Sea Treaty from the U.S. perspective.

Hufford, Ideological Rigidity vs. Political Reality:
A Critique of Reagan's Policy on the Law of the Sea,
2 Yale Law & Policy Review 127–166 (1983)

I. An Historical Overview

The Third United Nations Conference on the Law of the Sea [UNCLOS] was convened in 1973. These negotiations received continuous U.S. support throughout the Administrations of Presidents Nixon, Ford and Carter. By 1980, U.S. officials were predicting that a treaty effectively protecting U.S. interests could soon be adopted.

President Reagan's election, however, frustrated these predictions. Fearing that his new Administration would be forced to vote on an unacceptable treaty, President Reagan took the unprecedented step of withdrawing the

United States from UNCLOS in March 1981 to allow a thorough review of the Convention. By January 29, 1982 the review had been completed, and the President announced that the U.S. was ready to return to negotiations.

*   *   *

The proposed changes were so radical they were generally ignored. . . . By that time, however, the negotiations were effectively over.

*   *   *

On April 30, 1982 UNCLOS member nations adopted the Convention by a vote of 130–4, with 17 abstentions. Breaking from the traditional reliance in the Conference on consensus in decision-making, the U.S. asked for a recorded vote. Subsequently, it voted "no," along with Israel, Venezuela and Turkey. When the Convention was opened for signature on December 10, 117 nations signed on the first day—a record number, according to the General Counsel to the U.N., and a level of support unexpected by the Reagan Administration.

*   *   *

U.S. opposition to the Convention focuses on the regulation and use of the deep seabed beyond national jurisdiction. All activities in this area are to be regulated by the International Sea-Bed Authority (ISA), empowered to grant mining rights to both public and private ventures. An organization called the Enterprise will operate a "parallel system" for exploring and exploiting the ocean resources. Because the seabed is recognized as a "common heritage," all mining operators will be expected to contribute a portion of their revenues to the ISA. This is in addition to revenues expected from the states for resource development beyond 200 miles but within the continental shelf, and thus under national jurisdiction. To ensure international access to ocean resources, the Convention further requires mining contractors to sell to the ISA technology that cannot be obtained on the open market. The regulations for mining the deep seabed beyond national jurisdiction, and the procedures under which the Authority and the Enterprise will operate, are left to be developed by a Preparatory Commission (PrepCom). Although the U.S., despite its opposition to the treaty, is entitled to become involved in the PrepCom negotiations, the Reagan Administration has refused to participate.

NOTES

1. As of November 1983, there were 131 signatories to the Convention and 9 ratifications. The Convention will enter into force 12 months after ratification by the 60th nation. Kimball, PrepCom Concludes First Session, 8 Soundings 2 (Nov. 1982).

2. The U.N. had sponsored two previous conferences on the law of the sea. The first was held in 1958, adopting four treaties: the Convention on the Continental Shelf; the Territorial Sea and Contiguous Zone; the High Seas; and Fishing and Conservation of the Living Resources of the High Seas. The second conference, held in 1960, failed to accomplish its goal of determining the width of the territorial sea. The 1958 treaties can be found in C. Franklin, International Law Studies 1959–1960, The Law of The Sea: Some Recent Developments (Vol. 53, Naval War College Blue Book Series).

3. For a good review of the issues raised by the Law of the Sea Treaty, see Van Dyke & Yuen, "Common Heritage" and "Freedom of the High Seas," Which Governs the Seabed?, 19 San Diego Law Review 493, 527 (1982).

4. For the official position on the U.S "revisions" that were ignored by the other Convention members, see Presidential Statement on United States Participation in the Third United Nations Conference on the Law of the Sea, 1 Public Papers of Ronald Reagan 92 (Jan. 29, 1982). See also Whitaker, Outside the Mainstream, The Atlantic, October, 1982, at 21; Citizens for Ocean Law, U.S. Options on the Law of the Sea: The Preparatory Commission 1 (Dec. 1, 1982).

5. In an interesting article, Wertenbaker, A Reporter at Large: The Law of the Sea, The New Yorker, Aug. 1, 1983, at 42–44, the author points out that ending the negotiations was unnecessary. Although the Conference was coming to a close, the U.S. could have obtained a continuance in the negotiations to delay final consideration of the Convention while Reagan was reviewing his law of the sea policy. The U.S. had done just this in previous presidential transitions. The decision to withdraw was a surprise to most other nations as well as to the U.S. negotiating team.

DEVELOPED WORLD AND THIRD WORLD VIEWS ON SPACE DEVELOPMENT

As several of the excerpts that follow make clear, western economists see the need for property rights to ensure the orderly and efficient development of space resources. But as some of the other excerpts show, many developing country economists stress the need for equitable sharing of space resources and opportunities, to avoid the economic colonization of space along neo-imperialistic lines. This view is intimately tied to Third World perceptions of the economic basis for the developed world's wealth: the large-scale exploitation of natural resources. *See, e.g.,* H. Magdoff, The Age of Imperialism (1969); P. Jalee, The Pillage of the Third World (1965).

The first selection that follows, written by Edward R. Finch, Jr. and Amanda Lee Moore, reflects a minority position in the developed world: that the Moon Treaty is helpful to western interests, because it creates a framework for allocating development rights and settling disputes. As you can see from the excerpt, written by Art Dula, that follows that of Finch and Moore, other western commentators disagree sharply. They view the

Moon Treaty—and especially the "common heritage of mankind" principle—as a significant threat to space development.

The Dula excerpt, and the Wihlborg and Wijkman excerpt at the end
of this section, argue that space development will occur only if clear user
rights are established, and only if those rights are enforceable under a well-
defined liability scheme. Without such a system, the argument continues,
there is no incentive to develop space, since there is no way to insure that
each extra dollar spent in space is going to its most efficient use.

This kind of reasoning, of course, stands in stark contrast to the common
heritage principle, with its emphasis on international sharing of resources.
Unlike most Western commentators, Finch and Moore avoid discussing
the fact that sharing *presumes* the existence of something to share. In the
eyes of most developed-world commentators, when it comes to undeveloped
space resources, this is of course the key problem: there *is* nothing yet to
share or at least nothing much.

From this perspective, the "common heritage" principle is primarily
concerned with allocating profits from space development—what might be
termed "dividing the pie." (Note, however, that Article XI, paragraph 7
does mention other principles besides equity that must be taken into
consideration in developing the moon's resources, including "The *orderly*
and safe *development* of the natural resources of the moon," and "[t]he
expansion of opportunities in the use of those resources." (emphasis added).)
Meanwhile, as shown by the articles from "western" sources reproduced
below, the developed world has a different concern: what might be called,
to extend the metaphor, collecting the apples that go into the pie. That is,
those in the west are concerned primarily with creating incentives to *find
and develop* space resources; equitable sharing, in this view, is not a prime
concern until the resources have been identified and exploited.

One way to view the conflict between equitable distribution of resources
and incentives to develop them in the first place is to see it as a reflection
of fundamental cultural differences. For an example of western thinking,
consider the discussion in the Wihlborg and Wijkman excerpt, *infra,*
concerning the need for clearly-defined property rights to allow for efficient
space development. For some insight into the Third World perspective on
these issues, note the view of property implicit in the Rao excerpt *infra,*
which describes an alternative vision of the Common Heritage concept
made popular by advocates of the New International Economic Order.

**Finch & Moore, The 1979 Moon Treaty
Encourages Space Development,
Proceedings of the Twenty-Third Colloquium
on the Law of Outer Space 13–18 (1980)**

Understandings and Clarifications

The Moon Treaty should be signed by the US President and ratified by
the US Senate. However, certain legal understandings, which simply rei-

terate the US position already stated before various UN bodies, should be included. While clarifying the obligations assumed by the US, these understandings at the same time address pertinent issues raised by critics of the Moon Treaty provisions.

Subject to the approval of the House of Delegates of the ABA, the recently approved report by the Section of International Law of the American Bar Association includes four sample understandings: [Section of International Law, Report to the House of Delegates, American Bar Association, April 1980.]

"(a) It is the understanding of the United States that no provision in this Agreement constrains the existing right of governmental or authorized non-governmental entities to explore and use the resources of the moon or other celestial bodies, including the right to develop and exploit these resources for commercial or other purposes. In addition, it is the understanding of the United States that nothing in this Agreement in any way diminishes or alters the right of the United States to determine how it shares the benefits derived from exploitation by or under the authority of the United States of natural resources of the moon or other celestial bodies;

"(b) Natural resources extracted, removed or actually utilized by or under the authority of a State Party to this Agreement are subject to the exclusive control of, and may be considered as the property of, the State Party or other entity responsible for their extraction, removal or utilization;

"(c) The meaning of the term 'common heritage of mankind' is to be based on the provisions of this Agreement, and not on the use or interpretation of that term in any other context. Recognition by the United States that the moon and its natural resources are the common heritage of all mankind constitutes recognition (A) that all States have equal rights to explore and use the moon and its natural resources, and (B) that no State or other entity has an exclusive right of ownership, property or appropriation over the moon, over any area of the surface or subsurface of the moon, or over its natural resources in place. In this context, the United States notes that, in accordance with Articles XII and XV of this Agreement, States Parties retain exclusive jurisdiction and control over their facilities, stations and installations on the moon, and that other States Parties are obligated to avoid interference with normal operations of such facilities;

"(d) Acceptance by the United States of an obligation to undertake in the future good faith negotiation with other States Parties of an international regime to govern exploitation of the natural resources of the moon in no way prejudices the existing right of the United States to exploit or authorize the exploitation of those natural resources. No moratorium on such exploitation is intended or required by this Agreement. The United States recognizes that States Parties to this Agreement are obligated to act in a manner compatible with the provisions of Article VI(2) and the purposes specified in Article XI(7); however, the United States reserves to itself the right and authority to determine the standards for such compatibility unless and until the United States becomes a party to a future resources exploitation regime. In addition, acceptance of the obligation to join in good faith negotiation of such a regime in no way constitutes acceptance of any particular provisions which may be included in such a regime; nor does it constitute an obligation to become a Party to such a regime regardless of its contents."

In effect, these understandings clarify the obligations assumed by the US and emphasize the US position that the Moon Treaty recognizes that once lunar resources have been moved or extracted they may be considered the property of the extractor. Understanding (A) is similar to one attached by the US Senate when ratifying the 1967 Outer Space Treaty. [International Law Section Report, p. 7.] It should clarify as a matter of law the limits of any obligation assumed by the US in sharing benefits, and should legally protect the independence and flexibility of future US negotiators in deciding what, if any, specific obligations should be assumed in any new international resources exploitation regime.

Common Heritage Language

*   *   *

A review of the Moon Treaty's negotiating history supports the view that the term does not [imply] and need not lead to the use in a lunar resources regime of procedures and criteria developed in any other context. There is no generally accepted definition of this term. To quote one space law commentator, the phrase is "purely declaratory . . . and open to all interpretations." [Adrian Bucckling, "The Strategy of Semantics and the 'Mankind Provisions' of the Space Treaty," *Journal of Space Law*, 7:21 (Spring 1979).] Conversations with delegates to the Outer Space Committee reinforces [sic] the feeling that the phrase is in essence a continuation of the very general concept from the 1967 Outer Space Treaty of space as the "common province of mankind" with an attempt to move into language more commonly used in international law. In addition, to date, no two delegations have said the term means the same thing at any given time.

*   *   *

Advantage for Space Investment

. . . It may be stated that there is a clear advantage in the Moon Treaty for research and development for space manufacturing facilities, solar power satellites, and other large-scale manned space activities using lunar and other space natural resources. At the very least, a green light has been given for pilot projects in the ten years recommended before the first review of the Moon Treaty.

The more practical question is the investment of money, time and effort and how to obtain enough of each. The question of investment security to attract money will exist whether or not the US becomes a party to the

Moon Treaty. Such investment protection can only come from the US Government. It is not the province of a multilateral treaty, nor could it meaningfully be provided by such. Legislation encouraging exploitation of lunar resources, to be effective, would have to come from the US Congress, the way it has for mineral exploitation in the Law of the Sea.

NOTES

1. Finch and Moore state that no two countries have defined the "common heritage" in the same way. But note also that in arguing in favor of the Treaty, they defend the use of this language as "an attempt to move into [sic] language more commonly used in international law." Is it rational to defend the phrase on both these grounds?

2. Finch and Moore state that failure to ratify "would simply and devastatingly exclude the U.S. from legal entitlement to the benefits and protections included in the Moon Treaty." Are there alternative ways— e.g., a series of bilateral treaties—to achieve the same "benefits and protections"? *Cf.* U.S. Senate Committee on Commerce, Science and Transportation, Agreement Governing the Activities of States on the Moon and Other Celestial Bodies, Part 4, 96th Cong., 2d Sess. (1980), at 465 (stating, in summary of arguments against Moon Treaty, that, *inter alia,* it is "superfluous because the basic freedoms in space are already protected by the Outer Space Treaty," and "[n]o ongoing activities are constrained . . . but [it] . . . present[s] many possibilities for future constraints").

Dula, Free Enterprise and the Proposed Moon Treaty, 2 Houston Journal of International Law 3–33 (1979)

The Moon Treaty is vague, lengthy, and complex. Many of its critical terms are not well-defined.

*   *   *

"Exploitation" vs. "Use" of Natural Resources

One reason consensus was reached during the 1979 COPUOS session was that the Soviet Union accepted a Brazilian formulation of the treaty's "common heritage" language. This language is now in Article XI of the treaty: "The moon and its natural resources are the common heritage of mankind, which finds its expression in the provisions of this agreement and in particular in paragraph 5 of this article."

*   *   *

The United States, through Neil Hosenball, National Aeronautics and Space Administration's (NASA) General Counsel and chief U.S. representative to COPUOS, made a number of unilateral statements defining the United States' interpretation of several parts of the Moon Treaty. Two of these statements seem intended to contradict the clear language of the treaty regarding exploitation of space natural resources.

*   *   *

The clear language in Article VI of the Moon Treaty specifically permits scientific "use" of lunar resources. Conversely, equally clear language in Article XI states that as "exploitation" of those resources becomes feasible, negotiations for a new international legal regime must be begun. The U.S. position contradicts this treaty language by stating that the Moon Treaty places "no moratorium on the exploitation of the natural resources of the moon, pending establishment of an international regime."

*   *   *

In addition to limiting the "use" and "exploitation" of natural resources from space, the Moon Treaty goes to great length to deny any possible legal entity the capacity of owning any part of these resources.

*   *   *

On April 19, 1973 the U.S. representative to the COPUOS Legal Subcommittee unilaterally contradicted the clear meaning of the words "in place" appearing in an earlier working draft of the Moon Treaty:

> As is apparent from the text, this working paper excludes the concept of a pre-regime moratorium. References to the words "in place" in the first sentence of that paragraph . . . make this clear. More particularly, the words "in place" . . . are intended to indicate that the prohibition against assertion of property rights would not apply to natural resources once reduced to possession through exploitation either in the pre-regime period or, subject to the rules and procedures that a regime would constitute, following establishment of the regime. [Oversight Hearings on the Activities of the U.N. Committee on the Peaceful Uses of Outer Space: Hearings Before the Subcomm. on Space Science and Applications of the House Comm. on Science and Technology, 96th Cong., 1st Sess. at 90–100 (1979) (statement of Neil Hosenball, at 11).]

*   *   *

If the United States becomes a party to the Moon Treaty, the opportunities and prospects for private enterprise development of the resources of the Moon and other celestial bodies will be negligible if not non-existent. Specifically, the draft treaty would:

1. Create a moratorium on commercial exploitation of the resources of the [M]oon and other celestial bodies, until a second, much more comprehensive treaty for regulating resource activities is concluded;

2. Establish guiding principles for the negotiation of this second treaty which are completely antithetical to the commercial development of outer space resources by private enterprise; and

3. Thereby give the Soviet or Third World countries tremendous political control over the timing and direction of expanding commercial uses of outer space, as well as the question of whether to permit such uses.

The Administration, particularly the negotiators of this draft treaty, argue that United States public statements to the effect that the treaty does not establish a moratorium negate the implicit moratorium in the treaty. Unfortunately, such a moratorium is now contemplated in the treaty and underscored by the U.S. delegation's statements on the record. However, even if it is conceded that the United States' unilateral statements control the treaty's meaning, the fact remains that no private enterprise, or even a government, is going to invest billions of dollars in developing new commercial applications of space technology if most of the world disputes its legal right to deploy and profit from that technology.

It may be asserted that the guiding principles set out in the treaty for constructing the legal regime to control exploitation of outer space resources are empty phrases to be given later meaning. The Moon Treaty, however, must be considered in the context of international law and practice. These phrases all have a very well-defined meaning and have been exhaustively elaborated in other treaty negotiations. Since the Soviet Union first introduced a draft text on the Moon in 1971, the politics of resource development in areas beyond the territorial borders of nations have changed dramatically. The Law of the Sea Conference has moved to near-completion of a treaty establishing a deep seabed resource regime based on virtually identical guiding principles to those contained in the Moon Treaty. Examples of parallel provisions prove that such resources are the "common heritage of mankind," that their development should be orderly and rationally managed, and that the benefits (both financial and technological) should be equitably distributed.

Regardless of whether the Law of the Sea Treaty ever enters into force, the Third World has now developed a very sophisticated position on the content of an international resource regime that best serves its interests. Many informed observers will support the view that this detailed elaboration of these revolutionary new ideas reflects the international custom, practice, and consensus as to how so-called "common property" resources are to be regulated, managed, and developed.

The Draft Law of the Sea Treaty requires the collectivization of resource development through a global monopoly under the political control of a General Assembly-type body dominated by the Third World. It restricts the rights of states and private enterprise to carry out profit-making activities, by limiting these activities to an initial period during which the necessary technology is fully transferred to the monopoly. Finally, it provides for international regulation of production levels and prices in order to discriminate in favor of developing countries.

*   *   *

In summary, the Moon Treaty, if adopted as the basis for negotiating a future resource regime for the Moon and other celestial bodies, would borrow meaning from these precedents. There are many other imaginative approaches which would enable the nations of the world to cooperate peacefully in expanding the commercial applications of outer space technology to resource exploration and development. Good examples already exist for commercial utilization of outer space, and there is no reason why the United States should permit outer space resource development to be thrust into a quagmire of political principles derived from the "new international economic order."

In view of the enormous capital and technology requirements contemplated for the future industrialization of outer space, political stability for investments will be absolutely critical. If this treaty is ratified by the United States, however, any commercial application of outer space technology which involves use of Moon or other celestial resources will be subject to the greatest insecurity imaginable. While the spillover effect for other commercial activities in outer space cannot be fully predicted, it may be very significant.

**Specific Negative Implications
of the Moon Treaty for Free Enterprise**

*   *   *

[Another key] issue is the definition of "scientific investigations." To the extent that it excludes research and development activities undertaken by a commercial entity in the hope of future profit, paragraph 2 of Article VI would prohibit such an entity's using resource samples collected from the Moon and other celestial bodies either for research and development or for the support of its missions. Paragraph 8 of Article XI reinforces this apparent prohibition on the conduct of interim resource activities by states and persons who are not pursuing scientific purposes.

It is highly doubtful that the United States Department of State would support authorization of U.S. nationals to engage in the commercial exploitation of Moon resources prior to agreement on a new international regime, even if it is possible to make the legal case that the treaty does not prohibit these activities. State authorization is required under paragraph 1 of Article XIV (as it is under Article VI of the 1967 Treaty on Principles). An affirmative act by the United States to permit commercial development of the Moon's resources by private entities would probably require legislation and would be deemed an interference with the international negotiations by the United States State Department.

Finally, the practical effect of an international commitment to negotiate a new, unknown legal regime covering the Moon and other celestial resources will be to deter industrialists, and probably governments, from spending research and development dollars in related activities during the interim period. The precedent of the U.N. Conference on the Law of the Sea will convince them that Third World demands at the "Moon Conference" are going to be extreme, that existing investments may not be respected under the resulting treaty, and that the industrialized countries may not be very successful in negotiating a system of exploitation that permits commercial or industrial use of the resources under realistic terms and conditions.

*   *   *

For developing countries, "common heritage" means common ownership of the resources and majority control over their disposition. This translates into insistence that no single country, or entity under its control, has the independent right to use the commonly owned resource. Access to the resources must first be approved by the international community on the basis of one-nation, one-vote. As a result, the developing countries would collectively control who is allowed to exploit and use the resource. The concept of the "common heritage of mankind" does not, in the view of the Third World, recognize that industrialized countries with space technology should have a greater voice in regulating outer space resource development.

Paragraph 7 of Article XI further compounds the future negotiating difficulties of the highly industrialized countries with space technology. First, it establishes the principles of "orderly and safe development" and "rational management" of the Moon and other celestial resources. Most nations of the world interpret these principles as mandating central planning of resource development and international controls over resource uses and/ or marketing. In short, these principles are the antitheses of a free market approach to the exploitation and use of resources on the Moon and other celestial bodies. Today, many believe that free market economics in the traditional sense will have only a small role to play in space industrialization. Yet it may be short-sighted to concede in a binding treaty that the political will of the majority of nations, rather than market-oriented forces, should dictate the pace and substance of outer space resource development.

Second, the principle of "expansion of opportunities in the use of those resources" will ultimately evolve into a Third World position that access to the Moon and other celestial resources must be limited for industrialized countries, so that developing countries have a chance to participate. (The Soviet bloc can also use the principle to insist that Western and Soviet activities using the Moon's resources be kept at the same level of intensity.) The clearest evolution of this concept is found in the draft Law of the Sea Treaty which creates an international mining monopoly for half of the deep seabed's mineral resources, based on the argument that developing countries can only expand their opportunities to use the resources on a collective and subsidized basis.

Finally, the principle of "equitable sharing of benefits" could be interpreted to require a system of international taxation of any profits made by commercial resource developers. Since the term "benefits" is not restricted to the financial realm, the principle should dictate mandatory transfer to all countries of the technology used to exploit the resources.

*   *   *

Conclusions

*   *   *

Present space law, including the Moon Treaty, has been forged almost entirely out of high academic ideals in advance of any practical commercial reality. True space law, if it allows free enterprise to operate at all, will evolve to meet the needs of practical commercial ventures. In this author's opinion, practical business space law would, if not preempted, evolve shortly after space-based exploitation of basic resources and energy begins to yield substantial profits. History teaches that the transition between academic and practical legal regimes can be gradual or traumatic, but that such transitions inevitably occur.

Ominously, the world now spends far more for military purposes in space than for academic studies. Apparently the only remaining substantial possibility for free enterprise non-military development of space requires large scale commercial development of basic natural resources, *i.e.,* raw materials and energy from space. Only basic raw materials and energy from space can return a profit commensurate with the capital expense and risk that will be required to start up space industry. Only large scale development of these basic space resources can provide sufficient economies of scale to permit development of space as an industrial frontier by free enterprise capitalism.

Such large capital investments cannot be made by free enterprise without clear legal guidelines that allow commercial operations to exploit space resources for profit. Free enterprise institutions simply cannot make significant investments in space while they are under the threat of lawsuits over the meaning of treaty terms or *ex post facto* appropriation of their investments by a nebulous future international regime.

NOTES

1. Dula makes the point that the Third World countries could challenge the legality of U.S. enterprises initiated prior to the formation of an international space regime. As a practical matter, what form could these

challenges take? Keeping in mind the general principles of the 1967 Outer Space Treaty—especially that space is to be used for peaceful purposes— would it be legal for an international regime to mount a military challenge to unauthorized U.S. enterprises, or the enterprises of any country? *See also* Moon Treaty, Article 3. Without the threat of *military* action to back up any policing effort, how much of a disincentive to development is the possibility of hostile reaction by a future space regime?

2. Dula mentions that a space development regime could unilaterally expropriate non-authorized facilities and resources. One justification for this move could be that development whose benefits were not shared was in violation of Article 11(8) of the Moon Treaty, which requires that "*[a]ll* the activities with respect to the natural resources of the moon shall be carried out in a manner compatible with" the specific provisions of Article 11, i.e., an international regime, designed to facilitate an "equitable sharing," etc. Note in this regard that one way the U.S. government could mitigate the uncertainty associated with possible expropriation would be to establish a political risk insurance pool for space activities, similar to the Overseas Private Investment Corporation (OPIC), which provides political risk insurance for U.S. companies involved in overseas activities.

3. Throughout this article, Dula uses "the Soviet Bloc" and "the Third World" as interchangeable terms. Keep this in mind when reading the excerpt from Rao, *supra,* on Third World views of the Common Heritage Concept. Especially in light of the fact that the Soviet Union has joined the U.S. in refusing to sign the Moon Treaty, do you think Dula's categorizations are accurate? Also, bear in mind that the Soviet Union joined the U.S. in resisting the introduction of Common Heritage language into the Law of the Sea Treaty.

4. For an article that suggests an even more "libertarian" view of space, and condemns all space treaties that give states, but not individuals, rights in space, see Wassenbergh, The Unfreedom Under Outer Space Law, 10 Air Law 161 (1985). *But cf.* J. Fawcett, Outer Space: New Challenges to Law and Policy 121 (1984) (". . . perhaps no human activity has ever been so basically international").

Webber, Extraterrestrial Law on the Final Frontier: A Regime to Govern the Development of Celestial Body Resources, 71 Georgetown Law Journal 1426 (1983)

In 1969, when two United States astronauts landed on the Moon, Neil Armstrong proclaimed their success to be "one giant leap for mankind." Ten years later, the United Nations Committee on the Peaceful Uses of Outer Space (COPUOS) also took one giant leap for mankind—backwards. The committee reached an agreement, commonly known as the "Moon Treaty," which will, if given effect, significantly inhibit commercial exploitation of natural resources on celestial bodies.

*   *   *

The Moon Treaty Does Not
Eliminate the Problems of Colonialism

Prior to the establishment of the regime required by article XI paragraph 5, the Moon Treaty would permit a period of colonialism. During this period, each nation would be left free to follow its own interpretation of the treaty's provisions, and . . . these interpretations differ widely. Nations would interpret the provisions in their own interest instead of for mankind's benefit. Differing interpretations would increase the likelihood of conflict.

The problems of colonialism would also surface during the negotiations to establish the regime. The treaty expressly states that nations will perform the task of establishing the regime. Negotiations would be conducted under one-nation, one-vote procedures. This would pit conflicting national interests against each other. The developing nations would have the votes to push through a regime similar to the Sea Bed Authority. The space powers, however, which by then would have invested large amounts of capital and technology in development, could refuse to abide by such an agreement, claiming that it deviated from their longstanding interpretation of the provisions of the Moon Treaty. Unless the developing countries agreed to the interpretation of the space powers, the space powers would be likely to proceed with development unencumbered by the regime. The Moon Treaty, therefore, does little to abate the problems of colonialism.

*   *   *

The United Nations Is an Inappropriate Body
for Celestial Body Resource Development

Although the United Nations, through its committee structure, has contributed a great deal to the development of space law, it is not the appropriate organization to control the development of extraterrestrial resources. The United Nations is institutionally weak and incapable of enforcing any mandate. A slow and cumbersome body, it cannot respond effectively to conflicts among nations. In addition, because the United Nations deals with a wide range of activities, it would be unable to govern resource development on celestial bodies independent of terrestrial concerns. The involvement of terrestrial conflicts in celestial body decision-making would interject extraneous issues into the process, and burden and delay any decisions that were made. As a result, the United Nations could not provide the investment security necessary to foster the development of celestial body resources. . . .

Intelsat Does Not Offer an Adequate Model

A regime modeled after INTELSAT . . . would have serious flaws. Such a regime would engage in resource exploitation itself, create a monopoly, and freeze out independent public and private initiatives. These actions would violate the principle of free use. If an organization modeled after

INTELSAT has any role in the development of outer space, it should be as a participant within a legal regime, not as a governing body. In addition, the political conditions that led to INTELSAT's successful establishment have ceased to exist today. The organization's operational decisions are made by a committee in which each signatory's voting power is determined by its investment in and utilization of INTELSAT. Developed countries would not be able to gain similar control over a lunar regime under existing political conditions. INTELSAT was formed before the challenges by developing countries to the existing distribution of international economic power became an important influence in world politics.

Another reason that INTELSAT's success would not be transferable to a lunar regime is that INTELSAT provides telecommunication services, the value of which lies in their widespread availability. Nation-states have a mutual interest in the expansion of international communications. One country can not fully enjoy the benefits of the organization unless a significant number of other nations also participate. [Note: These benefits from broad participation, known as "network externalities," are a key feature of the telecommunications world. See Chapter 6, *infra,* for more on how such considerations shaped the structure of INTELSAT.] This is not true for celestial bodies, where the benefits can be profitably monopolized by one nation.

Finally, INTELSAT uses resources that, when the organization was created, were virtually limitless and did not threaten the natural resource markets dominated by the developing countries. In contrast, activities on the Moon will produce a vast supply of natural resources that potentially will compete with the resources of developing countries in terrestrial markets. The developing countries, therefore, would be threatened by a regime, dominated by the developed countries, that could diminish the value of their vital exports.

The Antarctica Treaty Does Not Offer an Adequate Model

The treaty to ensure the peaceful scientific exploration of Antarctica has been mentioned as a model for a celestial body regime. The Antarctica agreement, however, does not provide for an authority governing exploration and development, but only for a conference mechanism to permit consultations between signatories.

*   *   *

A Proposed Regime for Exploitation of Celestial Body Resources

. . . In order to consider the interests of mankind as a whole, as well as mankind's responsibility to reserve celestial bodies, a new type of regime is required. Mankind should establish an extraterrestrial regime for the sole purpose of controlling celestial body . . . development.

*   *   *

The regime should concentrate on facilitating the development of celestial body resources for the benefit of all mankind. In determining whether a particular resource should be extracted, the regime should consider economic benefits to mankind from exploitation, preservation of future rights of access to the body's resources, and protection of the environment of the celestial body. First, without the exploitation of resources, mankind will receive no benefits from celestial bodies. Second, the maintenance of free access is important in assuring lesser-developed countries that they will be able to use celestial body resources when they acquire the capability. Finally, mankind cannot rely solely on profit-motivated entities to protect the environment of celestial bodies.

The regime should institute a licensing system to ensure the benefit of mankind, future access, and environmental protection. An entity wishing to develop resources or use the surface of a celestial body in any way should be required to submit its proposal to the regime and the regime should have the authority to grant or deny the request. If the proposal met previously established criteria, the regime would issue a license. The license would cover only an area sufficient to allow an adequate return on investment, and would be subject, upon proof of adherence to established criteria, to renewal or revocation. The license would not confer any permanent property rights over the area. Only the resources exploited by the licensed entity would come under its exclusive control.

The primary goal of the licensing procedure should be to limit the domination of investing entities to an area that they can profitably exploit over a limited period of time, in a manner consistent with the benefit of mankind principle. For example, the regime could license a mining company to utilize a one square mile area over the course of one year, and simultaneously grant provisional options over adjacent square mile plots for the next ten years. So long as the entity's activities were consistent with the conditions of the license, the regime would renew it each year, so that the entity would always have rights to mine resources ten years into the future. This would provide the security necessary to induce investment without giving the investing entity control over a large land mass. Such a system would prevent foreclosure of a large area from newcomers.

The Regime Should Have the Power
to Tax Entities Utilizing Celestial Body Resources

The taxation of resource exploitation would be the regime's primary source of income. The regime should use the revenue to meet its administrative costs, conduct public research to improve the quality of human life on celestial bodies, learn more about the environment of celestial bodies, and discover information that might prove useful on earth. Information acquired by the regime would be available to all.

*   *   *

The Regime Should Not Attempt
to Redistribute Wealth Among Nations or Organizations

The Regime Should Not Attempt
to Redistribute Wealth Among Nations or Organizations

The only purpose of the regime should be to develop extraterrestrial resources for the benefit of mankind in accordance with the free access and environmental protection principles, not to redistribute wealth.

*   *   *

Participating Developers Should Be Given
Greater Input than Nonparticipants

Entities that participate in the development of celestial body resources have a greater interest in the effective operation of the regime than the rest of mankind, and consequently should have a greater input into the decisionmaking process than nonparticipants.

NOTES

1. Webber criticizes the role of the U.N. in the space development regime envisioned by the Moon Treaty, stating that U.N. involvement "would interject extraneous issues [i.e., "terrestrial concerns"] into the process" of making decisions. But what alternative international body could possibly eliminate the inclusion of "terrestrial concerns" in its decisionmaking? Even with voting weighted in favor of nations active in space, an international organization could be expected to reflect political and ideological tensions. Even INTELSAT, the international communications satellite consortium, has seen its share of political wrangling; a recent example is the controversy over U.S. establishment of a private communications satellite industry outside the auspices of INTELSAT. *See, e.g.,* 1 P. Meredith, G. Robinson, G. Raclin & R. de Seife, American Enterprise, the Law, and the Commercial Use of Space 22–24 (1986). This topic is discussed at length in Chapter 6, *infra,* as are the circumstances leading to INTELSAT's creation.

2. Webber states that "INTELSAT uses resources that, when the organization was created, were virtually limitless." This is somewhat misleading. The formation of INTELSAT can more accurately be described as an effort to centralize resources to create a facility that would be difficult for each nation to duplicate. *See* Sandler & Schulze, *The Economics of Outer Space,* 21 National Resources Journal 371 (1981). *See generally* Edelson, *Global Satellite Communications,* 236 Scientific American 58 (1977). Thus, it was the pooling of capital for creating what might be described as a "natural monopoly," rather than a lack of competition over communication frequencies, that led to the establishment of INTELSAT. For a detailed description of the negotiations leading up to the formation of INTELSAT, *see* R. Colino, International Telecommunication Satellite Organization (IN-

TELSAT), in 1 Manual on Space Law (N. Jasentuliyana & R. Lee eds. 1979), at 363–399.

3. Webber reaches an interesting conclusion by employing the logic of self interest often used by developing nation economists to describe the behavior of the U.S.: "activities on the Moon will produce a vast supply of natural resources that potentially will compete with the resources of developing countries in terrestrial markets." Thus the Note implies that a Third World–dominated space regime might act to *restrict* the output of space-derived resources to protect domestic markets for the same or complementary resources. Note that several considerations might mitigate this brand of protectionism: (1) the fact that the majority of the Third World countries each produces only a handful of natural-resource commodities, which makes it less likely they would have a unified economic interest in excluding or restricting any particular resource; and (2) the Moon Treaty itself states in Article 11(7) that one of the principles to be implemented by a space regime is "the expansion of opportunities in the use of [space] resources," which presumably would not be served by a restrictive self-interested policy of limited development. Nonetheless, Mr. Webber's point is well-taken.

Rao, Common Heritage of Mankind and the Moon Treaty, 21 Indian Journal of International Law 275–278 (1981)

The Agreement Governing the Activities of States on the Moon and Other Celestial Bodies, 1979, is largely addressed to regulate "exploration and use" of the Moon and other celestial bodies.

*   *   *

A point for consideration is whether it is permissible for a State Party to exploit, and thereby expropriate, the resources of the Moon, pending the establishment of an international regime. This issue assumes some significance in view of the fact that the developing countries did not insist on a provision for a moratorium on the exploitation of the natural resources of the Moon, pending the establishment of such an international regime like they did in the case of sea-bed resources.

*   *   *

[I]t appears that the absence of a moratorium clause in the Agreement amounts to licensing unilateral exploitation of the resources of the Moon, pending the establishment of an international regime and that the reference in Article 11(8) to Article 6(2) does not place any limit on the extent of commercial exploitation of natural resources of the Moon. These ideas come out clearly despite the contrived attempt to conform to Article 6(2). . . . [This became] all the more clear when the U.S. Representative approvingly referred, albeit impliedly, to the views bluntly presented earlier by the U.S. Representative to the Legal Sub-Committee of the UNCOPUOS on April 19, 1973:

The United States is not prepared to accept an *express* or *implied* prohibition on possible natural resources before the international conference meets and agrees on appropriate machinery and procedures [and] a treaty containing them take[s] effect.

That there is no express prohibition against a Member State exploiting the resources is apparent. The U.S. Representative, however, rightly anticipated one implied limitation (and there are many more) in Article 11(3) and then sought to explain it away in the following manner:

(T)he words "in place" in the first sentence of paragraph 2 are intended to indicate that the prohibition against assertion of property rights would not apply to natural resources once reduced to possession through exploitation either in the pre-regime period or following the establishment of the regime.

The views expressed by the U.S. Representatives lead to two propositions: one, there is no limitation on exploitation of the Moon's resources within the meaning of Article 6(2); and two, a Member State may not claim property rights on the natural resources of the Moon, but once the resources are collected or excavated, a Member State can hold possession of [them] and expropriate [them]. The tenability of these positions may briefly be examined.

Article 11(8) of the Agreement subjects all "activities with respect to the natural resources of the Moon" to article 6(2) (one such activity doubtless being the exploitation of natural resources of the Moon). Article 6(2) . . . states:

In carrying out scientific investigations . . . the States shall have the right to *collect on* and *remove from* the Moon samples of its mineral resources and other substances of the Moon in *quantities appropriate* for the support of their mission.

The main ingredients of the provision are: (1) the collection and removal of resources from the Moon are for samples to conduct scientific investigations; (2) the use of *appropriate quantities* of [the] Moon's resources is *permitted* only for scientific investigations; (3) the quantities so contemplated for the use in the latter category [are] *limited* to scientific investigation only; and (4) the expression "mission" is qualified by scientific investigations . . . .

The collection or removal or use of the resources of the Moon in all events is consequently confined to scientific investigations, and not beyond. How the U.S. Representative could read such expansive meaning into the provision, encompassing unlimited exploitation, even extending to commercial utilization, is indeed difficult to understand.

*   *   *

There is one more weighty reason as to why the resources of the Moon shall not be exploited for any reason other than for the common benefit of mankind. Article 11(6) of the Agreement ordains that once any such scientific investigations lead to discovery of any natural resources on the Moon, it shall be the duty of States Parties to inform the UN Secretary-General and the public and international scientific community to facilitate the establishment of the international regime. This provision is to be read with Article 11(5) under which the parties "hereby undertake" to establish an international regime to govern the exploitation of the natural resources of the Moon when such exploitation "is about to become feasible." The combined reading of the two provisions leads to the inevitable conclusion that on discovery of any resources in the Moon by any State Party or a group of States Parties . . . the conventional obligation to establish an international regime under Article 11(5) to govern the exploitation comes into operation soon thereafter. Explicit in this commitment—"hereby undertake"—is to agree for an agreement on the establishment of an international regime with the stipulated objective conditions.

NOTES

1. Notice that Rao's interpretation of the "scientific investigation" provision of the Treaty (Article 6(2)) is quite at odds with the official interpretation discussed in the first excerpt in this section. The issue boils down to this: in the absence of a *general* standard of conduct regarding how much material States can remove from the Moon, should the *specific* standard for scientific removal be read as (i) a general standard in disguise, or by implication, or (ii) a specific case with no bearing on the general case (i.e., of non-scientific removals), which suggests recourse to the general principles, including free use of the Moon and other celestial bodies (see Article 4(1), paragraph 1), that would tend to permit appropriation. Rao clearly buys argument (i); the preceding author, Webber, espouses (ii).

2. Rao's article can be read as an application of some new ideas in developing country economic theory, generally referred to as the New International Economic Order. The following Note is a brief summary of some of the substance of these ideas.

A NOTE ON THE NEW INTERNATIONAL
ECONOMIC ORDER

The New International Economic Order is a loose grouping of economic ideas made popular by a number of Third World economists. As formulated by the United Nations General Assembly, the New International Economic Order is intended, among other things, to "correct inequalities and redress existing injustices . . . eliminate the widening gap between the developed and developing countries . . . [and to give] preferential non-reciprocal treatment for developing countries, wherever feasible, in all fields of international economic co-operation whenever possible. . . ." Declaration on the Establishment of a New International Economic Order, May 1, 1974, G.A. Res. 3201, 6 (Special) U.N. GAOR Supp. (No. 1) at 3–5, U.N. Doc. A19559 (1974), reprinted in 13 I.L.M. 715, 716, 718 (1974). Scholars are in general agreement regarding the primary economic objectives of the proponents of the order: "[I]ncreasing LDCs' [Less Developed Countries'] control over their economic destiny; accelerating the LDCs' growth rate; tripling the share of global industrial production conducted in the LDCs by the year 2000; and narrowing the gap in per capita income between the developed countries [and the LDCs]." Kreinin & Finger, A Critical Survey of the New International Economic Order, 10 Journal of World Trade Law 493, 493 (1976). *See also* Gamble & Frankowska, International Law's Response to the New International Economic Order, 9 Boston College International & Comparative Law Review 257, 259 (1986).

The New International Economic Order has been described a number of ways. Some western observers see it primarily as a manifestation of the new Third World coalition in international law, which finds its expression primarily through the United Nations. *See, e.g.,* E. McWhinney, United Nations Law Making 22 (1984) (describing new era of "Third World–led" international law). From this perspective, the new order is said to reflect a "pluralistic" and "inclusive" set of norms growing out of shared aspects of Third World cultures. *Id.,* at 234. The emergence of the new order thus represents the beginning of a "transition in the world community, from an old system of world public order to a new one." *Id.,* at 3.

But proponents of the new order make it clear that they have in mind something more than a Third World–oriented system for resolving international disputes. They seek nothing less than a fundamental restructuring of the norms of international relations. One prominent spokesman for the new order, who writes in a style characteristic of many of its proponents, reflects this questioning of current norms in a passage describing the new order's view of the causes of underdevelopment:

Walt Rostow's theory [see his The Take-off into Self-Sustained Growth, 66 Econ. J. 25 (1956) and The Stages of Economic Growth (1961)] is well known. According to him, the Third World, which came late to industrialization, has already had the opportunity and will have the capacity to catch up with the countries whose development started earlier. Rostow, ignoring the phenomena of domination and imperialism, reduced underdevelopment to a mere question of backwardness . . . . This soothing belief in an automatic international redistribution of means and incomes in accordance with some sort of natural law is completely unrealistic, since it takes no account of the balance of power. The present international situation is characterized by an intensification of conflict and a widening of the differences in power between states, leading to balkanization rather than redistribution.

M. Bedjaoui, Towards a New International Economic Order 66–67 (1979). In light of the very rapid growth of many Third World nations since Bedjaoui wrote this, is his argument that inequalities are inherently self-sustaining especially credible?

As the McWhinney book, *supra,* makes clear, the new international economic theorists rely heavily on the United Nations as a platform from which to make their case. In fact, it seems likely that without the U.N., which allows so many small, underdeveloped countries to come together, there would have been no New Order movement. It is therefore a valid question whether the new alignment of power envisioned by these theorists is possible outside the bounds of a U.N.-administered system. If not, given the largely voluntary nature of the U.N., one must wonder whether the developed world will tolerate a fundamental U.N.-led restructuring of the international order. *Cf.* M. Benko, W. de Graaff & G. Reijnen, Space Law in the United Nations (1985). But even if this is a difficult prospect to envision, the effect of new order rhetoric on the domestic political scenes should not be underestimated.

NOTES

1. Later in the book quoted from above, Bedjaoui states that, since the developed nations of the world dominate the Treaty-making process, the Common Heritage concept "carries with it obvious dangers in that it could be applied in one direction only and be 'co-opted' by great powers to their exclusive advantage." M. Bedjaoui, *supra,* at 224. Recall that this is precisely the same fear voiced by American critics of the Common Heritage language in the Moon Treaty. Was it a major flaw of the Treaty drafters that they used language so flexible it gives rise to fears of adverse interpretation by both major groups of countries to the Treaty? Could a Treaty using less flexible language have ever been ratified by both groups? Can't opponents of a Treaty always imagine extremely adverse interpretations?

2. Bedjaoui's view of technology, which he also sets forth in the same book, is instructive of some of the basic precepts behind the New International Economic Order. "Technology," he states, "is the archetypal common heritage of mankind. . . ." M. Bedjaoui, *supra,* at 231. As such, it should be shared more readily by the "haves." Here we see the extreme concern with *distributional* issues—i.e., sharing—that characterizes so much of this new economic thinking. Without doubt there are strong equitable and even moral reasons for western countries to share technology. The problem is that an administrative structure that *forces* sharing entails a consequence that few would find palatable: there would inevitably be less to share.

In terms of western neoclassical economics, this is explained by appeal to a number of models. These attempt to capture the need for governmental intervention if technological innovation is to take place. Typically, the argument runs as follows: In the absence of government intervention, and assuming that a firm would find it impossible to keep new technologies secret, any firm that invests in research aimed at reducing costs or producing a new product will lose out to its rivals. The rivals will simply copy the new technology and achieve the same cost reduction or new product as the innovating firm. The difference, assuming that the costs of copying are substantially lower than the costs of research and perfecting the innovation, is that the rivals do not have to bear the costs of innovating. Thus, the innovating firm will find itself forced to price its output at levels that do not recoup its investment.

As a consequence, of course, neoclassical economic theory dictates that no firm will undertake research aimed at innovating. That is where government policy comes into play—to cure this instance of "market failure."

Government policy to encourage innovation can take many forms. For the most part, two instruments are used to achieve this goal: direct government funding of research (mostly basic research), and intellectual property protection (chiefly patents) for firms that create new products or cost-reducing processes. Intellectual property rights, by creating temporary monopolies over specific new technologies, provide the incentive required to encourage private firms to undertake costly research and development. For a good general review of these issues, see F.M. Scherer, Industrial Market Structure and Economic Performance (2d ed. 1980). For a discussion of other benefits of the patent system, see Kitch, The Nature and Function of the Patent System, 20 Journal of Law & Economics 266 (1977). In general, "diffusion of information" is one of the secondary benefits often associated with the patent system; it is furthered both by the limited duration of the patent grant (17 years in the U.S.) and by the requirement that each patent be published, with fully enabling details, upon issuance. *See* 35 U.S.C. §§ 100, 112 (1982).

It is important to note, however, that in contrast to the New International Economic Order envisioned by Bedjaoui and like-minded authors, the American patent system does not mandate the *direct* sharing of technology. Diffusion is expected to occur through the expiration of patents as well as the normal competitive process. Thus the *primary* goal of the patent system is to give an incentive to *create* new technologies; diffusion, or the sharing of benefits, is envisioned as an ancillary goal that will necessarily follow when firms take advantage of the incentive posed by patents.

A NOTE ON COMMON PROPERTY RESOURCES AND EFFICIENT ALLOCATION

Bedjaoui emphasizes the notion of common property resources, comparing space resources with technology (see Note 2 above) and even oxygen, which he correctly notes is "produced" in great quantities in the Congo and Amazon River basins, and used by all people on the planet. M. Bedjaoui, *supra,* at 235. Once again, his discussion reveals interesting assumptions behind the brand of developmental economics he espouses.

Western economists would have difficulty accepting the comparisons made by Bedjaoui. In the case of technology, the reasons are clear, as discussed in Note 2; at most, western economists view technology as essentially a "private good" with some "public goods" aspects. *See, e.g.,* Nelson, The Role of Knowledge in R&D Efficiency, 97 Quarterly Journal of Economics 453, 467 (1982). With respect to oxygen, it appears to be a classic example of what western economists would call a "public good"— that is, a good that (i) can be consumed by many without reducing the benefits to any user, and (ii) cannot be kept from potential users by any control or containment procedure. Other classic examples of public goods include sunsets and military protection. *See, e.g.,* R. Carnes & T. Sandler, The Theory of Externalities, Public Goods, and Club Goods 6 (1986).

Space resources are different. They have neither of the characteristics of public goods, nondivisibility (or non-exhaustibility) and nonexcludability. If one firm or nation strip mines one acre of lunar soil, no other firm or nation could follow on the same acre; the benefits would all go to the first firm. Likewise, it would not be impractical for a firm or a nation to build a fence or otherwise "stake a claim" to effectively exclude others from the area it wished to exploit.

Thus the comparisons Bedjaoui makes between oxygen and space resources do not work under conventional Western ideas about public goods. One point he raises, however, can be reconciled with traditional neoclassical analysis, and also finds expression in some provisions of the Moon Treaty: this is his allusion to the effect on Third World countries of developed nation consumption of oxygen and other environmental resources, an example of the economic concept of *externalities.*

In general, an activity that generates costs or benefits to firms or individuals not performing the activity is said to produce externalities. In some sense, the governments of Brazil and Zaire, by not cutting down all of the vast rain forests in their countries, are providing benefits to all the people on earth, since these rain forests produce a good portion of the oxygen in our atmosphere. (Of course, at the time of this writing at least, Third World countries *are* cutting down rain forests at a horrific rate, with consequences that may well turn out to be disastrous.) At the same time, Bedjaoui makes the point that the developed nations of the world, by burning hydrocarbon fuels, produce pollution, which damages the environment for everyone—an example of a negative externality.

The Moon Treaty makes an effort to minimize this form of negative externality in Article 7, which requires signatories to take measures to minimize the harmful impacts of their activities on the moon's environment.

Problems with a Common Resource Regime

Aside from the externalities problem identified above—which can be addressed as easily through a minimal regulatory scheme as through a common resource regime—there are a number of problems with the international development regime envisioned by Bedjaoui and reflected in certain provisions of the Moon Treaty. First, as we have discussed, it is not clear that space resources are the type of good commonly treated in the West under a centralized administrative regime; that is, they do not appear to be a classic public good. Second, as a result of the expense of exploiting these resources, the existence of a centralized, bureaucratic regime might well reduce or eliminate the incentives that would be required to entice private firms into space enterprises. That is, the excessive focus on distributional issues reflected in the Rao and Bedjaoui excerpts overlooks the fact that as of yet there are no benefits to distribute. Third, as a practical matter, a space development regime would be different from INTELSAT as regards the nature of the good they regulate. Because of the efficiencies of scale involved, INTELSAT's market is (or at least was, until recently) a natural monopoly; competing satellite communications systems did not make economic sense. The partners were thus forced by the nature of the market and the technology into banding together. (See Chapter 6, *infra*, for more on this topic.) This is not the case with space resources; there is no inherent reason why nations need band together to form a cooperative venture. Thus the centralized structure would have to be legislated *despite* the economic characteristics of the enterprise, not *because* of them.

On the other hand, economic theory also suggests that there might be some problems with a completely laissez-faire regime. If the most easy-to-exploit resources are located in a relatively small area on the moon, for instance, a substantial theoretical literature suggests that firms and nations will overutilize this area. *See, e.g.,* P. Dasgupta & G. Heal, Economic Theory and Exhaustible Resources (1979); R. Hardin, The Tragedy of the Commons, 162 Science 1243 (1968). *But cf.* Rose, The Comedy of the Commons: Custom, Commerce, and Inherently Public Property, 53 University of Chicago Law Review 711 (1986) (applying concept of "inherently public property" to describe modern land use law making some areas nonappropriable by private entities). It was to forestall such "land grabs" that the U.S. government instituted a "claiming" system for mineral deposits on federal lands in the nineteenth century. *See* I. C. Lindley, A Treatise on the American Law Relating to Mines and Mineral Lands Within the Public Land States and Territories 761–95 (3d ed. 1914). As a thought experiment, consider how such a claiming system might be structured for space. A helpful article, applying allocative economic principles to the problem of satellite frequency assignments, and suggesting the adoption of an auction system for frequency and satellite location resources, is Wihlborg & Wijkman, Outer Space Resources in Efficient and Equitable Use: New Frontiers for Old Principles, 24 Journal of Law & Economics 23 (1981); a portion of this article is reproduced *infra*.

The article just mentioned contains a very useful proposal regarding the reconciliation of efficiency and distributional considerations. Under the proposed scheme, all property rights over frequencies and satellite location would initially belong to a centralized agency. The agency would then auction off the rights to specific frequencies and locations, distributing the proceeds from the auction as it saw fit—e.g., by some "fairness" principle among members. As a second thought experiment, consider how this auction system might work in the context of space development. First, only those resources that are relatively easy to develop would be included in the centralized agency. Second, the agency would have to have some enforcement mechanism to punish non-members for transgressing on the agency's property rights. Third, the right to develop a particular resource would be time-limited, so that future bidders would have an opportunity to gain access to the same resource. Such a scheme would insure that the resources went to the highest bidder, and that no group of early bidders could monopolize resources long after the initial bidding. Such a regime would also solve the "tragedy of the commons" problem alluded to above.

In addition, since the bidding scheme would be independent of the system for allocating profits, it would in no way constrain the centralized agency from allocating its profits to assist less developed countries in achieving space capabilities or simply in developing their economic systems in general.

Do you think such a system would be compatible with the principles and provisions of the Moon Treaty? What position would you have to take on the two key interpretive issues in the Treaty—the meaning of "in place" resources and the "common heritage of mankind"—in order to espouse such a system? How would it square with the arguments and ideology associated with the New International Economic Order?

Note that, under the analysis set forth in the influential article by Ronald Coase, *The Problem of Social Cost,* 3 Journal of Law & Economics 1 (1960), an efficient allocation of resources can be achieved either by assigning property rights to private firms, or by shaping a liability rule making transgressors liable for damages inflicted on existing resource users. Either way would eliminate the necessity for a large-scale centrally administered regulatory agency. The assumption of no transaction costs, however, makes this analysis difficult to apply in many situations including outer space. (Imagine, for example, the problems that might arise if two or more claimants claim the same piece of moonscape to develop, or if one developer seeks to "buy out" all potential developers interested in one area.) The costs of resolving disputes, as well as of identifying and dealing with all relevant parties, are just two examples of transaction costs. Also, in the examples Coase runs through in his article, property rights are relatively easy to assign, e.g., to victims of pollution. It is less obvious how such rights should be assigned in the space context.

Wihlborg & Wijkman, Outer Space Resources in Efficient and Equitable Use: New Frontiers For Old Principles, 24 Journal of Law & Economics 23 (1981)

Space is the common property of mankind. Traditionally, access to common property resources such as the oceans has been open and free. This is appropriate for resources that are plentiful. At first glance, space appears to be not only abundant but infinite. However, future demand for space resources may soon make them scarce in the sense that an allocation mechanism will be needed for their efficient utilization. Satellites already perform traditional and new services using outer space resources, and plans for industrial ventures in space are under way. Space activities compete with more earthly activities for use of the scarce electromagnetic spectrum.

This paper demonstrates how the general principles of efficient markets easily can be extended to space resources. In fact, the market mechanism is particularly well suited to achieving efficient use of these resources given the difficulty for a central authority to obtain the necessary information. The paper is inspired by two seminal articles by R.H. Coase on the organization of economic activity. Our application is one of many possibilities: the same reasoning could be applied to other property resources.

*   *   *

II. Properties of Efficient Markets for Space Resources

This section argues that markets allocate rights to use orbit-spectrum resources more efficiently than do the nonmarket mechanisms currently in use. It considers three aspects of efficiency. First, efficiency means that a resource is allocated so that the marginal unit cannot be reallocated to another user without lowering value added. Second, an efficient system moves towards a new efficient allocation in the above sense after any disturbance such as an increase in demand or a reduction in production costs. These two aspects of efficiency will be denoted as *partial* efficiency in the markets for space resources. Third, and more general, an efficient system provides incentives for investment or research in new activities when they are expected to produce higher value added than do current activities.

As an economic resource, space consists of orbital positions and frequency bands. Efficiency requires that these can be combined freely. Currently they are sold as a unit with fixed coefficients. This is like assigning a radio station on earth a specific piece of real estate for a transmitter together with a frequency. Separate markets in frequency bands and orbit positions make it possible for all users of space locations and frequencies to trade the two separable economic resources until a Pareto-optimal situation is reached. In such a situation no user can change location and frequency without paying more than the potential gains generated by the new combination. Note, however, that in order for the markets for the resources to function efficiently, it must be possible to purchase a unit of one of the resources conditional on obtaining a certain unit of the other resource. Not only are the resources in general complementary but specific units of the two resources may be complementary.

[T]he markets for space resources should have the following properties: (a) complete allocation regime, (b) divisible and marketable user rights, (c) long contract periods, (d) well-defined liability rules.

*   *   *

A. Complete Allocation Regime

An allocation regime can be efficient only if it includes all resources that substitute for, or complement, each other. Thus, marketable user rights to resources in space must be defined to encompass substitutable modes of producing particular goods and services. For instance, long-distance communications can be transmitted by submarine cable, wire, and wireless as well as by satellite. Since real estate on earth is a well-priced and marketed resource, efficiency requires that scarce orbital positions, too, be priced in competitive markets. This allows a firm to compare the true costs of alternative locations for a relay station. If orbital slots remain free though scarce, too many resources will be invested in the building and launching of satellites.

*   *   *

[In addition,] the close substitutability between different parts of the [electromagnetic] spectrum necessitates that marketable user rights be defined for the entire spectrum—along the ground as well as in space—for the market system to be efficient.

B. Divisible and Marketable User Rights

The trade-offs facing users of the electromagnetic spectrum are more complicated than a simple choice between ground and space frequencies. Many trade-offs exist with respect to strength of signal, size of antennae, weight of satellites, precision in direction of the signal, and precision in the use of frequencies. Trade-offs occur between different geostationary orbits and other orbits and between the choice of orbit and all of the above aspects of frequency use. The length of time a frequency is used can also be traded off against location aspects and the different aspects of frequency use. The number of combinations among all these variables is immense.

*   *   *

C. Long Contract Periods

User rights may be purchased for either a limited or an indefinite period of time. While both formally are cases of leasing, a lease for an indefinite period of time in effect conveys a title of ownership to the lessee. How does the length of the contract period affect the efficiency of the market system? We show here that efficiency always prevails with indefinite user rights, while inefficiencies can be caused by time-limited user rights if the duration of the lease is shorter than the economic life span of the satellites. More specifically, it is the time-limit *combined with* costs for transforming the satellite to use by other firms and costs for transferring the satellite to other orbit-slots and/or frequencies that cause inefficiency.

*   *   *

Partial efficiency in the markets for space resources also prevails in cases involving *factor-specific equipment* with time-limited as well as indefinite user rights. Efficiency with respect to investment and research incentives presumes indefinite rights, however. To show this, consider how efficiency is achieved in the two cases after a technological change. For an *indefinite* user right the new firm must now bid a price that covers the present value of the incumbent's expected rent on the orbit slot and the frequency *plus* compensation to him for capital loss on the equipment. This is efficient because capital destruction should not occur unless new capital is so much more productive that the *increase* in value added covers the expected remaining value added on the old equipment. An identical situation will result with time-limited user rights. It is not sufficient for the new firm simply to bid more for the lease than the current holder pays, because the incumbent will be willing to increase his bid up to the point when he can no longer cover variable costs. The old factor-specific equipment therefore will not be taken out of service until it produces a negative value added at the bid-up price on the user rights. In this situation, the *increase* in value added on the new equipment covers the value added that will no longer be produced with the equipment that is taken out of service.

*   *   *

D. Well-Defined Liability Rules

The previous sections assumed that use of the spectrum is precise with respect to frequency and area affected, and that location of satellites in space is exact. These assumptions, however, are seldom valid. Users of the spectrum interfere with each other and space objects can collide. Thus social and private costs in the uses of the two resources can diverge.

A common regulatory response to such external effects is either to forbid the interference of one activity with others or to put specific technical limits on the external effects. The latter is particularly common in the use of common property resources. Well-known examples are quantitative regulations for air pollution by cars and factories or limits to the amount of waste products discharged in waters. Economists have often argued against specific technological constraints and instead have suggested the taxation of polluting activities. The advantage of this method is that those polluters whose costs of decreasing their pollution are lowest will do so first. The desired level of pollution is thus obtained at least cost.

Coase has argued [in The Problem of Social Cost, 3 Journal of Law & Economics 1 (1960)] that the so-called Pigovian approach [so-named after Arthur Pigou, 1877–1959, a noted English economist] is often inefficient. It may cost less for the activity harmed by pollution to reallocate or to protect itself than for the polluter to reallocate or decrease its emissions. Furthermore, Coase argued, an efficient allocation of resources could come about via market-induced negotiations without any intervention from regulatory agencies. Which system of reducing external effects is more efficient depends on information, transactions, negotiations, and enforcement costs— that is, on systems costs. . . .

We contend that most external effects in the uses of space resource can be reduced to efficient levels by market-induced negotiations once liability rules are defined and enforced. This is superior to a system of Pigovian taxes because most interferences in the uses of space resources occur between very few parties at adjoining frequencies or orbit slots. The external effects are then relatively "individualized" so that the costs of finding negotiating parties become relatively low for space resources. The Pigovian solution is superior on the other hand when external effects are "generalized," and many parties are affected by a particular activity so that the costs of starting and conducting negotiations are relatively high.

*   *   *

It follows from Coase's argument that an optimal degree of interference and collision risk can be brought about, whether or not a liability rule is defined, if no costs are involved in identifying potential sources of interference for uses of adjoining resources, in setting up negotiations, in conducting negotiations, and in enforcing an agreement. The definition of a liability rule will determine who bears the costs of adjusting to interferences; it will not affect the level of interference.

The optimal degree of interference would be reached even when current holders and new entrants interfere with one another. All parties would gain by negotiating mutual improvements in equipment until the costs of improvements exceed the gains. The assumptions under which this market solution would be reached are very restrictive, however. For instance, the users of adjoining frequencies and locations are assumed to know the degree of interference that will be caused by the new entrant. When this information is lacking, a liability rule is necessary or newcomers could benefit by installing low-quality, interfering equipment that is very expensive to modify once it is in use. Measures to decrease interference are likely to be much cheaper if they are implemented before the space objects are installed. Current users of adjoining frequencies and locations must pay a higher price, therefore, to reduce interference to an optimal level (as defined in the case with perfect information). If instead the new entrant were liable for damages caused by his satellite, he would be induced to start negotiations when the costs of modifying the equipment are at a minimum.

*   *   *

Choice of Management Regime: Efficiency and Equity Considerations

Is there any need for an international orbit and frequency authority, and, if so, what roles should such an authority have? This section concludes that an authority can contribute little to achieving *efficiency* once the institutional framework for complete markets exist. However, well-functioning international markets may require international trade and legal conventions. The main task of an international space resource authority is instead to achieve *equity* in the distribution of rents among nations. We suggest, therefore, creating an international condominium to auction the electromagnetic spectrum and the orbits and to distribute the resulting revenues.

The current regime has been called a squatters'-rights regime because ownership is distributed on a first-come, first-served basis. This is a misnomer in one important respect. Once a squatter's claim is secured, his property rights are complete and he can sell his farm to more efficient, more eager farmers or subdivide it for development. This was the case on the American frontier during the 1800s. While it is true that a user of orbit slots or the frequency spectrum is a squatter in the sense of claiming resources not used by anyone else, his claim and use of these resources do not grant him the right to sell all or part of them. His property rights are therefore circumscribed in an important respect which distinguishes the current regime from a true squatter's regime. Currently there are restrictions on the intranational transfer of user rights as well on their international trading. For example, the Federal Communications Commission must approve users of the electromagnetic spectrum in the United States.

A true squatters'-rights regime may be less efficient than auctioning user rights even when the conditions for efficient markets are fulfilled. One reason is that transfer costs between different orbits and frequencies may prevent a latecomer in space from obtaining an optimal position or frequency, since the resources cannot be claimed without physical presence. The complementary nature of orbit slots and frequencies emphasizes this inefficiency of the squatters'-rights regimes because a potential user of space resources cannot claim parts of the two resources simultaneously. An auctioning system could be designed in such a way that this complementarity could be recognized, however. . . . However, the major difference between a squatters'-rights regime and a resource auction is related to the

problem of equity rather than efficiency. We shall return to this issue below.
. . .

Thus, there is an important role for international conventions similar to those of the General Agreement on Tariffs and Trade (GATT). The optimal tariff argument suggests that one country could gain by restricting trade in its shares of the space resources if these were imperfect substitutes for the shares of other countries and possessed a comparative advantage in producing specific services demanded by other nations. Therefore, in an initial distribution of property rights no single country or small group of countries should be given a monopoly on specific space resources that it can exploit by imposing an optimal tariff.

Some nations may also wish to allocate all or parts of their resources in a spectrum for military purposes or for other services that are supplied by government authorities. The frequency spectrum can provide public goods, such as emergency communications and military services, which are nonmarketable, but this should not free the respective government authority from the market test of the willingness to pay for the use of a scarce resource. . . .

Inevitable interferences in the use of spectrum and orbit resources suggest the need for an international legal convention, because liability rules must be defined and enforced. Such a convention would not be necessary if enough national laws were directly applicable to the use of space resources. Lacking these, international interference requires an international legal framework that is accepted and enforced by all nations. Specification of such a legal framework would not be unique. Parallels exist in international law, such as the liability rules regulating collision at sea. Liability rules could either be accepted internationally and enforced by courts in individual nations, or the international authority could serve as a court for cases involving damages in the use of the frequency spectrum and the physical space resource. . . .

The major task of an international authority for managing space resources will be to distribute rents. When a nonreproducible resource becomes scarce, it generates rents. Discussion of the normative questions of who should enjoy these rents and how the desired distribution can be achieved has often been confused since space has traditionally been considered an international common property resource to which access is open and free. Property rights to the resource consequently have usually not been precisely defined and their rents have seldom appeared explicitly. The importance of rents is nevertheless illustrated by the struggle over property rights at the World Administrative Radio Conference (WARC–79) proceedings.

Allocating user rights through a regime of squatters' rights would resemble the acquisition of titles to gold and land during the westward push of the American frontier. Space would be a new frontier and firms and nations would rush to claim the most valuable orbit slots and frequencies. The best-equipped firms in the most technologically advanced nations could quickly claim valuable space property, and little of the rents would remain for other nations. Such a regime is unacceptable to most countries.

The current regime regulating access to the electromagnetic spectrum and orbits is similar to that traditionally used for commons. Governments apply for user rights to the International Telecommunications Union which grants such rights on a first-come, first-served basis for an unlimited time period. The applicant is in effect granted rents for the period of use. If entry were not regulated by this nonmarket method, rents would be dissipated through congestion and interference.

Some developing countries have proposed either that user rights be reserved for future use by countries that have no current use for them or that the electromagnetic spectrum and the satellite orbit be subdivided and title to its parts distributed among countries in an equitable manner. These two procedures are equivalent in terms of equity when user rights are accorded in perpetuity. However, unless markets for resale or subleasing of space resources are also allowed, greater equity is achieved at the expense of less efficiency since scarce resources will be hoarded for future use.

The auction method for allocating user rights as a way to ensure efficiency in resource use is consistent with any distribution of rents. The equity aspect of managing orbits and frequencies could therefore be separated from efficiency aspects.

NOTES

1. The authors suggest that an international authority is only necessary from an efficiency standpoint when so many activities are affected by some particular activity that liability rules and/or bargaining over property rights are not sufficient to reduce interference to an optimal level, that is, when there are excessive transaction costs. Is outer space sufficiently large to avoid the need for a centralized agency to achieve efficiency? Would it be wise to plan now for the day when interference between rival space developers is more likely? On the need to regulate communication via space satellite, see R. White & H. White, Jr., The Law and Regulation of International Space Communication 5–8 (1988); see also Chapter 6, *infra*. Note that the 1988 Space WARC (World Administrative Radio Conference), concluded as this book was in press, adopted a new regime for allocating geosynchronous orbital slots. This regime is discussed in Chapter 6.

2. The authors also note that equity, if not efficiency, requires an international "condominium" or central agency. Is it too early to worry about equity in space development? Is "fair development" an important enough principle to cause us to sacrifice "early development"? These are questions that will not die with the Moon Treaty; they are likely to be with us for a long time.

3. On these topics generally, see Coase, The Federal Communications Commission, 2 Journal of Law & Economics 1 (1959) and Coase, The Problem of Social Cost, 3 Journal of Law & Economics 1 (1960). Together with William Meckling and Jora Minasian, Coase wrote Problems in Radio Frequency Allocation (Rand Corp. 1963). Although this manuscript remained unpublished, the coauthors later published two important contributions. See William H. Meckling, Management of the Frequency Spectrum, 1968 Washington University Law Quarterly 26 (1968); and Jora R. Minasian, Property Rights in Radiation: An Alternative Approach to Radio Frequency Allocation, 18 Journal of Law & Economics 221 (1975). *See also* A.S. DeVany *et al.,* A Property System for Market Allocation of the Electromagnetic Spectrum: A Legal-Economic-Engineering Study, 21 Stanford Law Review 1499 (1969).

5

Other Treaties,
Agreements, and Issues

The preceding two chapters dealt with the overarching treaties governing activity in outer space. This chapter deals with a number of remaining treaties and issues that—although not necessarily of lesser importance—involve matters of less general application. Some, like the Liability Convention or the Rescue and Return Agreement, implement portions of the treaties described previously; others simply involve more specific topics. We will deal with the most important remaining space agreements at some length, and will at least touch on many other issues. We will also attempt to illustrate the ways in which different space agreements may interact in the context of a real-world fact situation.

THE LIABILITY CONVENTION

One major space law agreement that has seen dramatic application is the Convention on International Liability for Damage Caused by Space Objects of 1972, 24 U.S.T. 2389, T.I.A.S. 7762. That treaty provides detailed rules that flesh out the general liability provisions contained in the Outer Space Treaty of 1967 (see Chapter 3, *supra*). The Liability Convention is applicable to both military and civilian space activities of its signatory nations; it provides for absolute liability by launching states for damage caused by their space objects on the surface of the earth or to aircraft in flight (Article II), and liability based on fault where the damage is to space objects of another launching state elsewhere than on the surface of the earth (Article III). The launching state may, however, be exonerated where the injury is caused by the gross negligence or malice of a third party—for example, a terrorist bomb that causes a Space Shuttle explosion. The Convention also provides for joint and several liability where more than one launching state's space object, or space objects belonging to more than one launching state, are involved.

The Liability Convention has been applied in the real world amid rather dramatic circumstances: the crash in Canada of a Soviet satellite powered by a nuclear reactor. The following article by Alexander Cohen describes the satellite's crash and the legal and political response thereto. Cohen's article, part of a symposium on international incidents as a source of international law, shows how concrete events can shed considerable light on how different groups interpret international law.

Cohen, Cosmos 954 and the International Law of Satellite Accidents, 10 Yale Journal of International Law 78 (1984)

I. Problem

Falling satellites are an unavoidable hazard of space exploration: at the current level of technology, a certain number of satellites will inevitably fall out of orbit. Nevertheless, the traditional sources of international law provide little help in determining what norms would govern a situation in which a falling satellite causes injury. The 1978 crash of the U.S.S.R.'s Cosmos 954 satellite has shed some light on the normative expectations of states concerning satellite accidents.

From the events leading up to and following the crash of Cosmos 954, four governing norms emerged: (1) A state that becomes aware that one of its satellites will crash has the duty to forewarn a state that is in danger; (2) The state whose satellite has crashed in the territory of another state has the duty to provide that state with information (regarding the specifications of that satellite) to enable the endangered state to assess the dangers and act to counter them; (3) Special rules govern the duty to clean up the remains of a state's satellite that has crashed in another state's territory; and (4) The state whose satellite has crashed has the duty to compensate a state injured as a result of the crash.

II. Facts

The U.S.S.R. launched the nuclear-powered Cosmos 954 naval surveillance satellite on September 18, 1977. In late November or early December 1977, Cosmos 954's orbit became erratic. The U.S. soon calculated that the satellite would fall on or about January 23, 1978, although it was not known where it would land. In response, the U.S. initiated a series of secret meetings with the U.S.S.R. in mid-January 1978, during which the U.S.S.R. provided the U.S. with information about Cosmos 954's reactor. The U.S. also warned its NATO and Organization for Economic Cooperation and Development (OECD) partners that Cosmos 954 was expected to fall, and offered to help clean up any radioactive contamination that might result.

Cosmos 954 crashed to earth on January 24, 1978:

> [T]he satellite entered the earth's atmosphere intruding into Canadian air space at about 11:53 A.M. Greenwich Mean Time to the north of the Queen Charlotte Islands on the west coast of Canada. On re-entry and disintegration,

debris from the satellite was deposited on Canadian territory, including portions of the Northwest Territories, Alberta, and Saskatchewan.

U.S. President Carter notified Canadian Prime Minister Trudeau within fifteen minutes of the accident, and repeated the U.S. proposal of assistance. Trudeau accepted Carter's offer.

Some hours later, Canada asked the U.S.S.R. to provide information about the specifications of the Cosmos 954. The U.S.S.R responded that day by offering to help clean up Cosmos 954's remains. In contrast to its reaction to the earlier U.S. proposal, Canada declined the Soviet offer.

The joint U.S.-Canadian cleanup operation that resulted from this exchange, dubbed "Operation Morning Light," cost Canada nearly C$14 million, while the U.S. spent some U.S.$2–2.5 million. Canada billed the U.S.S.R. for C$6 million of its outlay on January 23, 1979, but did not seek reimbursement for the U.S. expenditure. The U.S.S.R. paid C$3 million to Canada on April 2, 1981, "in full and final settlement of all matters connected with the disintegration of the Soviet satellite 'Cosmos 954' in January 1978."

III. Conflicting Claims

Canada and the U.S.S.R. asserted different versions of the facts of the accident. First, the U.S.S.R. blamed the fall of Cosmos 954 on a mid-space collision. Academician L. I. Sedov explained that:

> On Jan. 6, 1978, for reasons that as yet remain unclear, sudden depressurization of the satellite took place outside the visibility zone of our facilities for tracking space objects. Judging from the fact that the depressurization process was very rapid, it can be assumed that the satellite collided in flight with some other body of natural or artificial origin. As a result the satellite's onboard systems went out of commission, it lost orientation, and began an uncontrollable descent.

Canada, in contrast, blamed the fall of the satellite on a faulty motor. "The U.S.S.R. admitted that Cosmos 954 had failed, and that it was not possible to lift the satellite into a much higher orbit, as had been planned in case of an emergency, because of failure of a rocket system."

Second, the U.S.S.R. claimed that Cosmos 954 had been completely destroyed during reentry. The official Soviet news agency (TASS) stated that, "in the afternoon of Jan. 24, 1978, the Kosmos–954 satellite entered the dense layers of the atmosphere over Northern Canada and ceased to exist." Notwithstanding this claim, Canada found charred pieces of the satellite that had returned to the ground.

Finally, the U.S.S.R. declared that the remains of Cosmos 954, if any, posed a minimal radiation hazard. According to Sedov, "[i]t was emphasized [to the Canadian government] that if individual fragments of the satellite did reach the earth's surface, only limited local pollution might occur, and only in the immediate area of the fall, and that this would require the application of ordinary decontamination measures." Canada, in contrast, found that "all but two of the fragments recovered were radio-active. Some fragments located proved to be of lethal radioactivity."

IV. Conflicting Conceptions of Lawfulness

The Cosmos 954 incident suggests that elites in Canada and the U.S.S.R. held divergent expectations of how states that are involved in satellite accidents should behave. These expectations concerned the substantive content of four governing norms: the duty to forewarn, the duty to provide information, the duty to clean up, and the duty to compensate for injury.

A. The Duty to Forewarn

It appears from the record that Canadian elites expected the Soviet Union to warn Canada as soon as the U.S.S.R. had discovered that Cosmos 954 might conceivably land in Canada:

> In the course of the day January 24, 1978, an official of the Department of External Affairs expressed to the Ambassador of the Union of Soviet Socialist Republics the surprise of the Government of Canada that the Government of the Union of Soviet Socialist Republics had failed to give notice of the possible re-entry of the satellite into the earth's atmosphere in the region of Canada, and, subsequently, of the imminent re-entry of the satellite.

Elites in Canada thus seemed to believe that the U.S.S.R was obligated to forewarn all potentially endangered states of the hazards posed by its falling satellite, no matter how remote the possibility of injury.

Soviet elites viewed the norm differently. They claimed that the U.S.S.R. had an obligation to warn only the United States of the impending crash of Cosmos 954:

> Calculations made on the basis of [Cosmos 954's] last orbits within the visibility range of our tracking facilities showed that if, because of the satellite's emergency condition, individual parts of the satellite were not fully consumed in the atmosphere and reached the earth's surface, they might fall into the open sea in the region of the Aleutian Islands. In this connection, the appropriate information was given to the U.S. government.

Two possible conceptions of the duty to forewarn may explain this asser-tion. First, Soviet elites may have interpreted the norm as a requirement that the U.S.S.R. warn the state in whose territory the satellite was most likely to crash. Alternatively, the U.S.S.R. may have agreed with Canada that the duty to forewarn required the notification of all potentially en-dangered states. Elites in the U.S.S.R. may not have believed, however, that they were required to notify these states directly if they were part of a political and military alliance hostile to the U.S.S.R. Rather, Soviet elites may have believed that the U.S.S.R. could discharge its duty under the norm by notifying the leading state in the hostile alliance—in this case, the U.S.—which would relay the warning to the other members of that alliance.

B. The Duty to Provide Information

Consistent with their position regarding the duty to forewarn, Canada's elites believed that the U.S.S.R. was under an obligation to disclose information. Canada repeatedly questioned the U.S.S.R. about Cosmos 954's specifications, and expressed frustration at the U.S.S.R.'s refusal to answer their inquiries:

> In this regard, Canada has requested the assistance of the Soviet authorities in furnishing information about the nature and characteristics of the nuclear core contained in the satellite. These requests have been conveyed on several occasions. . . . The Canadian authorities regret that they have not to date received answers to these questions.

Elites in Canada also expected that this information be publicly disclosed. Indeed, "Canada decided to publish the documents establishing the claim together with texts of its diplomatic exchanges with the Soviet Union on the matter. In so doing, the Canadian government departed from normal practice regarding the confidentiality of diplomatic communications."

Under the Soviet interpretation, however, the duty to provide information imposed a more limited burden. According to this interpretation, the U.S.S.R. was required to provide only the minimum degree of information that Canada needed to conduct a cleanup. In addition, the Soviet Union reserved the right to determine what that minimum included:

> In connection with the request made by the Canadian side for information regarding the power unit which was on board the Cosmos-954 satellite, the Embassy would remind that the necessary information about the satellite was already made available which, in the opinion of the Soviet side, is sufficient to organize and carry out effective search for possible consequences of its cessation to exist over Canadian territory.

The statements made in Pravda show that the U.S.S.R. also believed that any information it provided should be transmitted secretly. The Soviets chided Canada for the highly public manner in which Canada had handled the Cosmos 954 incident; they were particularly displeased at the fact that Canada did not notify them officially of its findings concerning the wreckage for two weeks, a considerable time after such information was released to the press. Indeed, the U.S.S.R. charged that Canada was using requests for information as a pretext for intelligence gathering. "The Soviet side finds it also necessary to note that some of the questions put by the Canadian side obviously relate to information which is outside the scope of the amount [sic] necessary to secure the health and safety of persons and the environment."

C. The Duty to Clean Up

In the Soviet view, the cleanup should be undertaken jointly by the injured state and the state that had launched the satellite. As the Soviet representative to the Scientific and Technical Sub-Committee of the UN Committee on the Peaceful Uses of Outer Space stated soon after the crash of Cosmos 954, "[i]f a satellite or any spacecraft, when it goes out of control should cause damage to another State, then the launching State is duty-bound to compensate for this damage: it is duty-bound to participate in the search and recovery of the debris of the satellite. . . ." Indeed, the U.S.S.R. repeatedly expressed frustration at Canada's refusal to allow it to participate in the cleanup.

Under the Canadian version of this norm, the injured state is entitled to choose which country or countries will carry out the cleanup. Accordingly, Canada turned down the U.S.S.R.'s offer of assistance but permitted its American ally to participate in the operation.

D. The Duty to Compensate for Injury

Canada evidently considered there to be a norm requiring the U.S.S.R. to make full payment for the cost of repairing the injury caused by its satellite. Although Canada eventually demanded only C$6 million in damages out of an expenditure of C$14 million, it clearly based its claim on the total cost of cleaning up the radioactive debris. Canadian elites also believed that the U.S. would help pay for the cleanup. If one conceives of the unreimbursed U.S. expenditure on the cleanup of US$2–2.5 million as a form of payment to Canada, the U.S. "paid" Canada C$2.5–3.125 million as a result of the crash of Cosmos 954. Canada never offered to repay the U.S. for its outlay on the cleanup, nor did it press the U.S.S.R. to do so.

Actions by Soviet elites showed partial disagreement with this interpretation. Unlike Canada, the U.S.S.R. viewed the duty to compensate for injury as an obligation to reimburse only the incremental costs that the injured state incurred in repairing the injury. Thus the Soviet officials who negotiated the U.S.S.R.'s payment to Canada "made it very clear that they wouldn't pay [Canadian] fixed costs." At the same time, the U.S.S.R.'s elites seemed to concur in the Canadian view that the U.S. should not be reimbursed for its role in the cleanup. The U.S.S.R., therefore, did not offer to reimburse the U.S. expenditure. Indeed, the Soviet refusal to pay Canada's "fixed costs" tends to suggest that the U.S.S.R. would have rejected a claim for U.S. cleanup expenditures.

V. International Appraisal

The conflicting expectations of elites in Canada and the U.S.S.R. were never appraised in a formal judicial setting. Nevertheless, their claims of what constitutes proper action by states that are involved in a satellite accident did receive widespread informal evaluation by a broad range of state and media elites. From the standpoint of norm creation, the crucial appraisals were those of elites in the United States.

The legal conceptions expressed by U.S. elites were much closer to those of Soviet than to those of Canadian elites. The United States assumed the burden of notifying its NATO and OECD partners, apparently without the U.S.S.R. having asked it to do so. Furthermore, the U.S. government never joined in Canada's public criticism of the U.S.S.R. for having failed to notify Canada of the impending crash of Cosmos 954. From this it would appear that the U.S. shared the Soviet view that the launching state was under a duty to forewarn only the leading state of a hostile alliance, and was not responsible for warning each of its political adversaries individually.

The United States also appeared to agree with the U.S.S.R. on the issue of how to interpret the second norm, the duty to provide information. U.S. elites interpreted this norm as an obligation to provide only that information needed to conduct the cleanup. Unlike Canada, the U.S. chose to question the U.S.S.R. about the specifications of Cosmos 954 in secret, and evidently expected only minimal compliance with American requests for information:

> [M]any American specialists were skeptical that the Soviet Union would provide any information about its out-of-control space satellite, when national security advisor Zbigniew Brzezinski, on Jan. 12, first raised the issue with Soviet Ambassador Anatoly F. Dobrynin. "Frankly, I thought they were likely to tell us to go to hell," said one administration specialist.

Again, the United States seemed to take the same view as the Soviets of the duty to compensate for injury. The U.S. never joined Canada in criticizing the U.S.S.R.'s payment to Canada as too small, apparently conceiving of the norm as imposing an obligation to reimburse the injured state only for the incremental cost of repairing the injury. Since the U.S. did not ask reimbursement for its share of the cleanup expenses from either Canada or the U.S.S.R., it would seem that the U.S. elites agreed with both countries that the U.S. was obliged to pay Canada under the norm.

While concurring generally in the Soviet formulations of the first three norms, the United States rejected the Soviet interpretation of the fourth, concerning the duty to clean up. There is no indication that the U.S. ever expected Canada to permit the U.S.S.R. to play any part in the cleanup operation. Nevertheless, the apparent difference in legal conceptions obscures the possibility that the two superpowers were motivated by similar concerns. It is not unreasonable to suppose, as did some Canadian observers, that each was anxious to participate in the cleanup chiefly to gather intelligence, or to prevent the other from doing so. The U.S. eagerness to examine what was left of Cosmos 954 was surely matched by Soviet desires to deny the U.S. just such an opportunity. It would therefore seem misleading to characterize the U.S. appraisal as an affirmation of free choice for the injured state. Rather, it appears to be an assertion of the right of the injured state to invite only its political allies to participate in the cleanup.

VI. Outcome

The norms established by the Cosmos 954 incident provide that the major satellite launching nations—the U.S. and the U.S.S.R.—notify each other of hazardous events due to satellite failure, relay information to facilitate damage control, assist their political allies in cleanup operations, and share the cost of compensating the state injured by a falling satellite, regardless of whose satellite caused the injury and regardless of fault.

The critical norm is that of joint compensation. This norm would appear to provide compensation only for the incremental costs of cleanup associated with the accident. It may also be limited in application to surveillance satellites.

Although it is possible that the payments made by the U.S. and the U.S.S.R. were *ex gratia* and, hence, devoid of normative content, at least the size of the Soviet payment tends to argue otherwise; in the context of negotiations with the U.S.S.R., a fifty percent settlement is apparently quite high. Indeed, that the U.S.S.R. paid anything is striking in light of the fact that it was not obligated to pay under the 1972 Liability Convention. That the U.S. paid its share without being at fault lends further support to the existence of this norm.

VII. Writer's Appraisal

The Cosmos 954 incident illustrates the paradox of satellite utilization: satellites simultaneously protect and endanger the international community. Reconnaissance satellites play a crucial role in maintaining the stability of the U.S.-U.S.S.R. nuclear balance. At the same time, nuclear-powered satellites present clear hazards, as the Cosmos 954 incident demonstrated.

One response to this problem would be to prohibit the use of those satellites that are most hazardous. At the time of the Cosmos 954 incident, President Carter suggested a ban on nuclear-powered satellites: "If we cannot evolve those fail-safe methods, then I think there ought to be a total prohibition against [nuclear-powered] earth-orbiting satellites. I would favor at this moment an agreement with the Soviets to prohibit earth-orbiting satellites with atomic radiation material in them."

A ban on nuclear-powered satellites does not seem a realistic solution. In the first place, the U.S. and the U.S.S.R. are unlikely to consent to a prohibition, because certain satellites must carry an on-board nuclear power source in order to perform their missions. Indeed, Canada's attempt, in the wake of the Cosmos 954 incident, to impose a new regime on the use of nuclear power sources in space through the United Nations Committee on the Peaceful Uses of Outer Space, has made little progress. In addition, the costs of such a ban might well outweigh its benefits in that restrictions on nuclear-powered satellites could conceivably destabilize the nuclear balance.

The norm of joint compensation that appears to emerge from the Cosmos 954 incident is a better answer to the paradox of satellite utilization. The states with the greatest investment in satellites are exposed to the greatest potential of liability, but that liability is limited, and is not such as to discourage satellite use. This norm takes into account the probability that some satellites will inevitably fall, by requiring payment regardless of fault. The outcome of the Cosmos 954 incident may well have had a positive effect on world order. The U.S. and the U.S.S.R. apparently recognized that it was in their mutual interest to cooperate rather than to turn the incident into a propaganda battle. The U.S. and the U.S.S.R. thus demonstrated their ability to take joint steps to deal with the dangerous items over which they exercise control. Their cooperation helps to increase the security of the two states and the world. While a price is paid for this security by the unlucky victims in such third states as Canada, the norm established by the incident provides at least for the payment of substantial reparations.

The use of nuclear-powered satellites will continue to threaten the earth with falling debris. The Cosmos 954 incident offers hope that cooperative measures can be taken to offset the damages that result, and to enhance global security in the satellite age.

NOTES

1. Although good practice calls for satellites carrying nuclear materials to be boosted into long-duration orbits at the end of their useful lives, accidents like the Cosmos 954 crash are likely to happen from time to time. In this context a strict liability regime makes sense. The operators of most satellites are likely to be either wealthy nations able to afford the cleanup cost out of pocket or (though there are currently no civilian applications for nuclear-powered satellites) corporations able to insure against loss. And, of course, the Outer Space Treaty of 1967 imposes ultimate liability for launches by non-governmental or intergovernmental organizations on the launching state or states. Since the countries involved tend to fly many satellites, a strict liability regime allows "spreading" of the total liability over a number of satellites. See generally G. Calabresi, The Cost of Accidents 39 *et seq.* (1970). Imposition of fault-based liability only as between space objects also makes sense from a "spreading" standpoint.

2. Note the magnitude of the costs involved in the Cosmos 954 cleanup, which by the standards of most earthbound disasters were relatively minuscule. Although the Liability Convention is important, misconceptions as to the magnitude of harm likely to result from satellite crashes are common. The Cosmos 954 crash, which involved a nuclear powered craft, nonetheless resulted in rather minor damages, something that should be borne in mind in the context of discussions concerning liability limits and insurance. While enormous damages are possible in some circumstances (for example, a loaded Titan, launched from Cape Canaveral, that crashes into the Vehicle Assembly Building while two Space Shuttles are being

prepared for launch—with possible damages in excess of $5 billion), most scenarios for such large sums involve launch accidents. Even in this setting, most risks are not great by earthly standards. A March, 1988 internal study by the Office of Commercial Space Transportation (see Chapter 8) concluded that the total chemical energy of three typical launch vehicles approximated that of a wide-body airliner. *See* Congress Moves Toward Subsidizing ELVs, Aerospace America, August, 1988, at 8. Launches are included within the Convention's coverage, but most launch accidents will take place within the launching state's own territory and involve its own nationals, a situation in which the Convention does not apply.

3. The Liability Convention is a detailed treatment of the 1967 Outer Space Treaty's liability provisions. Given the limited magnitude of damages likely to be covered by the Convention (compared to, say, the Chernobyl accident or to many other accidents that take place more frequently), such attention is surprising in some ways. Perhaps it reflects lawyers' fascination with liability issues, but it may also reflect a view by the non-spacefaring countries that space travel is an ultrahazardous activity for which the space powers (at the time of the Convention, limited to large and wealthy countries) should be held strictly to account—hence the different treatment of damages on earth as opposed to damage to other space objects. This view may change as more and more nations traditionally regarded as "third world" opinion leaders (such as India and Brazil) become active space powers themselves. If, as a result of this broader participation, space activity comes to be viewed as an economic mainstay of all nations rather than as a special activity only of the wealthy we may see a shift to limitations on liability such as exist in the maritime or aeronautical industries. For more on these and related liability issues in a private law context see Chapter 8, *infra*.

4. The Liability Convention makes no provision for punitive damages, indirect or consequential damages, or "moral damages," and discussions regarding these issues at the time of the Convention's drafting reached no conclusion. International law draws no clear distinction between "direct" and "indirect" harm as many nations' municipal law systems do. The United States did remark at the time that moral damage claims (that is, claims for insults to a nation's dignity or sovereignty) might be valid under some circumstances, a position supported by Hungary as well. There was no provision for punitive damages because the Convention provides for unlimited liability for actual damages, which was considered enough to provide adequate incentive for states to avoid unnecessary risks. For more on these and other topics relating to liability for space activity see Christol, International Liability for Damage Caused by Space Objects, 74 American Journal of International Law 346 (1980).

5. Article XI provides that a claimant state may present its claim under the Convention to the launching state without exhausting its local remedies under the law of the launching state. The claimant state is also given the option, however, of electing to proceed under the launching state's own

judicial or administrative procedures instead of the Convention; however, claims presented in such fora cannot simultaneously be made under the Convention. Where claims made under the Convention are disputed, there are provisions for arbitration (Article XIV).

6. The Liability Convention provides for strict liability in the case of harm to victims on earth, but for fault-based liability in the case of harm to other spacecraft. This is similar to the regime governing aircraft, where there is strict liability for injury to persons and property on the ground and fault-based liability with regard to other aircraft. *See* Restatement (Second) of Torts, Section 520A. This is entirely reasonable as an incentive for risk-minimizing activities. Persons on the ground can do little to protect themselves from crashing satellites, after all, and the low likelihood that any particular person or locality will be struck further dilutes any incentive to do so. Those who launch spacecraft, on the other hand, have considerable ability to reduce the chance that they will crash to the ground and harm individuals, and the certain knowledge that if they are allowed to crash in populated areas someone will be hurt. As among spacecraft operators, on the other hand, avoidance of injury is a mutual matter: the number of spacecraft is not that large, and all parties have the ability to avoid collision with one another.

The problem of space debris, discussed later in this chapter, may create considerable difficulty under the Liability Convention: since space debris (made up of fragments from defunct satellites, spent boosters, and space weapons tests) is a growing threat, but since it may be difficult to tell after a collision which nation's craft created the particular particle of debris causing damage, liability may be difficult to assign. Aside from this problem of proof, in order to recover the complaining party would have to show that (1) the accused party was negligent in either creating the debris or in failing to warn of its presence; and (2) that its own actions were not the primary cause of the injury. Given the difficulty of proving the origin of a particular piece of debris, a more workable solution might be for the space nations to contribute toward damage awards based on the proportion of space debris that each has caused, much as has been done in some pharmaceutical cases. *See, e.g.,* Sindell v. Abbott Laboratories, 26 Cal. 3d 588, 612, 607 P.2d 924, 937, *cert. denied,* 449 U.S. 912 (1980) (defendant's liability based on market share in offending product). For political reasons it is unlikely that such a compensation scheme would be agreed to, however, although it would have a valuable incentive effect as it would discourage nations from contributing to the amount of space debris in orbit.

7. Cohen speaks of "joint compensation" by the United States and the Soviet Union. This is an incorrect characterization, however. Although both the United States and the Soviet Union made payments to Canada, the payments were for differing purposes. The Soviet Union's payments were compensation under the Liability Convention; the U.S. payments and assistance were in exchange for access to intelligence data concerning Cosmos 954, an important military satellite. *See* W. Burrows, Deep Black (1986).

SPACE REMOTE SENSING

Use of satellites for earth observation is not a new idea: in 1946 a secret Douglas Aircraft/RAND Corporation report for the U.S. Army recommended making use of captured German rocket technology to launch reconnaissance satellites that could observe the Soviet Union and other potentially hostile nations. Douglas Aircraft Co. Inc. Report No. SM11827, Preliminary Design of an Experimental World-Circling Spaceship (May 2, 1946). By the early 1950s, even though the United States was years away from launching any kind of satellite, plans were already underway for orbital reconnaissance (see Chapter 1). *See also* P. Stares, The Militarization of Space: U.S. Policy 1945–84 (1985); W. Burrows, Deep Black: Space Espionage and National Security (1986). Civilian remote sensing did not get under way for some time afterwards, but by the 1970s it was already becoming a reality. On civilian remote sensing generally, see T. Lillesand & R. Kiefan, Remote Sensing and Image Interpretation (1987); R.M. Hord, Remote Sensing: Methods and Applications (1986).

Although such activities held the promise of more accurate maps, better crop and resource management, discovery of new deposits of mineral wealth, and more effective environmental monitoring, they also raised concerns on the part of two classes of nations: less developed countries who feared that corporations and developed nations would have unfair bargaining advantages regarding resources if they possessed such information, and totalitarian or authoritarian countries who regarded such sensing as an intrusion on their jealously guarded sovereignty. These fears led to considerable discussion in the United Nations and COPUOS, with results discussed in the articles below, which also provide some information regarding the technology behind and uses of remote sensing.

Logsdon & Monk, Remote Sensing from Space;
A Continuing Legal and Policy Issue,
8 Annals of Air & Space Law 409 (1983)

3. International and Foreign Policy Issues

The capability to make useful observations of all parts of the earth's land surface from orbit, using a U.S.-developed and operated satellite system, has provided a foreign policy opportunity for the United States. It has also created international demands that the United States, along with other potential operators of earth observation systems, be governed by a series of existing and emerging international obligations and principles related to remote sensing from space. These opportunities and obligations define an essential part of the context within which various scenarios related to a permanent U.S. remote sensing venture must be evaluated.

Current U.S. government policy with respect to the international aspects of remote sensing dates back to Richard Nixon's 1969 pledge before the

U.N. General Assembly that "this program will be dedicated to producing information not only for the U.S. but also for the U.N. community." In the years following this statement, the United States has put forth, and strongly defended against criticism, a policy of open and nondiscriminatory access on the part of all countries and their citizens to the product of the LANDSAT system. The United States has taken positive steps to implement Nixon's 1969 statement and its open access policy, ranging from permitting other countries direct access to LANDSAT spacecraft through their own ground stations to providing technical assistance to countries wishing to use LANDSAT information. Any attempts to reverse the policy—to change the expectations or to modify the patterns of use that have evolved over the past decade—will be certain to create international tension.

The current state of international thinking on remote sensing at the governmental level is perhaps best reflected in the report of the 1982 United Nations Unispace Conference. This report noted that although remote sensing is still in a "preoperational" stage, "it is only a matter of time—and a short time—before this very important application attains a completely operational status." Given this reality, the report recommended that "agreement should be reached on principles governing satellite remote sensing. Work to this effect . . . should be continued as a matter of priority, aimed at speedy agreement on such principles." In addition to a framework of general principles, concern was expressed that:

> Satellite operators should give assurance about continuity of data flows and provide indications about estimated lifetime [of] preoperational and operational systems in order to help all countries, in particular the developing countries. Compatibility of various systems and data formats is another important aspect. . . .

> Since remote sensing can collect data from all countries, it is therefore possible to use shared or internationally-owned remote sensing satellites. . . .

> It is suggested that a study be undertaken to assess the need for and the viability of a worldwide remote sensing system. Such a study could consider various ways of providing remote sensing data—including regional, bilateral, multilateral, and international arrangements—with the users bearing therefore the development, production, launching and operation costs of the satellites. Assuming that any one of these systems could provide assurance of continuity of data formats, avoid forced obsolescence of equipment, and enable the development and use of standardized data analysis software, the study should in particular indicate the comparative cost of such systems to the users vis-a-vis systems currently in operation and/or under development.

A persistent issue in international discussions is "a possible situation in which data are not available to the sensed State but are available for commercial and other forms of exploitation by another country." At the conference

Some delegations expressed serious concern regarding the dissemination of data collected by remote sensing satellites. While several developed and developing countries felt that such information should be freely available to an interested State, most delegations felt that the consent of the sensed State should be required before data could be released to a third State, organization, or third party. Some developing nations felt that the consent of the second State must be obtained before sensing, even if the information was not to be disseminated beyond the concerned States; some felt that in no case should the information be available to any State other than the sensor and sensed States. Most representatives expressing an opinion on the point agreed that priority in access to data must be accorded the sensed State.

The central points made by potential foreign users of land remote sensing products are:

The need for continuity in operation and overall system characteristics.

The need for guaranteed access at an acceptable price with provisions to avoid intrusions on national sovereignty.

The United States has attempted to deal with these pressures from the international community in ways that maximize the following U.S. policy objectives:

Maintaining U.S. leadership in space technology.

Assisting the economic and social developments of the developing countries.

Promoting international cooperation as a means of achieving common objectives as an example of the benefits of harmonious relationships among nations.

Ensuring U.S. ability to use space technology for its own national objectives, including operation of earth observation systems by both civil and national security agencies.

Enhancing the development of the U.S. economy by fostering new industries, new employment opportunities and new markets for U.S. firms.

In seeking to achieve these objectives the U.S. government has entered into a series of legal and political obligations. These include:

The provision of the Outer Space Treaty of 1967 that requires "States party to the Treaty" to "bear international responsibility for national activities in outer space, . . . whether such activities are carried on by governmental agencies or by nongovernmental entities," such nongovernmental activities "require authorization and continuing supervision by the appropriate State party to the Treaty."

A series of agreements negotiated with other governments to permit their access, under mutually agreeable terms, to the output of U.S. remote sensing satellites using foreign-owned and operated ground stations.

Through U.S. advocacy of the policy of open nondiscriminatory access in U.N. forums and otherwise, a fairly explicit obligation not to create either formal or informal (such as unaffordable prices or continuing changes in technical format or the system output) barriers to any country, organization or individual who wants to use the system, with all users receiving nondiscriminatory treatment.

Through negotiations in the International Telecommunications Union, agreement not to use the frequencies allocated for communicating remote sensing data streams to ground stations for any other purposes.

Given this melange of concerns, objectives and obligations, international issues suggested included:

a. Future International Negotiations

Over coming years, as remote sensing capabilities evolve, there are sure to be continuing international negotiations. These will take place in the United Nations, other permanent multilateral organizations, ad hoc . . . multilateral groups, or on a bilateral basis. Participation in these negotiations may vary, depending on the framework adopted for U.S. remote sensing activities. If a private sector option is selected, what international role, if any, will the private sector operator want the U.S. government to play? What role will U.S. government agencies believe is required to protect U.S. public interests?

b. Evolution of International Principles to Govern Remote Sensing

The interests of a commercial operator might sometimes conflict with the long standing U.S. policy in this area; one way of increasing the value of remote sensing products is to limit their dissemination. Another is by providing priority access to some users. The U.S. Department of Commerce Land Remote Sensing Advisory Committee recommended that there be a government requirement "that the operator, whether it be the government and/or the private sector, subscribe to the open sky policy—meaning that anyone, anywhere, in any country can purchase the data at equitable prices." The current government policy, as enunciated in President Reagan's space policy statement of July 4, 1982, is to "support the public, nondiscriminatory direct readout of data from federal civil systems to foreign ground stations and the provision of data to foreign users under specified conditions." The policy is silent on requirements for nongovernment systems.

One way to restrict access to remote sensing data is to adopt policies that are explicitly discriminatory. Another means is to price certain data (such as "quick looks") in ways that exclude some potentially interested users. This possibility has been noted by the international community; for example, a Romanian spokesman told COPUOS in the spring of 1983 of his concern about "the relatively new question of considering satellite remote sensing activities as operational, on a purely commercial basis, with the immediate consequence of augmenting by several times the costs of remote sensing products. Under these conditions, effective access to the data is practically possible only for developed countries."

How will considerations of cost recovery and commercial profit interact with an open access policy as an operational system evolves? Will system products be provided to poorer countries on a subsidized basis? What are the interactions among U.S. policy objectives vis-á-vis developing countries, the economic viability of an operational system and the general concern of avoiding tension? Although poorer countries may in the long-term have the prospect of receiving the most benefits from remote sensing, who will make the investments required for them to be effective users, and thus expand the market for the system? In the short run, would more expensive products from a private commercial system drive away non-U.S. users?

c. Meaning of U.S. Leadership in Space Technology

Current U.S. policy is to "maintain United States space leadership," particularly in "critical aspects of space, applications, and technology"; in these areas, the objective is "preeminence." The meaning of this policy with respect to remote sensing technology is unclear. Given the emerging foreign competition in the field, how will the U.S. government respond: by a continued program of R&D in the remote sensing area, keyed to staying ahead of competing systems; by reliance on the private sector to develop a superior system for the United States, without continuing government R&D subsidies; by providing subsidies or incentives beyond R&D to a commercial operator in order to help it best foreign competition and thus bring the benefits of a growing remote sensing industry (sales of equipment, training of non-U.S. personnel, consulting services, etc.) to the U.S. economy? Or is civil remote sensing not a "critical" area, and thus not one that requires U.S. leadership? What would be the costs in terms of more general foreign policy or economic objectives of a non-U.S. system dominating the world market for remote sensing? This could happen if no commercial system is established and the U.S. government withdraws from remote sensing activity after LANDSAT-5 reaches the end of its lifetime, or if the U.S. commercial venture is unsuccessful.

*   *   *

4. U.S. National Security Issues

It is a matter of public record that the United States uses earth observation satellites as one means of gathering intelligence information with respect to other areas of the world; these satellites are assets of extremely high value to U.S. national security interests. The capabilities of these satellites have also been extensively discussed, and in most parameters, they clearly exceed those available for civilian use. However, it is also reasonable to suggest that some information with intelligence significance can be extracted from existing civilian land observation satellites and that present national security systems may not duplicate all capabilities available in civilian satellites (for example, coverage in particular spectral bands). Thus, there are unavoidable national security aspects to the routine operation of a civilian land remote sensing system. In times of international tensions or crises, these aspects become more pronounced; the U.S. government will want to ensure that its national security agencies will be able to obtain immediate control over all earth observation systems.

Just as earth observation systems have both civilian and national security applications, the technologies on which they are based have "dual use" characteristics. Capabilities developed initially for national security purposes have potential relevance to civilian uses, and the technologies involved in sensors, data processing, image interpretation, etc., are sensitive in terms of export control regulations.

Given these realities, resulting national security issues include:

a. "Open Skies" Precedent and Ability
to Carry Out National Security Observations
One not quite incidental fallout from the U.S. policy of open, nondiscriminatory access to the products of civil earth observation systems is the creation of a climate in which all U.S. observation satellites can function without drawing protests from the countries of the world. Any modification of an open access policy, particularly by a private operator seeking competitive advantage or increased economic returns, could change this situation. For example, in the wake of the recent Administration announcement of its intent to transfer ownership and operation of civilian earth observation satellites to the private sector, one Canadian official indicated that his government was "very concerned," saying "we have a satellite looking down at our country and we don't call it a spy satellite because we have nondiscriminatory access to it. . . . But if we were charged 100 times as much by some company, then we might have to begin to wonder about this."

b. Tradeoffs Between National Security Interests
and Economic Competitiveness Concerns
Under continued government ownership and operation of the land remote sensing satellite system, past patterns of coordination between national security agencies and civilian agencies such as NASA and NOAA would likely persist. Some civilian sector objectives differ from those of the intelligence community, as illustrated by the conservative position adopted by national security agencies toward making advanced sensor capabilities available for civil sector use. On the whole, however, the relationship between the two sectors of the government has worked well. The potential for the transfer of the system out of government control does create serious questions regarding the extent of government supervision necessary and possible. National security-related areas for which a possible regulatory regime might engage itself include: spectral resolution, center frequency and tunable range; spatial resolution; geographic coverage; timeliness of data availability; tasking procedures and controls; and data dissemination policies.

The kind of quiet coordination that is possible within the government would be much more difficult to maintain in a relationship with a private sector entity. In the instance of private sector operation of the system, it becomes very important to recognize the need to temper national security considerations when designing an appropriate regulatory regime. Due regard must be given to the international market in which the private entity is operating, so that regulatory practices do not seriously erode the system's competitive position. A private operator may find, for example, that improved sensor characteristics may be required in order to keep itself economically solvent.

From the national security point of view, those sensor characteristics may present problems either in terms of revealing sensitive U.S. technological capabilities or in terms of providing images of the United States or other countries from which intelligence information could be extracted. If sensor capabilities were to be improved, then the intelligence community might want to involve itself in the process of determining appropriateness of data for dissemination. [NOTE: Precisely this issue has since arisen in the United States concerning civilian systems—see Chapter 8, *infra.*]

Reaching a balance between considerations of national security on one hand, and the need to develop a high performance, economically competitive system on the other, will continue to be a very difficult and complicated issue as land remote sensing satellite technology develops. Further aggravating this balance is the fact that U.S. national security interests and controls are in a large part derived from a different set of motivations and values than the potential security controls that might be applied to the French, European, or Japanese systems. Thus there is unlikely to be easy agreement among operators of remote sensing systems over what are acceptable limits on system performance from a national security perspective.

c. Export Control Regulations and Land Remote Sensing

There is heightened concern in recent years that U.S.-developed technology is being acquired by its adversaries and used as a major basis for their military capabilities. There is also recognition that the export of products and services based on advanced technology is a major source of positive U.S. balance-of-trade. Creating an operational U.S. land observation system aimed at dominating the international market brings with it an export control issue: will the United States aggressively seek to supply all elements required for other countries to participate in such a system, e.g., ground stations, computing capabilities and image interpretation capabilities, or will concern over the export of sensitive dual-use technologies limit the ability of the United States to capitalize fully on such a market opportunity?

National security concerns such as those embodied in the last two issues discussed above, in the context of a privately operated system, must be addressed within the framework of whatever regulatory regime is created to oversee such a system.

NOTES

1. Since Logsdon & Monk's article, the remote sensing industry has experienced considerable growth, with new entries from France (SPOT Image) and the Soviet Union (Soyuz Karta). In addition, a number of American media interests, spurred by the use of SPOT and LANDSAT images of the Chernobyl accident and scenes from the Iran/Iraq war, have discussed the possibility of a "MediaSat"—that is a civilian satellite with resolution approaching that of military reconnaissance satellites. This has created considerable debate within the United States already (see Chapter 8, *infra*); if such a satellite is actually launched (which is unlikely until well into the 1990s), it is likely to promote protests from a number of countries, although it appears that such a system would be legal under the new principles on remote sensing. *See* George Paul Sloup, MediaSat, Gray Reconnaissance, and the New United Nations Principles on Remote Sensing, paper presented at the 38th Congress of the International Aeronautical Federation, Brighton, U.K., October 10, 1987. *See also* Merges & Reynolds, News Media Satellites and the First Amendment, 3 High Technology Law Journal 1 (1988); Reynolds, The First Amendment and Satellite Newsgathering, The Air & Space Lawyer, Fall, 1987, at 3 *et seq.*

2. The U.S. law governing the operation of civilian remote sensing systems is the Land Remote Sensing Commercialization Act of 1984, Pub. L. 98–365, 98 Stat. 451, codified at 15 U.S.C. §§ 4201 *et seq.* and scattered sections of 49 U.S.C., implemented by regulations at 15 CFR 960 *et seq.* In keeping with the U.S. policies described above, it requires the operator to make all data available to parties on equal terms. While this may be good from an international relations standpoint, it might (as Logsdon & Monk suggest) make it difficult for a commercial operator to succeed in the marketplace. For more on these topics, see Chapter 8, *infra*.

3. In January of 1987 the United Nations Committee on the Peaceful Uses of Outer Space adopted new principles on remote sensing. The following excerpt from a paper by Professor DeSaussure explains why this latest round in the continuing debate over the legal status of remote sensing has not done much to settle matters.

Hamilton DeSaussure, Remote Sensing: The Interaction of Domestic and International Law. Paper presented at the 38th Congress of the International Astronautical Federation, Brighton, U.K., October 10–17, 1987

On January 22 of this year the General Assembly adopted principles relating to remote sensing of the Earth from space. The Principles had been drafted within and approved by the U.N. Committee on Peaceful Uses of Outer Space (COPUOS). The road to consensus within COPUOS

had been a long and tortuous one. The legal and political problems raised
by remote sensing activity were first examined at the First U.N. Conference
on the Peaceful Uses of Outer Space in Vienna in 1968. Argentina was
the first nation, in June 1970, to submit a formal draft to govern remote
sensing. A Working Group was then established with the Legal Subcommittee of COPUOS to work out rules which would be acceptable to the
COPUOS members. From the outset there was disagreement on fundamental principles pertaining to international law and state sovereignty. One
major dispute related to the question of prior consent. Argentina, Brazil,
and other Latin American countries believed that the states whose resources
were the subject of remote sensing had a proprietary right to the data
about their wealth derived from this new technique. Their position was
that certain U.N. resolutions providing that states have permanent sovereignty over their own natural wealth and resources were declaratory of
international law, and that information about these physical assets was
included in the concept of sovereignty. Therefore, the prior consent of the
surveyed state was necessary so as not to intrude upon sovereign rights.
. . . From the outset, the United States has rejected any notion that
international law requires the operator of a remote sensing system to secure
approval of the sensed states. The United States opposed the Argentine/
Brazil draft on the basis it was inconsistent with the provisions of the
Outer Space Treaty which provide that outer space shall be free for
exploration and use by all States without discrimination. A second major
dispute revolved around the right to have access and to disseminate the
data retrieved by remote sensing. The position of Latin American states,
following their view on sovereign rights, would accord a priority of access
to the retrieved data to the target state. In addition the target state would
have the final decision as to distribution to third parties. Again the United
States and other industrial nations were in opposition to any limitations
on the open dissemination of the acquired data. In the view of the United
States, this would conflict with the principle of free use. It would also be
contrary to the Universal Declaration of Human Rights which provides
for the freedom to receive and impart information regardless of frontiers.
Certain compromises between the opposing views were attempted within
the Working Group. One in particular was a joint proposal of the Soviet
and French delegates to divide into two classes data retrieved through
remote sensing. On the one hand, data acquired with a spatial resolution
of more than fifty meters would be classified as global and subject to an
open sensing and dissemination regime. Data retrieved through the use of
finer sensors, resolving objects of less than fifty meters, would be classified
as local. Local data would be subject to the control of the sensed state
which would decide on any distribution. Consensus on this compromise
could not be achieved in the face of the strong objections of the United
States to any curtailment of the open dissemination of basic data. Other
debated issues included the matter of defining the scope of remote sensing,
whether human activity was to be covered, any limitations on the spectral

resolution, and the role of the United Nations in supervising and regulating a remote sensing regime.

After debating these and other questions for seventeen years, consensus was reached within the Working Group in April 1986. The draft principles were approved by the full committee in June 1986 and were adopted by the General Assembly, as noted above, in January 1987. It is unfortunate the Resolution does not represent substantial progress in the development of a remote sensing legal order. This is not because of any lack of hard work by the COPUOS membership. The maximum level of agreement was achieved in a forum where consensus on all issues is required. Rather, failure to reach substantive agreement on crucial issues was the result of conflicting views on sovereignty, proprietary rights, freedom of information, and privacy. As the membership of COPUOS expanded and the increased value of the derived information became apparent, agreement on many of the ideological disputes became impossible. The result is a set of U.N. principles which are little more than a reaffirmation of those ideals incorporated into the major space treaties.

Principle I defines the term "remote sensing" as the sensing of the Earth's surface from space for the purpose of "improving natural resources management, land use and the protection of the environment." In the past some Soviet writers objected to including the word "environment" in the definition because that could be taken to encompass human activity as well. The United States and other western nations have interpreted "natural resources" to include the entire physical environment including human activity. Some earlier drafts omitted from the definition altogether a reference to the environment, while others did not include the phrase "the protection of. . . " . As finally approved, the scope of activity included in the definition remains an issue for unilateral determination. As will be seen below, the United States position seems to include human activity within the acceptable parameters of this activity.

Principle I also defines the terms "primary data," "processed data" and "analyzed information." *Primary data* is the raw data acquired by remote spaceborne sensors. *Processed data* means the products resulting from the enhancement of the primary data. *Analyzed information* means the processed data as transformed by its interpretation and combination with other information. These classifications are useful, but as it turns out from a reading of the entire resolution, not particularly significant since the rules for distribution as to each class seem to be the same. (See discussion of Principle XII.)

Principle II requires remote sensing activities to be carried out for the benefit and in the interests of all countries. This is virtually a word for word reaffirmation of Article I, paragraph 1 of the Outer Space Treaty. In conformity with the Outer Space Treaty, Principle I also provides that particular consideration be given to the needs of the developing countries. However there is no transformation of these general expressions into practical rules. Therefore, Principle II adds nothing to existing treaty law on the use of remote sensing.

Principle III is also redundant. It provides that remote sensing activities shall be conducted in accordance with international law, the U.N. Charter and other relevant treaties. The language is virtually identical to that of Article III of the Outer Space Treaty.

Principle IV provides that remote sensing will be conducted in accordance with the principles contained in Article I of the Outer Space Treaty. This requirement had already been stated in Principle II. However, Principle IV adds a provision which is not repetitious of prior treaty language and could leave the door open for further debate on the sovereign rights of the subjacent states. This is the provision that remote sensing activities shall be conducted with respect for the principle of full and permanent sovereignty of all states and peoples over their own wealth and natural resources. Further, this activity is not to be conducted in a manner detrimental to their legitimate rights and interests. Does this raise new issues regarding the U.N. Resolutions on permanent sovereignty over natural resources and the degree to which information about natural wealth is included within sovereign rights? Whether this language could imply any property rights in the target state, or a priority of access to the retrieved data, is far from clear. At the least, this language can rekindle debate as to what is included within a nation's resources and what is activity detrimental to the "legitimate" rights of surveyed states.

Principles V through VIII are mainly exhortations for participating states to cooperate. Joint ventures by two or more states shall be pursuant to "equitable and mutually acceptable terms" (V), through "feasible" agreements or arrangements (VI), upon "mutually agreed terms" (VII) or by international cooperation (VIII). All such provisions leave the specifics for participatory remote sensing activity to the future.

Principle IX usefully provides that states conducting remote sensing programs will inform the Secretary General of the U.N. of them "in accordance with Article IV of the Registration Treaty and Article XI of the Outer Space Treaty." Left open is the extent to which information must be supplied. It is interesting to compare the general obligation to inform the Secretary General of a remote sensing program under Principle IX, with the detailed information required by Article IV of the Registration Convention. . . . Principle IX also requires that "other relevant information will be provided to other states, particularly those developing states affected by this activity to the greatest extent feasible and practicable." Principle IX, standing alone, entitles the target state to nothing more than that which the sensing state wishes to make available. If any duty to disclose more than raw data exists, it must be found in Principle IV calling for respect for the principle of full and permanent sovereignty of all states over their own wealth and resources.

Principles X and XI place a positive duty on sensing states to disclose any information which could help another state avert or mitigate a natural disaster or avoid harm to the earth's natural environment. This would include more than the basic data. It would include the processed and analyzed product as well.

Principle XII is the heart of the U.N. resolution. It provides that the sensed state shall have access to the primary and processed data concerning its own territory *on a non-discriminatory basis and on reasonable cost terms* as soon as such data is produced (underscoring supplied). In addition, the sensed state shall also have access to available analyzed information concerning its territory on the same terms, with due regard to the need of the developing countries. The entitlement of the sensed state to all three categories (primary, processed, analyzed) is the same. The nondiscriminatory access provision seems to negate any inference drawn from the "permanent sovereignty over natural resources language" that subjacent states have proprietary rights. Sensed state entitlement is only on an equal basis with other states. It would have been helpful if this principle had elaborated somewhat more on the nature and full extent of the nondiscriminatory provision. When the sensing state, or a private entity under its national jurisdiction elects to retain exclusive possession of its data, can it for economic reasons deny it to target states, even the developing ones? Why should processed data be included in the duty not to discriminate, and the same not be said of analyzed information? Should the target state ever be denied the information about its own resources upon payment of reasonable costs?

Principle XIII requires operating states to consult with sensed states in order to make available opportunities for participation. The role of the private operator is not mentioned. When the State licenses a private operator, has the licensee a public duty to consult with the target state? If so, what must be disclosed? In which categories of data (raw, processed, analyzed) may the licensee place restrictions on the target state as to the use of the data? The level and depth of such consultations could be a matter for some disagreement. Presumably a private entity would not be enthusiastic about divulging all of its objectives, its know how, or the results of its investigations, or in entering consultations with officials of a foreign government.

Principle XIV recognizes state responsibility for national remote sensing activities in space whether conducted by government, non-governmental, or private entities and complies with Article VI of the Outer Space Treaty.

Principle XV provides for dispute resolution through "established procedures." It adds little to the notion that settlements should be in accordance with international law. Dispute resolution through a variety of possible alternatives from negotiation to international adjudication is well established in state practice and international decisions, but may not be relevant in the context of the private operator who will wish to settle his disputes within the framework of his own national legal system.

Perhaps the U.N. Principles have been left deliberately general and nonspecific in order that the states having control over remote sensing systems will have a large degree of flexibility in developing the rule of law. It is the proprietor states whose practices will largely shape the remote sensing regime of the future. The United States was the first nation to pronounce an open-skies policy for remote sensing activity. It is now taking the lead in setting forth a specific framework for the private enterprise operations. The United States launched the first remote sensing satellite in 1960. Since then the United States has launched five earth resource satellites, known as Landsats, with a sixth scheduled for delivery to a private company. . . . The United States is not alone in commercializing remote sensing. Sales from the French SPOT system of remote sensing are expected to exceed ten million dollars. According to the New York Times, the Soviet Government is also "seeking big profits" from commercial remote sensing ventures.

The Act went into effect July 17, 1984. The Secretary of Commerce was delegated responsibility for the Landsat system, including the orbit, operation and disposition of Landsats 1, 2, 3, 4 and 5. The Secretary was also made responsible for providing data to foreign ground stations pursuant to agreements between the United States and nations operating those stations. The Act provided for the licensing of private remote-sensing space systems under regulations to be promulgated. The National Oceanic and Atmospheric Administration (NOAA) was delegated the responsibility for drafting procedures for licensing private operators. In March 1986, NOAA published proposed rules and invited public comment. On July 10, 1987 the rules were made final and published. Many of the legal issues which had been debated within COPUOS while drafting the U.N. Principles, are covered in the Act and implementing rules (hereinafter called the Regulations). [For more on U.S. laws and regulations governing remote sensing, see Chapter 8.]

Since none of the multilateral space treaties cover remote sensing as a distinct regime, it is left to the practice of states to define the law in this area. The U.N. Resolution on Remote Sensing is simply too weak. Even if it were not, one state after another has declared that U.N. resolutions do not constitute binding obligations upon states.

*   *   *

Ever since the launch of Sputnik I in 1957, the development of customary rules has been fast moving. Technological advances, and the rapid expansion of state participation in space activity, demand certainty in the rules of space use. The centuries through which maritime law had time to develop is a luxury which cannot be afforded in outer space. It is left to states which pioneer the field of remote sensing to develop the law. By clearly placing civilian remote sensing in the private sector, the United States is the first state to establish a role for the private entrepreneur in this field. Commercial activity will expand into many areas of space exploration and use. The United States remote sensing legislation is a confirmation of that fact. In deciding the effect of domestic legislation on the development of maritime law, United States Supreme Court Justice Strong wrote more than a century ago that "many of the usages which prevail (in international law as to maritime navigation) . . . and which have the force of law, doubtless originated in the positive prescriptions of some single state . . . but which when generally accepted became of universal obligation." The birth of the United States Land Remote Sensing Act and its regulatory implementation, reflect the "positive prescriptions of a single state" which lay the cornerstone for a complete remote sensing regime enveloping both the public and the private operator.

[The principles themselves follow.]

Principles Relating to Remote Sensing of the Earth from Space

Principle I

For the purposes of these principles with respect to remote sensing activities:

(a) The term "remote sensing" means the sensing of the Earth's surface from space by making use of the properties of electromagnetic waves emitted, reflected or diffracted by the sensed objects, for the purpose of improving natural resources management, land use and the protection of the environment;

(b) The term "primary data" means the raw data that are acquired by remote sensors borne by the space object and that are transmitted or delivered to the ground from space by telemetry in the form of electro-magnetic signals, by photographic film, magnetic tape or any other means;

(c) The term "processed data" means the products resulting from the processing of the primary data, needed to make such data usable;

(d) The term "analysed information" means the information resulting from the interpretation of processed data, inputs of data and knowledge from other sources;

(e) The term "remote sensing activities" means the operation of remote sensing space systems, primary data collection and storage stations, and activities in processing, interpreting and disseminating the processed data.

Principle II

Remote sensing activities shall be carried out for the benefit and in the interests of all countries, irrespective of their degree of economic, social or scientific and technological development, and taking into particular consideration the needs of the developing countries.

Principle III

Remote sensing activities shall be conducted in accordance with international law, including the Charter of the United Nations, the [1967] Treaty on Principles Governing the Activities of States in the Exploration and

Use of Outer Space, including the Moon and other Celestial Bodies, and the relevant instruments of the International Telecommunications Union.

Principle IV

Remote sensing activities shall be conducted in accordance with the principles contained in article I of the Treaty on Principles Governing the Activities of States in the Exploration and Use of Outer Space, including the Moon and other Celestial Bodies, which, in particular provides that the exploration and use of outer space shall be carried out for the benefit and in the interests of all countries, irrespective of their degree of economic or scientific development, and stipulates the principle of freedom of exploration and use of outer space on the basis of equality. These activities shall be conducted on the basis of respect for the principle of full and permanent sovereignty of all States and peoples over their own wealth and natural resources, with due regard to the rights and interests, in accordance with international law, of other States and entities under their jurisdiction. Such activities shall not be conducted in a manner detrimental to the legitimate rights and interests of the sensed State.

Principle V

States carrying out remote sensing activities shall promote international cooperation in these activities. To this end, they shall make available to other States opportunities for participation therein. Such participation shall be based in each case on equitable and mutually acceptable terms.

Principle VI

In order to maximize the availability of benefits from remote sensing activities, States are encouraged, through agreements or other arrangements, to provide for the establishment and operation of data collecting and storage stations and processing and interpretation facilities, in particular within the framework of regional agreements or arrangements wherever feasible.

Principle VII

States participating in remote sensing activities shall make available technical assistance to other interested States on mutually agreed terms.

Principle VIII

The United Nations and the relevant agencies within the United Nations system shall promote international co-operation, including technical assistance and co-ordination in the area of remote sensing.

Principle IX

In accordance with article IV of the Convention on Registration of Objects Launched into Outer Space and article XI of the Treaty on Principles Governing the Activities of States in the Exploration and Use of Outer Space, including the Moon and Other Celestial Bodies, a State carrying out a programme of remote sensing shall inform the Secretary-General of the United Nations. It shall, moreover, make available any other relevant information to the greatest extent feasible and practicable to any other State, particularly any developing country that is affected by the programme, at its request.

Principle X

Remote sensing shall promote the protection of the Earth's natural environment. To this end, States participating in remote sensing activities that have identified information in their possession that is capable of averting any phenomenon harmful to the Earth's natural environment shall disclose such information to States concerned.

Principle XI

Remote sensing shall promote the protection of mankind from natural disasters. To this end, States participating in remote sensing activities that have identified processed data and analysed information in their possession that may be useful to States affected by natural disasters, or likely to be affected by impending natural disasters, shall transmit such data and information to States concerned as promptly as possible.

Principle XII

As soon as the primary data and the processed data concerning the territory under its jurisdiction are produced, the sensed State shall have access to them on a non-discriminatory basis and on reasonable cost terms. The sensed State shall also have access to the available analysed information concerning the territory under its jurisdiction in the possession of any State participating in remote sensing activities on the same basis and terms, taking particularly into account the needs and interests of the developing countries.

Principle XIII

To promote and intensify international co-operation, especially with regard to the needs of developing countries, a State carrying out remote sensing of the Earth from space shall, upon request, enter into consultations with a State whose territory is sensed in order to make available opportunities for participation and enhance the mutual benefits to be derived therefrom.

Principle XIV

In compliance with article VI of the Treaty on Principles Governing the Activities of States in the Exploration and Use of Outer Space, including the Moon and Other Celestial Bodies, States operating remote sensing satellites shall bear international responsibility for their activities and assure that such activities are conducted in accordance with these principles and the norms of international law, irrespective of whether such activities are carried out by governmental or non-governmental entities or through international organizations to which such States are parties. This principle is without prejudice to the applicability of the norms of international law on State responsibility for remote sensing activities.

Principle XV

Any dispute resulting from the application of these principles shall be resolved through the established procedures for the peaceful settlement of disputes.

RESCUE AND RETURN OF ASTRONAUTS

The Agreement on the Rescue of Astronauts, the Return of Astronauts, and Objects Launched into Outer Space of 1968, 19 U.S.T. 7570, T.I.A.S. 6599, expands upon the language in Article V of the Outer Space Treaty, which declares that astronauts are to be regarded as "Envoys of Mankind" and to be rendered "all possible assistance." (See Chapter 3.) The Agreement calls for a state in which a spacecraft crashes or a state operating in space that is in a position to assist astronauts in distress to conduct rescue operations (if it is a manned craft) and to speedily return both astronauts and hardware to the launching state.

The Agreement focuses (largely because of technological constraints at the time of its drafting) on earthbased events, though its language applies to space rescues as well. It leaves many questions unanswered, however: What if a rescued astronaut wishes to defect to the rescuing country? The Agreement's language is mandatory and does not admit of any exceptions based on the wishes of the astronauts involved, although other international law (such as the United Nations Charter and the Universal Declaration of Human Rights) at least seems to suggest otherwise. Some states signing the agreement reserved the right to grant political asylum to an astronaut. *See* U.N. Doc. A/AC.105/C.2/SR.87, 2 February 1968 pp. 10 *et seq.* (this position taken by Australia and France). The United States rejects this position, as do most nations, on the ground that requests for asylum may be coerced—particularly when the requestor is the victim of a recent space accident and may not be in full possession of his or her faculties. *See* U.N. Doc. A/AC.105/C.2/SR.86, 9 February 1968, at 8; U.S. Congress, Committee on Foreign Relations, Hearings on the Treaty on Outer Space, 90th Cong., 1st Sess. 1967 at 27. Other questions: How should rescue expenses be treated? Is the launching state obligated to reimburse the rescuing state? What if a rescue attempt is bungled—will the rescuing state be liable, or does some sort of Good Samaritan principle apply? Should there be such a principle, since rescue is mandatory? In light of these questions, it may be time for an update of the Agreement in order to avoid confusion or ill-will. This has been suggested by Nathan Goldman. Goldman, Transition or Confusion in the Law of Outer Space, in International Space Policy: Legal, Economic and Strategic Options for the Twentieth Century and Beyond 157, 162 (D. Papp & J. McIntyre eds. 1987).

REGISTRATION OF SPACECRAFT

The Convention on the Registration of Objects Launched into Outer Space of 1976, 28 U.S.T. 695, T.I.A.S. 7762, provides that each signatory shall maintain a registry of all objects that it launches into earth orbit or beyond. The launching state shall also provide to the Secretary-General of the United Nations information concerning each object on its registry, including: the name of the launching state or states, a designation or number, the location of the launch, the object's basic orbital parameters (including nodal period, inclination, apogee, and perigee), and the general function of the object. Nations are also to provide the Secretary-General with information regarding objects on their registry that have ceased to be in orbit.

Where an object is launched by more than one nation, the nations involved are to determine which of them shall register the object. This is not simply an administrative matter, since the state on whose registry the object is carried retains full jurisdiction and control over the object under Article 8 of the Outer Space Treaty of 1967—although Article 7 of the Space Treaty and Article I of the Liability Convention of 1972 do not assign responsibility on the basis of registry but on the basis of who is responsible for the launching of the spacecraft, and Article IV of the Liability Convention allows for joint and several liability in the case of multiple launching states. This leaves open the possibility of one nation having jurisdiction over an object (a matter of considerable significance with regard to manned craft, see U.S. Congress Office of Technology Assessment, Space Stations and the Law: Selected Legal Issues—Background Paper [1986]; Reynolds, Book Review, 27 Jurimetrics: Journal of Law, Science & Technology 431, 434–35 [1987]) while another bears international responsibility therefor. Although such matters are easily resolvable through negotiation, lawyers involved in such matters (for example drafting memoranda of understanding regarding joint missions or space stations) should bear such matters in mind. Typically, launch services contracts specify that the space object launched will be placed on the registry of a particular nation and provide that the launching entity will ensure that that is done. For more on this topic, see Chapter 8.

SPACE ENVIRONMENTAL MATTERS

Because the space environment is infinite in size, the very concept of worrying about maintaining the space environment seems absurd to many, particularly as (at the time of this writing) no life is known to exist beyond the Earth's biosphere. Yet in fact the outer space environment has already been the subject of considerable pollution, and some space environmental problems demand immediate attention if they are not to create serious problems here on earth.

Space pollution dates back to the dawn of the space age. In 1962 a series of very high altitude nuclear tests, code named Fishbowl, led to the creation of an artificial radiation belt around the earth that damaged a number of satellites and interfered with scientific experiments. At around the same time, Project West Ford, a misguided communications experiment, established a ring of copper dipole antennas around the earth; these were supposed to serve a primitive relay function by reflecting radio signals back to the surface. Radio astronomers raised a furor regarding these antennas, which threatened their observations. Because of negative public reaction, neither experiment has been repeated. For more on these and other issues see Gorove, Pollution and Outer Space: A Legal Analysis and Appraisal, 5 New York University Journal of International Law & Politics 53 (1972).

Another space environmental issue is the question of contamination, both "forward" and "back." "Forward contamination" occurs when, for example, microorganisms from earth are carried to other planets or celestial bodies. Such contamination could conceivably have disastrous effects: for example, if earth-based organisms were able to survive on the surface of Mars they could institute drastic and unplanned changes in its climate, as well as greatly complicating efforts by scientists to determine whether Mars supports life of its own. In order to prevent this from happening, space probes are sterilized prior to launch, a practice originated very early in the space age. *See* Horowitz, Sharp & Davies, Planetary Contamination I: The Problem and the Agreements, 155 Science 1501 (1967); Murray, Davies & Eckman, Planetary Contamination II: Soviet and U.S. Practices and Policies, 155 Science 1505 (1967); Sagan, Leventhal & Lederberg, Contamination of Mars, 159 Science 1191 (1968).

"Back contamination" involves the contamination of earth by foreign microorganisms (or conceivably other substances not necessarily "alive" by terrestrial standards but still capable of causing problems). Such contamination is unlikely for two reasons: first, there is (as of this writing) no evidence that life exists outside earth's biosphere, and second, any life that could live, say, on Mars or the Jovian moons would probably be poorly adapted to earth and hence not much of a threat. Still, earth history is full of cases in which whole peoples were decimated by the introduction of diseases to which they had no previous exposure, and science fiction is full of accounts of such horrors being brought to earth from space. In response to such fears, astronauts returning from the Moon were quarantined (along with their samples) in the Lunar Receiving Laboratory until scientists and physicians were certain that no contamination had occurred. *See* McClane, *et al.*, Lunar Receiving Laboratory, 155 Science 525 (1967).

Such precautions, in the case of future manned or unmanned missions, are required by the Outer Space Treaty, as discussed in Chapter 3, *supra.* Existing U.S. regulations designed to protect against extraterrestrial contamination are discussed in Chapter 8, *infra.* They do not, however, address other, more immediately pressing space environmental problems.

The most pressing such problem is the matter of earth orbital pollution, or space debris. As was mentioned earlier in this chapter in the context of liability issues, space near the earth is becoming filled with an increasing quantity of debris from spent boosters, defunct satellites, and the aftermath of space weapons tests. Since such debris travels at enormous speed (approximately 18,000 miles per hour in most cases), even small fragments can do enormous damage. Worse yet, collisions between space debris and other space objects create still more fragments, which themselves threaten to do damage.

At some point this process can become self-sustaining, a chain reaction known as the "Kessler effect" because the pioneering analysis was done by Donald Kessler. *See* Kessler & Cour-Palais, Collision Frequency of Artificial Satellites: The Creation of a Debris Belt, 83 Journal of Geophysical Research 2637 (1978). At present, it is impossible to tell how close we are to the creation of a self-sustaining debris belt, but it does appear that the artificial debris flux in near earth orbits exceeds the natural meteorite flux—meaning that already a spacecraft in those orbits is more likely to collide with a piece of space junk than with a natural meteorite. *See* Kessler, Earth Orbital Pollution, in Beyond Spaceship Earth: Environmental Ethics and the Solar System, 47, 48–49 (E. Hargrove ed. 1986); David Enrico Reibel, Prevention of Orbital Debris (paper presented at 38th annual congress of the International Astronautics Federation, Brighton, U.K., October 10, 1987). As of this writing, there is evidence that orbital debris is not merely a menace to navigation in space, but may in fact be working substantial changes in the near-earth space environment. *See, e.g.,* Konradi, Effect of the Orbital Debris Environment on the High-Energy Van Allen Proton Belt, 242 Science 1283 (1988). On space pollution issues generally, see Restatement (Third) of Foreign Relations Law § 601 (1987), esp. at note 6.

Not only does the proliferation of space debris pose a threat to space activities, but it could pose an even greater threat to those of us on earth. The United States and the Soviet Union (together with, increasingly, other powers) depend greatly on space resources to support military intelligence, early-warning, communications, and other functions. If, in a crisis, a key satellite were to be accidentally lost, that loss could be blamed on an adversary and could lead to a potentially-disastrous response. As space analyst Daniel Deudney has said, "The Archduke Francis Ferdinand of World War III may well be a critical U.S. or Soviet reconnaissance satellite hit by a piece of space junk during time of crisis." Deudney, Unlocking Space, Foreign Policy No. 53 at 91, 101 (Winter, 1983–84). For more on this and related topics see Reynolds, National Security on the High Frontier, 2 High Technology Law Journal 281 (1988).

Lastly, any discussion of space environmental matters would be incomplete without touching on the interplay between space and earth. Earth's environment is, of course, not really separate from outer space: sunlight comes in, heat is radiated away, and a substantial amount of extraterrestrial matter rains down every day in the form of meteors, cosmic dust, and so on. More to the point from a policy perspective, though, is the way in which space activity plays a vital part in managing environmental problems here on earth. The growth of an environmental movement on a massive scale stems in no small part from the dramatic impact of the Apollo mission photographs of earth, showing our planet as a small, fragile object amid a sea of blackness and emptiness and given the (not coincidental) nickname of "spaceship earth." The consequences of that particular change in attitudes have yet to be played out. For more on this see Hartmann, Space Exploration and Environmental Issues, 6 Environmental Ethics 227 (1984) and Beyond Spaceship Earth: Environmental Ethics and the Solar System (E. Hargrove ed. 1986).

On a more "micro" scale, space resources play an important role in recognizing and managing earth environmental problems. Satellite imagery, for example, was vital in identifying the Antarctic ozone hole, and is now being used by environmental groups to track industrial pollution, tropical deforestation, and many other important matters. In the future, as satellite costs come down and capabilities go up, we may see private environmental groups acquiring their own space remote sensing satellites in order to monitor and expose harmful activities by nations and corporations. In addition, it is likely that over the long term space and environmental goals will be seen as complementary, since space activity promises access to resources sufficient to avoid the depletion of the earth, and to knowledge sufficient to address many earthbound problems.

6

Space Communications

The importance of outer space to communications law stems from the use of satellites (almost exclusively in geosynchronous orbit) as relays for communications from one point on the earth to another, a use first proposed by Arthur C. Clarke in his famous *Wireless World* article of March, 1945. By the late 1950s communications satellite experiments were underway, although many believed that such satellites were unlikely to enter commercial use for decades at the very least. (For an interesting view of critics' fears that did not come true see A. Haley, Space Law and Government 190–212 (1963).) Those critics were proven spectacularly wrong: the first successful geosynchronous communications satellite was the NASA Syncom satellite of 1963, and the first commercial communications satellite in geosynchronous orbit was the Early Bird, launched in 1965. Within a very short time, the satellite communications industry became a global reality. For a time it appeared that that industry would be a near monopoly of the international communications satellite consortium, INTELSAT, but the forces of competition have caused satellite communications, at both the domestic and international levels, to become a business with many participants.

Like all other businesses, satellite communications is subject to regulation. The communications satellite industry is regulated at both the domestic and international level: at the international level there are two types of governance, the frequency and orbital slot assignments undertaken by the International Telecommunications Union (ITU) and its International Frequency Registration Board (IFRB), and the global requirements imposed by the INTELSAT agreement. At the domestic American level, regulation is by the Federal Communications Commission, which enforces its own rules and which has a number of responsibilities relating to the ITU and INTELSAT.

Although the distinction between international and domestic affairs is blurring in many areas, it is vanishing fastest in the area of communications regulation. For that reason, this chapter addresses both international and domestic regulation of international space communications. Following is a short description of the international regulatory mechanisms governing space communications (drawn in large part from R. White & H. White,

The Law and Regulation of International Space Communication (1988)), after which is a short discussion of domestic regulation. Then are excerpts from some government documents that provide considerable perspective on the nature of the regulatory process and the kinds of problems that come up.

SPACE AND INTERNATIONAL TELECOMMUNICATIONS

The principal body governing international communications in general is the International Telecommunications Union, a specialized agency of the United Nations which was originally formed as the International Telegraph Union in 1865 to coordinate the developing world telegraph network. The ITU has expanded its responsibilities over time to take account of the rapidly changing technologies of communications, and now governs communications via radio and cable, whether for broadcast or message service. Satellite communications, of course, are entirely by radio at present (though laser communications are a distinct possibility in the future) and hence are regulated as radio services.

The ITU's concern with regulation of radio service goes back many years. In the early days of radio communications, the lack of any frequency assignment mechanism led to substantial problems with interference, especially at sea and among the many and crowded nations of Europe. After some decades of wrangling over the problem, regulation of frequency use to avoid harmful interference was taken over by the ITU, with many technical aspects administered by its International Frequency Registration Board (which coordinates frequency use) and the International Consultative Committee on Radio (in French, the master language of the ITU, the *Comite Consultatif International des Radiocommunications* and hence abbreviated as CCIR). Following is a short description of the ITU's current composition.

Structure of the ITU

The constitutive document of the International Telecommunications Union is the International Telecommunications Convention. That document, as amended from time to time, sets out the purposes and structure of the Union. The ITU's goals include:

> to maintain and extend international cooperation between all Members of the Union for the improvement and rational use of telecommunications of all kinds, as well as to promote and to offer technical assistance to developing countries in the field of telecommunications;
>
> to promote the development of technical facilities and their most efficient operation; [and]
>
> to harmonize the actions of nations in the attainment of those ends.

In serving those ends, the Union's primary function is to regulate the world's international telecommunications so as to ensure an efficient and far-reaching global telecommunications system. In so doing, the Union is to:

> effect allocation of the radio frequency spectrum and registration of radio frequency assignments in order to avoid harmful interference between radio stations of different countries [and]

> coordinate efforts to eliminate harmful interference between radio stations of different countries and to improve the use made of the radio frequency spectrum.

International Telecommunications Convention, Nairobi, 1982, Article 4. In addition, the ITU is charged with the responsibility to foster international cooperation in assisting the developing countries with the development of their networks, with harmonizing the development of telecommunications facilities, with helping its members to organize international services so as to maintain rates at levels as low as possible consistent with an efficient international service, to promote efficient emergency communications services, and to undertake studies, adopt resolutions, formulate recommendations and opinions and collect and publish information concerning telecommunciations matters. *Id.* These provisions, like others contained in the Convention, are binding on the Union and its members, although individual countries may note reservations to any particular part of the Convention with which they disagree, at the price of being unable to enforce that part of the Convention against other nations.

The Convention may be (and is) updated and amended by the Plenipotentiary Conference of the Union. The Plenipotentiary Conference meets regularly (normally, every five years) and is the primary law-making body of the Union. Aside from the Convention itself, Plenipotentiary Conferences promulgate Resolutions (usually directing other bodies of the ITU to take particular actions), Recommendations (regarding actions that should be taken by member countries or the United Nations), and Opinions (which preserve the views and legal interpretations of the delegates to the Conference at which they are adopted, thus providing a sort of "legislative history").

In between Plenipotentiary Conferences, the Administrative Council of the Union meets once a year to address matters that cannot wait for attention from the full membership of the Union or that are too routine for such attention. The ITU also possesses a General Secretariat responsible for its day-to-day operations and for preparing for Plenipotentiary and Administrative meetings.

Also, from time to time, Administrative Conferences may be called to deal with special topics. These Administrative Conferences may be regional or they may be global. Space matters are addressed in Space World Administrative Radio Conferences (or Space WARCs) or, occasionally, in Space

Regional Conferences, or Space RARCs. Three geographic regions are able to call regional conferences: Region 1, which consists of Europe, Africa, the Middle East, the Soviet Union, and Mongolia; Region 2, consisting of the Americas, the Caribbean, and Greenland; and Region 3, consisting of Asia and the Pacific exclusive of Hawaii. World Administrative Conferences can make partial or complete revisions of the ITU Radio Regulations, while regional conferences may deal only with regional matters.

The ITU promulgates Radio Regulations which are binding on all members of the Union, although states can make reservations to particular parts of the Regulation subject to the principle that their domestic uses of frequencies may not cause harmful interference outside their borders. The Radio Regulations set out frequency allocations for different nations and for different services (*e.g.,* satellite direct broadcasting, satellite mobile communications, fixed satellite service, etc.). Interpretation of the Radio Regulations in case of dispute is entrusted to the International Frequency Registration Board (IFRB), which also maintains the Master International Frequency Register into which information concerning national assignments of frequencies is entered, and which provides technical assistance and promulgates technical standards and procedures. The IFRB is also responsible for recording the positions assigned by countries to geostationary satellites and for providing assistance in selecting those positions.

The International Radio Consultative Committee (CCIR) exists to provide technical advice on the setting of international standards. Although the CCIR standards are not binding on members, they are generally accepted in practice and incorporated into the Radio Regulations.

INTELSAT

Shortly after it became apparent that satellite communications were to have real utility, negotiations began to create an international agency that would provide international satellite communications services. The result was INTELSAT, an international consortium providing satellite communications among nations.

INTELSAT's structure and operation are governed by the Multilateral International Telecommunications Satellite Agreement of 1973, 23 U.S.T. 3813, TIAS 7532. At the time that that agreement was arrived at, INTELSAT had been operating for several years already, under an interim arrangement in which the U.S. participant in INTELSAT, the Communications Satellite Corporation (COMSAT), provided management and technical services. After the agreement, these services were gradually taken over by INTELSAT. INTELSAT had 112 member countries by the end of 1987, with membership continuing to grow slowly. Those countries are all part owners of INTELSAT, with their ownership share varying according to their use of INTELSAT facilities. INTELSAT's structure reflects its overall philosophy in favor of participation. It is governed by a Board of Governors, an Assembly of Parties, a Meeting of Signatories, and an Executive Organ. The Assembly of Parties consists of all member countries and meets biannually to decide issues of long-term importance. The Meeting of Signatories is made up of designated representatives of member countries; those representatives are telecommunications providers such as COMSAT from the United States. The Board of Governors meets four times a year to make executive decisions, while the Executive Organ, headed by a Director General, oversees the day-to-day operations of INTELSAT. INTELSAT is headquartered in the United States, in Washington, D.C. For more on the organization and operation of INTELSAT, see R. White & H. White, The Law and Regulation of International Space Communication 216–221; M. Kinsley, Outer Space and Inner Sanctums (1976). See Chapter 4 for economic analysis applicable to the establishment of INTELSAT as an efficient way to make use of shared orbit and spectrum resources.

The interesting legal and policy questions relating to INTELSAT grow out of two issues: its pricing structure and the requirement in Article XIV(d) of the Agreement requiring that parties establishing separate systems consult with INTELSAT to ensure technical compatibility and to avoid significant economic harm. Both issues have become items of considerable controversy over recent years.

The pricing policy is one of global averaging. Members of INTELSAT share revenues and adjust their investment amounts in proportion to their use of the system, as mentioned above. Under this system, therefore, the price that members pay for an INTELSAT circuit is approximately equal to the globally averaged cost of circuits throughout the INTELSAT system. Because the fixed costs of providing service are high and the marginal costs low, economies of scale are very significant. This results in a subsidy for thinly used routes (such as the Pacific and the Indian Ocean) and a "tax" on service over the heavily used routes such as those between the United States and northern Europe.

Although this subsidy was deliberate, in order to help move less-developed countries into the global village, it leads to considerable inefficiencies. On thin routes, the subsidy means that the network will be used more often than it would if prices were equal to costs, while on heavily-used routes the tax means that there will be less traffic than if prices were equal to costs. Of course, such an outcome was precisely the goal of the subsidy scheme when INTELSAT was organized, but as the more advanced nations find themselves increasingly struggling for economic competitiveness with the LDCs (and particularly those in the Pacific and Indian Ocean regions), whose costs in many areas are already lower, they increasingly seem to resent that subsidy, particularly given the increasing importance of telecommunications services in the growing information economy. For an excellent analysis of this topic see Kwerel & Pitsch, FCC Regulation of International Telecommunications Satellites and Cables, in 2 American Enterprise, the Law, and the Commercial Use of Space 119 (P. Mink ed. 1986); Federal Communications Commission, Office of Plans & Policy, Promoting Competition Between International Telecommunication Cables and Satellites (OPP Working Paper No. 19, January, 1986); U.S. Congress

Office of Technology Assessment, International Cooperation and Competition in Civilian Space Activities at Ch. 6 (1985). Similar issues have arisen in the U.S. domestic arena as a result of the breakup of AT&T. *See generally* Kahn, the Road to More Intelligent Telephone Pricing, 1 Yale Journal on Regulation 339 (1984).

Of course, as the LDC economies grow (something that, at this writing, appears likely to continue), so too will use of the parts of the INTELSAT network serving them, meaning that the problem may well solve itself within a decade or two. The question is whether the more advanced countries will be willing to continue the subsidy until things even out, given the level of economic competition that appears to be growing. The United States, at least, appears somewhat hostile to the subsidy, as the discussion of U.S. satellite policies later in this chapter shows. In addition, as Kwerel & Pitsch point out, maintaining the subsidy will be difficult for other reasons. The growth of fiber optic cable systems—which are not subject to restriction under the INTELSAT Agreement—will provide considerable competition for satellite services and will as a result force prices toward costs.

For the time being, however, the subsidy remains, and the Agreement requires that member nations take steps in the satellite field to avoid "significant economic harm" to INTELSAT. The following discussion outlines the way in which the United States has attempted to balance its general position in favor of free markets and against subsidies with the responsibilities growing out of its role in INTELSAT.

U.S. REGULATION OF SPACE COMMUNICATIONS

The United States regulates space communications involving its territory and nationals under a framework of both domestic and international law. The following excerpt provides an overview of that system.

Office of Commercial Space Policy, U.S. Department of Commerce, Space Commerce: An Industry Assessment 38–40 (1988)

The cornerstone of U.S. telecommunications law is the Communications Act of 1934 as amended [47 U.S.C. 151 (1982)]. It establishes the Federal Communications Commission (FCC) as the regulatory and licensing authority for non–Federal Government uses of the radio-frequency spectrum. Against this backdrop, the 1962 Communications Satellite Act (Satellite Act) [47 U.S.C. 701 (1982)] provides for the establishment of a global, commercial communications satellite system (now known as INTELSAT) and provides for the establishment of a private corporation, Comsat, as the sole U.S. participant and investor in the system. The Satellite Act requires Comsat to provide non-discriminatory access to the system for all authorized users [47 U.S.C. 731 (1982)]. Importantly, the Satellite Act states that it is not intended to preclude the establishment of communications satellites separate from INTELSAT that are determined to be in the national interest or required to meet unique governmental needs.

Three separate policies have been established to ensure that U.S. domestic and international satellite telecommunications activities are consistent with U.S. law and international agreements: (1) the U.S. Domestic Satellite Policy, which is intended to ensure a robust domestic satellite marketplace, (2) the Transborder Policy that applies to domestic systems used to provide incidental international services to neighboring countries, and (3) the U.S. Separate Systems Policy for satellite systems intended specifically to provide international public telecommunications services separate from INTELSAT. U.S. obligations under the INTELSAT Agreement were a major consideration in the creation of each of these policies.

In the early 1970s, the FCC adopted a policy of "open entry" for qualified domestic communications satellite systems (domsats) [35 FCC2d 86 (1970), *recon. granted in part,* 38 FCC2d 844 (1972)]. This policy, which is still in effect, is based on the concept that licensing all applicants meeting the FCC's established technical, legal and financial fitness requirements for obtaining a license will encourage the development of new technologies and services at lower costs to the public. These requirements have been tightened over the years as the number of domsats has increased and the orbit/spectrum resource has become more congested. The FCC has stated that if the number of domsat applications ever exceeds the orbital positions and spectrum available, it might have to resort to administrative selection procedures, such as comparative hearings, auctions or lotteries [48 Fed. Reg. 40,233 (Sept. 6, 1983)].

Use of U.S. domestic satellites for transborder services is governed by the U.S. Transborder Policy. The Transborder Policy was established by the Executive branch and the FCC to balance the efficiencies of using U.S. domestic satellites to provide service to neighboring countries within the footprint of the satellite, with the U.S. desire to avoid causing significant economic harm to INTELSAT. The Transborder Policy, established in 1981, requires: (1) a showing by the applicant that INTELSAT could not practically or economically provide the same services as the requested domestic satellite, and (2) consultation with INTELSAT pursuant to Article XIV(d) of the INTELSAT Agreement, prior to initiation of service [88 FCC2d 258 (1981)]. The FCC's transborder decisions to date have been limited almost exclusively to the authorization of video and private line voice and data services.

In 1984, the President determined that U.S. international satellite systems separate from INTELSAT (separate systems) are in the national interest. This determination was made in accordance with the 1962 Satellite Act and was accompanied by the conditions that (1) such systems may provide services only through the sale or long-term lease of space segment capacity for communications not interconnected with the public-switched network, and (2) at least one foreign authority must authorize use of each separate system and participate in consultations with the United States under the INTELSAT Agreement, to ensure technical compatibility with the INTELSAT system and avoid causing it significant economic harm. In 1985, the FCC used this determination and the conditions as the basis for its decision to license qualified applicants [101 FCC2d 290 (1985), *recon. granted in part,* FCC 86–144 (April 17, 1986), *further recon. denied,* 1 FCC Rcd. 439 (1986)].

The Transborder Policy has always been distinguished from the U.S. policy on separate international systems, because it only concerns U.S. domsats used to provide incidental services to nearby countries. The Separate Systems Policy, on the other hand, concerns satellites that are specifically intended to provide international services, and are considered a greater threat to INTELSAT's economic well-being. Unlike the separate systems policy, the Transborder Policy does not expressly prohibit interconnection with the public switched network, nor does it require the sale or long term lease of transponder capacity as a precondition to use. These differences, coupled with the recognition that INTELSAT has developed into a robust and highly profitable global communications satellite system, has prompted the Administration to initiate a comprehensive review of U.S. international satellite policy. This process is underway.

NOTE

The United States' decision regarding separate satellite systems was arrived at only after extensive study and considerable dissension. The following excerpt from an internal paper prepared by the Senior Interagency Group on International Communication and Information Policy explains the rationale behind the decision in considerable detail. A number of experts—not to mention those at COMSAT and INTELSAT—dispute its conclusions. For a good summary of their views see Sarreals, International Telecommunications Satellite Services: The Spirit of Cooperation versus the Battle for Competition, 26 Jurimetrics: Journal of Law, Science & Technology 267 (1986).

Senior Interagency Group on International Communication and Information Policy, A White Paper on New International Satellite Systems, February, 1985

Since 1983, several U.S. firms have filed applications with the Federal Communications Commission (FCC) to establish international communications satellite systems in addition to the global system owned by the International Telecommunications Satellite Organization (INTELSAT). Orion Satellite Corporation, International Satellite, Inc. (ISI), and Cygnus Corporation propose new transatlantic communications systems, and RCA

American Communications, Inc. (RCA) has applied to use capacity on a U.S. domestic satellite to provide international service. Pan American Satellite Corporation (PanAmSat) proposes to establish a system which would serve Latin America. In addition to existing and planned regional satellite systems independent of INTELSAT, other transoceanic satellite systems are under consideration abroad. Approved and proposed transatlantic submarine cable communications facilities, many of which are actually or potentially competitive with INTELSAT, are pending as well.

Focus of Report

The filing of U.S.-based satellite system applications with the FCC prompted action by the Executive branch, which has special responsibilities in this field under the Communications Satellite Act of 1962, as amended (47 U.S.C. 701 et seq.), including the responsibility to determine whether additional U.S. international satellite systems are "required in the national interest." The Senior Interagency Group on International Communication and Information Policy (SIG) reviewed U.S. international satellite policy to determine whether, and under what conditions, authorizing satellite systems and services in addition to INTELSAT would be: (a) consistent with prevailing U.S. law, practice, and international treaty obligations; (b) compatible with sound foreign policy and telecommunications policy goals; and, (c) in the U.S. national interest.

The Executive agencies represented on the SIG undertook a study and reached a unanimous position in favor of new entry, subject to certain limitations. A recommendation subsequently was made to the President by the Secretaries of State and Commerce. The President determined on November 28, 1984, that international satellite systems separate from INTELSAT were required in the U.S. national interest, subject to certain conditions. Specific criteria relating to the President's determination were then forwarded to the FCC by the Secretaries of Commerce and State jointly. See Appendixes A and B.

This report provides background information regarding the President's determination, and it also provides information on important regulatory and other parallel measures which are desirable to ensure that the Executive branch's fundamental policy goal—an efficient and responsive international communications environment—is achieved. The discussion here focuses on the major communications and information policy issues raised by the applications before the FCC. It addresses commercial, trade, and legal matters, and also examines major U.S. foreign policy interests and concerns.

*   *   *

I. The International Communications Marketplace Today

*   *   *

There are two principal international transmission modes: submarine cables and communications satellite facilities. The submarine cables which provide U.S. international service are owned collectively by AT&T, the IRCs [International Record Carriers], and their foreign correspondents. Seven transatlantic cables now terminate in the United States and an eighth, 38,000-circuit, fiber optic cable has been approved by the FCC. U.S. international satellite circuits are provided by Comsat, which has functioned as a "carrier's carrier" and holds a 23 percent interest in INTELSAT, the 109-nation organization that owns and manages the global satellite system. Comsat's investment share is adjusted annually to reflect U.S. use of the INTELSAT system.

*   *   *

U.S. Policy Goals

The international communications and information policy goals of the United States are the following:

- To enhance the free flow of information and ideas among nations;
- To promote harmonious international relations and contribute to world peace and understanding through communications;
- To promote, in cooperation with other nations, the development of efficient, innovative, and cost-effective international communications services responsive to the needs of users and supportive of the expanding requirements of commerce and trade;
- To ensure the continued technological and economic strength and leadership of the United States in the communications, information, and acrospace fields;
- To expand U.S. private sector investment and involvement in civil space and related activities;
- To promote expanded international trade and to ensure opportunities to U.S. firms to participate in such trade;
- To promote the continuing evolution of an international configuration of communications services that can meet the needs of all nations of the world, with attention toward providing such services to developing nations;
- To ensure efficient utilization of the geostationary orbit and the electromagnetic radio frequency spectrum;
- To promote competition and reliance on market mechanisms, as feasible, and to foster cost-based pricing, quality service, and more efficient use of resources; and,
- To ensure the needs of national defense, security, and emergency preparedness are satisfactorily met.

*   *   *

The INTELSAT system and the number of facilities which access INTELSAT's satellites have expanded rapidly. INTELSAT's 15 satellites today serve 173 countries, territories, and possessions directly or indirectly, and the organization leases satellite capacity to 26 nations for domestic services. Nineteen new earth stations and 39 new international communications antennas were added in 1982 alone. As of November 1984, there were 198 INTELSAT earth station sites and 293 international antennas in 157 countries, dependencies, and areas of other special sovereignty.

INTELSAT now handles about two-thirds of the world's transoceanic telecommunications traffic and most international television transmissions. Demand for full-time voice, record, and data services for INTELSAT grew by 18 percent in 1982; these services accounted for about 86 percent of the total satellite utilization revenue received by INTELSAT that year. The most recently published INTELSAT annual report states that INTELSAT expects continued strong growth of 15 percent annually on an expanded base of conventional international traffic over the 1988–2000 time period.

*   *   *

With the growth of the INTELSAT system, circuit charges have steadily declined. The annual charge for a 1965 INTELSAT I "Early Bird" half-circuit, for example, was $32,000, while the 1982–83 charge for an equivalent, though technically superior, half-circuit was $4,680. There is disagreement, however, over whether the substantial INTELSAT charge reductions over the past decades have been fully reflected in the prices which Comsat has charged U.S. international carriers or the prices which those carriers have charged their customers. At present, end-user prices for many international satellite services both here and abroad typically are between two to ten times INTELSAT's charges. U.S. international communications costs, moreover, often are very substantially above those for comparable domestic service.

INTELSAT has continued to grow and to prosper in an increasingly competitive international communications environment. Since 1981, the FCC has sanctioned certain international communications services using U.S. domestic satellite systems. At present, U.S. and Canadian satellites are used to provide certain services throughout North America and the Caribbean. Additional proposals for such transborder satellite service will be the object of consultations with INTELSAT. INTELSAT recently accelerated its plans and now offers a number of international communications services aimed particularly at meeting specialized and sophisticated business community needs.

Significance to Industry and Government

International communications services constitute an essential component of international trade today. Efficient and effective international communications are necessary to international finance, to facilitate the production and shipment of goods, and to manage U.S. off-shore operations, assets, and investments. International communications are also critical to the continued development of U.S. trade in services, which exceeded $40 billion in 1982. International communications, moreover, play a central role in facilitating the further economic development of less developed nations, thus permitting these countries to participate more fully in the world economy and contributing to peace, stability, and greater understanding.

Space communications is a major part of the aerospace industry, one of the world economy's most important "high-tech" or "sunrise" sectors, and an area where the excellence of U.S. manufacturing techniques and high technologies is reflected in the preeminence of the U.S. aerospace industry. U.S. aerospace trade is forecast to accelerate in 1985 as both exports and imports reach record highs. Aerospace exports should climb to a projected $18.9 billion, while imports will rise to $5.0 billion. The resultant trade surplus of $13.9 billion will be more than 30 percent above the level recorded in 1984. Total U.S. aerospace employment will rise an estimated 4 percent in 1985 to 739,000, with an estimated gain of 7 percent in the number of production workers.

Existing Policies and Objectives

*   *   *

The established foreign and domestic policies of the U.S. Government in this area seek to further the basic goals which are outlined above. These policies include:

- Adhering to the requirements and provisions of the Communications Act of 1934, as amended (47 U.S.C. 151 et seq.) and the 1962 Satellite Act, as amended (47 U.S.C. 701 et seq.);
- Complying with the terms of the INTELSAT Agreement (TIAS 7532) and all the privileges and obligations the Agreement provides its Parties and Signatories;
- Supporting INTELSAT as "a single global commercial telecommunications satellite system as part of an improved global telecommunications network" (Preamble, INTELSAT Agreement), and as a key element providing all countries of the world access to global communications services;
- Concurring in the development, separate from INTELSAT, of customized, regional, and transborder satellite services where technical or economic consultation, or both, is accomplished as required under the terms of the INTELSAT Agreement and such systems are consistent with the Agreement;
- Pursuing a nondiscriminatory satellite launch policy;
- Adopting domestic communications policies which emphasize reduced Government regulation, wherever feasible, and increased reliance on market forces in the provision of communications and information services;
- Advocating and adopting international communications policies which stress reliance on free enterprise, competition, and free trade, wherever

feasible, with full recognition that provision of international communications and information services involves joint undertakings among sovereign nations requiring mutually acceptable agreements to accommodate differing national policies;
- Supporting and fostering the development of a diversity of international communications technologies and modes, including fixed, mobile, and broadcast satellite, microwave, terrestrial and undersea cable, and optical fiber;
- Supporting and undertaking bilateral consultations and agreements, as well as multilateral deliberations in appropriate international forums, to ensure order and cooperation in the evolution of international communications and information services.

* * *

II. Institutional Limits On Competition

The United States since the early 1970s consistently has sought to reduce outmoded communications regulation and to eliminate unnecessary barriers to competition chiefly domestically, but internationally as well. Important changes and regulatory reforms have been accomplished. All recognize, however, that achieving a regulation-free international communications environment is not foreseeable at this time. There will remain significant U.S. limitations on competition in international communications as well as limits imposed by communications administrations abroad. Understanding some of these limits on potential competition is important to addressing the issues presented by the satellite applications pending before the FCC and reinforces our assessment that these applications imply continued evolutionary development, not radical or disruptive change.

Regulatory Constraints

There are, to begin with, a number of statutory requirements and limitations which bear on the level and intensity of potential competition in the international communications field. To enter the international communications satellite business, U.S. firms require FCC permission under title III of the 1934 Communications Act, provisions of title II of that Act (for would-be common carrier entrants), as well as provisions of the 1962 Satellite Act. The FCC is required by law to make an affirmative "public interest" finding prior to issuing construction permits and licenses to use the radio frequency spectrum. Considerable regulatory review of proposed systems typically is entailed. It is also relevant in this regard to note that given spectrum use limitations and international procedures governing the use of the geostationary orbital resource, there are significant technical constraints on possible entry into international satellite communications. [See generally *Orbital Locations,* 54 P. & F. Radio Reg. 2d 550 (1983); *Orbital Spacing,* 54 P. & F. Radio Reg. 2d 577 (1983); Robinson, *Regulating*

International Airwaves: the 1979 WARC, 21 Virginia Journal of International Law 1, 44 (1980).]

Entrants proposing to operate on a common carrier basis are subject to many provisions of title II of the 1934 Communications Act (e.g., 47 U.S.C. 214). Under title II, the FCC must generally find that the public interest, convenience, and necessity will be furthered by approving an additional international common carrier facility. Existing common carriers, moreover, must generally receive permission to make use of new facilities. As with other regulatory agencies, the FCC is required to weigh competitive factors when it functions as a "gatekeeper" with respect to common carrier communications. Under present law, however, the FCC may not legally authorize new common carrier systems simply to foster competition. It must instead make affirmative public interest findings that competition, for example, will spur technological progress, increase efficiency, and more rapidly expand customer choice.

Executive Responsibilities

In addition to the limitations on entry and competition contained in titles II and III of the Communications Act, section 102(d) of the Satellite Act recognizes the foreign policy, trade, and national security aspects of international satellite communications and provides that the President is responsible to determine whether additional international satellite systems are required to meet unique governmental needs or are otherwise required in the national interest.

The term "national interest" is not defined in the Satellite Act, but it encompasses considerations broader than those implicit in the FCC's regulatory "public interest" standard, a standard which the courts have ruled is not limitless. [See NAACP v. Federal Power Commission, 425 U.S. 662, 669 (1976); National Organization for Women v. FCC, 555 F.2d 1002, 1017 (D.C. Cir. 1977).] "National interest" is within the mandate of the Executive branch and includes such factors as general competition policy, whether entry will advance technological progress and innovation, promote U.S. international trade in goods and services, expand the international communications options available to the U.S. business community, and further overall U.S. spectrum management goals. Foreign policy and national security considerations are also important aspects of the national interest, and matters which are the Constitutional responsibilities of the Executive. The FCC in the past has generally deferred to Executive branch views on policies which are not directly within its regulatory purview. In sum, the "national interest" standard in the 1962 Satellite Act should be read as according the Executive branch responsibility to determine the compatibility of proposed international satellite systems with the broad range of U.S. programs and policies affected by such enterprises.

International Obligations

In addition to the limitations on competition implicit in the 1934 Communications Act and the special "national interest" criterion in the

1962 Satellite Act, U.S. international obligations are relevant. Certain responsibilities under Article XIV of the INTELSAT Agreement are also discussed in the Memorandum of the Legal Adviser of the Department of State which was transmitted to the FCC in 1984 and which is set forth as Appendix B to this report.

The INTELSAT Agreement entered into force for the United States on February 12, 1973. While the INTELSAT Agreement implicitly acknowledges that nations party to the Agreement retain the sovereign right to establish satellite telecommunications facilities separate from the INTELSAT system, the Agreement establishes: (1) a generalized obligation of the parties to act in a manner consistent with and in furtherance of the principles stated in the Preamble and other provisions of the Agreement (Article XIV(a)); and (2) a consultation process to be undertaken before a nation or its designated operating entity (a "Signatory") establishes, acquires, or utilizes separate, non-INTELSAT space segment facilities to meet its telecommunications requirements (Article XIV).

Article XIV(d) of the INTELSAT Agreement addresses the consultation obligation with regard to international public telecommunications services. In substance, it provides that a nation member or its Signatory shall furnish all relevant information to INTELSAT and shall consult with INTELSAT: (1) to ensure technical compatibility of the contemplated satellite facilities with the use of the radio frequency spectrum and the geostationary orbital space by the existing or planned INTELSAT satellites; and (2) to avoid significant economic harm to the global system of INTELSAT. At the conclusion of the consultation process, the INTELSAT Assembly of Parties (the principal organ of INTELSAT, composed of the representatives of all member nations) makes findings in the form of recommendations on the subjects of the consultation and further regarding the assurance that the proposed satellite facility will not prejudice the establishment of direct telecommunications links through the INTELSAT space segment among all the participants in the proposed system.

*   *   *

III. Foreign Policy Considerations
Regarding International Satellites

Addressing the issues raised by the proposed establishment of U.S. international satellite systems separate from INTELSAT requires consideration of U.S. foreign policy objectives. These objectives have been considered within the Executive branch and do not constitute an appropriate matter for independent determination by a regulatory agency. Here, however, the major foreign policy matters that were weighed are generally discussed to further understanding of the President's determination.

In his September 1983 letter to Chairman Charles H. Percy of the Senate Committee on Foreign Relations, Secretary of State George P. Shultz reiterated the basic foreign policy objectives of the United States in international communications, and they are similar to those enumerated in detail above: "To promote an environment in which ideas and information can flow freely among nations, to support the advancement of international commerce through the efficient and innovative use of communications resources, and to expand information access and communications capabilities of developing countries."

The 1962 Satellite Act reflects these objectives and others which have been furthered through our participation in developing and supporting the INTELSAT system. INTELSAT's manifest success has:

- Provided a dramatic example of U.S. leadership in the peaceful use of space in the interest of all countries;
- Contributed to meeting evolving U.S. commercial needs for efficient international communications services;
- Provided developing countries with improved communications at reasonable and affordable rates;
- Confined the Soviet INTERSPUTNIK system to a relatively small portion of the world;
- Supplied developing countries with access to the geostationary orbit and satellite radio frequencies; and,
- Provided benefits to U.S. companies through open international procurement for the international system's space communications equipment and services.

Permitting U.S. international satellite systems separate from INTELSAT, however, could:

- Bring new diversity and flexibility to international communications;
- Create or expand markets in new areas, such as customized, data, and video services;
- Provide incentives for INTELSAT and its Signatories to be more efficient and innovative; and,
- Permit outside financial sources to undertake high-risk, speculative ventures, thereby enabling INTELSAT to concentrate its resources on further extending basic services through prudent financial management.

*   *   *

Access to the Geostationary Orbit

How all nations can enjoy "equitable access" to the geostationary satellite orbit and to the associated radio spectrum is a major concern within the International Telecommunication Union (ITU). The results of the ITU's consideration of this issue at the upcoming World Administrative Radio

Conference on the Use of the Geostationary Satellite Orbit and the Planning of the Space Services Utilizing It (Space WARC) in August 1985 and June 1988 [are] important to the United States and many other countries. INTELSAT's role in meeting developing countries' communications needs could make it a critical, if indirect, participant in the resolution of this issue on terms acceptable to ITU member nations. [See Chapter 4, *supra*, for a discussion of economic rationales for INTELSAT's role. The outcome of the 1988 Space WARC is discussed in this chapter, *infra*.]

For more than a decade, some developing countries have sought a guaranteed share of the geostationary orbit and the radio spectrum allocated to space services. They maintain that unconstrained growth of commercial satellite communications systems could exhaust the geostationary orbit and the frequencies currently available. Fearful of losing their share of what they understand to be limited global resources, developing countries in 1983 inscribed "equitable access" provisions into the ITU Convention. By the 1979 WARC, they were determined to write new rules for the use of the geostationary orbit and associated radio spectrum and obtained a commitment for the two-part Space WARC in the 1980s.

The availability of INTELSAT has not eliminated developing country demands for equitable access to the geostationary orbit and related spectrum. Nevertheless, its existence offers an alternative to the implementation of costly national satellite systems. So long as low-cost and technically attractive service is available through an international organization which accommodates the sovereignty interests of each country, there is added hope that developing countries may meet some of their needs through INTELSAT.

The proliferation of communications satellite systems already in progress, moreover, will heighten the importance of INTELSAT's role in frequency conservation. Increasing demand for the radio spectrum is hastening the development and implementation of innovative technologies which expand the capacity of the geostationary orbit resource and permit greater efficiency through multiple uses of the same frequency. Large-scale space platforms and other techniques have the potential to increase frequency usage efficiency by perhaps 50- to 100-fold; INTELSAT's multinational consolidation of demand—domestic, regional, and transoceanic—will thus have particular attraction. With these considerations in mind, the United States lent strong support at the October 1982 INTELSAT Assembly of Parties to the principle of domestic service using INTELSAT facilities, despite European opposition.

An indication of the developing countries' growing stake in INTELSAT can be found in INTELSAT's evolution toward playing a larger role in the provision of domestic satellite service. In 1974, Algeria proposed to lease INTELSAT capacity for enhancement of its domestic telecommunications network. Today, some 26 countries use INTELSAT to provide domestic service. INTELSAT has responded to this demand by committing itself to include planned domestic capacity, as opposed to relying solely on preemptible, spare capacity, in future generations of satellites. It has also developed higher power satellites that are compatible with the small earth stations that have proved most economical for domestic service.

*   *   *

U.S. Role in INTELSAT

The U.S. role in INTELSAT continues to be strong, although it has changed over the past 20 years. The U.S. investment share has decreased from 61 to 23 percent; hence the U.S. weighted vote in the Board of Governors has decreased to the current 23 percent. An international secretariat of some 600 INTELSAT staff now manages the system rather than Comsat. A U.S. citizen was recently elected Director General of INTELSAT. INTELSAT no longer purchases almost all of its equipment from U.S. manufacturers, although the United States still supplies about 70 percent of INTELSAT's purchases. The United States is the host country for the INTELSAT headquarters.

The United States has been and should continue to be a strong leader and contributor to the INTELSAT system. Changing technology, competitive economics, and diversifying user needs, however, have created a new international telecommunications environment. There is a manifest trend toward coexistent, separate national and regional satellite systems. This does not obviate the continued need for a global system providing an essential core for public-switched international communications. The 1962 Satellite Act and the INTELSAT Agreement both specifically anticipated communications satellite systems outside INTELSAT, and provided the flexibility to allow for and to respond to such systems.

*   *   *

INTELSAT faces growing competition from new fiber optic cables, which may constitute a more significant challenge to it than separate satellite systems. The transatlantic cable (TAT-8) planned for 1988 by AT&T and the IRCs, Teleglobe Canada, and European telecommunications administrations will have a capacity equivalent to about 38,000 telephone circuits, as previously noted, and nearly quadruple the current submarine cable capacity across the North Atlantic. This fiber optic cable, moreover, will have technical capabilities, including the ability to transmit high-quality video signals, which existing submarine cables lack.

A "status quo approach" often has short-term appeal and merit from a foreign policy standpoint. Change inherently creates pockets of concern in the complex environment of international relations. By its very nature, however, telecommunications is uniquely amenable to change. The issues associated with international telecommunications cannot and will not stand still. They are driven by technology—and technology, in turn, is driven by continuing innovation and evolution.

U.S. policy leaders 20 years ago could not easily have envisioned the exponential expansion of communications horizons through new technology which has subsequently occurred. They did, however, anticipate the need for flexibility to develop the then-uncharted telecommunications frontier.

NOTES

1. The U.S. policy on separate systems is dependent on a number of use restrictions in order to be effective, primarily the requirement that separate satellite circuits not be connected to the public switched network. This presents two problems, one potential, the other unavoidable. The potential problem lies in the FCC's legal authority to enforce such restrictions. The history of telecommunications regulation over recent years has been made up primarily of the demise of such restrictions. *See* Hush-A-Phone Corp. v. United States, 238 F.2d 266 (D.C. Cir. 1956); Use of the Carterfone Device, 13 FCC2d 420 (1968); MCI Telecommunications Corp. v. FCC, 561 F.2d 365 (D.C. Cir. 1977), *cert. denied,* 434 U.S. 1040 (1978) (usually known as *Execunet I*); MCI Telecommunications Corp. v. FCC, 580 F.2d 590 (D.C. Cir.), *cert. denied,* 439 U.S. 980 (1978) (*Execunet II*). *See generally* Comment, Competition in the Telephone Equipment Industry, 86 Yale Law Journal 538 (1977). On the other hand, these restrictions are likely to be on firmer ground than those based simply on a desire to shape domestic markets. That is because the Communications Act, in Section 301, prohibits any radio transmission except in accordance with the Communications Act and applicable regulations, while Section 303(r) of the Act authorizes the FCC to prescribe such restrictions and conditions as may be necessary to carry out the Act or to effectuate U.S. obligations under treaties or conventions relating to radio or wire communications. Since the INTELSAT Agreement clearly qualifies as a "treaty or convention" it may be possible to sustain the use restrictions imposed on separate systems.

The unavoidable problem is technology. Given the complex structure of modern networks, both public and private, virtually any system above the tin-can-and-string level is likely to connect with the public network at some point and policing such interconnections has proven virtually impossible. *See* P. Huber, The Geodesic Network: 1987 Report on Competition in the Telephone Industry (1987) at Chs. 2, 16. The FCC has had little luck in dealing with the problem of "leaky PBXs," in which private networks allow callers to place "local" calls in distant cities without paying long distance access charges, see MTS and WATS Market Structure, Second Supplemental Notice of Inquiry and Proposed Rulemaking, 77 FCC2d 224, 241 (1980); In the Matter of Amendment of Part 69, 2 FCC Rcd. 7441 (1987). Separate satellite operations are likely to pose similar problems. Whether the leakage that exists will be sufficient to pose a significant risk of economic harm to INTELSAT is unclear—certainly such risk will not materialize until separate satellite systems have been around for many years.

2. The White Paper mentions the problem of geosynchronous orbital slot allocation. The problem is that satellites may not be placed too close together without harmful interference. The appropriate spacing interval has dropped over the years as technology has improved, from five degrees to only two at the time of this writing. Further reductions are likely over time, increasing the number of satellites that can be accommodated. Nonetheless, many less-developed countries fear that they may be left behind and that by the time they are ready to launch their own satellites there will be no room for them. A variety of measures have been suggested to deal with this; the economic theory involved is discussed in Chapter 4 in the more general context of common resource allocation.

The 1985 Space WARC proposed principles to deal with this problem, including a guarantee of access and a guarantee that resources would be allocated on an equitable basis. The details of administration were left to be worked out in the 1988 Space WARC.

After this book went to press, the 1988 Space WARC reached a conclusion that, though less elegant than many academic proposals, achieved the sort of pragmatic solution for which the ITU has traditionally been known. The plan is marked by (1) guaranteed orbital slots for developing nations and (2) recognized access rights for current satellite operators for at least 20 years. The 937 delegates, representing 120 nations, voted to establish 480 national slots for nations that so far have not filed applications for domestic systems in the fixed satellite service. Nations are not guaranteed specific slots, but are guaranteed access within a suitable segment of the geosynchronous arc. Most countries, including the United States, were very pleased with the outcome: Theodore Brophy, chair of the U.S. Space WARC delegation, pronounced it a "major breakthrough." *See* Space WARC Guarantees Rights of Existing and Planned Satellite Systems, Communications Daily, October 11, 1988 at 1. For the full text of the agreement, see International Telecommunications Union, ORB-88 Final Acts (1988).

3. In actually implementing the recommendations set out in the White Paper, the FCC made some significant alterations and clarifications. First, it adopted a one-year lease requirement in place of the five-year requirement recommended. It also clarified that although the separate systems could not provide any switched services (such as ordinary Message Telephone Service (MTS), telex, telegrams, and high-speed switched data) they could provide all nonswitched services, including video and private line service. Under no circumstances, however, are the systems allowed to interconnect to the switched network, even on a store-and-forward basis. And the Commission promised to strictly enforce these restrictions and to monitor international telecommunications to ensure that they are not being violated. Establishment of Satellite Systems Providing International Communications, 101 FCC2d 1046 (1985). Nonetheless, the interconnection requirement will be very difficult to enforce and some "cheating"—whether deliberate or accidental—is inevitable.

4. As a signatory to the INTELSAT Agreement, the United States was forced to consider whether its separate satellites decision implicated concerns covered by the INTELSAT accord and whether as a result consultation with INTELSAT was mandated. The following legal opinion from the State Department's Legal Adviser, reproduced in its entirety except for the summary, explains the U.S. view of the subject.

Department of State
The Legal Adviser
Washington, D.C. 20520

MEMORANDUM OF LAW
The Orion Satellite Corporation and International
Satellite, Inc. Applications for International
Satellite Communication Facilities

Background and Question Presented

The Orion Satellite Corporation (Orion) and International Satellite, Inc. have applied to the FCC for authority to provide privately owned international satellite communications facilities to customers on a commercial basis. Orion argues that its system, which would sell or lease transponders to major business users on both sides of the Atlantic, is subject to coordination with INTELSAT only for technical compatibility with the INTELSAT system. The essence of its argument is that it does not propose common carrier services and only such services are "public international telecommunications services" which require coordination with INTELSAT for avoidance of significant economic harm as well. Although International Satellite, Inc. (ISI) argues that its system will not cause significant economic harm to INTELSAT, it does not explicitly concede that its system is subject to coordination under Article XIV(d) of the INTELSAT Agreement.

These applications present the following threshold legal question under the INTELSAT Agreement of 1971, TIAS 7532:

Do the Orion and ISI proposals involve the use of non-INTELSAT space segment facilities for international "public telecommunications services" within the meaning of Article XIV(d), requiring coordination with INTELSAT for both technical compatibility *and* the avoidance of significant economic harm, or do they propose "specialized telecommunications services" under Article XIV(e) which require coordination for only technical compatibility?

*   *   *

Analysis

1. *Authorization of a space segment to provide public international telecommunications services requires technical and economic harm coordination with INTELSAT.*

Under the definitive INTELSAT arrangements, the United States has an obligation, set out in the Agreement's preamble and made operative by Article XIV, to help maintain a single global commercial international telecommunications system as part of an improved global telecommunications network. The obligations extend to what is defined in the Agreement as the "space segment" of INTELSAT. This includes the satellites and related facilities and equipment which are required to support the operation of the satellites.

While available for other purposes, the INTELSAT Agreement contemplates use of the INTELSAT space segment essentially for international public telecommunications. It expressly permits parties to use non-INTELSAT space segment facilities to provide public domestic services [Article XIV(c)] or specialized services [Article XIV(e)] after coordination with INTELSAT solely for technical compatibility. The use of non-INTELSAT space segment for international public telecommunications services [Article XIV(d)] is contemplated after consultation with INTELSAT to ensure technical compatibility and to determine that the services will not cause significant economic harm to the INTELSAT system. Article XIV(g) totally excepts non-INTELSAT space segment facilities used solely for national security purposes. The XIV(d) and (e) provisions are the crux of the issue.

The coordination requirements of Article XIV are a key element of the general obligation of INTELSAT members to help maintain INTELSAT as a single global telecommunications network. The INTELSAT Agreement negotiating history shows that Article XIV was a compromise between the desire of certain European countries, led by France, that the Agreement allow for possible "regional" satellite systems, and the desire of the United States that other international satellite systems be precluded. France, in fact, proposed that INTELSAT be only a federation of regional systems. Several definitions of what would constitute a regional system were put forward, but none was adopted in the final text. It appears that the negotiators felt that the economic harm test incorporated in Article XIV(d) for international public telecommunication services made a definition unnecessary.

2. *"Public telecommunications services" are not limited to "common carrier services."*

The INTELSAT Agreement, Article I(k), defines public telecommunications services as follows:

"Public telecommunication services" means fixed or mobile public telecommunication services which can be provided by satellite and which are available for use by the public, such as telephony, telegraphy, telex, facsimile, data transmission, transmission of radio and television programs between approved earth stations having access to the INTELSAT space segment for further transmission to the public, and leased circuits for any of these purposes; but excluding those mobile services of a type not provided under the Interim Agreement and the Special Agreement prior to the opening for signature of this Agreement, which are provided through mobile stations operating directly to a satellite which is designed, in whole or in part, to provide services relating to the safety or flight control of aircraft or to aviation or maritime radio navigation.

The applicable rules of international law governing the interpretation of international agreements do not sustain the view that the term "public telecommunications services" means only services analogous to those considered "common carrier" in United States telecommunications law. In interpreting an international agreement, the general rule is that the terms of the agreement will be given their ordinary meaning in the context of the entire agreement and in light of its object and purpose, unless it can be established that the parties intended a special meaning to attach. The rules call for taking into account as well, *inter alia,* any subsequent practice in the application of the treaty. Secondary sources of interpretation can be resorted to in order to confirm the resulting interpretation or to resolve ambiguities. These secondary sources include the agreement's preparatory work and the circumstances of its conclusion. The purpose of all the rules is to establish the agreed intent of the parties, as reflected in the text. (See the Vienna Convention on the Law of Treaties, Articles 31 and 32, which the United States accepts as a generally accurate statement of the applicable international law on the interpretation of international agreements.)

Applying these rules, we note first that, while it was certainly contemplated that access in the United States to the INTELSAT space segment would be made through common carriers, there is nothing in the text of the INTELSAT Agreement which links or limits the concept of "available to the public" in the definition of "public telecommunications services" to the concept of common carriage, which is essentially a United States domestic regulatory concept. Nor is there anything in the text which links or limits that concept to the analogous term "public correspondence," used in the ITU Radio Regulations, where it is defined as: "any telecommunication which the offices and stations must, by reasons of their being at the disposal of the public, accept for transmission." Radio Regulations, Chapter I, Article 1, Section 5.1.

The text of the INTELSAT definition appears to be largely self-contained and susceptible of a reasonable meaning in context without resorting to the special meaning given the term in the regulatory framework of one of the participants or in a different agreement which defines an analogous term for a different object and purpose. Article I(k) defines "public international telecommunications services" by reference to types of services, e.g., telephony and telegraphy, which were services to which the public had access at the time of the INTELSAT negotiations. It appears to use the phrase "available for use by the public" to make clear that new telecommunications services which satellites could provide would fall under the INTELSAT mandate as they came into public use. This construction of the phrase "available for use by the public" appears to be in accord with INTELSAT's practice in interpreting the concept of public telecommunications services over the years.

The definition itself appears to contemplate expressly that such services will be considered "public" even when offered via the leasing of a circuit by INTELSAT through one of its members. There is no requirement that the lease be only to a common carrier rather than an entity or small group of entities for their own communications needs.

The strongest argument for the interpretation put forth by Orion is that the concept "public telecommunications" and the analogous term "public correspondence" were in use at the time of the INTELSAT negotiations in both the U.S. domestic telecommunications field and in the ITU Radio Regulations, a broad multilateral telecommunications instrument with which all the participants in the INTELSAT negotiations were familiar. In both those settings it denoted, *inter alia,* availability to the public at large, not just selected customers, a key element of common carriage. However, that fact does not appear to be sufficient to establish legally that the parties to the INTELSAT Agreement intended to so link and limit it, in light of a number of factors:

First, there are many different definitions of "public."

Second, within the telecommunications authorities and administrations of most of the participants in the INTELSAT negotiations, provision of circuits dedicated to the user's own communications are considered part of the public network, and wholly "private" systems are not a feature.

Third, the practice of the parties in the application of the INTELSAT Agreement includes the authorization of circuits dedicated to direct use by an end user, not merely circuits for use by a carrier offering telecommunications services to the public at large.

Fourth, it has not been U.S. practice under the INTELSAT Agreement to equate "public" with "common carrier." The FCC has held entities purchasing transponders not to be common carriers, yet the services they provided have been coordinated with INTELSAT as domestic public telecommunications services under Article XIV(c).

Fifth, the concept of common carriage, as it existed in the United States at the time of the INTELSAT Agreement, is itself shifting as formerly regulated services are deregulated and new services come on stream in a deregulatory climate. For example, in the *Computer II* decision, the FCC decided to forbear from regulating computer processing type services which, nevertheless, are services offered to the public and are not "private" services.

Finally, the theory that "public international telecommunications services" under the INTELSAT Agreement do not include the provision of a space segment on a commercial basis to users who own or lease individual transponders on the satellite would allow any INTELSAT member to authorize the establishment of such a space segment *even if it were to do significant economic harm* to INTELSAT. This would appear to run counter to the object and purpose of the Agreement, the maintenance of a "single global commercial satellite telecommunications system," to provide the space segment required for expanded "international public telecommunications services of high quality and reliability to be available . . . to all areas of the world." [Preamble, Article III and Article XIV(a).]

The Orion application cites INTELSAT's non-discrimination provision as an indication that "public telecommunications service" under INTELSAT means carrier service. However, the "non-discrimination" clause cited by Orion, which occurs in the Preamble to the INTELSAT Agreement, clearly refers to the requirement of the Agreement that services be available on a non-discriminatory basis to the nations, large and small, developed and developing, who are members of INTELSAT. This is consistent with the non-discrimination policy in the Communications Satellite Act. It does not refer to a requirement that INTELSAT be restricted to services made available to all members of the potential user public in participating states on a non-discriminatory basis.

3. *Although a private non-commercial space segment might not require economic harm coordination with INTELSAT, the proposals are not for such service.*

There is no indication that the development of purely private space telecommunications systems was considered by the negotiators of the INTELSAT Agreement or that such limited satellite systems would, in any event, be likely to cause significant economic harm. Nevertheless, from the INTELSAT Agreement's Article 1(k) reference to leased circuits and the overall object and purpose of INTELSAT as a single "commercial" telecommunication system, one might logically infer that the INTELSAT Agreement does not require economic harm coordination for a privately-owned satellite system in which all the capacity is dedicated to the communications needs of its owner. However, the proposals do not involve a privately-owned satellite for exclusive owner use.

While not necessarily dispositive of the INTELSAT interpretation issue, neither Orion nor ISI proposes a genuinely private facility even in U.S. regulatory terms. The FCC's regulations on private radio systems are found in 47 CFR Part 90. The services most analogous to those proposed to be provided by Orion and ISI are found in Subpart D, Industrial Radio Services. These are services which have been established by companies to satisfy their own communications needs. For example, a pipeline transmission company has been permitted to establish a private communications system to serve itself along its right of way. The Commission's regulations (Subpart M) permit companies operating these private systems to provide services to others, or permit any person to provide private services to any person eligible for licensing under Subpart D. However, the Subpart M regulations permit the arrangements only on a "not-for-profit, cost-shared basis." Both Orion and ISI intend to sell or lease satellite transponders, and to maintain satellite control centers and furnish telemetry, tracking, and control functions for a profit. Neither Orion nor ISI will therefore be a private system as those systems are defined in the FCC regulations.

4. *The proposals are not for the type of services which the "specialized services" category, requiring no economic harm coordination, was intended to include.*

The INTELSAT Agreement, Article I(1), defines "specialized telecommunications services" as:

> telecommunications services which can be provided by satellite, other than those defined in paragraph (k) of this Article ["public telecommunications services"], including, but not limited to, radio navigation services, broadcasting satellite services for reception by the general public, space research services, meteorological services, and earth resources services.

While the category of "specialized services" might be a catch-all to assure that any service which is not a public service would, nevertheless, be technically coordinated with INTELSAT under Article XI(e), the drafters had certain kinds of exceptions in mind for its principal content. The negotiating history of the INTELSAT Agreement gives clear guidance that "specialized" as opposed to "public" services were intended to comprise principally those services, excluding generalized telecommunications, under the direct control of governments as a matter of special national policy (such as direct broadcasting) or services provided by governmental or intergovernmental entities incident to their functions. The negotiators intended to permit members and intergovernmental organizations full freedom to provide such services outside of and without regard to the economic well-being of INTELSAT. Numerous references in the negotiating history indicate that, before INTELSAT undertakes specialized services, it should consult with the U.N. specialized agencies already involved in providing such services, such as the International Civil Aviation Organization (ICAO) or the International Maritime Consultative Organization (IMCO).

The data and TV services that Orion and ISI propose to offer are not specialized services within the sense of that term as used in the INTELSAT Agreement.

Conclusion

While the issue is not free from doubt, the proposals would appear to contemplate providing public international telecommunications and require coordination with INTELSAT both to avoid economic harm and for technical compatibility.

NOTES

1. The U.S. separate systems are not the only systems outside of IN-TELSAT. There has been consultation with INTELSAT regarding other systems, such as the European system EUTELSAT, the Indonesian Palapa system, the Arabsat consortium, Algeria's use of the Soviet Intersputnik system, and the use of U.S. domestic satellites to connect the United States with Canada, Mexico, and Bermuda. A complete survey of the ever-changing array of new satellite consortia is beyond the scope of this book; for more information on these see R. White & H. White, The Law and Regulation of International Space Communication (1988). Although these systems vary, the issues they raise are generally the same as those explained above—competition for scarce spectrum, economic harm to existing systems, and national sovereignty.

2. Having decided to license separate satellite systems, the United States faced greater difficulties in implementing its decision. The domestic telecommunications of virtually all nations other than the United States fall under the supervision of Postal Telephone and Telegraph authorities, or PTTs. These organizations, as monopolists, tend to be hostile to competition, and since they are usually regulators as well as providers they are able to do much to obstruct the entry of new providers into their markets. They do this not because of concern about economic harm to INTELSAT, but because they fear competition with their lucrative participation in the international cable business, and because they fear that U.S. deregulation, if too successful, might spill over into their own markets. For a discussion of many of these issues see Rein *et al.,* Implementation of a U.S. "Free Entry" Initiative for Transatlantic Satellite Facilities: Problems, Pitfalls, and Possibilities, 18 George Washington Journal of International Law and Economics 459 (1985); Godwin, The Proposed Orion and ISI Transatlantic Satellite Systems: A Challenge to the Status Quo, 24 Jurimetrics: Journal of Law, Science & Technology 297 (1984).

The PTTs' position is probably untenable over the long run, given the growing importance of flexible and inexpensive telecommunications services to international competitiveness—efforts, for example, to maintain jobs within the telecommunications establishments of particular nations will be superseded by concern for maintaining the competitiveness of the economies of those nations as a whole. That is because the importance of information industries to the overall economy of a nation far exceeds their value in terms of the jobs and national income that they create directly on their own. *Cf.* Bresnahan, Measuring the Spillovers from Technical Advance: Mainframe Computers in Financial Services, 76 American Economic Review 742 (1986) (estimating that consumer benefits from computers used in financial services far outweigh benefits to computer companies); T. Howell *et al.,* The Microelectronics Race (1988). Thus, obstructionist telecommunications regulation intended to keep out foreign competition will be seen as the equivalent of destroying roads and harbors in order to reduce imports of foreign television sets—effective in a narrow sense, perhaps, but suicidal from a broader perspective. All nations can be expected to learn this lesson sooner or later—although pressures for protection of domestic telecommunications jobs are likely to be substantial in many cases.

DIRECT SATELLITE BROADCASTING

Broadcasting in general has the capability of transcending national boundaries, something that naturally concerns those who desire to maintain control over the dissemination of information within their domains. Satellites, however, offer the possibility of broadcasting to many nations at once in a way that no other technology does. Although shortwave radio may travel around the world, the signals that television depends on are limited by line of sight. From a satellite, however, an enormous portion of the earth is within view, so that three satellites in geosynchronous orbit can blanket the entire planet. Given that television is generally seen as a more powerful medium than other broadcast services, the possibility of Direct Broadcast Satellite (DBS) television has created considerable concern among those governments who see it as their right to control the kinds of information that their citizens may receive.

As a result, DBS has been on the agenda of the Legal Subcommittee of the Committee on the Peaceful Uses of Outer Space since 1968—and, indeed, was discussed in COPUOS as early as 1964. Such discussions, though often heated, have achieved little. Generally, the Soviet Union, together with many other authoritarian regimes, has championed principles demanding that no broadcasts be made to any state without its prior consent. Western nations, and particularly the United States, have on the other hand favored a far more open approach. The United States in particular has taken the position that such broadcasting should be limited only to the extent necessary to ensure that copyright and trademark laws are observed and to avoid harmful interference with other broadcast signals.

Not surprisingly, given the political makeup of the globe, the United States' position is distinctly in the minority. Nonetheless (and probably fortunately), the consensus procedure within COPUOS has meant that no principle could be agreed to. However, the United Nations General Assembly and the United Nations Educational, Scientific and Cultural Organization (UNESCO) have adopted positions (which do not have binding force) that reject the United States approach in favor of a more restrictive one.

Arguments in favor of such a position are often couched in terms that avoid politics and stress the need for "cultural sovereignty" or a "New International Information Order." (For an interesting and thorough discussion of these issues from a Third World perspective, see Addis, International Propaganda and the Developing Countries, 21 Vanderbilt Journal of Transnational Law 491 (1988).) While we do not mean to minimize cultural concerns, and we recognize that most international news organizations *do* possess a generally Western orientation, the fact is that politics form the real motivation for most governments' hostility to DBS. Most governments in the world are decidedly authoritarian, and even many governments that *are* generally democratic have a tendency to try to control the nature and amount of information to which their citizens have access. The Soviet Union's history is well known, but even the United States—unquestionably the world's leading champion of open access to information—has had a somewhat checkered record in that regard. *See generally* L. Powe, American Broadcasting and the First Amendment (1987) on this topic. Wherever their employ, the instinct of bureaucrats and politicians is to protect their jobs and promote their interests by using the power of the state to silence their enemies and proclaim their own views. In some countries they are restrained in this tendency by domestic laws or political ideologies; in others they have free rein.

The existing international law (or its aspirational equivalent) is quite clear, though. Article 19 of the Universal Declaration of Human Rights, which has been assented to (if not necessarily followed) by virtually every nation in the world, provides that:

> Everyone has the right to freedom of opinion and expression; this right includes freedom to hold opinions without interference and to seek, receive and impart information and ideas through any media and regardless of frontiers.

Nations should not be permitted to depart from this principle in the DBS context simply because a novel technology is involved. Although governments often attempt to control new communication technologies to a degree that would not be tolerated with regard to those that are more established, if history teaches anything it is that governments are not to be trusted, *under any circumstances,* with control of their citizens' right to receive and impart ideas. Such control is almost inevitably abused, and the results of such abuse are consistently worse than the consequences of freedom—at least from the viewpoint of the governed.

Fortunately, however, the rapid dissemination of technology and the continued progress in the field of electronics that have marked this century will make control of satellite broadcasting less and less feasible. Already, at the time of this writing, satellite dishes capable of receiving programs from communications satellites not intended for broadcasting at all are widespread, both within the United States and throughout the third world. Given time, the size and cost of such facilities (already well within the limits of individuals and small organizations) will likely become small enough that even concerted government efforts to stamp them out will be fruitless—and the widespread presence of video recorders, even within East Bloc countries, already ensures that any program received can be widely circulated. As satellites specifically designed for broadcast purposes grow common, reception will become easier and censorship even more difficult.

Furthermore, the growth of two-way satellite technologies will undoubtedly allow the spread of inexpensive portable uplink equipment, meaning that incriminating evidence of (say) a massacre of civilians in a remote region can be sent to the world within minutes regardless of efforts by the regime in power to prevent it.

This is as it should be. As the Universal Declaration of Human Rights recognizes, free exchange of ideas is a basic human right. The explosion of information technologies in the late 20th century has made it steadily easier to realize that right, and the importance of those technologies to national economic competitiveness has meant that nations cannot for long resist their spread without paying a fearsome price. While the technologies of space communication will not in themselves make tyranny impossible, they will make its task far more difficult, and ensure that its actions do not escape notice and censure in the world community. The benefits from this will far exceed the costs.

Although the DBS debate has generated far more heat than light, it does offer a fascinating (if not especially encouraging) view of how the international system responds to new technologies. For more on this topic, including good histories of the debate, see R. White & H. White, The Law and Regulation of International Space Communication (1988), especially at Chapter 9, E. van Bogaert, Aspects of Space Law 223 *et seq.* (1986), and Paul, Images from Abroad: Making Direct Broadcasting by Satellites Safe for Sovereignty, 9 Hastings International & Comparative Law Review 329 (1986).

7

Space-Related International Trade Issues

Throughout the 1980s, space industries began to take on a more commercial tone. With the entry of the European Arianespace as a quasi-private commercial entity, competition for satellite-launching business began in earnest. At first, such competition was between NASA's space shuttle and Ariane, but after the 1986 *Challenger* tragedy that competition became more widespread. Pursuant to the Commercial Space Launch Act of 1984 (Pub. L. 98–575, 98 Stat. 3055, codified at 49 U.S.C. § 2601 *et seq.*), as amended in 1988, the U.S. government had already begun the process of establishing a private sector commercial launch industry. The enormous disruption created by the *Challenger* accident and by unfortunately timed problems with other launch systems accelerated this process, and focused attention on the importance of a diverse and robust U.S. launch capacity. Meanwhile, the Soviet Union and the People's Republic of China began aggressively marketing launch services on their own launch vehicles, while new entrants, including Japan, Brazil, and India appeared on the horizon.

Similarly, growing competition was developing in the payload sector. European satellite manufacturers, having gained experience with the early *Symphonie* communications satellite in the mid-1970s, became more and more involved in the satellite construction field, while a French concern, Spot Image, entered the private remote-sensing field in competition with the United States' EOSAT. India began building and launching its own remote sensing and communications satellites, Brazil began moving toward entry into that area, and Japanese executives were heard talking excitedly about the prospects for Japanese "hegemony" in satellite telecommunications, to the discomfiture of their commercial rivals in other nations. Despite calls for the development of "rules of the road" for international trade in space goods and services, the stage at this writing is obviously set for a series of trade disputes in the area, disputes for which existing international trade law is clearly inadequate, whether embodied in international agreements or U.S. municipal law.

Because at this writing we are only now on the verge of such disputes, this chapter will not attempt a microscopic dissection of existing international trade law, such as it is, nor will it attempt to foresee all of the possible disputes in the offing. Instead, it will examine the reasons why such disputes are likely to occur, will discuss the forces that will tend to shape them, and will suggest some things that might be done to reduce the magnitude of the problem and to safeguard U.S. national interests. In addition, this chapter discusses the impact of U.S. and international technology controls on space industries and activities.

ECONOMICS OF SPACE INDUSTRIES

Although the term "space industries" encompasses a wide variety of enterprises, from launch services to microgravity manufacturing to telecommunications, such industries have, in broad, some important elements in common. First, they tend to be at or near the cutting edge of technological development. Second, they tend to be characterized by substantial economies of scale. Third, they tend to be of considerable importance to both "upstream" industries (that is, suppliers) and "downstream" industries (that is, customers)—for example, the telecommunications satellite industry is a consumer of many high technology products, as well as a key input for long distance telephone companies and television networks. And fourth, space industries are often of "dual use" character, having both civilian and military applications which are largely inseparable—for example, the technologies involved in entering the civilian launch industry are little different from those needed to construct ballistic missiles capable of carrying nuclear warheads, a fact not overlooked by the Indian and Brazilian governments, or their neighbors.

Aside from their military implications, space industries are strategic in an economic sense as well, for the reasons listed above. Nations involved in marketing space goods and services do so for the opportunity to gain economies of scale, to move up the learning curve, to drive development of key technologies, and to gain hard currency and international prestige. Although these are all legitimate and even desirable goals, they do pose problems from an international trade standpoint, since they may be better served by national strategies involving pricing below cost ("dumping") and unfair government subsidies than by strategies based solely on commercial competitiveness. Dumping and subsidization are generally considered unfair practices in international trade; however, they are often engaged in by nations (particularly mercantilistic or non-market economies) for strategic reasons. Such behavior is likely in a number of space-related areas, particularly the launch services field, and is hence likely to lead to disputes. For more on these economic issues see Reynolds & Merges, Toward an Industrial Policy for Outer Space: Problems and Prospects of the Commercial Launch Industry, 29 Jurimetrics: Journal of Law, Science & Technology 7 (1988).

To provide a bit of the flavor of such disputes, and to allow a bit of perspective on the discussion to follow, we reproduce here excerpts from one recent international dispute over international trade in the launch services field. Following those excerpts is a discussion of how U.S. law and existing international trade agreements apply to trade in space-related goods and services, and some observations for the future.

The Transpace Section 301 Petition

As the move toward commercialization of the launch services market began to get underway, several companies were organized to enter that market. Unfortunately for these entities, market prospects were difficult: NASA shuttle launches were still subsidized, and NASA's only active competitor, the European consortium Arianespace, was meeting NASA's prices in an effort to attract business. Since NASA was backed by the U.S. treasury, and Arianespace by the scarcely less formidable resources of the major European countries, it was difficult for entities that had to make a profit to compete. One of the new companies, Transpace Carriers, Inc., thus filed a so-called "Section 301 petition" with the United States Trade Representative. The following discussion will make clear why Transpace chose that approach, after which are excerpts from both the petition and the Presidential determination stemming from it.

**Reynolds & Merges, Toward an Industrial Policy
for Outer Space: Problems and Prospects
of the Commercial Launch Industry,
29 Jurimetrics: Journal of Law, Science & Technology 7 (1988)**

Because of the likely importance of price in this market, new foreign competitors can be expected to price aggressively, and even to dump, in order to obtain market share and scale economies. Existing U.S. trade laws, however, are not admirably suited to the problem of unfair trade in launch services. The antidumping law, Section 731 of the Tariff Act of 1930 as amended [19 U.S.C. § 1673(1) (1988)], focuses on "a class or kind of foreign merchandise" that "is being, or is likely to be, sold in the United States at less than its fair value." Launch services almost certainly would not be found to be "merchandise" for the purpose of this provision, nor is it likely to be found that a foreign launch provider, by contracting with a U.S. customer, has "sold" anything "in the United States." Similarly, U.S. countervailing duty law [19 U.S.C. § 1671 (1988)] provides for imposition of a duty in response to "a subsidy with respect to the manufacture, production, or exportation of a class or kind of merchandise imported or sold (or likely to be sold) for importation, into the United States." Both laws also apply an injury test, although in the case of the countervailing duty law the injury requirement is omitted as to countries not party to the GATT subsidies code. Because these laws were designed to deal with traditional trade in goods, they are poorly suited to dealing with predatory pricing in the launch services field.

Somewhat more success might be expected under Section 301 of the Trade Act of 1974 as amended [19 U.S.C. § 2411 (1988)]. Among other things, Section 301 allows the President to "take all appropriate and feasible action within his power" in response to any foreign practice that "is unjustifiable, unreasonable, or discriminatory and burdens or restricts United States commerce." Unlike the antidumping and countervailing duty laws, Section 301 explicitly applies to services as well as merchandise, and grants the President sweeping power to respond via duties, restrictions on foreign services, and actions in trade sectors other than the one in dispute. Thus (for example) predatory pricing in Chinese launch services might be penalized via a ban on imports of Chinese textiles or agricultural products.

Despite the power and flexibility of Section 301, however, there is surprisingly little enthusiasm among space and international trade lawyers for its application to launch services. This is because in 1985 the United States refused to take action against the European Space Agency in response to the petition by Transpace Carriers, a U.S. launch company. Despite this refusal to act, however, Section 301 may profitably be applied to the future, given the changes in the industry, in U.S. practice, and in the degree and nature of foreign competition. However, trade legislation specifically aimed at launch services *would* be beneficial, not least as a signal to foreign providers that the United States takes the matter seriously.

Another possible solution, which we endorse, would be to pursue multilateral trade talks regarding launch services with all other spacefaring nations. Some such talks have been going on informally already; these could be expanded into a full-scale trade agreement governing launch services, or perhaps incorporated into the current round of negotiations under the General Agreement on Tariffs and Trade. Such talks are certainly worth pursuing and such an agreement, if well-drafted, would be worth concluding. In general, though, the effectiveness of such agreements in preventing unfair trade practices has not been stellar; at best they prevent the most egregious abuses, at worst they simply introduce market distortions that ultimately harm the competitiveness of domestic industries. To survive in the long run, U.S. launch services industries need to be better than their foreign competitors, which means that the launch technology they employ must be more efficient and at least as reliable.

**Before the Office of the United States
Trade Representative Chairwoman, Section 301 Committee;
Petition Seeking Presidential Action Under Section 301
of the Trade Act of 1974 as amended (19 U.S.C. § 2411, et seq.)
by Transpace Carriers, Inc. against the Governments of
Belgium, Denmark, France, Germany, Ireland, Italy,
the Netherlands, Sweden, Spain, Switzerland and
the United Kingdom and Their Space-Related Instrumentalities**

This petition is filed on behalf of the civil expendable launch vehicle services industry, by Transpace Carriers, Inc. ("TCI") pursuant to § 301 *et seq.* of the Trade Act of 1974, as amended, 19 U.S.C. § 2411, *et seq.* (Supp. III 1979) (hereinafter "the Act") and 15 C.F.R. § 2006.0(b) (1982). This petition contains all information reasonably available to petitioner.

The subject of the petition are acts, policies and practices undertaken by the Member States of the European Space Agency ("ESA"), *i.e.,* Belgium, Denmark, France, Germany, Italy, Ireland, the Netherlands, Spain, Sweden, Switzerland and the United Kingdom, and their space-related instrumentalities, that are unjustifiable, unreasonable or discriminatory and that burden or restrict United States commerce in trade in services within the meaning of section 301(a)(2)(B) of the Act. Specifically, the above-referenced governments and their instrumentalities, particularly the French national space agency, Centre National d'Etudes Spatiale ("CNES"), are subsidizing the activities of a French company, Arianespace, S.A., which is in direct competition with petitioner in the provision of civil expendable launch vehicle services to customers in the United States and third countries.

The specific subsidy practices of which petitioner complains, include:

— The two-tiered pricing of launch services offered by Arianespace. Member States of ESA have agreed to pay 25% to 33% per "launch" more than is charged to the export market for the same services.

— The provision of launch and range facilities and services and/or personnel at no charge, or unreasonably low cost, to Arianespace by the French national space agency, CNES. The cost of launch and range facilities and services represents approximately one-third of the total cost of a launch.

— The provision of CNES administrative, management and/or technical personnel to Arianespace either at no charge or at rates that are unreasonably low.

— The subsidization of mission insurance rates which Arianespace customers would otherwise pay.

As a beneficiary of such subsidy practices, Arianespace has been able to offer launch services to United States companies and third country customers at rates which are substantially less than those charged to Member States of ESA and substantially below those prices that Arianespace would be able to charge in the absence of subsidization. This unfair competitive advantage has resulted in lost sales to petitioner and price suppression, if not depression, of bid prices. Furthermore, it poses a serious threat to the establishment of a United States commercial launch services industry.

Petitioner therefore requests, pursuant to section 301(a) of the Act, that the President take all appropriate and feasible action within his power to obtain the elimination of such acts, policies or practices that are unjustifiable, unreasonable or discriminatory and that burden or restrict this important new service industry, and to take such other action as is sanctioned by section 301(b) of the Act.

In particular, petitioner requests the President to seek the immediate discontinuance of the two-tiered pricing policy for Arianespace launches observed by the Member States of ESA, the elimination of the cost-free or below-cost support in facilities, services and personnel provided by the French national space agency, CNES, and the subsidization of mission insurance rates, such that all outstanding and future Arianespace bids for launch services reflect actual costs plus a reasonable profit for each launch. Pending the elimination of such acts, policies and practices, the President is requested to retaliate by prohibiting Arianespace U.S.A. from advertising and marketing its services in the United States and by imposing economic sanctions against the goods and services of the Member States of ESA.

NOTE

Under Section 301, action is not mandatory. The United States Trade Representative, whose office is part of the Executive Office of the President, investigates and makes a recommendation to the President, who determines whether or not to act. Although time limits vary depending on the allegations involved, the President must in no case take longer than 12 months to respond. The President's determination, along with the reasons behind it, is then published in the Federal Register. Because the language of Section 301 is permissive, not mandatory, the President may be swayed by political considerations unrelated to trade issues. (Legislation under consideration at the time of this writing would reduce the amount of discretion under Section 301 and would shift the decision from the President to the United States Trade Representative. These changes are unlikely to have major impact in the space context.) Many have criticized Section 301 on this ground, and on the basis that it does not clearly define the conduct to which the President is permitted to respond. *See, e.g.,* Hansen, Defining Unreasonableness in International Trade: Section 301 of the Trade Act of 1974, 96 Yale Law Journal 1122 (1987). There is no right to appeal from a determination not to act, but petitioners may withdraw their petition in order to avoid a negative determination. Although negative determinations do not have a binding precedential effect, they represent a distinct burden on further efforts by the petitioner and thus are to be avoided where possible.

In the case of the Transpace petition, the result was a negative determination: the President found that the practices complained of were not sufficiently different from those of NASA at the time. A major influence on this decision was the absence of any viable domestic commercial launch industry: although Transpace and others were attempting to obtain business, none had signed a launch contract and many doubted whether they could succeed on a commercial basis. (Of course, given the need to compete with NASA and Arianespace at artificially low prices, this may well have been true.) It is unlikely that this negative determination would be a bar to a future proceeding if circumstances justified, however: there is now a substantial and growing U.S. launch industry, and NASA is no longer competing for commercial launch contracts. Certainly Transpace's experience is no reason for international trade and space lawyers to despair of *ever* using Section 301 in response to unfair foreign practices in the space field, despite the negative determination excerpted next.

Determination Under Section 301
of the Trade Act of 1974, 50 Fed. Reg. 29631 (July 22, 1985)

Pursuant to Section 301(a) of the Trade Act of 1974, as amended (19 U.S.C. 2411(a)), I have determined that the practices of the Member States of the European Space Agency (ESA) and their instrumentalities with respect to the commercial satellite launching services of Arianespace, S.A. are not unreasonable and a burden or restriction on U.S. Commerce. While Arianespace does not operate under purely commercial conditions, this is in large measure a result of the history of the launch services industry, which is marked by almost exclusive government involvement. I have determined that these conditions do not require affirmative U.S. action at this time. But because of my decision to commercialize expendable launch services in the United States, and our policies with respect to manned launch services such as the Shuttle (STS), it may become appropriate for the United States to approach other interested nations to reach an international understanding on guidelines for commercial satellite launch services at some point in the future.

Reasons for Determination

Based on a petition filed by Transpace Carriers, Inc. (TCI), the United States Trade Representative (USTR) initiated an investigation on July 9, 1984, of the European Space Agency's policies with respect to Arianespace S.A. Arianespace is a privately owned company, incorporated under the laws of France for the purpose of launching satellites. Arianespace's shareholders include the French national space agency, and aerospace companies and banks incorporated in the ESA Member States.

The Petitioner alleged that 1) Arianespace uses a two tier pricing policy whereby Arianespace charges a higher price to ESA Member States than to foreign customers; 2) the French national space agency (CNES) subsidizes launch and range facilities, and services and personnel provided to Arianespace; 3) the French national space agency subsidizes the administrative and technical personnel it provides to Arianespace; and 4) Arianespace's mission insurance rates are subsidized. In addition to these allegations, the U.S. also investigated three other areas: government inducements to purchasers of Arianespace's services; direct and indirect government assistance to Arianespace; and, Arianespace's costs and pricing policies.

Our findings with respect to these allegations are set forth below. Many of the factual allegations were not supported by evidence on the record. While other allegations were substantiated, the practices were not sufficiently different from U.S. practice in this field to be considered unreasonable under Section 301.

*   *   *

Since there are no international standards of reasonableness for launch services, we have compared ESA practices to United States practice, and to reasonable commercial practices. The ESA practices are not sufficiently different from those of the U.S. to be actionable under Section 301. This determination is not an endorsement of ESA practices. Our policies in this area are now undergoing revision, and in the future we may wish to reexamine ESA's practices and their effect on U.S.G. launch services. At that time it may be in our mutual interest to engage in international discussions aimed at establishing appropriate guidelines for the commercial launch industry.

The determination shall be published in the Federal Register.
RONALD REAGAN

THE WHITE HOUSE
Washington, July 17, 1985

NOTES

1. At the time of this writing, there are informal talks going on between the United States, the Europeans, and various other governments regarding the establishment of "rules of the road" for trade in launch services. The goal is to determine what conduct should be regarded as fair and unfair in promoting a nation's launch business. This is made more important by the complete absence of any international agreement covering launch services. This absence may be remedied during the upcoming round of negotiations over the General Agreement on Tariffs and Trade (GATT)'s coverage of service industries, although prospects at this writing do not appear especially hopeful.

2. The Transpace petition involved subsidies that (although they may have been real) were difficult to quantify and hard to separate from activities that any responsible government could be expected to engage in—such as safety inspections, assistance in planning launch ranges, etc. And the prices charged by Ariane were not dramatically lower than those charged for launches on what was then its only competitor, the Space Shuttle. Future trade disputes are more likely to deal with purely state-operated launch services, such as the Soviet or Chinese are beginning to market.

3. International trade lawyers refer to sales of products or services at prices below the seller's cost as "dumping." The following excerpt explains why dumping is considered an unfair practice in international trade, and why nations engage in what, at first glance, may seem like a counterproductive practice: selling goods for less than they cost.

Glenn Reynolds & John Ragosta, International Trade in Launch Services: Some Problems and Solutions

Although dumping seems beneficial to consumers in the short run, since they are able to buy at below the seller's cost, it is very harmful to national economies in the long run. Dumping allows the producing country to achieve sales volumes great enough to produce substantial scale economies and dramatic moves up the learning curve, giving that country tremendous long-term advantage over competitors. Such moves up the learning curve can produce a near-insurmountable advantage in high technology capital-intensive industries—just as, in a different context, the money spent on air mail subsidies in the 1920s and 1930s allowed the U.S. aircraft industry to "bootstrap" itself into levels of efficiency that produced 50 years of American predominance in aviation.

And where dumping targets a particular "bottleneck" sector, it can allow other, more profitable sectors to flourish, often to the extent that revenue from those sectors offsets the cost of the dumping. For example, Japanese dumping of computer memory chips has allowed them to virtually eliminate the U.S. industry in that area; now it appears that they are manipulating supplies and prices of those chips to disadvantage U.S. competitors in high value-added sectors that depend on memory chips, such as whole computers, disk drives, and custom chips. While the United States is now, after the fact, working diligently to respond to Japanese chip-dumping, Japan has leveraged its advantage into other markets, gained in violation of international trade rules, that it could effectively control for years.

In the same way, one might imagine the Japanese exploiting a similar position in the launch services area to disadvantage U.S. satellite manufacturers, remote-sensing operators, etc. There is certainly no question that the Japanese hope to compete in the payload sector as well as in the launch services arena—in fact, Teruo Masuda, a senior section officer of C. Itoh's information systems and technology department, was recently quoted as saying "We have to have hegemony in satellite telecommunications," a goal that in light of recent Japanese successes should send shivers up the spines of U.S. satellite manufacturers. A decisive advantage in the launch services area, however achieved, could substantially help Japan in achieving such control.

NOTE

The above excerpt embodies new economic thinking about international trade. Classical and neoclassical economists maintain that nations cannot be harmed by dumping or subsidization on the part of competitors. Many economists are now arguing that this may not be the case, at least with regard to key "strategic industries." For a good survey of such thinking, see Strategic Trade Policy and the New International Economics (P. Krugman ed. 1986); R. Gilpin, The Political Economy of International Relations (1987) esp. at 215–230; Tyson, Ask The Right Tough Questions About America's Strategic Industries, Harvard Business Review, November-December 1988, at 103; Krugman, Import Protection as Export Promotion: International Competition in the Presence of Oligopoly and Economies of Scale, in Monopolistic Competition and International Trade (H. Kierzkowski ed. 1984); Krugman, New Theories of Trade Among Industrial Countries, 76 American Economic Review 343 (1983). *See also* R. Nelson, High Technology Policies: A Five Nation Comparison (1982); Mowery & Rosenberg, The Commercial Aircraft Industry, in Government and Technical Progress: A Cross-Industry Analysis (R. Nelson ed. 1982). For an article applying many of these ideas in the context of international trade in launch services see Reynolds & Merges, Toward an Industrial Policy for Outer Space: Problems and Prospects of the Commercial Launch Industry, 29 Jurimetrics: Journal of Law, Science, & Technology 7 (1988).

EXPORT CONTROLS AND TRADE IN SPACE-RELATED GOODS AND SERVICES

The earlier part of this chapter deals with space-related international trade issues from the perspective of ensuring that U.S. industry enjoys all possible opportunities to sell its goods and services abroad, an avowed goal of the U.S. government. Set against this U.S. policy, however, are a group of laws and regulations designed to restrict the availability of those same goods and services. These laws and regulations, collectively known as "export controls," are intended to protect U.S. national security and promote U.S. foreign policy interests by preventing the export of U.S. goods, services and technical information to specified countries. In general, U.S. export controls focus on controlling products, services and data of U.S. high technology industries, including U.S. space and space-related industries, which could contribute significantly to the military potential of U.S. adversaries. In order to protect such items from diversion, some form of license is generally required to export or reexport them to almost any destination in the world (Canada is a special exception), including the United States' closest allies.

Obviously, U.S. export controls offer considerable potential for conflict with another important policy, that of promoting U.S. trade, either by denying to U.S. companies access to potential markets or, more typically, by imposing burdensome license requirements that impede the ability of U.S. companies to make sales in already established markets. *See, e.g.,* Committee on Science, Engineering & Public Policy, Balancing the National Interest: U.S. National Security Export Controls and Global Economic Competition (1987) esp. at pp. 7–6, 6–11 (finding that overcomplex and overinclusive U.S. export control regulations impede domestic innovation and harm ability of U.S. firms to compete in international markets). See also Gerjuoy, Controls on Scientific Information Exports, 3 Yale Law & Policy Review 447 (1985). The recently enacted Omnibus Trade and Competitiveness Act of 1988 includes a number of provisions that are intended to simplify licensing requirements for exports to Western Europe, Japan and other Free World destinations where most purchasers of U.S. goods and services are located. Pub. L. No. 100-418, §§ 2414–2423, 102 Stat. 1107, 1347–1359 (1988). Whether this objective will be achieved is difficult to predict, however, as the strictness with which the United States applies export controls is more a function of U.S. policy requirements than of the legal infrastructure upon which controls are based.

On the other hand, export controls may themselves be used in service of the goals of promoting U.S. trade—for example, restrictions on the export of U.S. satellite technology may be used to frustrate foreign dumping of launch services by depriving the offending foreign country of payloads. Using export controls in this fashion is, however, a two-edged sword. While restrictions on export of U.S. technology may accomplish important goals in the short run, they encourage foreign nations reliant on that technology to work harder to achieve independence, ultimately undermining U.S. leverage *and* creating new competition in international markets. In addition, to the extent that export controls are seen as a tool for maintaining U.S. economic position rather than as a means of promoting international security, cooperation from allied nations—which is absolutely essential if export controls are to be effective—is likely to diminish markedly.

Maintaining international security is, of course, the primary purpose of export controls, and it is an important purpose in the context of many space goods and services. Many space-related technologies are of considerable military importance: for example, any nation capable of launching satellites (or even sizable suborbital payloads) is capable of delivering nuclear warheads via ballistic missile. At the time of this writing, a number of nations have such a capability or are likely to acquire it in the near future; such nations number not only the traditional space powers but also the European nations, the People's Republic of China, Japan, India, and Brazil, with more entrants (perhaps including Israel and South Africa) likely. It is no coincidence that many of these nations possess (or are developing) nuclear weapons technology as well.

U.S. and international efforts to limit the spread of nuclear weapons technology have been a qualified success to date. Although some nations have acquired nuclear capabilities, that number has been smaller than many expected in the 1960s and no nation since World War II has exploded a nuclear weapon in anger. This has been made possible by a system of international controls on nuclear technology that, although far from seamless, have served (in combination with political pressure) to restrict the transfer of such technology considerably.

The United States and other nations have recently attempted to institute a similar regime (discussed *infra*) with regard to technologies capable of delivering nuclear warheads, but the prospects for success there are much less. There are two key reasons for this grim scenario. First, the agreement comes much later in the day: many nations have already developed or acquired basic launch technology, making it harder to keep the lid on matters—particularly as that technology is, overall, less difficult than that embodied in nuclear weapons. The German V-2, which was the first liquid-fuelled rocket of any real consequence, would have sufficed as a nuclear delivery vehicle. Second, the "dual use" character of many space technologies means that they necessarily appear in various commercial incarnations that are virtually impossible to control entirely. The modern industrial world is so dependent on precision machining, high-strength and high-temperature alloys, sophisticated avionics, and other technologies that, collectively, constitute "space launch technologies" that a complete ban on exports would constitute technological and market suicide. Some seepage is thus inevitable. Despite controls, then, the primary barrier to the spread of nuclear missile technology is likely to be political pressure from the more advanced countries. Whether those nations possess the political will to exert that pressure in the face of other (often conflicting) policy goals is unclear.

In the meantime, however, export controls remain in existence, and it is likely that they will be of some use in retarding, if not halting, the spread of nuclear missile technology. The following section provides a brief overview of existing controls.

Existing Export Controls

The current U.S. and international export control regime constitutes one of the most confusing and technically demanding areas of law practice. The export of commercial space products, services and technology, for example, is generally controlled under the provisions of the State Department's International Traffic in Arms Regulations (ITAR), 22 CFR pts. 120–130 (1988), which govern the licensing of exports and reexports of "defense articles and services," *i.e.,* goods or services that are "inherently military in character" and consequently included on the U.S. Munitions List. *Id.,* § 120.3. Not all space-related products fall under the ITAR, however. Certain commodities intended for commercial space applications are exempt from ITAR control and instead fall under the Commerce Department's Export Administration Regulations (EAR), 15 CFR pts. 370–399 (1988), *as amended by* 53 Fed. Reg. 37751 (Sept. 28, 1988) (recodifying EAR as 15 CFR pts. 770–799), which are designed to control "dual use" items, *i.e.,* items that can be used for both military and commercial applications. *Id.,* § 399.1. The fact that the purchaser of these commodities may be a military entity is not necessarily relevant to whether a space-related product is considered a "defense article" or a "dual-use" item. 22 CFR § 120.3.

Given the overlap between the ITAR and the EAR, it is often difficult to determine which controls are applicable in a given case. Indeed, export control practice requires not only a substantial knowledge of the technology involved, but the necessarily arbitrary practice of classifying technologies and destinations results in an administrative practice of case-by-case evaluation of license applications, with predictably arbitrary and variable results. Worse yet from the perspective of lawyers and their clients, some international export control agreements (for example the recent multinational agreement on nuclear missile technologies) are actually secret, necessitating the partial secrecy (and/or the considerable ambiguity) of many implementing regulations. Leaving aside the dubious constitutionality of subjecting U.S. citizens to bodies of secret law, this practice unavoidably adds additional layers of complexity.

In dealing with these problems, and export controls generally, it is strongly recommended that space lawyers and businesspeople seek experienced and qualified specialist counsel in the export control field; export controls lawyers, meanwhile, are urged to consult closely with space counsel and clients, as complete knowledge of the industry and its overall legal environment is essential to dealing with its export control problems.

Even when such experts in export controls are employed, however, it is highly beneficial for those involved in space industries to have some general knowledge of the export control area. Following is a brief outline of key issues in the area. It focuses on the application of controls under the EAR, but is equally applicable to the ITAR. Note, however, that there is considerably less flexibility under the ITAR to make an export without first obtaining specific written approval from the U.S. government.

McFadden, Snyder & Schoettler, The Structure of Export Licensing, in 1 The Commerce Department Speaks 379 (D. Riggs ed. 1987)

II. Principles Relating to Export Licensing

A. THERE IS NO INHERENT RIGHT TO EXPORT. With limited exceptions, the export from the United States of all commodities is prohibited, "unless and until" a license for export is issued by the Department of Commerce. 15 C.F.R. § 370.3 (1987). Thus, most business transactions involving the export of goods will be subject to government regulation and require some form of government approval.

B. THE PROHIBITIONS AND RESTRICTIONS ON U.S. EXPORTS ARE FAR-RANGING. Many prohibitions, such as munitions requirements, 22 C.F.R. §§ 120.1–130.17 (1987), and foreign assets controls, 31 C.F.R. §§ 500.101–545.807 (1987), are independent or overlapping with the

Export Administration Regulations. 15 C.F.R. §§ 368–399.2 (1987). As discussed in Section III A. *infra*, there are at least seven agencies other than the Department of Commerce involved in the regulation of exports. Approval of an export transaction by one agency does not necessarily relieve an exporter of the burden of obtaining approval or a license from other agencies which may have responsibility for control of the item to be exported.

C. TECHNOLOGY AND INFORMATION AS WELL AS GOODS ARE SUBJECT TO U.S. EXPORT CONTROLS. Some of the U.S. government's most critical concerns about export controls relate to the transfer of proprietary know-how. *See id.* §§ 379.1–379.10 (rules on export of technical data). In any international business transaction, special attention should be given to compliance with regulations governing technical data.

D. U.S. EXPORT CONTROLS ARE APPLIED ON AN EXTRATERRITORIAL BASIS. U.S. export control regulations cover not only the export, but also the reexport of goods and technology that have been transferred from the United States. *Id.* § 370.2 (definition of "reexport"). The transfer of U.S. origin goods and technology between two foreign countries must generally comply with U.S. export controls. Depending upon the transaction, obtaining U.S. permission to reexport may be the responsibility of the U.S. exporter or the party who initially received the export.

E. WHAT CONSTITUTES AN EXPORT MAY NOT ALWAYS BE WHAT IT SEEMS. The Export Administration Act defines "export" to include not only the shipment of goods or technology beyond U.S. borders, but also the transfer of goods or technology within the United States to an affiliate or embassy of a controlled country or a transfer of such items either within or outside the United States with the knowledge or intent that the items will be shipped, transferred or transmitted to an unauthorized recipient. 50 U.S.C. app. § 2415(5) (1982 & Supp. III 1985). There is no general definition of "export" in the Export Administration Regulations, although certain activities are defined to be exports in various parts of the Regulations. *See, e.g.,* 15 C.F.R. § 379.1(b)(ii) (1987) (definition of export of technical data for purposes of Part 379 of the Regulations). Thus, a practitioner must exercise care when applying the export control laws to ensure that the scope of export licensing requirements is clearly understood.

F. THE REACH OF U.S. EXPORT CONTROLS IS EXTENSIVE. Sanctions for violations of export control rules may be imposed on persons and firms within the United States and outside its borders. *Id.* § 370.1 (definition of "person or firm"). Even if it is not subject to U.S. jurisdiction, an entity can be affected by U.S. sanctions in that all U.S. firms can be prohibited from dealing with it. *Id.* § 387.12. Further, persons related by ownership, control, position of responsibility, affiliation or other connection to a violator may be subjected to sanctions. *Id.* § 388.3(b). Even where a party was not involved in the violation, his property may be seized and subjected to forfeiture if the property was, or was intended to be, exported in violation of export controls. *Id.* § 387.1(b)(4).

G. THE U.S. GOVERNMENT EXERCISES BROAD DISCRETION IN ADMINISTERING EXPORT CONTROLS. This wide discretion is due largely to the national security dimensions of export controls, as well as the technical nature of product classifications. The judgment of U.S. government officials in these particular areas is accorded great deference.

H. PENALTIES FOR EXPORT VIOLATIONS CAN BE SEVERE. In addition to criminal fines and imprisonment, administrative sanctions may include the denial of export privileges, ineligibility as a recipient of U.S. exports or reexports (*i.e.,* being placed on the so-called Denied Party List), and exclusion from practice before the International Trade Administration. *Id.* §§ 387.1, 388.3. As a practical matter, these administrative sanctions could well prevent a company from engaging in any international operations. Hence, they represent a powerful incentive for businesses to comply strictly with U.S. export controls.

I. EXPORTERS CAN BE HELD STRICTLY LIABLE FOR CERTAIN EXPORT CONTROL VIOLATIONS. Exporters are strictly liable for violations of a license issued to them. *Id.* § 387.9. Engaging in transactions from which a denied party may, directly or indirectly, obtain any benefit is a violation regardless of whether the person had any knowledge or reason to know that the denied party would benefit. *Id.* § 387.12(a)(2)(iii). This strict liability standard, coupled with potentially severe sanctions and broad governmental discretion, places a high premium on careful compliance with U.S. export control laws.

J. MULTILATERAL AND BILATERAL CONTROLS MAY APPLY TO U.S. EXPORTS. In some cases, governmental consultation must be made with the Coordinating Committee (COCOM), an informal group of Western nations which have mutually agreed to coordinate their export control policies concerning exports to certain Communist countries, before the U.S. government will approve an export license application. In addition, some exports to COCOM countries and countries such as India, the People's Republic of China and Switzerland, may require special import certifications to be issued by the relevant foreign government. *Id.* §§ 375.3, 375.4–375.7. This requirement can often have a crucial effect on the time necessary to secure license approval.

K. THERE ARE A VARIETY OF FORMS OF EXPORT AUTHORIZATION. Some items may be explicitly exempt from licensing, such as commodities destined for Canada. *Id.* § 385.6. For most exports, however, one of two export authorizations are needed: A *general license*, which is simply standing authority to export and requires no special application or approval with respect to any U.S. government entity; and a *validated license*, which requires specific application and governmental approval of transactions for a specific time period. *Compare id.* §§ 371.1–371.22 (general license rules) *with id.* §§ 372.1–372.13 (validated license rules).

L. AN EXPORTER'S RIGHT TO APPEAL AN ADVERSE LICENSING DECISION IS EXTREMELY LIMITED. Adverse decisions rendered by the Export Administration may be appealed only to the Assistant

Secretary of Commerce for Trade Administration; there is no right to an appeal outside of the Department. *Id.* § 389.2.

M. EXPORT LICENSING IS HANDLED ON A CASE-BY-CASE BASIS. License applications and decisions are treated on a confidential basis. Prior licensing decisions, therefore, are not generally available to exporters to utilize for precedential value in support of new applications. The principal evidence beyond the facts of a particular application that may be used to justify government approval relates to foreign availability—the existence in uncontrolled foreign sources of items of sufficient quantity and comparable quality.

N. EXPORTERS ARE REQUIRED TO MAINTAIN COMPLETE RECORDS OF EXPORT TRANSACTIONS FOR A PERIOD OF AT LEAST TWO YEARS. *Id.* § 387.13(e). On applications presenting new or difficult questions of interpretation, it is especially important for counsel to document the supporting steps and rationale. This includes records relating to the technical characteristics of commodities or technical data as well as the applicability of the Export Administration Regulations.

NOTES

1. From reading the above, it should be obvious that many space-related transactions will require close cooperation between export control counsel, clients, and counsel with expertise in space law and space industries. Because of the broad sweep of export controls and the "dual use" character of many space technologies, virtually any transborder shipment of space-related hardware or technical information is likely to raise export control issues. Leaving aside such obvious elements as launch vehicles, many other space technologies—such as satellites, radiation-hardened chips (essential for space vehicles, but with obvious military implications), and telemetry gear—are treated as "munitions" for export purposes. 22 CFR § 121.1. Given the stiff penalties that can result from illegal exports, it is very important that all technology transfers in the space area be scrutinized for export control compliance.

As mentioned above, such transfers need not involve any shipment of goods (or even data) across borders. For example, disclosure of technical data needed to mate a communications satellite to a foreign launch vehicle, even if such disclosure is made within the United States to a representative of the foreign launch provider, and even if the satellite itself is manufactured abroad, could qualify as an "export" of technical data. Leaving aside the question of the treatment of data that is classified and therefore subject to special controls, see Dep't of Defense, Industrial Security Manual for Safeguarding Classified Information (1987), the mere disclosure within the United States of non-classified data controlled by either the ITAR or the

EAR can be subject to export license requirements if the disclosure is made to a foreign national or with the intent or knowledge that the data will be released to a foreign national or taken out of the United States. *See, e.g.,* 15 CFR § 379.2.

A broad definition of the term "export" raises special concerns for companies offering launch services, because the launch of a vehicle could be considered to be an export from the United States. Indeed, prior to enactment of the Commercial Space Launch Act in 1984, a launch was considered an export subject to ITAR licensing requirements. S. Rep. No. 656, 98th Cong., 2d Sess. 17–18 (1984). Section 21(b) of the Commercial Space Launch Act, however, specifically provides that the mere launching of a payload or a vehicle cannot, solely by reasons of the launch, be considered an export under any export control law. Pub. L. 98–575, § 21(b), 98 Stat. 3055, 3063 (1984) (codified at 49 U.S.C. app. § 2620). In accordance with Section 21(b), the ITAR now specifically excludes the launch of a payload or vehicle from its definition of export. 22 CFR § 120.5. Interestingly, however, there is no definition of export in the EAR and thus a launch of a payload or vehicle is not specifically excluded from the EAR's provisions. Nonetheless, the scope of Section 21(b) of the Commercial Space Launch Act is sufficiently broad to preclude the application of controls under the EAR as well as under the ITAR.

2. The new U.S. regulations designed to limit the spread of technology usable for missiles capable of delivering nuclear weapons (implementing an agreement between the U.S., Canada, France, West Germany, Italy, Japan, and the U.K.) are far reaching. They require a "validated license" for export of equipment and technical data to every country except Canada. Requiring a validated license, rather than a general or special license, means that each shipment must be separately approved. The term "missiles capable of delivering nuclear weapons" is defined as "rocket systems (including ballistic missile systems, space launch vehicles, and sounding rockets) and unmanned air vehicle systems (including cruise missile systems, target drones, and reconnaissance drones) capable of delivering at least a 500 kilogram (kg) payload to a range of at least 300 kilometers." Export Administration Regulations, § 376.18(a) (December, 1987).

Since a validated license is required, exports will be reviewed on a case-by-case basis. This is likely to prove complex and time-consuming since the regulations cover 26 commodity classifications (including aircraft electronics, radiation- and temperature-hardened computer chips, vibration test equipment, and analog-to-digital converters), many of which have important civilian applications. *See* EAR Supplement No. 4 to Part 379 (October 1, 1987) at pp. 6–7. It is unclear how successful these controls will be in preventing the spread of nuclear missile technology. Although modern nuclear missiles certainly depend on components of the sort described in the regulations, the power of nuclear weapons allows missile designers substantial leeway in terms of accuracy and means that even relatively primitive vehicles (such as the German V-2 of World War II) can deliver nuclear weapons. Thus, although the regulations may make it somewhat more difficult to construct nuclear missiles, they by no means make it impossible.

8

The Law of Private Commercial
Activities in Outer Space

Although many of the topics in prior chapters contain material that touches on non-public activities in space, most of the discussion has centered on public law issues. For instance, private entities play a major role in the space satellite communications industry, but our discussion in Chapter 6 focused primarily on the governance structure and international dimensions of such quasi-public bodies as INTELSAT and the ITU. Likewise, Chapter 7, on space-related trade issues, emphasized the applicability (or lack thereof) of the international legal regime established by the General Agreement on Tariffs and Trade (GATT), as well as trade disputes arising under the trade laws of the United States.

In this chapter, we turn our attention to issues of private law that are of importance to commercial activities in space. We are concerned here not with the large-scale legal regimes that govern the interactions between States in space, but rather with the law that governs the smaller-scale interactions between private parties' space activities. (Actually, as you will see, the fact that national governments still dominate most sectors of the space "industry" means that one of the private parties to a space-related transaction may be a State; but the legal issues involved—contracts, torts, and the like—are still *private,* bilateral legal issues.)

Thus in this chapter we address the following topics:

- Jurisdiction: Which country's law applies to private space activities?
- Tort law: How are private parties, as opposed to governments, to be compensated for damage suffered as a result of accidents in outer space?
- Contracts: What special problems are presented by private agreements concerning space activities—primarily commercial launch contracts?
- Intellectual Property: How are inventions made in space protected under U.S. patent law?
- Administrative law: How are private commercial space activities regulated by the U.S. government?

We turn now to the first of these topics, jurisdiction.

JURISDICTION

The following excerpt is from an Office of Technology Assessment (OTA) study of the legal aspects of space stations. It concisely summarizes the major jurisdictional issues raised by space activities.

Office of Technology Assessment, Space Stations and the Law: Selected Legal Issues 25–32 (1986)

Jurisdiction over Space Station Activities

This section examines the concept of jurisdiction and explains how it might be applied to private and government-owned space stations.

A. The Concept of Jurisdiction

Jurisdiction is a legal concept used to describe a state's right to take action—e.g., to prescribe and enforce rules of law—with respect to a particular person, thing, or event. In its inception, the principle of jurisdiction was primarily territorial, deriving from the belief that the power of a nation to act within its own borders was "necessarily exclusive and absolute . . . susceptible of no limitation not imposed by itself." [Comments of Chief Justice Marshall in *Schooner Exchange v. McFaddon,* 7 Cranch [11 U.S.] 116, 136 (U.S. 1812).] But the actions of nations have rarely been limited to their territory. As a result of international trade and travel, and military and political cooperation and competition, the concept of jurisdiction had to expand to comprehend the myriad interactions of states. [The following paragraph is from a footnote in the original.]

Although there are many jurisdictional rationales, all require that there be some genuine link between the state and the persons, property, or events over which jurisdiction is claimed. States have traditionally sought to assert jurisdiction on certain bases or principles. As usually identified, these include:

1. *The Territorial Principle*—A state may exercise jurisdiction with respect to an act occurring in whole or in part in its territory.

2. *The Nationality Principle*—A state may exercise jurisdiction with respect to its own national, wherever he may be.

3. *The Protective Principle*—A state may exercise jurisdiction with respect to certain types of acts wherever, and by whomever, committed where the conduct substantially affects certain vital state interests, such as its security, its property, or the integrity of its governmental process.

4. *The Universality Principle*—A state may exercise jurisdiction with respect to certain specific universally condemned crimes, principally piracy,

wherever and by whomever committed, without regard to .the connection of the conduct with that state.

5. *The Passive Personality Principle*—A state may exercise jurisdiction with respect to any act committed outside its territory by a foreigner which substantially affects the person or property of a citizen.

(S. Houston Lay, Howard J. Taubenfeld, The Law Relating to Activities of Man in Space, The University of Chicago Press, 1970).

Jurisdiction must be exercised some*where,* with respect to some*thing or person.* [J]urisdiction cannot be applied to the high seas or to outer space [except insofar as a nation may exercise jurisdiction and control over a ship *on* the high seas or a space object *in* outer space] because these areas are considered *res communis* under international law and therefore are not "places" that can be appropriated by claim of sovereignty. However, the 1967 Outer Space Treaty declares that a nation may exercise jurisdiction and control over objects in space, much as a nation may exercise jurisdiction over a ship at sea. Objects in space and ships at sea are treated (with some important limitations) as if they were part of the territory of the country on whose registry they are entered and whose flag they fly. [The legal fiction that ships on the high sea and space objects in orbit are like "floating islands" has not been universally accepted. The U.S. Supreme Court, in *Cunard S.S. v. Mellon* (262 U.S. 100) [at 123], referred to the floating island theory as "a figure of speech, a metaphor."]

B. Extent of National Jurisdiction

International law recognizes a nation's jurisdiction over its citizens, its territory, territorial waters and airspace, and those ships and aircraft which it has registered. Whether nations have, through the exercise of their domestic laws, actually extended their jurisdictions to the full extent allowed by international law is a more complicated question.

With reference to U.S. jurisdiction over space activities, it will be important to distinguish between what the United States is capable of doing and what, through congressionally enacted legislation, it has already done. Absent a specific statement of congressional intent, U.S. courts have been reluctant to give extraterritorial reach to certain domestic laws. For example, in *McCulloch v. Sociedad Nacional de Marineros de Honduras* [372 U.S. 10; 83 S. Ct. 671 (1963)], the Court was asked to decide whether U.S. labor laws would apply to ships registered in Honduras and owned and operated by the Honduran subsidiary of a U.S. corporation. The Court noted that Congress had the "constitutional power to apply the National Labor Relations Act to the crews working foreign-flag ships, at least while they are in American waters," but decided that the resolution of the case depended on "whether Congress exercised that power." The court held: "to sanction the exercise of local sovereignty in this 'delicate field of international relations there must be present the affirmative intention of the Congress clearly expressed.' . . . Since neither we nor the parties are able to find any such clear expression, we hold the [National Labor Relations] Board was without jurisdiction. . . ."

Similarly, in *United States v. Cordova* [89 F. Supp. 298 (E.D.N.Y. 1950)], the Court was asked to decide whether an assault committed in a U.S. flag airplane flying over the high seas was within the admiralty and maritime jurisdiction as described in the then current U.S. Criminal Code (18 U.S.C.A. Sec. 451). [At the time, 18 U.S.C.A. Sec. 451 stated that the admiralty and maritime jurisdiction of the United States extended to "American vessels on [the] high seas."] Although the Court noted that "Congress could, under its police power, have extended federal criminal jurisdiction to acts committed on board an airplane owned by an American national. . . ," the applicable legislation (18 U.S.C.A. § 451) spoke only of "vessels" on the "high seas." The Court then concluded that "'vessel' . . . evokes in the common mind a picture of a ship, not of a plane," and that no case or legal principle would "justify the extension of the words 'high seas' to the air space over them." [*Cordova* involved the interpretation of a criminal statute; therefore, under U.S. law, the statute was strictly construed. Not all statutes are strictly construed. For example, the Death on the High Seas Act [41 Stat. 537] (46 U.S.C. 761) [(1982)], which provides a remedy for wrongful death occurring "on" the high seas, has been interpreted by several Federal courts to apply to tortious conduct "over" as well as "on" the high seas. *See:* D'Aleman v. Pan American Airways, 259 F.2d 493 [(2d Cir. 1958)].]

The U.S. statute defining the "special maritime and territorial jurisdiction of the United States" for criminal jurisdiction has since been modified to resolve the problem presented in *United States v. Cordova* and to try to anticipate those problems which might arise in future space activities. [18 U.S.C.A. Sec. 7.] Currently, this special jurisdiction includes:

1. . . . any vessel belonging in whole or in part to the United States, or any citizen thereof, or to any corporation created by or under the laws of the United States. . . .

5. Any aircraft belonging in whole or in part to the United States, or any citizen thereof, or to any corporation created by or under the laws of the United States, . . . while such aircraft is in flight over the high seas, or over any other waters within the admiralty and maritime jurisdiction of the United States. . . .

6. *Any vehicle used or designed for flight or navigation in space and on the registry of the United States pursuant to the [1967 Outer Space Treaty] . . . and the [Registration Convention] . . . while that vehicle is in flight . . .* [emphasis added]

7. Any place outside the jurisdiction of any nation with respect to an offense by or against a national of the United States.

Given the restrictive interpretation of the U.S. jurisdiction presented in the *McCulloch* and *Cordova* cases, it is possible to imagine further problems even under the revised Criminal Code. For example, is a large, manned space vehicle "used or designed for flight or navigation in space"? If so, then paragraph 6 of the Criminal Code (above) would include a space station within the "special maritime and territorial jurisdiction" of the United States. However, since space stations have attributes which differ from those of space transportation vehicles—e.g., their size, complexity, multinational nature, duration in orbit, etc.—[the code provisions] might be more applicable to shuttle-type vehicles. If space stations did not meet the requirements of paragraph 6, they still might be included under the general provisions of paragraph 7. . . .

In the future, it is entirely possible that some space stations will be privately owned. It is also possible that space stations owned in whole or in part by U.S. nationals or corporations will be registered in other countries. A state is generally considered to have jurisdiction to prescribe (though not necessarily enforce) rules of law regarding the conduct of its nationals wherever that conduct occurs. [Restatement (Second) of Foreign Relations Law of the United States, Sec. 30, American Law Institute, 1965.] The extension of U.S. law to privately owned space stations that were registered in other countries would be complicated by the fact that the law of the state of registry might conflict with that of the United States. This could cause problems since the United States, under article VI of the Outer Space Treaty, would remain responsible for the acts of its nationals in space.

Finally, should the United States have the right to exercise its jurisdiction in a particular instance, it would still be necessary to decide how to share power between the Federal government and the individual States. This generally means deciding: 1) whether the grant of jurisdiction in a particular case is exclusively limited to Federal courts or is shared with the state courts, and 2) whether the individual States would be allowed to pass laws in this area. [Some laws may have to be exclusive (e.g., registration laws and laws pertaining to the spaceworthiness of spacecraft); other laws might be amenable to concurrent State/Federal jurisdiction (e.g., criminal and tort law pertaining to individuals on board).] The Judiciary Act of 1789 granted Federal courts exclusive jurisdiction over *in rem* (action against the vessel) admiralty questions. However, *in personam* (action against the owner of the vessel) maritime cases can be brought in State courts. [Maritime causes of action brought *in personam* in State courts must rely on maritime law and not the common law of the State of the forum. (See: *Garret v. Moore McCormack,* 317 U.S. 239 (1942).) Justice Black, writing in *United Fruit* (365 U.S. 731) [1961], noted that "Article VI of the Constitution carries with it the implication that wherever a maritime interest is involved, no matter how slight or marginal, it must displace a local interest, no matter how pressing and significant." The supremacy and uniformity doctrines that prevail in maritime law could be applied to law in outer space.] Similar grants or restrictions of the jurisdiction of Federal and State courts may be necessary for cases involving space activities. In addition, Congress may choose to limit the ability of States to pass laws in certain areas while allowing State courts to apply Federal law. For example, the Federal Aviation Act [49 U.S.C. 130, *et seq.*] limits the right of States to legislate with respect to commercial air travel; however, State courts share with Federal courts the ability to interpret the Federal Aviation Act. The "Commercial Space Launch Act" [49 U.S.C. §§ 2601–2623], establishes a Federal licensing mechanism but notes that the "authority of States to regulate space launch activities within their jurisdictions, or that affect their jurisdictions, is unaffected by this Act. . . ."

To summarize, the issue of jurisdiction is fundamental to the application of U.S. laws to space activities. The fact that international law would allow an extension of U.S. jurisdiction in a particular instance does not mean that such an extension has occurred. Laws meant to regulate U.S. domestic activities may not apply to U.S. space activities (just as the U.S. criminal laws did not apply to the *Cordova* case) unless Congress has clearly established its intention to so extend these laws. Should international law allow an extension of U.S. jurisdiction and should Congress establish its intention to take advantage of such an extension, it would still be necessary to decide whether Federal laws would preempt State laws with respect to space activities, and whether jurisdiction was shared by both Federal and State courts.

C. Jurisdictional Alternatives for Governments.

A space station could have at least four different types of legal status, making it either:

1. *a national space station* under the jurisdiction and control of a single nation; [Space stations owned by private sector entities and registered under the laws of a single state would also fall in this category. A space station that was owned by a U.S. national but registered in another country would fall in this category but would raise a more complicated set of legal issues.]
2. *a multinational space station* under the joint jurisdiction and control of several nations;
3. *a multinational space station* the individual modules of which are under the independent jurisdiction and control of separate nations; or
4. *an international space station* under the jurisdiction and control of an international governmental organization similar to INTELSAT.

Under each of these options, the rights and liabilities of the U.S. Government and its citizens could be substantially different:

1) *U.S. Jurisdiction and Control.* To avoid the controversy and complexity of cooperative international ownership and operation, the United States may wish to retain complete control over the space station. Assuming the space station is owned and registered solely by the United States under the terms of the 1976 Registration Convention, its legal status would be similar to that of a ship or airplane flying the U.S. flag. As discussed

above, ships [Restatement (Second) of Foreign Relations Law of the United States, Sec. 28(1), American Law Institute, 1965] and aircraft [1944 Convention on International Civil Aviation, 61 Stat. 1180; T.I.A.S. 1591] have the nationality of the state in which they are registered. The United States would have the sole power to make and enforce rules of law regarding the operation of such a space station as long as such rules did not violate international law. Presumably, the United States would coordinate many of these rules with the foreign participants in the space station.

As discussed above, Congress could apply U.S. laws to the activities aboard a U.S. space station, but in the absence of clear congressional intent such laws might not be independently applied by the courts.

2) *Joint Jurisdiction and Control.* Nations considering investing a substantial portion of their financial, technical, and human resources in the space station may wish to jointly own and register it through some type of international joint venture. Under current international law, joint *registration* (as distinguished from ownership) of space objects is not provided for. Article VIII of the 1967 Outer Space Treaty establishes the principle that "A State . . . on whose registry an object launched into space is carried shall retain jurisdiction and control over such object." [1967 Outer Space Treaty, article VIII.] The 1976 Registration Convention maintains that where two or more states may be considered "launching states" [defined in Article I of the Registration Convention as: (i) A State which launches or procures the launching of a space object; (ii) A State from whose territory or facility a space object is launched], "they shall jointly determine which one of them shall register the object . . . bearing in mind the provisions of article VIII." [The Registration Convention, Article II.] Under the Registration Convention then, participants in a joint space endeavor must choose which one shall be the registering state. Nonetheless, the Registration Convention also states that such a joint determination is to be without prejudice "to appropriate agreements concluded . . . among the launching States on jurisdiction and control over the space object and over any personnel thereof." [Ibid.]

Therefore, nations wishing to jointly own and jointly exercise jurisdiction and control over a space station can follow the Registration Convention's suggestion to engage in an agreement separate from the actual registration.

It is not clear now—and may not be clear until a body of case authority is available—just how "appropriate agreements" would modify the "jurisdiction and control" granted by article VIII of the Outer Space Treaty. The Registration Convention is patterned after maritime law. The 1958 Convention on the High Seas states that a ship may only sail under one flag and, save in exceptional circumstances provided for by treaty, the flag state has exclusive jurisdiction on the high seas. [2 U.S.T. 2312; T.I.A.S. 5200.] Article 71 of the 1958 Convention states:

1. Ships shall sail under the flag of one State only and, save in exceptional cases expressly provided for in international treaties, or in these articles, shall be subject to its exclusive jurisdiction on the high seas. . . .

2. A ship which sails under the flag of two or more States, using them according to convenience, may not claim any of the nationalities in question with respect to any other State, and may be assimilated to a ship without nationality.

Article 92 of the 1982 United Nations Convention on the Law of the Sea contains language almost identical to the language of the 1958 Convention. [The United States is not a party to the 1982 Convention.] Both maritime law and space law hold that registration implies jurisdiction. Similarly, both bodies of law allow this presumption of jurisdiction to be rebutted by specific agreements between the concerned parties. Although this practice has not been extensively used in maritime law it could be used for the space station.

3) *Jurisdiction and Control Over Independent Modules.* It is possible that nations may wish to join together to form a space station, yet retain control over their individual contributions. A space station could conceivably be composed of different modules, each owned, registered, and under the jurisdiction and control of separate countries. Common elements of the station such as power modules might be owned separately and shared through specific agreement (option one, above) or jointly owned (option two, above).

In such an environment, each module would be under the jurisdiction and control of the country that owned, operated, and registered it. The problems with registering the common elements of such a station would be similar to those encountered in option two.

4) *Jurisdiction and Control by an International Organization.* Assuming nations would wish to avoid some of the problems caused by concurrent national jurisdictions, it is possible that an international organization similar to INTELSAT could be formed to own, operate, and register the space station. Since such an organization would not be able to develop a completely independent body of law to regulate space activities, it would still be necessary to decide which national laws or combinations of national laws would apply to the organization.

Such an organization could have quasi-legislative powers (subject, of course, to the concurrence of the member states) similar to those held by INTELSAT. Such powers would allow the organization to make normal operational, management, and safety decisions without the need to renegotiate separate agreements among the member states.

NOTES

1. The OTA Report notes that the "floating island" theory of jurisdiction has not been universally accepted, citing Cunard S.S. Co. v. Mellon, 262 U.S. 100, 123 (1923). In that case, however, the Supreme Court went on to say that

The jurisdiction which [the "floating island" theory] is intended to describe arises out of the nationality of the ship, as established by her domicile, registry and use of the flag, and partakes more of the characteristics of personal than of territorial sovereignty. [Cites omitted.] It is chiefly applicable to ships on the high seas, where there is no territorial sovereign; and as respects ships in foreign territorial waters it has little application beyond what is affirmatively or tacitly permitted by the local sovereign.

Id.

The Registration Convention (discussed in Chapter 3), in conjunction with the Outer Space Treaty, provides for jurisdiction-by-registry for "space objects" in much the same way ships are required to be registered under the international law of the sea. *See* H. Meyers, The Nationality of Ships (1967); M. McDougal & W. Burke, The Public Order of the Oceans (1962). *See also* Chapter 2 (discussing maritime analogies generally). And, given that the Outer Space Treaty prohibits declarations of sovereignty over territory in space, national jurisdiction in space is highly analogous to the personal jurisdiction found by the Court in the *Cunard S.S.* case. That is, assertions of jurisdiction are based not on declarations of territorial sovereignty but instead on the nationality of the persons (or, in this case, spacecraft) involved, and the nation of registry has jurisdiction under the Registration Convention.

2. The OTA Report refers to the principle of single state registration enunciated in both the Outer Space Treaty and the Convention on the High Seas. *See* Geneva Convention on the High Seas, art. 5, April 28, 1959, 13 U.S.T. 2312, T.I.A.S. No. 5200 (entered into force on September 30, 1962). *See also* Restatement (Second) of Foreign Relations § 28 (1965). On jurisdiction over aircraft, *see* The Convention on International Civil Aviation of December 7, 1944, 61 Stat. 1180. The Report also refers to the fact that both the Outer Space Treaty and the Convention on the High Seas appear to allow states and private parties who jointly operate a space or sea-faring vessel to stipulate which country shall have jurisdiction over the endeavor. In this connection, consider the following passage, taken from one of the most detailed studies ever made of jurisdiction in outer space:

[N]o hard and fast rules as to who the state of registration should be, would suffice. In fact, the framework must be flexible so as to admit of optional arrangements for registration between the parties concerned *inter se.* . . . For the sake of peace, order, and good government in outer space, a rebuttable presumption and legal obligation should be created to the effect that the State from whose territory the space object was . . . launched . . . shall register the object and give adequate notification thereof. . . .

I. Csabafi, The Concept of State Jurisdiction in International Space Law 22 (1971). *See also id.,* at 18 (Soviets recommended a flexible, consensual registration regime in connection with the 1967 Outer Space Treaty). On the problems that will have to be faced when modules from different countries are assembled in space to form a "new" composite craft or vessel, see Glazer, Domicile and Industry in Outer Space, 17 Columbia Journal of Transnational Law 67, 73–74 (1978) (discussing how composite spacecraft such as international space labs would be treated in light of Outer Space Treaty's references to "space objects").

3. In certain circumstances, primarily when a "flagless" and thus stateless ship is involved in criminal activities on the high seas, a state may exercise jurisdiction outside its territory over people who are not nationals of that state. *See* Rivard v. United States, 375 F.2d 882 (5th Cir.), cert. denied, 389 U.S. 884 (1967); Rocha v. United States, 288 F.2d 545 (9th Cir.), cert. denied, 366 U.S. 948 (1961); 6 M. Whiteman, Digest of International Law 278 (1968). *See generally* Landau, Extraterritorial Penal Jurisdiction and Extradition, 29 International & Comparative Law Quarterly 274 (1980); Restatement (Second) of Foreign Relations Law of the United States §§ 10–19 (1965). Presumably, the same principle would apply to criminal activities in space, including the fanciful situation of "space pirates" preying on lawful space stations or settlements. For a critique of recent developments in this theory of jurisdiction, see Comment, Stateless Vessels and the High Seas Narcotics Trade: United States Courts Deviate from International Principles of Jurisdiction, 9 Maritime Lawyer 273 (1984).

4. For a well-argued plea for the formation of an international convention to address legal issues concerning the governance of permanent manned space colonies, see Vereshchetin, Legal Status of International Space Crews, 3 Annals of Air and Space Law 545 (1978). *Cf.* G. Robinson & H. White, Jr., Envoys of Mankind: A Declaration of First Principles for the Governance of Space Societies (1986) (discussed in Chapter 9).

5. Even if an international treaty on jurisdiction were established— whether it governed temporary or permanent activities—the U.S. Congress would be free to override its terms by statute. See Lobel, The Limits of Constitutional Power: Conflicts Between Foreign Policy and International Law, 71 Virginia Law Review 1071, 1072 (1985) (describing current law and proposing that certain trends away from the current law toward making international law binding are to be encouraged and furthered). *See also* Casenote, Congressional Power to Abrogate the Domestic Effect of a United Nations Treaty Commitment: *Diggs v. Shultz* (D.C. Cir. 1972), 13 Columbia Journal of Transnational Law 155 (1974) (describing case where plaintiffs claimed that the United States was violating specific treaty commitments by resuming trade with Rhodesia in violation of a U.N. Security Council resolution; Court dismissed action in part because Congress can override treaty obligations by enacting a subsequent clearly inconsistent statute); Note, Security Council Resolutions in United States Courts, 50 Indiana Law Journal 83 (1974). The theory behind this rule is that Congress is free to abrogate treaty obligations since it has plenary power over domestic affairs, and that the U.S. should be subject to punishment in the international sphere by whatever enforcement mechanisms operate there. *See* Lobel, *supra,* 71 Virginia Law Review 1071, 1073. The same reasoning has been applied by some commentators who argue that the President is free

to abrogate international obligations, e.g., by Executive Order. *See* L. Henkin, Foreign Affairs and the Constitution 221–22 (1972).

6. The OTA Report refers to a number of occasions when U.S. Courts have declined to extend U.S. jurisdiction to non-territorial events or objects in the absence of clear Congressional authorization. Courts have also been reluctant to consider a treaty an operative component of U.S. law unless (1) Congress has passed clear implementing legislation or (2) the treaty on its face provides clear standards and other guidance on how it is being implemented—i.e., it is "self-executing." *See, e.g.,* Foster v. Neilson, 27 U.S. (2 Pet.) 253 (1929); Man Hing Ivory & Imports v. Deukmejian, 702 F.2d 760 (9th Cir. 1983); 14 G. Hackworth, Digest of International Law § 29 (1943) (discussing history of doctrine). Some commentators have argued that the phrasing of certain provisions of the Outer Space Treaty renders it non-self-executing. *See* S. Gorove, Studies in Space Law: Its Challenges and Prospects 145 (1977); Menter, Jurisdiction Over Man-Made Orbital Satellites, 2 Journal of Space Law 19, 22 (1974) (noting that Article VI of the Treaty states that "[t]he activities of non-governmental entities in outer space . . . shall require authorization and continuing supervision by the appropriate State Party to the Treaty," and that this could be interpreted as requiring implementing legislation). On the other hand, Congress has exercised jurisdiction over U.S. registered space objects through such statutes as the Federal Criminal Code (discussed in the OTA Report excerpt), the Communications Satellite Act of 1962 (47 U.S.C. §§ 701–744 (1964)), and the National Aeronautics and Space Act of 1958 (42 U.S.C. §§ 2451–2484 (1982)). Also, the act of registering a space object and reporting it to the United Nations could be viewed as sufficient implementing action under article VIII of the Outer Space Treaty (re: jurisdiction); by analogy, the very act of attributing national character to an ocean-going vessel by registering it in a particular country is said to authorize the state of registry to exercise jurisdiction over it. *See* M. McDougal, Foreword to B. Boczek, Flags of Convenience at xii (1962); *see also* H. Meyers, The Nationality of Ships (1967). In any event, for practical reasons it is generally conceded that the U.S. does have jurisdiction over "space objects" listed on its registry. *See, e.g.,* Cunningham, Space Commerce and Secured Financing—New Frontiers for the U.C.C., 40 Business Lawyer 803, 816 (1985). *But cf.* De Saussure & Haanappel, A Unified Multinational Approach to the Application of Tort and Contract Principles to Outer Space, 6 Syracuse Journal of International Law & Commerce 1, 4 (1978) (arguing that jurisdictional provision of Outer Space Treaty is of only limited effect without implementing legislation in common law countries).

7. There is usually a choice of law provision in a contract for commercial space activities, such as the ones excerpted later in this chapter. Note that some courts look with disfavor on contracts that attempt to divest them of jurisdiction. For example, a French citizen has a statutory right to resort to the French judicial system even if she was damaged on foreign soil or by a foreigner. The French Civil Code, Article 14, provides:

An alien, even one not residing in France, may be summoned before the French courts for the fulfillment of obligations contracted by him in France; he may be brought before the French courts for obligations contracted by him in a foreign country toward French persons.

Fr. C. Civ. art. 14, *reprinted in* H. DeVries, N. Galston, & R. Loening, Materials for the French Legal System 2 (2d ed. 1977). Note that under French law, "obligations" refers to tortious as well as contractual obligations.

TORT LAW

At the outset, one should be careful to distinguish private tort law from the kind of internationally established liability adopted in the 1972 Liability Convention (discussed in Chapter 5). The latter type of liability attaches to *states* by virtue of the language of the Convention; it was designed to provide a means of settling liability claims between rival states. The claims of the Canadian government against the Soviet Union for cleanup costs associated with the crash of the Soviet Cosmos 954 Satellite (described in detail in the excerpt from Cohen in Chapter 5), for instance, are the type of claims dealt with in the Liability Convention. In addition, the Outer Space Treaty and the Liability Convention provide for state-level liability for damage caused by space objects of one state to another state or its natural or juridical persons. Outer Space Treaty, Article VII. Under these treaties, the launching state is liable for damage caused by any launches from its territory—from the government itself, corporations, or even individuals. The treaties establish that the launching state is absolutely liable for damage on Earth or in the air between Earth and outer space. (See Chapter 1 for a discussion of the end of airspace and the beginning of outer space.) But when the damage is "caused elsewhere than on the surface of the Earth to a space object of one launching state or to persons or property on board such a space object by a space object of another launching State," liability will result only if the damage is due to the fault of the "defendant" launching State or persons for whom it is responsible. Liability Convention, Article III. *See generally* G. Zukhov & Y. Kolosov, International Space Law 106 (B. Belitzky trans. 1984) (Soviet view).

In the excerpt that follows, taken from the same OTA Report excerpted earlier in this chapter, the law governing private activities after launch is discussed:

Office of Technology Assessment, Space Stations and the Law: Selected Legal Issues 44–50 (1986)

A. Applicable Law

As people begin to live and work in space, incidents of damage caused by intentional actions or negligence are certain to occur. Individuals seeking compensation for damage to property or personal injury may look either to international space law or to the tort laws of their own or other nations. Unfortunately, none of these courses of action is without difficulty. Current international space laws are little more than agreed fundamental principles, and no efficient mechanisms exist for applying these principles to specific cases. National tort laws, on the other hand, are well developed but vary drastically from country to country. In the United States, certain elements of tort law are not even consistently applied among the different States. Furthermore, some States have recently enacted legislation that limits the recovery of certain types of damages in tort suits.

1) International Law

. . . Article VI of the Outer Space Treaty provides that states party to the treaty bear "international responsibility for national activities in outer space," and that the activities of "nongovernmental entities" (i.e., individuals, corporations, etc.) "shall require authorization and continuing supervision by the appropriate State Party to the Treaty." Article VII of the Outer Space Treaty declares that a launching state is "internationally liable for damage to another State Party to the Treaty or to its natural or juridical persons. . . ." The 1973 Liability Convention restates and expands on the principles established in article VII of the Outer Space Treaty and provides specific procedures for making and settling claims.

Although the Outer Space Treaty and the Liability Convention establish several key principles—e.g., absolute liability for damage on Earth or in the air, and liability of the launching state for either government or private sector activities—both treaties leave a great many questions unanswered. Three important problems raised by the current international space liability regime are:

Uncertain applicability to activities aboard space stations. There is considerable doubt as to whether the Liability Convention could ever be applied to injury or damage caused by persons participating in space station activities. Article VII states that the Convention does not apply to either the "nationals of [the] launching state" or "foreign nationals . . . participating in the operation of that space object. . . ." This [OTA Study] previously examined four different ways to own, operate, and register a space station. No matter which of these was chosen, it is likely that the participants would either be "nationals of [the] launching state" or "foreign nations . . . participating in the operation of that space object. . . ." Therefore, the Liability Convention would not apply. For example, under article VII of the Liability Convention, if a U.S. astronaut were killed by the negligence of either another U.S. astronaut or a foreign astronaut, the family of the U.S. astronaut could not file a claim for damages under the Liability Convention because the United States was the "launching state."

Lack of attention to damage caused by, and the liability of, individuals. [*See* Hamilton DeSaussure, P.P.C. Haanappel, "A Unified Multinational Approach to the Application of Tort and Contract Principles to Outer

Space," Syracuse Journal of International Law & Commerce, vol. 6, No. 1, summer 1978.] Both the Outer Space Treaty and the Liability Convention focus on damage caused by space objects rather than on damage caused by individuals in space. This is understandable because the primary concern of the drafters was probably to offer some degree of protection from falling or colliding space objects. The crash of the radioactive Soviet satellite, Cosmos 954, in Canada was an example of the kind of injury best suited to the protections of the international treaties.

On a space station, however, individual personal injury actions resulting from intentional actions or negligence are likely to predominate. A good example of the Liability Convention's lack of attention to the role of individuals in space can be seen in its application of the doctrines of "strict" and "fault" liability. According to the terms of the treaty, a launching state whose space objects cause damage on the surface of the Earth or to aircraft in flight is strictly liable for the damage caused. States whose space objects cause damage to other objects in space are liable only after fault has been established. However, no such division between strict liability and fault liability is made with respect to individual conduct.

It is generally held, at least in common law countries, that strict liability applies to certain abnormally dangerous conditions and activities. [DeSaussure and Haanappel, *supra.*] Since, at present, most space activities might be regarded as "abnormally dangerous," one might argue that "fault" should play a diminished role in space. [It might be argued that eliminating the necessity to prove fault and thereby forcing all actors in space to cope with a strict liability scheme would be socially desirable for many of the same reasons that strict liability is used on Earth; that is, to make those engaged in dangerous activities liable for the consequences of such activities.] However, such a requirement could diminish the pursuit of commercial space opportunities by placing a heavier liability burden on these activities. On the other hand, one could also argue that all persons on the space station are to some degree engaged in an "abnormally dangerous" activity and that this is quite different from the situation on Earth where the injured party might not be a participant in the activity in question. [The following paragraph was in a footnote in the original.]

Maritime law offers some interesting insights into the question of liability for injury to individuals on board a space station. Under maritime law, the shipowner must furnish a vessel that is seaworthy in all respects. (*see* Mitchell v. Trawler Racer, Inc., 362 U.S. 539.) The shipowner's duty is nondelegable and the fact that the shipowner used "due diligence" to make the vessel seaworthy is no defense if a member of the ship's crew is injured by some defect. What constitutes a defect has been broadly construed, and so has the question of who is a seaman for the purpose of bringing an unseaworthiness action.

The concept of "seaworthiness"—or in this case, "spaceworthiness"— may eventually be a useful addition to space law, as it could serve to protect space workers and transfer the risk of liability to the spacecraft owner, who presumably, is in a better position to assess the risks of a particular activity.

With respect to liability as *between* spacefarers, the concept of fault may be more useful. How fault would be determined and what defenses would be permitted (e.g. contributory negligence, fellow servant rule, assumption of risk) are some of the most challenging questions that are likely to accompany the development of a tort law for space.

No efficient mechanism for resolving disputes between individuals. Serious questions exist as to whether current international laws could be applied to assist individuals. The 1967 Outer Space Treaty and the Liability Convention establish no cause of action, no courts, no rules of procedure, and no method of enforcing even agreed resolutions. Lacking such mechanisms, claimants are forced to rely on the diplomatic procedures commonly used between nations.

Article VIII of the Liability Convention requires that the state—not the injured person—present the claim to the "launching state"—not the person who caused the injury. Because nations and not individuals are involved, under article IX, claims for compensation must be presented "through diplomatic channels." If the two states in question do not have diplomatic relations then the claimant may present its claim through another state or through the Secretary General of the United Nations. Assuming that a claim has been filed and diplomatic negotiations have failed for a year, then article XIV authorizes the parties to set up a "Claims Commission" composed of three members (the two parties and an agreed chairman).

2) National Tort Laws

Perhaps in anticipation of the problems mentioned above, the drafters of the Liability Convention stated in article XI that: "Nothing in this Convention shall prevent a State, or the natural or juridical persons it might represent, from pursuing a claim in the courts . . . of a launching state." Indeed, given the vague nature of the Liability Convention as compared with the well-defined state of domestic law, it would be unlikely that any individual would ever use it to obtain compensation for injury. [*See, e.g.,* March, "Dispute Resolution in Space," 7 Hastings International and Comparative Law Review 211 (1983).]

Having acknowledged this, it is then necessary to inquire which domestic laws would be applicable to a given case. Whenever individual relationships transcend the boundaries of one jurisdiction, conflicts arise concerning the applicable substantive law, the jurisdiction of national courts, and enforcement of foreign judgments. For example, every nation has its own methods for choosing the law applicable in a specific case. The most common of these are:

The *lex loci delecti,* that is, the law of the place where the offense occurred. Outer space, being *res communis* and, therefore, not subject to national law, has no clear "law of the place." Whether or not the *lex loci delecti* rule can be applied to the space station will depend on how nations agree to exercise jurisdiction and control over the space station.

The *lex fori,* that is, the law of the forum where the case is brought. This approach could be used on the space station, but again, would depend on how questions of jurisdiction and control are resolved.

The law of the state having the greatest interest. This rule—probably the prevailing U.S. standard—looks to which state's contacts with the incident are the most substantial and applies the relevant laws of that state. Because of its flexibility, this rule could have the greatest applicability to space station activities.

An important alternative (at least in contract, if not in tort cases) would be for the parties to stipulate both the applicable national law, and the applicable forum. This practice is frequently followed in multinational business contracts. This approach has two major defects. First, such stipulations would constrain only those who signed them. As space stations become larger, employing greater numbers of people, it may be impossible to anticipate and draw up contracts to cover all the interpersonal relationships that could develop. Second, some courts look with disfavor on contracts that attempt to divest them of jurisdiction. [See the introduction to this chapter.]

Given the current level of space activity, another solution to the problem of liability might be to negotiate interparty waivers of liability. The limitation of such agreements is that they only cover signatories. Interparty waivers of liability were used in the 1973 Spacelab Agreement [Space Laboratory: Cooperative Program, 24 U.S.T. 2049; TIAS 7722], the 1985 Memorandum of Understanding (MOU) regarding Phase B of the space station negotiations [*See* "Memorandum of Understanding Between the National Aeronautics and Space Administration and the European Space Agency for the Conduct of Parallel Detailed Definition and Preliminary Design Studies (Phase B) Leading Toward Further Cooperation in The Development, Operation and Utilization of a Permanently Manned Space Station," June 3, 1985], and are regularly used in shuttle launch agreements.

Article 11(A) of the Spacelab Agreement, for example, provides that the United States "shall have full responsibility for damage to its nationals . . . [resulting from] . . . this agreement." The ESA nations accept a similar "responsibility" under this article. In other words, the United States would not sue ESA for damage to U.S. nationals or property and vice versa. However, article 11(C) acknowledges that in the event injury is caused to persons not party to the agreement, ". . . such damage shall be the responsibility of . . . [the United States or ESA] . . . depending on where the responsibility falls under applicable law." The 1985 space station MOU between NASA and ESA extends the interparty waiver of liability to the Phase B contractors and subcontractors; however, third parties are still not covered under the agreement.

B. Future Developments

Current international space law will continue to be an effective means for allocating responsibility and liability for incidents which occur between nations. For example, should a space object of one nation fall on the territory of another nation or should one nation's space object collide with a space object of another nation, the principles found in the 1967 Outer Space Treaty, the Registration Convention, and Liability Convention will, when combined with serious diplomatic efforts, be sufficient to resolve these problems. As space activities increase and technologies grow more complex, some refinement of these principles will probably be necessary; nonetheless, the existing framework is workable *when applied to national activities.*

Unfortunately, the legal regime for redressing individual grievances resulting from space activities is not nearly so well established. As discussed above, international space law, with its heavy reliance on diplomacy, is too unwieldy for most tort actions between individuals, and negotiated interparty waivers of liability do not address the problem of third-party plaintiffs.

National tort laws, although well defined, differ considerably and no consensus exists on when to apply the law of one or another nation. The actions necessary to resolve this problem vary with time:

Short-term solutions (shuttle activities). Because the shuttle carries multiple and often multinational payloads, NASA has had to develop policies regarding both liability between mission participants (interparty liability) and liability with respect to parties unrelated to the mission (third-party liability). [*See* Maj. Bruce A. Brown, "Commercial Law and Liability Issues of the Space Transport System," 23 Air Force Law Review 424 (1982–83) discussed in the notes at the end of this excerpt.] With respect to interparty liability, the standard shuttle launch agreement contains a mutual covenant not to sue similar to the one found in the Spacelab Agreement.

To cover the possibility of third-party suits, NASA also requires shuttle payload owners to purchase insurance to protect against damage to property and injury to persons unrelated to the space activities. This third-party insurance would, for example, be used to compensate individuals on Earth for damage they sustained as a result of de-orbiting space debris.

The liability procedures currently used by NASA are sufficient while the U.S. Government operates the shuttle, the shuttle crews are small and well-disciplined, and commercial insurance is available. As space activities become more complex and numerous, existing procedures will have to be reexamined.

Medium-term solutions (government space stations). Liability issues on the first generation of government-owned space stations could be handled by using the methods similar to those NASA now employs on the shuttle. The space station owner and operator, whether it be one nation or a consortium of nations, could require all other nations to waive their right to sue each other and require all participants to self-insure or purchase commercial insurance for third-party claims.

As space stations grow in size and complexity and become staffed by civilian employees, it will probably be necessary to develop more flexible rules for compensating individuals injured in space. A logical next step might be to negotiate international agreements similar to the NATO Status of Forces Agreements that would designate which nation's laws would apply in which situations. As mentioned above, it is not clear whether all national courts would feel constrained to respect these contracts.

Long-term solutions (private space stations and beyond). Eventually, space travel will be quite common and individuals may visit neighboring space stations much as we now visit neighboring countries. A rule could develop which places on the space traveler the burden to know the law of the place visited; that law would govern all civil and criminal actions resulting from the traveler's visit. Alternatively, nations may strive to achieve international uniformity in the application of "conflicts rules." The 1955 "Hague Convention on the Law Applicable to the Sale of Corporeal Movable Objects" . and the 1973 "Hague Convention on the Law Applicable to Products Liability" are examples of such attempts. In the 1973 Products Liability Convention, nations agreed to apply the law of the habitual residence of the victim, or subsidiarily, the law of the place where the damage has occurred. Similar international agreements for applying Earth law to space activities may be necessary. Finally, nations may attempt to create a uniform substantive tort law system for activities in outer space. [International aviation law conventions such as Warsaw (49 Stat. 3000; T.I.A.S. 876; UNTS 11) and Rome (310 U.N.T.S. 181) might serve as models.]

NOTE ON LIABILITY: APPROACHES AND STANDARDS

A number of theories have been advanced regarding the open legal questions concerning private party liability identified by the OTA Report. The consensus seems to be that space activities should give rise to absolute liability (i.e., liability without fault) where they are the proximate cause of personal or property damage on earth or in earth airspace. *See, e.g.,* A. Haley, Space Law & Government 237–240 (1963); Haanappel, Product Liability in Space Law, 2 Houston Journal of International Law 55 (1979). What these proposals do, in effect, is to import the principles of international liability developed in the major treaties into the private law of torts. Thus the same principles that apply to accidents between space objects of two nations would be made to apply to accidents between individuals or between individuals and a single national. Extending the analogy further would require one to advocate a fault-based liability regime for accidents occurring in space, in keeping with the treatment of space mishaps in the

Outer Space Treaty and Liability Convention. For more on these nation-to-nation liability issues, see Chapter 5.

The strict liability principle for space launches is based on the notion that these are "ultrahazardous activities," that is, activities which "necessarily involve a risk of serious harm to the person, land or chattels of others which cannot be eliminated by the exercise of utmost care" and which are "not a matter of common usage." Restatement of Torts § 520 (1938), Restatement of Torts (Second) §§ 519, 520 (1977). In the book cited above, noted early space lawyer Andrew Haley made the point that early in the history of aviation courts held that airflight, and even balloon flights, were ultrahazardous, but that a negligence standard for airflight conduct had since become the dominant rule. A. Haley, *supra,* at 238–39. This rule was stated in the Uniform Aeronautics Act, a codification of the negligence standard adopted by twenty-four states. *See* Prentiss v. National Air Lines, Inc., 112 F. Supp. 306, 308 (D.N.J. 1953). *See also* Boyd v. White, 128 Cal. App. 2d 641, 651, 276 P.2d 92, 99–100 (1954) (expressing general view that airplane is not inherently dangerous instrument when handled by a competent pilot). *But see* Restatement (Second) of Torts § 520A (1977) (maintaining strict liability standard despite authority to the contrary). From his review of the historical record, Haley concluded that,

> the operator of a rocket range or service in the years to come can expect that his activities will be viewed by the courts as being ultrahazardous and that, at least until such operations become commonplace, he can expect to be held liable for damage caused by an errant rocket although he is free from negligence. As technology advances and rockets become less of a novelty, it is probable that the rule will be changed and that, as in the case of aircraft, liability will be based solely on fault.

Id., at 239–40 (footnotes omitted). *But cf.* Deem, Liability of Private Space Transportation Companies to Their Customers, 51 Insurance Counsel Journal 340, 350–51 (1984) (collecting cases where testing of high performance aircraft and rocket motors gave rise to strict liability for property damage on the ground, *e.g.,* from noise and vibrations stemming from supersonic flight). Note that Haley was writing in the era prior to the Outer Space Treaty of 1967 (discussed in Chapter 3) and the Liability Convention of 1972 (discussed in Chapter 5). Note also that the liability standard for the operation of aircraft has become less important in light of the growth of strict product liability for defective products, including airplanes and related equipment. *See, e.g.,* Herndon v. Piper Aircraft Corp., 716 F.2d 1322 (10th Cir. 1983); Nesselrode v. Executive Beechcraft, Inc., 707 S.W.2d 371 (Mo. 1986); D. Barry, Choice of Law Problems in General Aviation Accident Cases: Liability and Damages, in General Aviation Accident Litigation 65 (Practicing Law Institute 1986) (PLI Litigation and Administrative Practice Course Handbook Series Litigation No. 312). *See generally* Priest, The Current Insurance Crisis and Modern Tort Law, 96 Yale Law Journal 1521 (1987) (discussing drastic increases in insurance premiums necessitated by rapidly escalating damage awards in tort cases, including those based on strict liability); Brody, When Products Turn Into Liabilities, Fortune, March 24, 1986, at 18; Wall Street Journal, January 21, 1986, at 31, col. 5. *Cf.* Dillingham, Developments and Trends in Aviation Insurance, 21 Tort Insurance Law Journal 44 (1985).

Nevertheless, negligence of one type or another is often asserted as an alternative basis of liability in aircraft accident cases. *See, e.g.,* Brooks v. United States, 695 F.2d 984 (5th Cir. 1983); *In re* Air Crash Disaster Near Chicago Ill., 500 F. Supp. 1044 (N.D. Ill. 1980), *aff'd in part and rev'd in part,* 644 F.2d 594 (7th Cir. 1981), *cert. denied,* 454 U.S. 878 (1981). *Cf.* Product Liability in Air and Space Transportation (K. Bockstiegel ed. 1978). In fact, the standard of care differs from state to state in the United States. *See* P. Foss & R. Adams, Pre-Trial Strategy in American Air Disaster Litigation, 14 Transportation Law Journal 327 (1986) (describing different standards of care and attempts by counsel to bring cases in more "favorable" states).

Although the amount of damages a private firm may have to pay is unlimited, several factors—some in place, others only possibilities—have the potential to limit damages. First among these is the regulations establishing the amount of insurance a firm must carry to legally launch a private payload into space. Although many launch service companies have substantial assets (*e.g.,* Martin Marietta, McDonnell Douglas, or General Dynamics), some are small "start-ups" for whom the insurance coverage is for all practical purposes a ceiling on liability. Note, however, that there is some reason to believe that a court would "pierce the corporate veil" if it found that a launch company was too thinly capitalized given the risk inherent in its activities. This is one reason why there is so much interest in limiting liability in the launch industry.

The second factor that may limit damage awards is the possibility of legislation to place explicit limits on damages that may be collected in the event of a space launch disaster. This would be analogous to the Price-Anderson Act of 1957, Pub. L. No. 85–256, § 4, 71 Stat. 576 (1957), *as amended by* Act of September 29, 1965, Pub. L. No. 89–210, § 1, 79 Stat. 855 (1965) *and* Act of December 31, 1975, Pub. L. No. 94–197, §§ 2–14, 89 Stat. 1111 (1975) (codified at 42 U.S.C. § 2210 (1976)). The Price-Anderson Act limits the liability of nuclear energy companies in the event of a disaster. The Act has been criticized, however, as an unfair subsidy of a dangerous industry—a criticism not likely to be as effective against the space industry. *See* Brauer, The Price-Anderson Act: A Constitutional Meltdown of Tort Liability, 8 Hastings Constitutional Law Quarterly 731 (1981).

Some commentators have called for a Price-Anderson Act for outer space activities. See A. Dula, Management of Interparty and Third-Party Liability for Routine Space Shuttle Operations, in Space Shuttle and the Law 93 (U. Miss. L. Center, Monograph Series No. 3, 1980). See also Bosco, The United States Government—One Example of the Need for a Uniform

Liability Regime to Govern Outer Space and Space-Related Activities, 15 Pepperdine Law Review 581 (1988) (pointing out widely divergent damages that would be paid to third party claimants from different states in suits against the government for a space-related disaster, and calling for unified tort claims regime for space-related accidents). In his paper Dula also calls for (1) *mandatory* cross-waivers of liability among all parties to commercial space contracts; (2) amendment of the NASA Authorization Act to permit NASA to indemnify users of the space shuttle against the risk of loss of satellites and other payloads; and (3) a budget for on-the-spot settlement of claims against NASA for property damage on earth due to launch operations. The second of these proposals was adopted by NASA; Section 2458b of the NASA Act now reads as follows:

42 U.S.C. § 2458b. Insurance and Indemnification

(a) Authorization

> The Administration is authorized on such terms and to the extent it may deem appropriate to provide liability insurance for any user of a space vehicle to compensate all or a portion of claims by third parties for death, bodily injury, or loss of or damage to property resulting from activities carried on in connection with the launch, operations or recovery of the space vehicle. Appropriations available to the Administration may be used to acquire such insurance, but such appropriations shall be reimbursed to the maximum extent practicable by the users under reimbursement policies established pursuant to section 2473(c) of this title.

(b) Indemnification

> Under such regulations in conformity with this section as the Administrator shall prescribe taking into account the availability, cost and terms of liability insurance, any agreement between the Administration and a user of a space vehicle may provide that the United States will indemnify the user against claims (including reasonable expenses of litigation or settlement) by third parties for death, bodily injury, or loss of or damage to property resulting from activities carried on in connection with the launch, operations or recovery of the space vehicle, but only to the extent that such claims are not compensated by liability insurance of the user, provided that such indemnification may be limited to claims resulting from other than the actual negligence or willful misconduct of the user. Pub. L. 85–568, title III § 308, 93 Stat. 348; Pub. L. 96–48, § 6(b)(2), Aug. 8, 1979.

New legislation, discussed in the notes accompanying the 1984 Commercial Space Launch Act, *infra,* has been passed to provide additional limits on liability. Unfortunately, it was passed after this book went to press, so it is not excerpted here. The notes, *infra,* provide a clear outline of the liability limits' operation, however, and the policy issues analyzed here remain just as relevant as before. The Office of Commercial Space Transportation, which is the central federal agency responsible for regulating the commercial space launch industry, has expressed its intention to exercise flexibility in its review of launching companies' insurance arrangements, which review is authorized by Executive Order 12465, Feb. 24, 1984, and the Commercial Space Launch Act, Pub. L. 98–575, codified at 49 U.S.C. §§ 2601–2623 (1982 & Supp. II (1985)). This is in keeping with a number of comments the Office received in response to an Advanced Notice of Proposed Rulemaking on the topic of minimum insurance requirements for commercial space launches. *See* 50 Fed. Reg. 19280–01, May 7, 1985. Consider also the comments of the authors of this book, reproduced in the following excerpt:

Comments on Proposed Regulations Governing Third-Party Liability Insurance for Commercial Space Launch Activities; Docket No. 43098

From: Glenn Reynolds & Robert Merges
        Yale Law & Technology Ass'n
        Yale Law School, New Haven, CT

I. Introduction and Background

Our approach in these comments reflects our belief that the rapid commercial development of outer space is the best way to produce a stable and wealth-producing regime in that region. That thesis is developed in our article, *The Role of Commercial Development in Preventing War in Outer Space,* 25 Jurimetrics Journal 130 (1985). For another, more recent, discussion of this argument, see Daniel Deudney's *Forging Missiles into Spaceships,* 2 World Policy Journal 271 (1985).

Because we believe that the speedy development of outer space resources is essential for both economic and political reasons, we advocate a flexible, pragmatic approach to the formulation of policy. Considerations of ideology, however sincerely or deeply held by policymakers, should give way to the overriding need to develop space resources as quickly as possible. We suggest that analogies drawn from the development of the railroads during the nineteenth century, the United States shipping industry before the Civil War, and the British shipping industry through the turn of the century can be very helpful if carefully and intelligently used.

II. Comments

A. *Need for the Insurance Requirement:* Establishment of financial responsibility for space launch enterprises is essential if public support for such activities is to exist, though other private activities (large-scale transport of liquefied natural gas, for example) are in fact substantially more hazardous to the public (at least in a worst-case scenario) than private space launches are likely to be. It is likely, however, that private space launches will be initially perceived by some sectors as very risky. Requirement of adequate third-party insurance will help allay this perception.

B. *Amount of Coverage Required:* We favor the use of risk analysis as a method of establishing the amount of coverage required. Private commercial launches should not pose particularly stiff challenges to risk analysis; launches are likely to be over predictable paths, from ascertainable sites, using launch vehicles of known characteristics. Use of risk analysis to set requirements has the additional advantage of helping to provide insurance carriers with helpful data for their own actuarial calculations. At the very least, we believe that risk analysis should be used to determine whether the "maximum amount of insurance commercially available at reasonable rates" is grossly excessive or inadequate. We believe that the $500 million dollar figure used for shuttle payloads is inapplicable to private launch services as its main objective is the protection of NASA and other payload owners. The use of analogies to space shuttle activities is probably inappropriate generally, as the shuttle is simply too different a launch vehicle for profitable comparisons to be made. Analogies to expendable launch vehicles are likely to be more helpful, since all private launch operations in the near future will be using ELVs.

Specific Answers to the Questions under III.D.:

*   *   *

(2) *Should insurance levels be set by class of vehicle?* This depends on other regulatory practices. If DOT plans to regulate launch sites and payloads so closely as to eliminate substantial variation in risk among different sites and cargoes, then this practice night be a helpful way of simplifying the insurance regulations. However, it would be helpful to know what is meant by "class." If Delta rockets are one class, and Titans another, then the use of class regulations might be accurate, but would have limited value in terms of simplification. On the other hand, if "liquid fueled boosters" are a class, things would be simplified substantially, but at considerable cost to actuarial accuracy. However, since the main source of danger to third parties is likely to be the launch vehicle itself, rather than payloads, it may be that a few classes (e.g., large liquid fueled boosters) will be sufficient, as long as the level of reliability among boosters within a class does not vary widely.

*   *   *

D. *Risk Retention:* We believe that high levels of risk retention are appropriate as an incentive to safety, as long as such risk retention is not expected to discourage investment.

E. *Government Involvement:* While DOT does not intend to provide for governmental subsidy in this regard, we believe that such a policy, though generally wise, should not be carried too far. In light of the shortage of insurance capital generally (witness the shortage of satellite insurance money, for example), it may be appropriate for the federal government to serve as an "insurer of last resort" if sufficient coverage is not available through private carriers. In light of DOT's role in launch licensing and safety requirements, the federal government should have sufficient information to perform this function adequately. Such a last-resort role would prevent valuable economic activity from being frozen out because of insurance problems.

LIABILITY FOR DAMAGE TO CARGO

So far, we have been focusing on the various theories that have been invoked to establish liability for personal injury and property damage arising from aircraft accidents. But what legal standards apply in the event that cargo *on board* an aircraft is damaged?

In the case of aircraft, goods damaged on international flights are covered by the Warsaw Convention, which limits liability to $9.07 per pound or a maximum of $75,000. *See* Reukema, No New Deal on Liability Limits for International Flights, 18 International Lawyer 983 (1984) (describing Supreme Court case refusing to abrogate liability limits of Warsaw Convention); Note, Torts—Liability Limitation Under the Warsaw Convention, 50 Journal of Air Law & Commerce 155 (1984).

As for cargoes in space, no binding rules have yet emerged, but firms and governments have begun to follow certain practices that may eventually be codified. For the most part, the standard procedure is that both parties to a space launch agreement agree to hold each other harmless for damage that may occur. See the Launch Services Agreement excerpted later in this chapter. *See also* Brown, Commercial Law and Liability Issues of the Space Transportation System, 23 Air Force Law Review 425, 431 (1982–1983). *Cf.* Comment, Liability of Private Space Transportation Companies to Their Customers, 1983 Brigham Young University Law Review 755 (1983). Of course, this waiver has no effect on the claims of third parties. *See* Wolcott, Some Aspects of Third Party Liability in Space Shuttle Operations, 13 Akron Law Review 613, 615 (1980). One commentator has explained the rationale behind this "no-fault, no-subrogation, inter-party waiver of liability," as it is called, in the following terms:

> Although insurance coverage becomes more readily available in increasingly favorable terms with the passage of time [in a developing industry], there is some concern about the ability of the insurance industry to underwrite such enormous risk potential. Since the covenants also protect a user from another user, the participation of small users is fostered by eliminating the necessity

for a user of a $50,000 package to take out a liability policy to cover damage done by his package to the rest of the users' packages and the [spacecraft] itself in an amount which could exceed nine figures. Finally, such a policy serves to simplify risk allocation among NASA and all users. It is important to note that the cross-waiver provision resulted from lengthy negotiations and discussions with representatives of the insurance industry and prospective users.

Brown, *supra,* 23 Air Force Law Review 425, 431.

By waiving liability, these agreements skirt a number of issues that may arise in the future. One is the status of commercial launch vehicles. Under standard commercial law analysis, a transporter of goods is either a "common carrier" or a private carrier. The distinction is well described in the article by Deem, *supra:*

> A common carrier has been defined as "one who, by virtue of his calling, undertakes, for compensation, to transport personal property from one place to another for all who may choose to employ him, and everyone who undertakes to carry for compensation all persons indifferently, is as to liability, to be deemed a common carrier." Because it is held to a standard of care higher than that for ordinary negligence,
>
>> the common carrier is regarded as a practical insurer of the goods against all losses of whatever kind with the exception of (1) those arising from what is known as an act of God, and (2) those caused by the public enemy; to which modern times have added (3) those arising from the act of the public authority, (4) those arising from the act of the shipper, and (5) those arising from the inherent nature of the goods.
>
> A private carrier or contract carrier, as opposed to a common carrier, does not undertake to carry for all persons indiscriminately but only for those with whom he wishes to contract.
>
>> Subject to statutory restrictions, state or federal, concerning performance of a transportation service none of which are applicable here, a person has the right to engage in the business of a private carrier. He asserts that right when, seeking all potential business as avidly as any other businessman desirous of a profit, it is yet his practice to treat each individual shipment on a separate basis and accept or reject it as wished and on terms and at rates satisfactory to him at the time.
>
> [Home Ins. Co. v. Riddell, 252 F.2d 1, 4 (5th Cir. 1958).] [Importantly,] a private or contract carrier is held to the traditional standard of due care.
>
> During the early years of the space transportation era, it is doubtful that a space carrier would be considered a common carrier. Space carriers are not likely to hold themselves out to the public to transport goods into space for all persons. . . . This practice of contracting each shipment on a separate basis is one factor indicating that a transportation company is a private carrier rather than a common carrier. Additionally, space carriers are more likely to be considered private carriers because they will tend to serve a unique limited class of persons, satellite users, rather than the public at large.
> . . .

Presumably, absent contrary state or federal regulation, space carriers could remain private carriers even in a well-developed space transportation industry [with substantial volume] if they contracted separately for each carriage and did not hold themselves out to the public to transport goods or persons into space indiscriminately.

51 Insurance Counsel Journal 340, 355.

THE *CHALLENGER* DISASTER

Because of the mutual waivers of liability for damage to goods that proliferate in space launch agreements, many observers were surprised to learn that the victims of the Space Shuttle *Challenger* disaster had not signed any waivers at all. As a consequence, the estates of these victims were free to pursue claims against both NASA and the government contractors responsible for the defective rocket engine seal that led to the disaster. *See generally* M. McConnell, Major Malfunction (1987). All these claims have now been settled. But they may prove instructive for future space-related suits (which we hope never arise).

While it would be impossible to review all the intricacies of these actions for recovery on behalf of the *Challenger* victims' estates, several points are worth noting.

First, there were three classes of people aboard the *Challenger:* (1) military personnel, (2) NASA personnel, and (3) one civilian. Because the Federal Employees Claim Act (FECA) applies exclusively to federal employees operating within the scope of their duties, it was the only source of recovery available to the first two classes of claimants against the government. And the Act makes it clear that no recovery can be had by military personnel killed in the line of duty. *See* Feres v. United States, 340 U.S. 135, 146 (1950); *cf.* Comment, The *Feres* Doctrine: Has it Created Remediless Wrongs for Relatives of Servicemen? 44 University of Pittsburgh Law Review 929 (1983) (criticizing *Feres* doctrine). The lone civilian on board the Shuttle (Christa McAuliffe) was not covered by this provision, however, and her estate did reach a settlement with the government.

As for the other two claimants in the case, they pursued claims solely against the government contractors in the case, primarily Morton Thiokol. Because Thiokol appeared to be negligent in its decision to recommend launch of the Shuttle on that fateful, cold morning in January, and because the rocket seals were defective in the first place, all three claimants had strong cases under both negligence and strict product liability theories. Personal Conversation with Ronald D. Krist, attorney for several victims' estates, July 26, 1988.

It is difficult to predict what effect the reportedly large settlement in the case will have on future insurance practices and/or space activities in general. One effect, however, is likely to be far greater care in deciding whether launch conditions are safe. Waivers of liability may also be introduced at some point.

CONTRACTS RELATING TO OUTER SPACE

Although a host of contracts could be described as "space-related," including those between NASA and its subcontractors or between those subcontractors and their suppliers, we will consider here only those contracts that directly relate to launch services. This is one of the few major areas of truly space-related commerce where enough contracts have been negotiated and signed to allow any room for generalizing about principles, trends, etc. Thus, although we will briefly discuss such agreements as space insurance contracts and NASA Joint Endeavor Agreements, our primary focus will be on launch service contracts.

With NASA now out of the commercial launch business for the most part, most launch agreements are now between a private company desiring to have a payload (usually a satellite) put into orbit and a private launch services company. Keep in mind, however, that these are not the only parties with an interest in the agreement. The purchase of launch services, for example, is quite often financed by banks; these banks may actually be providing the early payments to the launch services company, with the purchaser to repay the banks out of revenue generated by the satellite. In addition, the government is directly involved as well: at present, it still has a monopoly on launch sites.

Launch agreements reflect the involvement of these additional parties in a variety of ways. Since banks may be making early payments, they are especially interested in the payment schedule (i.e., the percentage of the contract price due at each stage of preparation for the launch), as well as the provisions governing liquidated damages for early termination, re-flight schedulings in the event of a mishap, etc. The government, for its part, shows up in the agreements in a standard provision reminding the parties that it has priority in the use of the launch sites.

Launch service contracts are fairly elaborate in their coverage of issues, though actually quite short relative to other commercial agreements for transactions of similar value ($100–200 million). This is due primarily to the fact that the commercial space launch community is so small, and to the shared belief in the community that the high uncertainties of space activities, rather than one's negotiating partner, are the true adversaries. In any event, the typical launch agreement includes provisions on (1) allocation of the risks of loss, (2) safety and accident prevention, (3) payment schedules, (4) performance criteria, (5) rescheduling arrangements in the event of delay, and (6) miscellaneous matters, such as termination and dispute settlement procedures, nondisclosure covenants, and choice of law. In addition, the agreement may include detailed appendices describing (1) the payload, and (2) if the payload is a satellite (as is usually the case), the exact orbit it is to be placed into.

The following excerpt is a shortened and somewhat simplified "hybrid" of a number of different Launch Services Agreements. While it is not nearly complete enough to serve as a model in an actual launch for payment transaction, it does serve as a useful introduction to the launch contract. (The authors thank Dennis Ahearn of Davis, Graham & Stubbs of Washington, D.C., who has negotiated a number of launch services agreements, for his assistance in this section.)

Contract for Launch Services

This contract is made and entered into by and between _____ Launch Co. (hereinafter, referred to as "Contractor") and _____ Co. (hereinafter called "Customer").

Article 1—Services to be Provided

1.1 In consideration of the mutual promises and covenants herein contained, the parties hereto agree as follows:

The Contractor shall furnish and the Customer shall accept _____ launch(es), including associated launch services, for the launch of a Customer-Furnished Satellite(s) from Cape Canaveral Air Force Station, Florida, United States of America, utilizing a _____ Launch Vehicle as set forth in Annex 1, entitled, "Commercial Launch Services Statement of Work," which is attached hereto and made a part hereof.

Article 2—Launch Schedule

The planned launch date will be established by mutual agreement of the parties at least twenty-four (24) months in advance of each launch date, subject to the requirements of the U.S. Government.

Article 3—Launch Schedule Adjustments

This Article addresses adjustments to the launch schedule. The Customer will give written notice of any desired change in the launch schedule as soon as possible. In the case of a request for postponement of the launch date by the Customer, the Customer will propose a new launch date. Within two weeks of receipt of the written request of the Customer of a launch schedule adjustment, the Contractor will inform the Customer whether a launch opportunity exists as requested or will propose an alternately available launch date. The Customer has thirty (30) days following receipt of the Contractor's proposition to give its written agreement.

Postponement requests by the Customer, for other than those specified in Article 9, shall not exceed a total of twelve (12) months for each satellite launch under this Contract. In the event a single postponement or cumulative postponements by the Customer exceed twelve (12) months, the Contract shall be subject to renegotiation, or termination.

Each postponement by the Customer that occurs twenty-four (24) months or less prior to the launch date is subject to the liquidated damages indicated in Table 3-1.

TABLE 3-1
Launch Delay Liquidated Damages

Months Prior to Launch Date 1st Day to Last	Percent of Launch Service Price in Firm Fixed January 1987 U.S. Dollars
24	1
23	1
22	2
21	2
20	3
19	3
18	4
17	4
16	5
15	5
14	6
13	6
12	7
11	7
10	8
9	8
8	9
7	9
6–1	10

Should the tanking of the launch vehicle be started or already achieved prior to the receipt of the Customer postponement request, the Customer will pay an amount of 375,000 January, 1987 U.S. Dollars to cover the cost of propellants and retanking labor, in addition to any other postponement fees.

In addition to delays for causes set forth in Article 9, the Contractor has the right to postpone the launch, without being subject to termination under Article 16, for the following reasons:

- Reflight launches for other Customers;
- Rescheduling of launches of other Customers with earlier scheduled launch periods;
- Technical difficulties;
- Weather and launch safety conditions which do not permit launching;
- Requirements of the U.S. Government and the maintenance of appropriate clearances between flights;
- Postponement request(s) by another Customer occupying the same launch quarter set forth in this contract.

Postponements requested by the Contractor that exceed a total of twelve (12) months, and are not the result of the reasons enumerated in [the preceding] Paragraph, and occur in twenty-four (24) months or less prior to the launch date shall be subject to the same liquidated damages indicated in Table 3–1.

Article 4—Payment

The Customer will make an Initial Payment for each satellite to be launched as set forth in Article 1, equal to 10% of the Contract Price (less any deposit, if applicable) within thirty (30) days of the effective date of this contract.

The balance of the payments for each satellite launch as set forth in Article 1 shall be paid in twelve (12) quarterly payments beginning thirty-three (33) months prior to the launch date with each payment being due the first week of each calendar quarter, and the final payment due at the time of the launch.

Article 5—Reflight or Refund Option

The Customer must specify, at the time of Contract execution, whether a refund or reflight is desired.

In the event of total failure, constructive total failure or partial failure, implementation of this Article shall be based on the findings of the Failure Review Board. The findings of the Failure Review Board shall be transmitted to the Customer in writing.

The Failure Review Board shall consist of personnel skilled in the Contract technical disciplines necessary to assess the failure, its cause, and necessary corrective action, if any, required for future launches.

Reflight launch(es) for a Customer-Furnished satellite will be provided for the satellite, if for any reason, without limitation after intentional ignition, the launch vehicle fails, but excluding partial failures, to deliver the Customer-Furnished Satellite into orbit as specified in Annex 1 [describing the orbit].

In the event, the following conditions apply to a reflight election by the Customer:

a. The reflight launch will be no later than eighteen (18) months after the confirmation of the launch vehicle failure, by the Failure Review Board.

b. Reflight election does not include the replacement cost of the satellite.

If the Customer shall elect a reflight, within the conditions set forth above, the Contract Price set forth in Article 4 shall remain unchanged.

In the event of a failure of the reflight launch, no further reflight will be provided under this Paragraph.

No reflight under this Paragraph is available in the event of a partial failure.

Article 6—Termination

Should the Customer find it necessary to suspend the work indefinitely, or cancel the launch requirement, the Contractor's services may be terminated, following at least thirty (30) working days written notice from the Customer. Upon receipt of the Customer's notice of termination, the Contractor shall take the appropriate steps to stop the work in an orderly manner and to terminate outstanding obligations and commitments.

As a cancellation fee, the Contractor shall retain all prior payments made by the Customers plus all amounts remaining due to the Contractor and, in addition, all rights relating to the ownership of all materials under this Contract shall remain with the Contractor.

Article 7—Government Priority

The Customer and Contractor recognize and agree that the U.S. Government will have priority in the use of Government and contractor property and personnel for a launch, if such becomes necessary. In such event, all scheduled commercial launches will be rescheduled to accommodate the Government's need.

Neither the Contractor nor the U.S. Government shall be liable to the Customer for any costs or damages, including consequential damages, arising out of a delay caused by the U.S. Government priority.

NOTES

1. The payment, liquidated damages, and launch schedule provisions are usually the subject of vigorous negotiations between launch service companies and users. From the launch services company point of view, it is essential that the contract protect against some of the risks of cancellation by a user. Cancellation or postponement is very costly to the launch company, because preparing for a launch requires substantial investment that is difficult to recoup immediately due to the specialized interfaces between payloads and rockets and to the relatively "thin" market for launches in any given time period. Thus, unlike the seller of a standard commodity, the launch company cannot simply sell to an alternative customer in a well-defined "spot market" and thereby recoup its investment.

2. Review the Termination provision of the preceding agreement (Article 5). Do you think it favors the launch company or the user? Would this agreement be classified as a Contract of Adhesion by modern-day courts, in light of contemporary contract principles? Keep in mind that the excerpted agreement is a composite contract for a hypothetical large company in the launch services business. It is only one side's opening salvo in negotiations, and may be changed in the course of the contracting process. (There is a "battle of the forms" even in the space arena.)

3. Of the many provisions this sample agreement leaves out, perhaps the most important are (1) the allocation of risks and liabilities due to loss or damage, and (2) performance guarantees on the part of the launch provider. The next excerpt contains an elaborate provision on risk allocation that is similar to ones that appear in launch service contracts.

As for performance guarantees, they will vary with individual contracts. The basic issues, however, are (1) whether the launch service provider will guarantee *any* performance, and (2) if so, in the case of satellites, whether the guarantee will end when the satellite reaches the end of the primary launch vehicle stage or whether it will extend until the satellite reaches its final, operational orbit—typically after an auxiliary booster has fired it into final position. This is, of course, a matter of detailed negotiation between the User and the launch provider, and thus also between the User and its bank(s), and they in turn with their insurance company. Note carefully the provisions relating to performance guarantees in the next excerpt, which is taken from an agreement between NASA and a user of the space shuttle.

SAMPLE LAUNCH AGREEMENT

Based on Agreement Between the United States of America Represented by the National Aeronautics and Space Administration and Satellite Business Systems for Launch and Associated Services, Launch Agreement No. 1009–001, Effective Date: June 17, 1980

Preamble

This Agreement is entered into between the United States of America represented by the National Aeronautics and Space Administration (hereinafter called "NASA") and Satellite Business Systems, a general partnership (hereinafter called the "User"), and sets forth the terms and conditions under which NASA will furnish Launch and Associated Services to the User for the launching of SBS telecommunication spacecraft (hereinafter called the "Spacecraft") into earth orbits.

Article II—Description of Services to Be Provided by NASA

1. Definition of Launch and Associated Services

[In addition to the basic launch, NASA agrees to provide services which will consist of:]

d. [P]roviding, at no additional cost to the User, one reflight of the Shuttle (hereinafter called "Shuttle Reflight Launch") for each Payload launch provided [under this Agreement], and for each Shuttle Reflight Launch prior to which the User has paid to NASA an additional Reflight Premium . . . in accordance with . . . this Agreement, if the events described in both Subparagraphs 1.d.(1) and 1.d.(3) below or in both Subparagraphs 1.d.(2) and 1.d.(3) below occur. . . .

(1) through no defect of the Payload or fault of the User, the User's contractors or subcontractors or the upper stage contractor (i) Payload operations do not result in the Deployment of the Payload, if the Payload is intended to be Deployed, (ii) Payload operations do not commence, if the Payload is not intended to be Deployed, or (iii) the Payload is Jettisoned after liftoff of the Shuttle and (iv) such launch, if itself a Shuttle Reflight Launch, is covered by an additional reflight premium paid by the User to NASA as defined above.

(2) the Payload is Deployed and the Deployment deviates from the specifications defined in the Payload Integration Plan . . . , unless NASA conducted the Deployment without actual knowledge prior to Deployment, based solely on United States Government instrumentation and data, that the ensuing Deployment would deviate from the specifications . . . , or unless NASA received such knowledge at a time when Deployment activities could not be safely halted.

(3) the particular Payload is returned to the launch site and provided to NASA in a flightworthy condition or another substantially identical Payload is provided by the User. . . .

Article V—Allocation of Certain Risks

1. General

a. To the extent that a risk of Damage, as defined below, is not dealt with expressly in this Agreement, the United States Federal Law shall govern the allocation of such risk between the User and the United States Government.

2. Third Party Liability

a. The User shall obtain, at no cost to NASA, insurance protecting the User, the United States Government and, to the extent the United States Government is liable to reimburse them for costs they incur for Liability, the United States Government's contractors and subcontractors from any third party Liability for Damage arising out of the performance of this Agreement.

b. The User shall obtain, at no cost to NASA, insurance protecting the User, the United States Government and, to the extent the United States Government is liable to reimburse them for costs they incur for Liability, the United States Government's contractors and subcontractors from any third party Liability for any Damage resulting from a deployable Payload element following Deployment.

c. The insurance policy may take into account the agreement by NASA, the User and other identified persons, in Paragraph 3. below, not to make a claim for Damage under the conditions described therein. The policy may exclude from coverage the Liability of an insured to his own employee.

d. The amount of insurance and the terms and conditions of such insurance to be purchased pursuant to this Paragraph 2. shall be agreed to by the User and NASA in view of the insurance available in the world market at a reasonable premium. Notwithstanding such agreement by NASA, the User shall have the responsibility to meet the requirements in Subparagraphs 2.a. and 2.b. above. Such insurance shall not be required in an amount in excess of 500 million dollars (U.S.).

3. Damage to Persons or Property Involved in STS Operations

a. To simplify the allocation of risks among NASA and all users of the Space Transportation System and to make the use of the Space Transportation System feasible for the use and exploration of outer space by all potential users, the parties agree to a no-fault, no-subrogation inter-party waiver of liability under which each party agrees to be responsible for any Damage which it sustains as a result of Damage to its own property and employees involved in [Space Shuttle] Operations during such operations, which Damage is caused by NASA, the User or other users involved in STS Operations during such operations, whether such Damage arises through negligence or otherwise. Thus, if NASA's property, while involved in [Space Shuttle] Operations, is damaged by the User or another user, NASA agrees to be responsible for that Damage and agrees not to bring a claim against or sue any user. Similarly, if any user's property, while involved in these Operations, is damaged by NASA or another user, the user whose property is damaged agrees to be responsible for that Damage and agrees not to bring a claim against or sue NASA or another user. It is the intent of the parties that this inter-party waiver of Liability be construed broadly to achieve the intended objectives.

b. NASA obligates itself to require all users of the Space Transportation system and third parties as described in Subparagraphs 3.1., 3.b., and 3.c. above to agree to an identical waiver of Liability as described therein.

NOTES

1. Of critical importance in this Agreement is precisely what NASA agrees to. In Article I, NASA, like the private carrier in the agreement excerpted earlier, agrees to provide a launch, or a "Shuttle Reflight" in the event that certain contingencies occur. These are, (1) "Through no defect of the Payload or Fault of the User," the Payload is not "Deployed" or doesn't work, or (2) "the Deployment deviates from specifications." In any event, even if (1) or (2) occurs, NASA is not obligated to try again unless the Payload, or a replacement, is returned to the launch site prior to a reflight. In other words, NASA bears the risk of an improper deployment, so long as it is not the User's fault.

But what if something goes wrong prior to deployment, or after deployment but prior to positioning of the satellite in an operational orbit? (This latter possibility is quite important since satellites typically require an additional boost to place them in useful orbits, which are higher than the Space Shuttle's highest operational orbit.) In these events, the basic message of the Agreement to the user is: you're out of luck.

In the first place, the Agreement gives NASA the right to suspend and postpone a launch for a variety of reasons; since neither party is liable for the other's consequential damages under Article V, the risk of loss due to any delay falls on the user of launch services. *See* Footer, Legal Issues and Answers for Commercial Users of the Space Shuttle, 13 Transportation Law Journal 87 (1983). Secondly, NASA retains the right to "jettison" the user's payload if, in its sole discretion, it concludes that this must be done for reasons of safety or mission success. (However, if a NASA review later concludes that NASA's decision to jettison was unwarranted, the user is entitled to a new launch—but not, one should note, to compensation for the jettisoned item.) Third, "deployment" is so defined that NASA is required to provide a reflight only if it is responsible for the faulty deployment, which includes the caveat that NASA is *not* liable if it conducted the deployment without knowledge that it would be faulty, such knowledge to be "based solely on United States Government instrumentation and data." Thus, NASA has to *knowingly* bungle the deployment to be liable.

Finally, as noted above, NASA's responsibility ends with the successful deployment of the satellite. But that is not equivalent to a working satellite; it has to be in a proper orbit normally much higher than the Shuttle's. Therefore, NASA also does not bear the risk of a faulty "upper stage" in the satellite's final booster mechanism. As Footer notes, "[a] guarantee for the higher orbit would require an additional cost to be sustained by the user [in the form of] an additional fee for 'optional' services or by an additional premium for insurance." *Id.*

2. Another critical element of the Agreement concerns NASA's requirement that the user obtain insurance. As we mentioned earlier in this chapter, Congress in 1979 gave NASA the right to limit the required insurance to reasonable amounts, and to indemnify launch users who could not obtain the appropriate amounts of insurance. Nonetheless, in the Agreement excerpted above, NASA required launch users to provide $500 million worth of insurance for third-party losses. *See* Article V, Section 2(d). Interestingly, this is precisely the figure that many in the insurance industry reportedly identified as the maximum amount of insurance that would be available in the world market per user, per shuttle mission. *See* Footer, Legal Issues, *supra. But see* P. Blassel, Space Projects and the Coverage of Associated Risks, 10 The Geneva Papers on Risk & Insurance 51, 78 (1985) (reporting that one U.S. insurance broker, with NASA's assistance, had set up a syndicate offering up to $1 billion of coverage for all users of a given shuttle flight). *See generally* Margo, Some Aspects of

Insuring Satellites, 1979 Insurance Law Journal 555 (1979). On space insurance issues as of the time of this writing, see 100th Cong. 2d. Sess. S. Print No. 100–112, Insurance and the U.S. Commercial Space Launch Industry (July, 1988).

3. A problem of interest, though largely theoretical in application so far, is how one would go about perfecting a security interest in a satellite or other space object—e.g., research facilities in orbit. The problem is that the property is not in any state, so the rules governing the perfection of security interests under the U.C.C. are difficult to apply. For a thorough article that suggests a number of important considerations, see Cunningham, Space Commerce and Secured Financing—New Frontiers for the U.C.C., 40 Business Lawyer 803 (1985).

4. Another species of space contract of importance in commerce is an expendable launch vehicle commercialization agreement. This is an agreement between a private company and a government launch facility—for example, the Eastern or Western Space and Missile Centers of the U.S. Air Force, at Cape Canaveral and Vandenberg Air Force Bases, respectively. Under the Commercial Space Launch Act of 1984, Pub. L. 98–575, 98 Stat. 3055, codified at 49 U.S.C. §§ 2601–23 (1982 & Supp. III 1985), government agencies connected with space are directed to make their facilities available to private companies and to assist in any way the development of the private industry. (In addition, the 1984 Act established a centralized "one-stop" agency for regulatory approval for the private space launch industry, codifying Executive Order 12465, which created the Office of Commercial Space Transportation within the Department of Transportation; this is discussed in the final section of this chapter.) In general, these commercialization agreements make the government's launch facilities available to private companies essentially "at government cost." The idea behind the legislation was that the government should make its resources available to private sector entrepreneurs to spur the growth of this important young industry. As might be expected, the government requires fairly elaborate waivers of liability. But on the whole, the space launch industry has applauded this government program.

A similar species of agreement is the NASA Joint Endeavor Agreement (JEA). Under these agreements, which have been used primarily to foster the materials processing in space industry, NASA agrees to underwrite a certain portion of the costs of pre-launch and launch services. The basic goal is to foster the development of the materials processing industry, to help "grow" a major customer that will help keep NASA's shuttle and non-shuttle flights fully booked in the future. Some agreements actually involve an explicit "fly-now-pay-later" arrangement.

INTELLECTUAL PROPERTY

As the prospect of research activities on space platforms, in orbital laboratories, and on board reusable orbiting vehicles has moved from the realm of speculation to reality, the issue of whether U.S. patent law applies to research in space has also moved to the fore. As of this writing, there has not yet been a successful legislative response to this problem. But the progress of a bill that originated in the House of Representatives, together with the strong and unified support of the interest groups involved, means that this Bill (or one like it) will probably pass soon. Thus it is important to understand the issues that this legislation was designed to address.

The following excerpt from the House Report on H.R. 2725, introduced June 11, 1985, is a good introduction to these issues.

U.S. House of Representatives, 99th Cong., 2d Sess., Rept. 99–788, Part 1, August 13, 1986

The Committee on the Judiciary, to whom was referred the bill (H.R. 4316) to amend title 35, United States Code, and the National Aeronautics and Space Act of 1958, with respect to the use of inventions in outer space, having considered the same, report favorably thereon without amendment and recommend that the bill do pass.

Purpose

The purpose of the legislation is to amend title 35 and the National Aeronautics and Space Act to assure adequate patent protection to inventions made in outer space. The bill provides a clear, definite and understandable set of rules for determining when and how U.S. patent law applies in outer space.

Introduction

H.R. 2725 was originally suggested in legislative form by the National Aeronautics and Space Administration (NASA).

*   *   *

The major impetus for this legislation is the expanded availability of commercially relevant activities in outer space. . . .

Patents in Space: Current Law

United States Law

There are no patent rights under the common law; therefore obtaining or enforcing a patent is governed by Title 35 of the United States Code. Whoever invents or discovers any new and useful process, machine, manufacture, or composition of matter, or any new and useful improvement thereof, may obtain a patent therefor. [35 U.S.C. 101.] For infringement of a patent, remedy is by a civil action. [35 U.S.C. 281.] Such laws are territorial in nature, although the statutory definition of "United States" as "the United States of America, its territories and possessions, is descriptive rather than limiting." [35 U.S.C. 101(c).] The Supreme Court has stated that our patent system makes no claim to extraterritorial effect and was not intended to operate beyond the limits of the United States. [Deepsouth Packing Co. v. The Laitram Corporation, 406 U.S. 518, 531 (1972).] As a result, there is general agreement that "The laws relating to inventions and patents have no extraterritorial effect." [Statement of S. Neil Hosenball, General Counsel, National Aeronautics and Space Administration, in Patents in Space: Hearing Before the Subcomm. on Courts, Civil Liberties, and the Administration of Justice of the House Comm. on the Judiciary, 99th Cong., 1st Sess. 5 (1985).]

There appears to be controversy about whether the patent laws can be given extraterritorial effect in the sense that they can apply to United States flag ships on the high seas and United States aircraft in airspace above the high seas. Courts have held that patent laws apply to any place under United States jurisdiction. [See Gardiner v. Howe, 9 Fed. Cas. 1157 (1865).] This theory of jurisdiction has even led one legal commentator to conclude that national patent laws thereby extend to all places over which sovereign rights are exercised, such as man-made installations on the continental shelf used for exploration and exploitation of the shelf, ships flying the national flag, aircraft registered in the country, and manned spacecraft over which it exercises sovereign rights. [Stauder, Patent Protection in Extraterritorial Areas (Continental Shelf, High Seas, Air Space, and Outer Space), 7 International Review of Industrial Property & Copyright Law 470, 478 (1976) (reprinted in Hearings, at 119, 127).] On the other hand, one court created a "fiction," finding that for the purpose of the patent laws, ships and planes are to be considered as United States territory. This holding has been criticized [See, for example, Decca Limited v. United States, 544 F.2d 1070, 1073–74 (Ct. Cl. 1976)] by one court as a "judicial prop" to be avoided if a case can be decided on other grounds. [Ocean Science & Engineering, Inc. v. United States, 595 F.2d 572, 574 (Ct. Cl. 1979).] . . .

Thus, with respect to extending patent laws to space vehicles, two possibilities exist. First, several cases concerning "reduction to practice" of an invention have found either that testing is or has to be done on the Earth, or that the invention is an integrated instrumentality with the control point on Earth. For an invention intended ultimately for use in outer space, some type and degree of testing on Earth may be sufficient to constitute an actual reduction to practice under patent law. [Kempf, Reduction to Practice of Space Inventions, 50 Journal of the Patent Office Society 105, 111 (1968).] If an invention is of such magnitude that it necessarily extends beyond the United States, such as a satellite system which can be viewed as the operation of an integrated instrumentality with its control point in the United States, the inventive act has been considered as occurring in the United States. [Rosen v. National Aeronautics & Space Administration, 152 U.S.P.Q. 757 (1966).] Under either of such findings the patent laws would be applied territorially. Second would be the more difficult instance where an invention is intended for sole use in outer space, is only tested there, is not part of an integrated instrumentality, and perhaps is invented on a flight that is a joint effort with another nation. In such event, the application of the patent laws could only be justified by invoking sovereign jurisdiction. [Thus, an invention made aboard an orbiting space vehicle might arguably be within the patent law of the state of registry, which owns and controls the vehicle. Saragovitz, The Law of Intellectual Property in Outer Space, 17 Idea 86, 88–94 (1975).] Even if there are other nationals on board, since jurisdiction rather than nationality would be the governing factor, the passengers would arguably be subject to the laws of the state of registry. If the flight is a joint effort, the particular circumstances of the project as a whole would have to be examined to find United States involvement sufficient to constitute grounds for an infringement action in the United States. [Hughes Aircraft Co. v. Messerschmitt-Boelkow-Blohm, 562 F.2d 580 (5th Cir. 1980).]

It would also seem possible to argue that the policy reasons for not giving the patent laws extraterritorial effect are not present in situations involving outer space. "A major reason for this limitation is the avoidance of interference with the sovereignty of other countries, which may have patent laws that differ from those of the United States." [Statement of Professor Donald S. Chisum, in Hearings, at 18.]

International Law

Assuming that it can adequately be demonstrated that the United States patent laws apply to flag vessels on the high seas and to United States aircraft in flight above the high seas, would or could that analogy be extended to include United States spacecraft in outer space? In other words, does the United States exercise sovereign jurisdiction over such a craft and its crew and passengers? Answers do not appear clear or convincing.

At least three distinct postures can be taken on the issue. First, under a free space concept as declared in the Outer Space Treaty, the state of registry of an object launched into outer space retains jurisdiction and control over such object and its personnel while in outer space. Registry of a spacecraft is similar to the registry of an ocean going vessel. The analogy between space law and the law of the sea is obvious. As one commentator put it:

> It is submitted that whenever the United States constructs and orbits a spacecraft, any legally relevant events, such as the operation and testing of an invention in its intended functional setting, come within the jurisdiction of the United States patent law.

[Kempf, Reduction to Practice of Space Inventions, 50 Journal of the Patent Office Society 105, 105, 119–120 (1968).]

Additional support for this position may be gleaned from the [Outer Space Treaty], establishing absolute liability of the launching State for damages, and the Registration Convention, which requires a launching State to enter each launching in an appropriate registry. "As a result, the Registration Accord proves to be thoroughly suitable as a foothold for the determination of applicable law. The prerequisite for the application of the law of the recording state to bodies in outer space under its jurisdiction and control is concrete, of course, and an explicit or at least implicit extension of the national law to these space bodies operating in the extraterritorial region." [Beier and Stauder, Space Stations and Intellectual Property Law (1985) (reprinted in Hearing, at 67, 79).]

An excerpt from the House Bill referenced in the Report is set out below.

H.R. 2725, 99th Congress, 1st Session

A BILL

To amend title 35, United States Code, and the National Aeronautics and Space Act of 1958, with respect to the use of inventions in outer space.

Be it enacted by the Senate and House of Representatives of the United States of America in Congress assembled,

Section 1. Space Inventions.

(a) AMENDMENTS TO TITLE 35, UNITED STATES CODE.—(1) Chapter 10 of title 35, United States Code, is amended by adding at the end thereof the following: "§ 105. Inventions in outer space

"Any invention made or used in outer space on an aeronautical and space vehicle (as defined in section 103(2) of the National Aeronautics and Space Act of 1958 (42 U.S.C. 2452(2)) under the jurisdiction or control of the United States shall be considered made or used within the United States for purposes of this title."

From the point of view of U.S. patent law, a patent in space amendment would serve three purposes: (1) insuring that research conducted in space could be protected by *some* country's patent law; (2) guaranteeing that space-based inventions are not subject to the subtle but important burdens placed on U.S. patent applicants whose inventive work was done outside the U.S.; and (3) making infringement done in space susceptible to liability under the patent laws. *See* U.S. Congress, Patents in Space, Hearings Before the Subcommittee On Courts, Civil Liberties and the Administration of Justice, Comm. on the Judiciary, 99th Cong., 2d Sess., June 13, 1985 at 4–6 (Statement of S. Neil Hosenball, General Counsel of NASA).

The Hearings on the Patents in Space Bill provide ample description of how the Bill would have furthered all three goals. On the topic of jurisdiction, reference was frequently made to the Outer Space Treaty and Registration Convention, which, as we have discussed, provides a means for states to assert jurisdiction over space activities. *See id.*, at 17.

Regarding the Bill's second goal, insuring "U.S. treatment" for inventions made in space, one must understand several basic points to see why the Bill was important. The first of these is that, under U.S. patent law, foreign inventive activity is treated differently than domestic activity. In general, under U.S. law (though not under most countries' patent law), a patent will issue to the first person to invent the product or process he claims in his patent. (In most countries, the patent goes to the first person to file a patent application on the product or process.) The first to invent is said to have "priority" over others claiming the same invention. Priority is determined by reference to certain key events—conception, reduction to practice, and diligence. A person cannot, under U.S. law, establish any of these events by reference to activity in a foreign country. 35 U.S.C. § 104 (1982); *see* 3 D. Chisum, Patents § 10.03 (1978 & rev. 1988). For example, if A Co., a foreign company, conceives and reduces to practice a satellite stabilizing mechanism outside the U.S. in early 1986, but does not file a patent application until late 1987, and B Co., a U.S. company, conceives and reduces to practice the same invention in late 1986 but files a patent application in early 1987, B Co. will have priority. This is in contrast to the situation where both A Co. and B Co. do their research in the U.S.; then A Co., as the first to invent (i.e., conceive and reduce to practice), would get the patent. Although this has been criticized for good reason, see Chisum, Foreign Activity: Its Effect on Patentability under United States Law, 11 International Review of Industrial Property & Copyright Law 26, 28–33 (1980), it is still U.S. law. The Patents in Space Bill assures that no U.S. company will be in the position of A Co. in the example above after conducting research in space. This is by virtue of Section 1 (adding proposed Section 105 to the patent statute), providing that "Any invention *made* or used" in space "shall be considered made or used within the United States" (emphasis added).

The second reason why "U.S. treatment" of patents based on space research is important is that foreign activity can affect the patentability of an invention in light of the "prior art" in the field. An invention must be both novel, in the sense that no identical invention exists in the legally recognized prior art, and "nonobvious," i.e., more than a simple extension of what was known from the prior art. 35 U.S.C. §§ 102, 103 (1982). Patent law distinguishes sharply between domestic and foreign activities for purposes of determining what falls within the prior art. For instance, patents and printed publications, no matter where they originate, are prior art, but items previously known, used, or invented by another—i.e., non-written prior art—are within the prior art only if they occur within the United States. 35 U.S.C. § 102. Thus in our example, if U.S. patent law does not apply to space, and B Co. conceived of and reduced to practice its invention in space, A Co., the foreign company, can argue that B Co.'s prior invention in space does not bar A Co.'s invention from patentability.

The third major effect of the Patents in Space Bill concerns infringement, discussed in the following excerpt from written testimony in the House hearings by a preeminent patent scholar, Donald Chisum of the University of Washington:

> Infringement of a United States patent is defined as the unauthorized making, using, or selling of the invention "within the United States." 35 U.S.C. Section 271(a).
>
> There is case authority that use of an invention aboard a vessel owned and operated by United States citizens on the high seas is use within the United States. Gardiner v. Howe, 9 F. Cas. 1157 (No. 5219) (C.C.D. Mass. 1865). The analogy between ships on the high seas and craft in outer space is a strong one. In reversing a rejection of a process that could only be practiced on the moon, the Board of Appeals of the Patent and Trademark Office relied on this analogy. Ex parte McKay, 200 U.S.P.Q. 324 (P.T.O. Bd. App. 1975). The rejection was based in part on 35 U.S.C. Sec. 154, which provides that a patent grant shall confer exclusive rights "throughout the United States." Citing Article VIII of the Outer Space treaty, the Board reasoned that "A patent grant under 35 U.S.C. 154 by the United States for a process to be carried out on the moon by personnel subject to its jurisdiction is thus not inimical and at variance with the indicated section of the statute."
>
> On policy grounds, extension of the scope of a United States patent to activity abroad a spacecraft under United States jurisdiction is fully justified. It is true that United States patent laws have no direct extraterritorial effect. See Deepsouth Packing Co., 406 U.S. 518 (1972). A major reason for this limitation is the avoidance of interference with the sovereignty of other countries, which may have patent laws that differ from those of the United States. However, having separate patent systems for each country of the world is a necessary evil at best since technology by its very nature flows easily to wherever it may be effectively utilized. Extending the scope of U.S. patents into space will not conflict with the policies of any other sovereign.
>
> Denial of patent protection in space will create a partial "free ride" for those who use new technology that can be utilized in space and a total "free ride" for those who use new technology that can only be utilized there. Denial of patent protection in space may also cause economic inefficiencies. Expensive new technology that has primary utility in space will be developed internally only by those companies or entities with enough resources to make direct effective usage of such technology aboard space vehicles. Small entities, universities, etc. would not be able to obtain effective patent protection that could be licensed to others.
>
> It should be recognized that extension of patent protection to spacecraft under United States jurisdiction will have direct implications for the United States government given its control and involvement in most activity in space. By statute, the United States is subject to suit for reasonable compensation

when an invention "covered by a patent of the United States is used or manufactured by or for the United States." 28 U.S.C. Sec. 1498(a).

As noted above, the language of the proposed new Section 105 is not entirely clear. It speaks of an "invention" being "made or used" in space being considered as though it is the United States for purposes of title 35. Literally, that would cover infringing acts of making and using (though not selling, which is a separate infringing act). Placement of the section after Section 104 may support at least a litigable argument that it relates only to priority and patentability. The matter could be made clearer by placing the substance of the amendment in the existing Section 100(c) definition of "United States."

Hearings, *supra*, at 18–19 (Written Statement of Professor Donald Chisum).

PROTECTING TRADE SECRETS IN SPACE

**Reynolds, Book Review, 27 Jurimetrics:
Journal of Law, Science & Technology 431 (1987)
(Reviewing Office of Technology Assessment,
Space Stations and the Law (1986))**

Intellectual Property

The background paper next addresses the protection of intellectual property in outer space. Unfortunately, however, the authors' concept of intellectual property seems limited to patent law, which is the only subject discussed. While the patent discussion is interesting and provocative, there are other aspects of intellectual property that present problems just as interesting, and at least as thorny, as those discussed with regard to patents. For example, in most people's minds the commercial activity to which the space station has the most to contribute is manufacturing. While patents obviously are involved in manufacturing processes, it is unavoidably true that most improvements to manufacturing processes—including those of great value—are incremental in nature and hence often not patentable.

Those improvements are instead protected under trade secret law, and by precautions against disclosure. But trade secret law is state law, not federal law, and it is far from clear which (if any) state's trade secret law would apply to a U.S. space station. The regime that would govern a multinational space station in which different modules fall under the jurisdiction of different nations boggles the mind, especially when manufacturing processes might be carried out in more than one module, and when rights of access among modules would be guaranteed to all occupants of the station. Since the station will be small, and occupants will unavoidably have many opportunities to learn about secret processes carried out on board, some sort of contractual scheme seems necessary if those processes are to be protected. It would have been helpful if the OTA had addressed such issues.

It certainly would have helped me, anyway, since I confess to being stumped. I *do* have a suggestion as to what could be done with a U.S. station, or perhaps with regard to the parts of the station governed by the United States. With regard to those circumstances, Congress could [federalize and] extend the Uniform Trade Secrets Act to govern manufacturing processes in outer space, or provide that a particular state's law (say, that of the state from which the station is launched) would govern. This would provide some protection to secret manufacturing processes employed or developed abroad a U.S. station, but I'm not sure that much can be done to protect such secrets in the context of a multinational station. This may encourage companies involved in manufacturing processes to make use of free-flying packages whose secret components are sealed in black boxes, so that those servicing them from the station will be unable to gain access to any secret information. I don't know whether this will place a substantial burden on experiments in space manufacturing or not; much will depend on the nature of the processes experimented with.

ADMINISTRATIVE LAW: REGULATION AND DEREGULATION OF SPACE ACTIVITIES

In this final section we consider a number of conceptually related yet distinct legal problems raised by space activities—those relating to government regulation.

The chief legislative initiative on space regulation was the Commercial Space Launch Act of 1984, Pub. L. 98–575, 98 Stat. 3055, codified at 49 U.S.C., §§ 2601 *et seq.* For the most part, the Commercial Space Launch Act attempts to support the private launch industry by (1) streamlining the regulatory approval process governing space activities, and (2) admonishing all branches of the government to support the industry in whatever ways possible. The following excerpt is from the Act:

Commercial Space Launch Act of 1984, 49 U.S.C. §§ 2601 *et seq.*

§ 2601. Congressional findings

The Congress finds and declares that—

*   *   *

(6) provision of launch services by the private sector is consistent with the national security interests and foreign policy interests of the United

States and would be facilitated by stable, minimal, and appropriate regulatory guidelines that are fairly and expeditiously applied; and

(7) the United States should encourage private sector launches and associated services and, only to the extent necessary, regulate such launches and services in order to ensure compliance with international obligations of the United States and to protect the public health and safety, safety of property, and national security interests and foreign policy interests of the United States.

*   *   *

§ 2604. General responsibilities of the Secretary and other agencies

(a) Duties of Secretary [of Transportation]

The Secretary shall be responsible for carrying out this chapter and in doing so shall—

(1) encourage, facilitate, and promote commercial space launches by the private sector; and

(2) consult with other agencies to provide consistent application of licensing requirements under this chapter and to ensure fair and equitable treatment for all license applicants.

*   *   *

§ 2605. Requirement of license for private space launch operations

(a) Geographical restrictions

(1) No person shall launch a launch vehicle or operate a launch site within the United States, unless authorized by a license issued or transferred under this chapter.

(2) No United States citizen . . . shall launch a launch vehicle or operate a launch site outside the United States, unless authorized by a license issued or transferred under this chapter.

(3)(A) No United States citizen . . . shall launch a launch vehicle or operate a launch site at any place which is both outside the United States and outside the territory of any foreign nation, unless authorized by a license issued or transferred under this chapter. The preceding sentence shall not apply with respect to a launch or operation of a launch site if there is an agreement in force between the United States and a foreign nation which provides that such foreign nation shall exercise jurisdiction over such launch or operation.

*   *   *

§ 2607. Licensing requirements

*   *   *

(c) Waiver

The Secretary may, in individual cases, waive the application of any requirement for a license under this section if the Secretary determines that such waiver is in the public interest and will not jeopardize the public health and safety, safety of property, or any national security interest or foreign policy interest of the United States.

§ 2608. License application and approval

(a) Application procedures

Any person may apply to the Secretary for issuance or transfer of a license under this chapter, in such form and manner as the Secretary may prescribe. The Secretary shall establish procedures and timetables to expedite review of applications under this section and to reduce regulatory burdens for applicants.

§ 2614. Use of government property

(a) Authority of Secretary

The Secretary shall take such actions as may be necessary to facilitate and encourage the acquisition (by lease, sale, transaction in lieu of sale, or otherwise) by the private sector of launch property of the United States which is excess or is otherwise not needed for public use and of launch services, including utilities, of the United States which are otherwise not needed for public use.

(b) Acquisition and payment by private sector

(1) The amount to be paid to the United States by any person who acquires launch property or launch services, including utilities, shall be established by the agency providing the property or service, in consultation with the Secretary. In the case of acquisition of launch property by sale or transaction in lieu of sale, the amount of such payment shall be the fair market value. In the case of any other type of acquisition of launch property, the amount of such payment shall be an amount equal to the direct costs (including any specific wear and tear and damage to the property) incurred by the United States as a result of the acquisition of such launch property. In the case of any acquisition of launch services, including utilities, the amount of such payment shall be an amount equal to the direct costs (including salaries of United States civilian and con-

tractor personnel) incurred by the United States as a result of the acquisition of such launch services.

*   *   *

(c) Establishment of assurances to protect United States from liability, loss, or injury

The Secretary may establish requirements for liability insurance, hold harmless agreements, proof of financial responsibility, and such other assurances as may be needed to protect the United States and its agencies and personnel from liability, loss, or injury as a result of a launch or operation of a launch site involving Government facilities or personnel.

§ 2615. Liability insurance

Each person who launches a launch vehicle or operates a launch site under a license issued or transferred under this chapter shall have in effect liability insurance at least in such amount as is considered by the Secretary to be necessary for such launch or operation, considering the international obligations of the United States. The Secretary shall prescribe such amount after consultation with the Attorney General and other appropriate agencies.

§ 2616. Enforcement authority

*   *   *

(b) Power to investigate, inspect or seize

In carrying out this section, the Secretary may—

(1) make investigations and inquiries, and administer to or take from any person an oath, affirmation, or affidavit, concerning any matter relating to enforcement of this chapter; and (2) pursuant to any lawful process—

(A) enter at any reasonable time any launch site, production facility, or assembly site of a launch vehicle, or any site where a payload is integrated with a launch vehicle, for the purpose of inspecting any object which is subject to this chapter and any records or reports required by the Secretary to be made or kept under this chapter; and

(B) seize any such object, record, or report where there is probable cause to believe that such object, record, or report was used, is being used, or is likely to be used in violation of this chapter.

NOTES

1. For general commentary on this Act, see Note, The Commercial Space Launch Act: America's Response to the Moon Treaty? 10 Fordham International Law Journal 763 (1987).

2. In response to their experience in the first few years of commercial space activities, launch service companies led a movement to amend the Commercial Space Launch Act in two crucial respects: First, they attempted to have the insurance provision (§ 2615) amended to explicitly limit the amount of insurance required. The proposed change, embodied in H.R. 4399 and S.2395, the Commercial Space Launch Act Amendments of 1988, 100th Cong., 2d Sess., would require that damage to *government property* be insured for no more than $100 million or "the maximum . . . available on the world market at a reasonable cost, whichever is less." H.R. 4399, § 4(a); S. 2395 § 16(a)(1)(B)(ii). The proposed amendments would also limit insurance for damages to *third parties* to $500 million or the maximum available at a reasonable cost, again, "whichever is less." H.R. 4399 § 4(b); S.2395 § 16(a)(1)(A)(ii). With current insurance costs running some 20% of the total value of the launch services and payload combined, it is difficult to determine whether the "reasonable cost" language in the amendments would free the parties to a launch agreement to reduce insurance coverage from the current *de facto* requirement of $500 million. (But note one factor that suggests this new limitation would not affect insurance costs: most of the costs of insurance go to insuring against the risk of losing the payload, rather than against the risk of injuring third parties.) In addition, the amendments provide for free reflights for payloads "bumped" from the space shuttle. *See* S.2395 § 5(c)(2). Of course, competitors of the "bumped" companies object to this proposal, as do those who would otherwise get the launch business. The Defense Department has also objected to this provision as too costly. *See* Hearings on the Commercial Space Launch Act Amendments of 1988, U.S. Senate Subcomm. on Science, Technology and Space of the Committee on Commerce, Science and Transportation, 100th Cong., 2d Sess. (May 17, 1988) (Statement of Thomas S. Moorman, Jr., Director of Space and SDI Programs, U.S. Air Force), at 6–7. NOTE: After this book went to press, the above Amendments were passed and signed by the President. *See* Commercial Space Launch Act Amendments of 1988, Pub. L. 100-657, 102 Stat. 3900 (1988). On launch insurance generally, see 100th Cong. 2d Sess. S. Print No. 100-112, Insurance and the U.S. Commercial Space Launch Industry (July 1988).

Under the Commercial Space Launch Act of 1984, the Secretary of Transportation was free to delegate his or her authority to other officers in the Department. This was done almost immediately, and that is how the Department of Transportation's Office of Commercial Space Transportation (OCST) was born in its current form.

The following regulations are those most recently promulgated by OCST. They are excerpted below to give a flavor of the Office's authority, as well as its regulatory approach.

Rules and Regulations
Department of Transportation
Office of Commercial Space Transportation
14 CFR Ch. III
Commercial Space Transportation: Licensing Regulations
53 Fed. Reg. 11004, Monday, April 4, 1988

SUMMARY: The Office of Commercial Space Transportation is publishing final licensing regulations for commercial launch activities. These regulations constitute the procedural framework for reviewing and authorizing all proposals to conduct non-Federal launch activities, including the launching of vehicles, operation of launch sites, and payload activities that are not licensed by other Federal agencies.

DATE: This rule becomes effective April 4, 1988. [From 14 C.F.R. §§ 400–499 (1988)]

§ 405.1 Monitoring of Licensed and Other Activities.

Each licensee shall allow and cooperate with Federal officers or employees or other individuals authorized by the Director to observe licensed activities, including launch sites, production facilities or assembly sites used by any contractor or a licensee in the production or assembly of a launch vehicle and in the integration of a payload with its launch vehicle.

§ 405.3 Authority to Modify, Suspend or Revoke.

. . . . (b) If the Office finds that a licensee has substantially failed to comply with any requirement of the Act, any regulation issued under the Act, the terms and conditions of a license, or any other applicable requirement, or that public health and safety, the safety of property or any national security or foreign policy interest of the United States so requires, the Office may suspend or revoke any license issued to such licensee under this chapter.

§ 405.5 Emergency Orders.

The Office may immediately terminate, prohibit or suspend a licensed launch or launch site operation if the Office determines that—

(a) Such launch or operation is detrimental to public health and safety, safety of property, or any national security or foreign policy interest of the United States; and

(b) The detriment cannot be eliminated effectively through the exercise of other authority of the Office.

*   *   *

SUBCHAPTER C—LICENSING

§ 411.1 General

The Office of Commercial Space Transportation may issue and transfer licenses authorizing launches, the operation of launch sites, or both.

§ 411.3 Review Procedures

(a) The evaluation of license requests for unmanned launches involves two reviews, Safety Review and Mission Review, designed to address in the most effective and least burdensome manner the two general areas of Federal concern: (1) the efficacy of the proposed safety operations to support safe preparation and launch of a launch vehicle and any payload; and (2) significant issues affecting United States national security interests, foreign policy interests, or international obligations which might be associated with the proposed launch. These reviews may be conducted independently of each other and in whichever order, sequential or concurrent, is more appropriate to the needs of the applicant.

*   *   *

§ 411.5

(b) . . . If an applicant proposes to contract for the services of a Federal range or a private launch site operated under the authority of a license issued by the Office, safety approval will ordinarily be given once the applicant has been accepted by a range or site capable of handling the launch activity proposed.

PART 413—APPLICATIONS

*   *   *

§ 413.5 Application.

(a) Form. Applications shall be in writing and filed in duplicate with the Office of Commercial Space Transportation, S–50, 400 Seventh Street, SW, Washington, DC 20590. Attention: Applications Review Branch.

(b) Types. Applications to the Office may request issuance or transfer of a license authorizing a launch or the operation of a launch site. Applications may also be made, separately and in advance of a license application, requesting an approval or determination that must be secured before a license can be issued or transferred.

§ 413.7 Confidentiality.

(a) Information or data submitted to the Office may be designated as confidential by the person or agency furnishing such data or information.

§ 413.9 Review of Applications.

*   *   *

(c) Applications found by the Office to be incomplete or so speculative as to make review inappropriate will be returned to the applicant with a statement of the reasons therefor.

(d) Once an application is accepted, the Office initiates an appropriate review in light of the specific action requested in the application. . . . [T]he Office shall consult with the Department of Defense on all matters affecting national security and with the Department of State on all matters affecting foreign policy, including the issuance or transfer of each license.

(e) The Office makes a determination on an application as expeditiously as possible but, in the case of a license application, not later than 180 days after receipt of such application.

§ 413.17 Certain Rights Not Conferred by License.　　　　'

No license shall confer any proprietary, property, or exclusive right in the use of any airspace, Federal launch facility, or Federal launch support facility. Issuance of a license does not affect the authority of the Federal Communications Commission under the Communications Act of 1934 (47 U.S.C. 151 *et seq.*) or the authority of the Secretary of Commerce under the Land Remote-Sensing Commercialization Act of 1984 (15 U.S.C. 4201 *et seq.*).

§ 413.19 Substantial and Significant Changes in Information Furnished to the Office.

(a) Each applicant is responsible for the continuing accuracy and completeness of information furnished to the Office to support a pending application or which formed the basis for any approval, determination or licensing action by the Office. Whenever such information is no longer substantially accurate and complete in all significant respects, or whenever there has been a substantial change as to any matter of decisional significance to the Office, the applicant shall, as promptly as possible, submit a statement furnishing such additional or corrected information as may be appropriate.

*   *   *

PART 415—LAUNCH LICENSES

§ 415.3 When a Launch License is Required.

(a) The launch of a launch vehicle from U.S. territory by any person, or from outside U.S. territory by any individual or any corporation, partnership, joint venture, association or other entity organized or existing under the laws of the United States or any state, must be authorized by a license issued under this part.

(b) The launch of a launch vehicle by a foreign corporation or other entity controlled by a United States citizen . . . at any place which is both outside the United States and outside of the territory of any foreign nation when there is no agreement in force between the United States and a foreign nation which provides that such foreign nation shall exercise jurisdiction over such launch, must be authorized by a license issued under this part.

(c) The launch of a launch vehicle by any foreign corporation or other entity described in paragraph (b) of this section from the territory of a foreign nation, when there is in force an agreement between the United States and such foreign nation concerning the exercise of jurisdiction by the United States over such launch, must be authorized by a license issued under this part.

§ 415.9 Standard Conditions.

. . . Standard conditions in licenses include requirements for the licensee to do the following:

(a) Secure at least the minimum amount of third-party liability insurance specified by the Department;

(b) Adhere strictly to specified range safety regulations and procedures;

(c) Comply with requirements concerning pre-launch record keeping and notifications, including those pertaining to Federal airspace restrictions and military tracking operations; and

(d) Comply with Federal inspection, verification and enforcement requirements.

Subpart D—Environmental Impacts of Launch Activities

§ 415.31 General.

In accordance with the requirements of the National Environmental Policy Act, 42 U.S.C. 4321, *et seq.* (NEPA), the Council on Environmental Quality Regulations for Implementing the Procedural Provisions of NEPA, 40 CFR Parts 1500–1508, and the Department of Transportation's Procedures for Considering Environmental Impacts, DOT Order 5610.1C, the environmental impacts of licensing commercial launch activities are required to be considered by the Office. The effects of most projected commercial launch activities are already addressed in the Office's programmatic environmental assessment or in environmental impact statements for existing launch sites. The Office will determine whether a proposed launch activity is adequately addressed in these documents. Applicants may be required to provide additional information concerning the environmental effects of a proposed launch activity.

THE LAND REMOTE SENSING COMMERCIALIZATION ACT

Besides the Commercial Space Launch Act and ensuing OCST regulations, there is another piece of legislation which, with its accompanying regulations, affects one big segment of the commercial space business: the Land-Remote Sensing Commercialization Act of 1984, Pub. L. 98-365, 98 Stat. 452, codified at 15 U.S.C. §§ 4201 *et seq.* (1982 & Supp. III 1985). The basic aim of this legislation was to (1) "privatize" the marketing and sale of remote sensing data gathered by U.S.-owned Landsat Satellites, and (2) provide launch licensing procedures for private-sector enterprises that wish to enter the remote sensing business.

Remote sensing is a general term used to describe satellite-based systems that take precise images of the earth's surface for use in such applications as weather prediction and tracking, natural resource location and inventory (e.g., timber and oil and gas deposits), environmental monitoring, and general observation (e.g., by the news media, following natural disaster or international conflict stories). *See* Reynolds, Satellite Newsgathering and the First Amendment, The Air & Space Lawyer, Fall, 1987 at 1; Joyner & Miller, Selling Satellites: The Commercialization of LANDSAT, 26 Harvard International Law Journal 63 (1985); Diederiks-Vershoor, Current Issues in Remote Sensing, 1984 Michigan Year Book of International Legal Studies 305 (1984).

The following excerpt is a condensation of the Commercialization Act.

Land Remote Sensing Commercialization Act of 1984
[From 15 U.S.C. (1982 & Supp. III 1985)]

§ 4201. Congressional Findings

The Congress finds and declares that—

(1) the continuous civilian collection and utilization of land remote-sensing data from space are of major benefit in managing the Earth's natural resources and in planning and conducting many other activities of economic importance;

*   *   *

(5) the broadest and most beneficial use of land remote-sensing data will result from maintaining a policy of nondiscriminatory access to data;

(6) competitive, market-driven private sector involvement in land remote sensing is in the national interest of the United States;

(7) use of land remote-sensing data has been inhibited by slow market development and by the lack of assurance of data continuity;

(8) the private sector, and in particular the "value-added" industry, is best suited to develop land remote-sensing data markets;

(9) there is doubt that the private sector alone can currently develop a total land remote-sensing system because of the high risk and large capital expenditure involved;

*   *   *

§ 4212. Contract for Marketing of Unenhanced Data

(a) Provisions of Contracts

In accordance with the requirements of this subchapter, the Secretary [of Commerce], by means of a competitive process and to the extent provided in advance by appropriation Acts, shall contract with a United States private sector party (as defined by the Secretary) for the marketing of unenhanced data collected by the Landsat system. Any such contract—

(1) shall provide that the contractor set the prices of unenhanced data;

(2) may provide for financial arrangements between the Secretary and the contractor including fees for operating the system, payments by the contractor as an initial fee or as a percentage of sales receipts, or other such considerations;

(3) shall provide that the contractor will offer to sell and deliver unenhanced data to all potential buyers on a nondiscriminatory basis;

(4) shall provide that the contractor pay to the United States Government the full purchase price of any unenhanced data that the contractor elects to utilize for purposes other than sale, except in the case of research and development activities conducted in accordance with section 4264 of this title;

(5) shall be entered into by the Secretary only if the Secretary has determined that such contract is likely to result in net cost savings for the United States Government; and

(6) may be reawarded competitively after the practical demise of the space segment of the Landsat system, as determined by the Secretary.

(b) Specification that Contractor May Use, Maintain, Repair or Modify Elements of Landsat System

Any contract authorized by subsection (a) of this section may specify that the contractor use, and, at his own expense, maintain, repair, or modify, such elements of the Landsat system as the contractor finds necessary for commercial operations.

*   *   *

§ 4241. General Authority

(a) Licensing Private Sector Parties; Authority of Secretary; Limitations

(1) In consultation with other appropriate Federal agencies, the Secretary is authorized to license private sector parties to operate private remote-sensing space systems for such period as the Secretary may specify and in accordance with the provisions of this subchapter.

(2) In the case of a private space system that is used for remote sensing and other purposes, the authority of the Secretary under this subchapter shall be limited only to the remote-sensing operations of such space system.

(b) Grant of License; Conditions

No license shall be granted by the Secretary unless the Secretary determines in writing that the applicant will comply with the requirements of this chapter, any regulations issued pursuant to this chapter, and any applicable international obligations and national security concerns of the United States.

(c) Review of Applications by Secretary

The Secretary shall review any application and make a determination thereon within one hundred and twenty days of the receipt of such application. If final action has not occurred within such time, the Secretary shall inform the applicant of any pending issues and of actions required to resolve them.

(d) Denial of Licenses; Secretary to Refrain
from Denying to Protect Licensees from Competition

The Secretary shall not deny such license in order to protect any existing licensee from competition.

REMOTE SENSING REGULATIONS

Under the terms of the Act, the Secretary of Commerce delegated his authority to make regulations to the National Oceanic and Atmospheric Administration (NOAA), an arm of the Department of Commerce. The following is an excerpt from NOAA's regulations on remote-sensing business licensing:

Civilian Remote Sensing Licensing Regulations
[from 15 C.F.R. §§ 960.9 et seq. (1988)]

§ 960.9 Review Procedures

(a) The Administrator shall immediately forward a copy of any application or a summary thereof to the Department of Defense, the Department of State, and any other Federal agencies determined to have a substantial interest in the proposed activity, such as the National Aeronautics and Space Administration, and the Department of Transportation. . . .

*   *   *

(e) Within sixty days of receipt of a complete application, each Federal agency consulted under paragraph (a) of this section shall recommend approval or disapproval of the application in writing.

(1) If the Secretary of Defense or the Secretary of State determines that an application may not be approved without modifications or conditions consistent with national security concerns or international obligations, the determination shall clearly state why the modifications or conditions are necessary to accomplish the intended purpose.

(2) If any other agency recommends disapproval, it shall state why it believes the application does not comply with any law or regulation within its area of responsibility and how it believes the application may be amended or the license conditioned to comply with the law or regulation in question.

§ 960.10 Timely Approval or Denial of Application and Issuance of License.

*   *   *

(b) If the Administrator denies the application, he or she shall provide the applicant with a concise statement in writing of the reasons therefor.

*   *   *

§ 960.11 Criteria for Approval or Denial

Before approving an application and issuing a license or an amendment to a license, the Administrator shall find in writing that:

(a) The licensee will operate the system in a manner consistent with national security and the international obligations of the U.S.;

(b) The licensee will make available unenhanced data to all potential users on a nondiscriminatory basis. . . .

In making the findings required by paragraph (a) of this section, the Administrator shall be entitled to rely upon the written recommendations of the Departments of Defense and State described in § 960.9(e).

CRITICISMS OF REMOTE SENSING REGULATIONS

A number of commentators have criticized the breadth of NOAA's discretion under these regulations, and its ability to deny permission to launch a private system or use it if it threatens "national security." These commentators have argued that this amounts to a prior restraint under established First Amendment principles. The following excerpt captures the flavor of these criticisms:

Merges & Reynolds, News Media Satellites and the First Amendment, 3 Boalt High Technology Law Journal 1 (1988)

Although military planners might well prefer to exclude news media satellites and reporters from reporting many topics, and might have their jobs made appreciably easier by that exclusion, they may do so only when the interests involved are of sufficient immediacy and importance to pass muster under the first amendment. The fact that the information in question is being gathered via a novel technology is irrelevant: the first amendment was not drafted in contemplation of many new technologies, from telephones to offset printing presses to personal computers. Nor is it sufficient to assert, as some have done, that we live in a perpetually dangerous world and cannot afford to limit the discretion of national security officials by imposing first amendment restrictions on their actions. The choice between taking every conceivable action to promote "national security" ends, and balancing those ends against the importance of preserving essential freedoms, has already been made.

In a way, the advent of civilian imaging technology brings the history of space surveillance full circle. In the earliest days of enthusiasm for space, satellites were one of the benefits identified by early visionaries—private citizens—who encountered more than a little difficulty in selling their ideas to governments. But now that the technology has matured to the point that private interests might be able to afford it, the U.S. government has begun drawing a line around space and declaring it off limits, or at least subject to a level of regulation that would not be tolerated on earth.

And there is irony here on another level as well. The U.S. has long championed an "Open Skies" approach to space reconnaissance; this was in fact an important element shaping early U.S. space policy. While this approach has been taken to mean that space overflight should be open to spacecraft from all countries, satellite technology has now become routine enough to put space within the reach of entities other than countries—private firms, for example, including the media. As a consequence, for the first time the U.S. is being forced to decide just how open it really wants the skies to be.

In that sense, this is just another in a long line of problems posed by new information technologies from the time movable type was invented to the present. The instinct of governments confronted by new technologies is generally to bring them under control (or at least try to do so), especially when those technologies are closely related to matters of power and politics. That instinct is generally wrong, though, at least in nations, like ours, with a tradition of free expression. The proper course is to remain faithful to that tradition, even in the context of new technologies.

Fortunately, the first amendment is flexible enough to accommodate new situations without sacrificing important interests. In this instance, an approach consistent with the first amendment would be to identify subjects and occasions for which media satellite imaging would be inappropriate—troop ship departures and secret military installations, for example—and to prohibit publication of such images, rather than threatening to place a blanket ban on media access to satellite technology.

NOTE

The debate over the "Mediasat" regulations, as they have been called, is only the first of many that will take place as the governmental monopoly over space technologies erodes. As costs drop and capabilities rise, private organizations—such as news organizations, arms control groups, and human rights and environmental advocates—will begin to make greater and greater use of space technologies. This trend is likely to cause considerable consternation within and among various world governments, but it is unlikely that they will be able to do much about it. For more on remote sensing in an international context see Chapter 5.

EXTRATERRESTRIAL CONTAMINATION

One possible barrier to civilian plans for extracting resources from the Moon or other celestial bodies is found in existing regulations governing extraterrestrial exposure. Under these regulations, 14 C.F.R. §§ 1211.100 *et seq.,* (1988) any person who has had contact with any other celestial body, *or* who has been in contact with a person or object who has done so is to be quarantined. The length of the quarantine, and the decision whether or not to quarantine, are left to the discretion of the NASA Administrator, although the Regulations *do* provide that any person quarantined shall "be given a reasonable opportunity to communicate by telephone with legal counsel or other person of his choice." 14 C.F.R. § 1211.104(b)(5).

Although these regulations were drafted to deal with astronauts and artifacts returning from the Moon—or actually with autograph hounds and publicity seekers who might violate the quarantine to which the astronauts had already agreed anyway—they might be applied under other circumstances. Their applicability is unclear: Section 1211.100 states that the regulations establish "NASA policy, responsibility and authority to guard the Earth against any harmful contamination or adverse changes in its environment resulting from personnel, spacecraft and other property returning to Earth after landing on or coming within the atmospheric envelope of a celestial body." On the other hand, Section 1211.101 provides that the "provisions of this part apply to all NASA manned and unmanned space missions which land on or come within the atmospheric envelope of a celestial body and return to the Earth."

Thus, the applicability of these regulations to non-NASA missions, or in the (rather unlikely) circumstances of an alien spacecraft landing, is unclear. Those planning non-Governmental missions to the Moon or asteroids would be well-advised to consult with appropriate officials in advance. In general, the U.S. obligation under the 1967 Outer Space Treaty to prevent harmful contamination of the earth argues in favor of reading the Regulations' applicability broadly, as does the potential magnitude of any harm resulting from such contamination, however unlikely. Of course, anyone quarantined should retain all other constitutional liberties—need to avoid contamination would not, for example, justify holding someone *incommunicado.* For more on contamination, both "forward" and "back," see the environmental discussion in Chapter 5.

9

Some Issues of the Future

Most of this book has addressed issues of space law that are either of current application or that are likely to be applied in the near future—satellite broadcasting, or patents for space inventions, for example. This chapter, however, deals with issues of space law that are likely to have less immediate application, though in the case of at least one—the governance of space societies—a surprisingly large amount of work has already been devoted to the problem. Not only is the issue extensively treated in the two seminal works of space law, Andrew Haley's *Space Law and Government* (1963) and Myres McDougal, Harold Lasswell, and Ivan Vlasic's *Law and Public Order in Space* (1963), but it has also been the subject of considerable attention in later years.

GOVERNANCE OF SPACE SOCIETIES

Space Settlements and the Law:
Address of Justice William J. Brennan, Jr.,
American Law Institute Annual Dinner, May 21, 1987

Always with us are changes and developments in the law, new terrain to be explored, understood, grappled with, fought for and constantly reassessed and applied under fire. So I thought it would not be inappropriate tonight, in this year of the Bicentennial of the Constitution, if I said something of an important new emerging area of the law that is knocking at the door and demanding our attention. I refer to space law. I confidently predict that we'll soon have to grapple with the question: what law should govern, not only the relationship between earth (particularly the United States) and space societies but, perhaps more importantly, what law should govern within space societies themselves and among space inhabitants who will people space communities. . . .

A worrisome concern these days is the Earth's population explosion. The New York Times recently stated in an editorial: "In July 1986 the world's population, which didn't top a billion until 1850, passed the 5 billion mark. The Population Institute warned that the 5 billion may be 10 billion by 2028." Perhaps the development of space communities may be at least a partial answer to these worries. If then, we accept, as I am persuaded we must, that space colonization is inevitable, and that we should therefore prepare for it, what are just some of the legal problems we should be thinking about? . . . Here are some: since Earth is part of space and in space and is part of the Cosmos, space societies can't sever their ties with Earth. Is Earth then to determine the shape or nature of governance in space? If so, isn't space then just a new continent, as was our own when the Mayflower landed, to be explored as was our own by several nations—the Spanish, the French, the Portuguese, the English? Should any law then be made for a space society in advance of actual settlement? . . . What is the best historical model—the Mayflower Compact, the Articles of Incorporation of the British East India Company or whatever? . . . If the United States creates a society populated by U.S. citizens, what federal law should govern that society. . . . [d]oes the constitution follow the flag so that its protections are available to every resident of the space settlement?

*   *   *

Indeed, the American Law Institute itself co-sponsored in November 1981 the International Conference that debated issues on Doing Business in Outer Space: Legal Issues and Practical Problems. Moreover, Congress has extended federal criminal laws to punish criminal conduct on the Moon or other celestial bodies and in space craft outside the Earth's atmosphere. Indeed, a few district court and state court decisions have extended American domestic law to the solution of outer space problems. And doubtless, too, many lawyers here tonight have already had occasion to counsel clients on space law. But I suggest that the actual establishment of space settlements will confront the profession with enormous new responsibilities that we ought to prepare for as thoroughly as we can. For it is accepted by all of us, I am sure, that the United States must be, and must become unequivocally committed to space exploration and exploitation and the settlement of space by Americans. Our very survival requires no less. We have to keep in mind that Russians, Japanese, Europeans, and South Americans also have asserted interests in outer space.

The Smithsonian Institution Press recently published a lengthy and erudite treatment of this topic, G. Robinson & H. White, Envoys of Mankind: A Declaration of First Principles for the Governance of Space Societies (1986), and followed it up with a series of conferences cosponsored with Boston University's Center for Democracy. Many individuals, including such luminaries as Justice Brennan, Professor A.E. Dick Howard, and journalist Walter Cronkite, participated in this process, which culminated in a draft declaration of principles. The following excerpt discusses some issues behind both the book and the conference.

Ragosta & Reynolds, In Search of Governing Principles, 28 Jurimetrics: Journal of Law, Science & Technology 473 (1988)

In fact, the central point of *Envoys of Mankind* is that space is a different environment from any that we have known before, and that laws governing the behavior of people, and societies, in space must take those differences into account. This point is more subtle than it seems—as the authors note, different environments do not simply present legal problems of their own (as, for example, the dry climate of the American West led to new doctrines of riparian law); they also change the very nature of the societies and human beings to whom the laws apply.

*   *   *

There is considerable evidence already, in the nonspace context, that Robinson and White are right to take seriously the impact of new environments on human behavior and governance. Experience with Antarctic bases and other isolated environments where significant numbers of people must work together demonstrates that traditional methods of organization— particularly hierarchical structures modelled on established military systems—simply do not work well in such circumstances:

> A winter base in Antarctica is a unique world, where the cook often has greater prestige than the officer-in-charge and the radio operator can have more influence than an established scientist. The traditional hierarchical structure of the military, and of government as a whole, breaks down. . . . This was a controversial and embarrassing realization for the Navy. Flexible authority and sharing of tasks among everyone are vital. . . . This can run against the grain of highly specialized scientists and career military officers. The absence of women was also a factor. Navy traditions excluded females from the continent, and this increased tensions. . . .
>
> Some lessons have been learned. With great reluctance, the Navy eventually allowed women on the continent. . . . A more flexible organizational structure is tolerated, and private enterprise is now providing some services and personnel. . . . The Antarctican experience reminds us that the dangers of mutiny or psychosis in a space station or colony are as real as the threat of meteors or solar flares.

[Lawler, Lessons from the Past: Toward a Long-Term Space Policy, in Lunar Bases and Space Activities of the Twenty-First Century 757, 762– 63 (W.W. Mendell ed. 1985).]

Likewise, the experience of many earthbound colonial efforts demonstrates the problems created by attempts to graft old or poorly thought out social systems on new environments. One such example is in the early years of Australia, where the transition from a penal colony to full fledged settlement was fraught with difficulties stemming from excessive meddling by distant authorities and by local military authorities' lack of skill in building up a civilian economy. Many others abound.

For more on how space environments may differ and on what their unique characteristics may be, *see* Rambaut, The Social and Physical Environment of Space Stations and Colonies, in Beyond Spaceship Earth: Environmental Ethics and the Solar System 263 (E. Hargrove ed. 1986). This excellent book, published by the Sierra Club, contains essays on a wide variety of issues relating to space exploration, the environment, and human society. *See also* Crosby, Life (with all its problems) in Space, in Interstellar Migration and the Human Experience 210 (B.R. Finney & E.M. Jones eds. 1985).

Robinson and White set out at the end of their book a draft treaty relating to the governance of space societies. This effort aroused sufficient interest that the Smithsonian Institution, in cooperation with the Center for Democracy at Boston University, organized a symposium on the topic, which made a further effort at the task. The symposium's final effort is reproduced below; Ragosta & Reynolds, *supra,* analyzes a slightly earlier draft.

Declaration of First Principles
for the Governance of Outer Space Societies

Preamble

On the occasion of the Bicentennial of the Constitution of the United States of America and in commemoration and furtherance of its values we, the undersigned petitioners,

Bearing witness to the exploration and inevitable settlement of outer space;

Recognizing the universal longing for life, liberty, equality, peace and security;

Placing our trust in societies that guarantee their members full protection of law, due process and equal protection under the law;

Reaffirming our faith in fundamental freedoms;

Mindful, as were our nation's founders, of the self-evident truth that we are endowed by our Creator with certain inalienable rights;

Recognizing the responsibility of a government to protect the rights of the governed to exist and to evolve;

Do assert and declare in this petition the intrinsic value of a set of First Principles for the Governance of Outer Space Societies and, at the beginning of this third century of nationhood under our Constitution, resolutely urge all people of the United States of America to acknowledge, accept and apply such First Principles as hereinafter set forth.

Article I

A. The rule of law and the fundamental values embodied in the United States Constitution shall apply to all individuals living in outer space societies under United States jurisdiction.

B. Appropriate constraints upon and limitations of authority shall be defined so as to protect the personal freedom of each individual, such as the right to reasonable privacy, freedom from self-incrimination, freedom from unreasonable intrusion, search and seizure, and freedom from cruel and unusual punishment.

C. Toward this end, the imperatives of community safety and individual survival within the unique environment of outer space shall be guaranteed in harmony with the exercise of such fundamental individual rights as freedom of speech, religion, association, assembly, contract, travel to, in and from outer space, media and communications, as well as the rights of petition, informed consent and private ownership of property.

D. The principles set forth here should not be construed to exclude any other such rights possessed by individuals.

Article II

A. Authority in space societies, exercised under principles of representative government appropriate to the circumstances and degree of community development, shall reflect the will of the people of those societies.

B. All petitions to the United States Government from outer space societies under its jurisdiction shall be accepted and receive prompt consideration.

C. The United States shall provide for an orderly and peaceful transition to self-governance by outer space societies under its jurisdiction at such time as their inhabitants shall manifest clearly a belief that such a transition is both necessary and appropriate.

D. In response to aggression, threats of aggression, or hostile action, outer space societies may provide for their common defense and for the maintenance of essential public order.

E. Outer space societies shall assume all rights and obligations set forth in treaties and international agreements, relevant to the activities of such societies, to which the United States is a party and which further freedom, peace and security.

F. The advancement of science and technology shall be encouraged in outer space societies for the benefit of all humanity.

G. Outer space societies shall protect from abuse the environment and natural resources of Earth and space.

The Declaration is easy to critique, though such an effort could just as easily be unfair to its drafters: it is difficult to draft principles for the governance of societies that do not yet exist, and whose outlines are only hazily apparent at this stage in history. These difficulties do not make the

effort worthless, but rather dictate the form in which it should be undertaken. Here, however, the Declaration has problems: it is an unwieldy
mixture of the general and the specific. Where it is specific, it is often
counterproductive: the statement that "fundamental values" embodied in
the Constitution should apply to space societies under U.S. jurisdiction
might be read as meaning that non-fundamental values would not apply.
As discussed in Chapter 8, *supra,* the U.S. Constitution applies to all
activities in outer space under U.S. jurisdiction. By their use of the term
"fundamental values" the drafters may have had in mind the *Insular Cases,
see* Balzac v. Porto Rico, 258 U.S. 298 (1922), De Lima v. Bidwell, 182
U.S. 1 (1901), Dooley v. United States, 182 U.S. 222 (1901), Armstrong v.
United States, 182 U.S. 243 (1901), Downes v. Bidwell, 182 U.S. 244 (1901);
see also J. Cabranes, Citizenship of the American Empire (1979), Baldwin,
The Constitutional Questions Incident to the Acquisition and Government
by the United States of Island Territory, 12 Harvard Law Review 393
(1899) (U.S. Constitution applicable to territories), Langdell, The Status of
Our New Territories, 12 Harvard Law Review 365 (1899) (U.S. Constitution not applicable to territories), Lowell, The Status of Our New Possessions—A Third View, 13 Harvard Law Review 155 (1899) (U.S. Constitution's restraints on government would apply, but other constitutional
provisions applicable only in territories that are "incorporated" into United
States). But those cases, of somewhat dubious reputation nowadays if still
possessed of considerable authority, are not applicable to outer space
societies. In the *Insular Cases* the Supreme Court was attempting to deal
with new territories, already settled by others, with their own preexisting
customs and laws, that had to be integrated into the United States. Space
societies under U.S. jurisdiction, on the other hand, would be established
by Americans from the beginning (with jurisdiction automatically flowing
from the Outer Space Treaty), and would be far more analogous to Antarctic
bases than to Puerto Rico or the Philippines in the aftermath of the
Spanish-American War.

The Declaration also contains language that seems disturbingly similar
to the "saving clauses" in many other nations' bills of rights. The United
States Constitution does not provide that the guarantees of individual
liberty are to be balanced against the good of the community; courts do
this, of course, in extraordinary circumstances, but with some reluctance
and usually with bad results. *See, e.g.,* Korematsu v. United States, 323
U.S. 214 (1944) (upholding internment of Japanese-Americans during World
War II); Aleinikoff, Constitutional Law in the Age of Balancing, 96 Yale
Law Journal 943 (1987) (warning against dangers in balancing approach
where important rights are at stake); Leff, The Leff Dictionary of Law: A
Fragment, 94 Yale Law Journal 1855, 2123–24 (1985) (definition of balancing warns of "the extreme dangers of too facile a use of 'balancing' in
a system of justice"). Such balancing, where engaged in, should be done
with as much reluctance as possible; the language chosen in the Declaration,
calling for the balancing of "community safety and individual survival
within the unique environment of outer space" to be "guaranteed in

harmony with the exercise of . . . fundamental rights" is a trap. Although it may have been meant otherwise by the drafters, it is an invitation to engage in unnecessary balancing, balancing that is likely to be at the expense of those the Declaration is meant to protect. It is true that the outer space environment is a unique one, but no more so than many other environments in which human beings operate. Commanders of nuclear submarines operating beneath the polar icepack are nonetheless constrained by the Constitution, as are instruments of the United States government operating in foreign countries. *See* Ragosta, Aliens Abroad: Principles for the Application of Constitutional Limitations to Federal Action, 17 New York University Journal of International Law & Politics 287 (1985); Ragosta & Reynolds, In Search of Governing Principles, 28 Jurimetrics: Journal of Law, Science & Technology 473, 485–86 (1988).

Where the Declaration is not specific, it is often so general as to be meaningless, or at least unclear. For example, Article IIA says that authority in outer space societies should reflect the will of the people of those societies. But virtually *all* wielders of authority claim that they do so in the name of, and reflecting the will of, the people. And the Declaration's treatment of self-government is unclear as well: it does not make clear whether the transition to self-government means one of complete independence as a new sovereign nation, or simply the inclusion of the space society as a self-governing but not sovereign entity such as Puerto Rico or (speaking practically, regardless of states' rights rhetoric) any one of the United States.

Here a bit more specificity would have been nice. If space societies are to become fully independent, then some measure such as Article 73 of the United Nations Charter, which provides for the gradual independence of Trust Territories, might be a good model. In fact, since the 1967 Outer Space Treaty extends the principles of international law and the U.N. Charter to outer space, Article 73 appears already to apply to space societies: it simply states that members of the U.N. who "have or assume responsibility for the administration of territories whose peoples have not yet attained a full measure of self government" are to promote self government and respect fundamental human rights for the inhabitants thereof. Although Article 73 was written with Trust Territories and territories formerly administered under Mandates from the old League of Nations in mind, its language does not exclude application to space societies as well. If, on the other hand, "self-governance" simply means ending a colonial or territorial status while remaining a part of the United States, then the model by which Western territories were admitted to the Union might be a better one. The Declaration's drafters would have been better off clarifying their intent and drawing upon one or the other of these models.

This is not to criticize the Declaration unduly. The effort was a worthwhile one, and helps set the stage for further effort along these lines, with plenty of time left to iron out the kinks before the problem becomes pressing. For an alternative version that answers many (though not all) of the above criticisms see Ragosta & Reynolds, In Search of Governing Principles, 28 Jurimetrics: Journal of Law, Science & Technology 473 (1988). Like the United States Constitution, the draft set out therein pays more attention to restrictions on government activity than to affirmative statements of rights. Consider this, however: In space societies, individuals will be far more dependent upon their governments for the basic necessities of life than they are on earth. In such a context, are affirmative statements of rights—to food and air, for example—more appropriate than they are on earth? Or are earth inhabitants actually almost as dependent, making the lack of such rights a defect, rather than a virtue in the U.S. Constitution? For an expression of this view, see Black, Further Reflections on the Constitutional Justice of Livelihood, 86 Columbia Law Review 1103 (1986).

The following excerpt, from another recent speech by Justice Brennan, discusses and compares various recent efforts in this field:

Remarks of William J. Brennan, Jr., Associate Justice, Supreme Court of the United States, at Bicentennial Conference of Judges of United States Courts of Appeals October 26, 1988

Let me return now to the Declaration of First Principles that the Smithsonian Conferences produced last year. That Declaration was not the only effort in its field. Another, entitled a proposed "Treaty Governing Social Order of Long-Duration or Permanent Inhabitants of Near and Deep Space" (which I shall refer to as the Convention to distinguish it from the Declaration), was advanced in a book "Envoys of Mankind" by George S. Robinson and Harold M. White, Jr. Both the Convention and the Declaration have come under sharp criticism in a review of "Envoys of Mankind" by John A. Ragosta and Glenn H. Reynolds, lawyers practicing in Washington, D.C. [Ragosta & Reynolds, In Search of Governing Principles, 28 Jurimetrics: Journal of Law, Science & Technology 473 (1988).] The criticism of the Declaration may be more serious. While concluding that the Declaration has much to recommend it because it focuses directly on affirmative statements of fundamental and political rights, the review comments:

"The Declaration appropriately guarantees civil and political freedoms that should govern all actions in space of earth and space inhabitants. Such principles can guide analysis of legal issues that arise in whatever context and provide guidance for a discussion of rules for governance of space societies. Unfortunately, the Declaration has a fatal flaw. The Declaration is written solely from the perspective of the United States, failing . . . to understand the critical role that the political relations of all Earth nations will have on space inhabitants. . . . We do not believe that the Soviet Union, France, China, or any other spacefaring nation will look with favor on principles formulated in such a manner. It is simply not productive to seek to establish principles for laws and government in space that will certainly be perceived by the world's leader in space habitation (the Soviet Union, alas, not the United States) as either irrelevant or insulting."

Having decided that both the Convention and the Declaration were flawed, Messrs. Ragosta and Reynolds offered their own version of a "Declaration of Rights and Principles for the Governance of Space Societies." Their guidelines emphasized focus on the space inhabitants, not an attempt to defuse or resolve all the possible conflicts of Earth nations in space. Accordingly, their focus was on man's exploration and ultimate inhabitation of space, not simply one nation's space activities, and in that respect avoided unnecessary historic, political and cultural ties to one nation. They believe that the Declaration cannot itself be a system of laws and governance but should stop with fostering such a system. Finally, they too would have the Declaration recognize that there are fundamental principles that should apply to governance of any human society.

It's very obvious that neither the Convention nor the two Declarations come even close to being the last word on the subject. As the reviewers observed, "All of the work done to date constitutes little more than a preface to the task of working out a scheme of governance for space societies." But whether permanent human presence in outer space is likely in the near term, or likely only in the distant future, apparently [space societies] are going to be a reality with which we must deal.

And the study of space societies may have a big dividend for Earth. As Walter McDougall has noted, the great age of earth exploration stimulated a burst of inquiry into the laws governing nations and led to our modern system of international law. In the same way, inquiry into the rules that should govern societies in space is likely to provide fresh insights into the governance of societies here on Earth, a field in which, to judge by current events, there is certainly room for progress. This is particularly true because many of the most salient characteristics of space societies, such as strong dependence on sophisticated technology, problems with maintaining environmental quality, the need for people to work together smoothly under stress in close quarters, and the dependence of inhabitants on their society for basic necessities such as food, water, air, and communications, are in many ways simply exaggerations of characteristics already present (and growing) in Earth societies. By studying the problems of space societies we gain a window into not just their future, but our own.

I won't see the day when a code of laws for space communities will become an urgent necessity. Perhaps few of you may see that day. But we can be glad that responsible quarters are beginning to give thought to the law and space communities. For, to repeat President Reagan's admonition, "America must lead the effort to colonize space, because in the next century leadership on Earth will come to the nation that shows the greatest leadership in space."

NOTES

1. Space governance (like the other issues discussed in this chapter) is likely to seem remote and of no immediate concern to many. It is possible, of course, that it is a problem that will never arise at all—over the next few decades, only a modest degree of mismanagement of the world's economy, resources, and political environment will be necessary in order to ensure that human beings will lack the ability to live in outer space, or even to reach it at all, for many years afterward if not forever. On the other hand, if such problems are avoided, the human species (given its expansionist nature) will almost inevitably reach the point at which space societies of some sort become a reality. At that point, they will likely draw on the works of scholars in previous centuries, just as the American colonists drew on the works of political theorists ranging from Aristotle to Locke in formulating their system of government.

There are already rudimentary principles of space governance. *See, e.g.,* 14 C.F.R. §1214.702 (granting space shuttle commander legal authority to maintain order and discipline in flight); 18 U.S.C.A. §451 (West supp. 1988) (extending U.S. criminal jurisdiction to outer space for some purposes). For more on existing U.S. "black letter" law applying to in-space activity see Chapter 8, *supra* and U.S. Congress Office of Technology Assessment, Space Stations and the Law: Selected Legal Issues (1986); *see also* Reynolds, Book Review, 27 Jurimetrics: Journal of Law, Science & Technology 431 (1987) (reviewing OTA space stations paper); Kanowitz, American Labor Law and the United States Space Shuttle, 34 Hastings Law Journal 715 (1983); Robbins, The Extension of United States Criminal Jurisdiction to Outer Space, 23 Santa Clara Law Review 627 (1983). As experience develops and new problems are encountered, those principles will grow by accretion, and it is even possible that self-governing space societies will be arrived at by a process so gradual that it will hardly be noticed. New legislation, passed after this book went to press, ensures that space governance issues will continue to receive study. Language added to the 1988 NASA Authorization Act requires NASA to report regularly to Congress on the prospects for human settlement in space and on various topics pertaining to such space settlements, including "sociological and legal issues." S. 2209 (100th Cong. 2d Sess.), Pub. L. 100-685, 102 Stat. 4083 (1988).

2. In many ways, as Justice Brennan notes, the problems of space societies are likely to be simply exaggerated versions of those faced by earth societies. In a space society, each member will have the potential to severely disrupt the environment, perhaps threatening all others—just as on earth, terrorists, or incompetents, have similar abilities now: witness the accidents at Bhopal, Chernobyl, and elsewhere. In a space society, each member will be dependent on her society for food, air, communications, housing, and all of the other requirements of life—just as on earth, virtually the entire population is coming to depend on the transportation and

communications networks for the delivery of everything from food to medicine to crucial weather information. And, in a space society, it will be a great challenge to balance this interdependence between society and individuals in a way that preserves individual freedoms that we think important—just as on earth, striking that balance is a challenge that many governments and peoples find almost insuperable. Fortunately, however, if they are to flourish space societies—like societies on earth—will find themselves more and more dependent on their members' creativity and best efforts, providing an incentive to find that balance. Because of this relationship between space societies and earthbound ones, study of the governance of space societies is likely to have profound uses on as well as off the planet. By examining ways in which people may live in space in the distant future, we may come up with answers—or at least questions— that are of help in determining the way people will live on earth in the next century.

CONTACT WITH EXTRATERRESTRIALS

If governance of space societies may seem a remote issue to some, then possible contact with extraterrestrial beings may seem remoter still, and with some reason. After all, human history has already seen several space stations, but (leaving aside various never-confirmed reports) no contact at all with beings not of this earth. Nonetheless, the possibility has (perhaps for that very reason) intrigued many fine minds. The issue is surveyed exhaustively in A. Haley, Space Law and Government ch.12 (1963) and M. McDougal, H. Lasswell & I. Vlasic, Law & Public Order in Space ch.9 (1963), as well as E. Fasan, Relations with Alien Intelligences (1970). Since there has been no gain in experience and no law made since those volumes were published, we refer the reader to them for detailed treatment, pro- viding only a short summary of the issues here.

The first question with regard to extraterrestrial life is whether it exists at all. At the time of this writing, opinions on the subject vary among experts, but those opinions are of limited worth because they are based on so little evidence. What evidence exists is largely negative. Since 1960 scientists have been listening on various radio frequencies, but without detecting any signal that appears connected with intelligent life. In addition, the earth's own man-made radio signals have been steadily expanding out into the galaxy, offering the possibility that alien beings' first indication that there is life on earth might come from their reception of *Gilligan's Island* episodes. Whether those aliens would conclude, on that basis, that earth life is intelligent is a matter of opinion. For whatever reason, however, there has been no response. On the search for intelligent life and its implications as of the time of this writing see Easterbrook, Are We Alone? The Atlantic Monthly, August, 1988, at 25.

The negative results achieved to date do not rule out encounters with extraterrestrial life, of course. Efforts so far have merely scratched the surface, the Universe being a rather large place and the number of radio frequencies virtually limitless. And there is always the possibility that we are simply going about it all wrong. It may be that alien beings, once encountered, will consider efforts at communicating via radio odd, if not downright bizarre. Perhaps some fluke in mankind's technological evolution has caused us to overlook a method of interstellar communication that other species rely on, leaving us in the position of an FM radio owner in a town where all the stations are AM—or, perhaps more accurately, of a primitive tribesman climbing to the top of a microwave relay tower to look for smoke signals.

What is certain is that any contact with extraterrestrial life will have a major impact on earth cultures. Earth societies are only now beginning to encompass fully the idea that inhabitants of other nations might be as human as they; it is unclear whether humankind is ready to extend similar consideration to beings with whom we share no genes. And, depending on differences in biology and culture, it may be difficult to determine whether what we have encountered is alive at all, or whether it is intelligent: witness the ongoing debate over just how intelligent dolphins (hardly different from us, on any kind of a cosmic biological scale) really are.

Assuming, however, that we are in no doubt as to these threshold matters, encounters with extraterrestrial life will involve either contact with intelligent beings or contact with "lower" life forms possessing no intelligence, or intelligence on the order of domestic animals (though we stress that such determinations may be quite difficult to make). In the case of the latter, legal questions will essentially be those of environmental law and cruelty to animals: how to avoid harming the habitats of exotic life while taking advantage of opportunities to study, or perhaps farm or otherwise exploit, that life without cruelty. *See generally* Callicott, Moral Considerability and Extraterrestrial Life, in Beyond Spaceship Earth: Environmental Ethics and the Solar System 227 (E. Hargrove ed. 1986).

If we encounter intelligent beings, on the other hand, a number of questions arise. First, the entire environment for relations will be determined by questions of power: are we dealing with beings to whom we are measurably superior in science, technology and military might? To which we are measurably (or perhaps immeasurably) inferior? Or roughly equivalent? Yet again, we note that in practice determining which is the case may be extraordinarily difficult: by any measure of military might Cortez and Pizarro were in a far inferior position to the Aztec and Inca societies that they conquered and destroyed, but by chance their strengths were precisely those needed to exploit their victims' cultural weaknesses.

If contact is made with beings substantially inferior to us in power, we must decide which of many human models we will follow. Will we become ruthless exploiters like the Spanish Conquistadores? Will we attempt to incorporate the aliens into our own civilization via a mechanism like that of Article 73 of the UN Charter, which provides for trust territories? Or will we establish rules designed to minimize interference with alien societies? Note that the Outer Space Treaty of 1967 expressly acknowledges that general international law, including the United Nations Charter, is applicable to activities in outer space. This means that the nonaggression principle contained in Article 2(4) of the charter (along with the rest of international law) is applicable to activities in outer space and, at least arguably, with regard to alien societies.

These are the most remote issues of this rather remote topic. In order to contact intelligent beings of less development than our own, we must go to them, which is likely to be difficult since there is no evidence of any life in our solar system beyond the earth's biosphere (though the possibility of such life continues to exist, based on present knowledge). Beings of greater development than our own—or perhaps even those whose development is roughly equivalent to our own except for a degree of superiority in space transportation—may instead come to us. How we shall deal with them poses fewer moral dilemmas, but greater practical difficulties.

Such beings may be friendly or hostile. Some writers on the topic fear that the latter is more likely. As Gregg Easterbrook says:

> The most disquieting aspect of natural selection as observed on Earth is that it channels intellect to predators. Most bright animals are carnivores: stalking requires tactics, pattern recognition, and, for social animals, coordinated action, all incubators of brainpower. Though the martial heritage of mankind has been exaggerated in popular fiction (there's no proof, for example, that our Cro Magnon ancestors waged war against the vanished Neanderthals), it's reasonably certain that the forebears of modern *Homo Sapiens* were hunters, and it's definite that man has been savage during the historical era. This isn't much of a testimonial to "intelligence" [as a civilizing influence].

Easterbrook, *supra,* at 37. On the other hand, even if such beings were friendly (at least by their own lights) we might be well to be concerned, as we might not appreciate any favors they chose to do us. And it is entirely possible, if they are alien enough, that the terms friendly or hostile might mean little as applied to them.

In this context, Haley proposes a principle of "Metalaw" that constitutes a revised Golden Rule: "Do unto others as they would have you do unto them." As Haley says, "To treat others as we would desire to be treated might well mean their destruction." A. Haley, Space Law and Government 395 (1963). Obviously there are limits to such a principle, which appear when the interests of the others begin to collide with our own (science fiction fans might call this the "Klingon Corollary"). And there is, naturally, no guarantee that other civilizations would adopt the same view.

As always, McDougal, Lasswell & Vlasic are more concerned with matters of power than Haley. They outline a number of possible scenarios in which aliens quarantine the earth (as too violent), or in which groups on earth conspire with aliens (or even with dissident groups within alien societies) in various sorts of power-bloc games, or in which even an inferior earth attempts to use balance of power diplomacy (setting rival alien groups against one another) to maintain its independence. It is to be hoped that such eventualities remain as remote as they now seem; if they become concrete, it might be worthwhile to examine the ways in which earth societies have dealt with more powerful foreign rivals, either by absorbing conquerors (as the Chinese and Indians have done) or by absorbing selective aspects of foreign culture (especially technology) while retaining their own essential character (as the Japanese have done).

Even where superior alien beings are demonstrably friendly by our own standards of judgment, their impact on our society may be enormous and not always positive. The realization that other intelligent beings exist would undoubtedly create considerable consternation within many religions, for example. It would also have major secular effects: note how important an effect was created simply by the Apollo photographs of earth from a distance, showing our planet not as the vast expanse we were used to imagining but as a small fragile ball in an enormous universe, its atmosphere so thin as to be barely visible. The result was a tremendous growth in environmental consciousness that has not reached its end yet. *See* Hartmann, Space Exploration and Environmental Issues, 6 Environmental Ethics 227 (1984) on this impact of the space program. Although the impact of learning that we are not alone in the Universe is difficult to estimate, it would likely be greater still. As Easterbrook says:

> A stock assumption is that the first question we would send to an extraterrestrial radio operator would be something like "How do you build a 10,000 megajoule charged particle beam?" Consider the ramifications if instead the question were "Have you seen God?" Many religions expound variations on what Christians call the kingdom of God—the idea that human travails and celestial suffering of evil are a transitory state of affairs, to be replaced by perfect justice when God manifests Himself and takes active control of events. . . . So if any long-lived alien race we might contact testifies that it has walked the cosmos for thousands of millennia without encountering God or obtaining divine grace, a lot of air would rush out of the faiths we Earthlings practice. If, on the other hand, the aliens have met the absolute and will tell us the specifics, human society will shake to its foundations.

Easterbrook, *supra,* at 38. *Cf.* Cobb, Theology and Space, in Beyond Spaceship Earth: Environmental Ethics and the Solar System 291 (E. Hargrove ed. 1986).

Of course, religious fanatics on earth might reply that God exists only for us, not for those unwashed heathens from Tau Ceti—and aliens who claim to have seen God may have entirely different ideas about what that means, or may be lying, either because they think that is what we want to hear or in order to take advantage of the opportunity to make human society "shake to its foundations."

If the beings encountered are themselves (by humans' own reckoning) markedly superior, the problems created may be more dramatic yet. Though earth cultures vary in their assessment of their own superiority or inferiority in relation to other cultures, there is general consensus that humankind represents the top of the heap not only in terms of sophistication or technological development, but from a standpoint of moral worth. Were we to encounter creatures who seemed to us (as occasionally appears in science fiction films) almost angelic, would we be inspired to emulate them, or would we despair of attaining their perfection and give up trying? And how would it affect our assessment of our own interests? Robert Nozick has argued in favor of a sliding scale of worth, beginning with inanimate matter and continuing onward through plants, animals, and ultimately humans. But he admits of the possibility of alien beings who are (or at least seem to be) superior to humans, and suggests that this would pose unusual problems for moral philosophy, problems for which it is unprepared:

> Some theological views hold that God is permitted to sacrifice people for his own purposes. We also might imagine people encountering beings from another planet who traverse in their childhood whatever "stages" of moral development our developmental psychologists can identify. These beings claim that they all continue on through fourteen further sequential stages, each being necessary to enter the next one. However, they cannot explain to us (primitive as we are) the content and modes of reasoning of these later stages. These beings claim that we may be sacrificed for their well being, or at least in order to preserve their higher capacities. They say that they see the truth of this now that they are in their moral maturity, though they didn't as children at what is our highest level of moral development.

R. Nozick, Anarchy, State & Utopia 46–47 (1974). Nozick concludes that currently popular moral frameworks offer no answer in these circumstances. *See also* R. Nozick, Philosophical Explanations 417 (1981) and Tooley, Would ETIs [ExtraTerrestrial Intelligences] Be Persons? in Extraterrestrial Intelligence: The First Encounter (J. Christian ed. 1976). It seems unlikely that many would be persuaded by this argument, but if humans *were* to be convinced that aliens were morally superior (say, by aliens who demonstrated their goodness but who refrained from spoiling their image with arguments that they may morally sacrifice us to serve their own interests) the impact could be enormous and devastating, much like (but worse than) the dispiriting effect of European conquest on many less advanced peoples. (For an illustration of this impact see C. Turnbull, The Lonely African (1962).) On the other hand, human beings might be inspired by the aliens' example, as a sign that it is possible to do better than we have done historically.

By our discussion of the moral implications of contact with superior beings we do not mean to suggest that there are no significant moral issues associated with meeting beings who (again, by our own estimation, which may well differ from that of the beings we meet) are inferior to or on a par with us. However, existing moral frameworks governing our treatment of animals or our treatment of other human beings address similar issues. With regard to relations with superior beings, the only framework that we have that even begins to address the topic is religion. Various religions treat the matter differently, sometimes portraying humans as clever tricksters who can (and who are heroic when they do) deceive supernatural entities with powers greater than their own, and sometimes demanding strict obedience to the slightest whim of those entities. But religions, by their nature, tend to be specific with regard to *which* superior beings they describe; they do not set out general rules for dealing with such beings and they generally involve beings who are not merely superior, but supernaturally so.

Although it may be that any sufficiently advanced technology will *seem* supernatural, it is unlikely to be so, and few are likely to believe that it is. Indeed, given the number of alien-contact movies that have been made to date and their impact on the popular consciousness, it is more likely that angels visiting the earth would be greeted as extraterrestrials than that extraterrestrials visiting the earth would be greeted as angels. Nonetheless, contact with beings who appeared vastly superior to us would have a dramatic, and perhaps crushing, impact on human society, and cushioning that impact, or channelling it in productive ways, would be a major task for governments and opinion leaders worldwide.

On a narrower scale, the introduction of alien customs, technologies, goods, and ideas would also be likely to have a disruptive impact on earth life. Authorities would be faced with difficult problems as to how they could smooth and ease those disruptions while allowing the necessary accommodations with individual and academic freedom and with the general principles of an open world society. A variety of legal problems, some picayune and some interesting, would also arise. For example, most murder laws forbid only the killing of a human being. Thus, the killing of even an intelligent and cultured extraterrestrial, however human-seeming in behavior or (even) appearance, would probably be legally indistinguishable from killing someone's dog—or perhaps subject to even less control, as many states specifically forbid dog-killing by unauthorized persons. On another front, existing regulations requiring quarantine of anyone contacting extraterrestrial matter (discussed at the end of Chapter 8) would come into play, as dramatized in the movie *E.T.* Given the excitement attendant upon contact with alien beings, however, most such legal questions are likely to be pushed to the side at least at first, and we do not consider them worth addressing at any length here.

Finally, at the extreme end of the remoteness continuum lies a favorite idea of science fiction writers: the possibility of incorporating the earth or parts of it into some sort of overarching organization, whether called a "United Federation of Planets" or whatever. McDougal, Lasswell & Vlasic discuss this issue at some length, but seem to treat it as a purely diplomatic issue when in fact (although the diplomatic problems would be far more apparent) there would be legal difficulties as well. The United Nations

Charter makes no provision for UN membership in other organizations, meaning that any treaty bringing the earth into a larger organization would have to be negotiated piecemeal to encompass the hundreds of different sovereign entities on the planet, a task sure to prove difficult and divisive. Alternatively, the United Nations Charter could be amended (with the consent of its member governments) to allow it to represent all nations and to enter into appropriate agreements. Getting agreement on such a task might be marginally easier, and somewhat less divisive.

From the standpoint of United States law, even a treaty making the United States a member of such an organization would be open to later abrogation by legislative efforts. *See* L. Tribe, American Constitutional Law 225–26 (2d ed. 1988) and sources cited therein. As a result, only a constitutional amendment could place the United States into an organic relation with a greater body. In the current political climate such an amendment could never be obtained with regard to membership in a purely earth-centered organization, raising doubts as to how voters would view membership in any sort of interstellar organization—indeed, U.S. membership in the United Nations, which entails no loss of sovereignty, is controversial enough at times. Fortunately, this issue is unlikely to arise in the near future, so any detailed speculation regarding current laws and political attitudes is likely to prove pointless.

10

Conclusion

The Earth is the cradle of the mind, but one cannot remain in the cradle forever.
Konstantin Tsiolkovsky

In the introduction to his excellent history of the space age, . . . *the Heavens and the Earth: A Political History of the Space Age* (1985), Walter McDougall compares humankind's emergence into outer space to the emergence of the first lungfish from the oceans. Though dramatic, this comparison is not overdrawn. The emergence of humanity into spaces beyond the earth represents a real qualitative change in human existence. Over the next centuries, if affairs on earth are not too badly mismanaged, humanity will spread to a variety of locations outside the earth, carrying with it parts of earth's biosphere as it goes. Some writers, indeed, have suggested that this is humanity's real role: if one believes, as adherents of the so-called *Gaia* hypothesis do, that life on earth can in many respects be viewed as one meta-organism, then humanity's role may in large part be that of meta-gamete, carrying the seeds of life to new environments where it could not have evolved, and which it could not have reached, in other ways.

Whether one accepts this description or regards it as so much science fiction, there can be no question that the expansion of humanity into outer space will be a drama and a challenge for which there is no real counterpart in recorded history. The great age of earth exploration is the closest analog, but although European discoverers played a vital role in uniting the globe into one network of commerce and communication, they "discovered" mostly places that were already inhabited by human beings, although in their rather ethnocentric view the discoverers did not always recognize that fact. By contrast, in exploring space explorers really do go "where no man has gone before," to use the stirring (if a trifle sexist) language of one popular television program.

Some of the consequences of this expansion will be beyond the purview of space law; they will instead constitute basic changes in the way we view ourselves and our world. To a degree this has already taken place: the Apollo photographs of the earth as seen from the moon have had dramatic and lasting effects on earth-based views of politics and the environment.

Writing prophetically (as usual) in 1959, Arthur C. Clarke described this effect:

> We all know the narrow, limited type of mind which is interested in nothing beyond its town or village, and bases its judgments on these parochial standards. We are slowly—perhaps too slowly—evolving from that mentality toward a world outlook. Few things will do more to accelerate that evolution than the conquest of space. It is not easy to see how the more extreme forms of nationalism can long survive when men begin to see the Earth in its true perspective as a single small globe among the stars.

A. Clarke, The Challenge of the Spaceship 7–8 (1959). In addition, the adventure involved in meeting the challenges of expanding into space is likely to energize all of earth society. The following excerpt discusses how this might happen.

Reynolds, Structuring Development in Outer Space: Problems of How and Why, 19 Law & Policy in International Business 433 (1987)

I think that we should also look at the more immediate effects of space development on those of us left behind. . . . Everyone shares in the excitement of a frontier's opening, and its dynamism filters back into everyday life. Many historians believe that the dynamism and vigor of the East Coast business community during the mid- and late nineteenth century resulted from the psychological effect of the western frontier. [For the most widely known of such arguments, see F.J. Turner, The Frontier in American History 1–38, 290–311 (1920).] In the same way, it may be that much of the dynamism and vigor of U.S. society in the 1960s was a product of the excitement generated by the moon program, and that much of the malaise and pessimism of the 1970s grew out of the U.S. retreat from outer space in that decade.

These examples are far from the only ones available. Perhaps the most striking example of the opening of a new frontier energizing a whole society is that of Europe at the opening of the Age of Discovery. In his classic biography, Samuel Eliot Morison describes the impact of Columbus' discovery on a continent sunk in despair and stagnation:

> At the end of the year 1492 most men in Western Europe felt exceedingly gloomy about the future. Christian civilization appeared to be shrinking in area and dividing into hostile units as its sphere contracted. For over a century there had been no important advance in natural science, and registration in the universities dwindled as the instruction they offered became increasingly jejune and lifeless. Institutions were decaying, well-meaning people were growing cynical or desperate, and many intelligent men, for want of something better to do, were endeavoring to escape the present through studying the pagan past. . . .

Yet, even as the chroniclers of Nuremberg were correcting their proofs from Koberger's press, a Spanish caravel named *Niña* scudded before a winter gale into Lisbon, with news of a discovery that was to give old Europe another chance. In a few years we find the mental picture completely changed. Strong monarchs are stamping out privy conspiracy and rebellion; the Church, purged and chastened by the Protestant Reformation, puts her house in order; new ideas flare up throughout Italy, France, Germany and the northern nations; faith in God revives and the human spirit is renewed. The change is complete and astounding. "A new envisagement of the world has begun, and men are no longer sighing after the imaginary golden age that lay in the distant past, but speculating as to the golden age that might possibly lie in the oncoming future."

Christopher Columbus belonged to an age that was past, yet he became the sign and symbol of this new age of hope, glory and accomplishment. His medieval faith impelled him to a modern solution: expansion.

[S. Morison, Admiral of the Ocean Sea: A Life of Christopher Columbus 3 (1979).] Perhaps a major worldwide commitment to outer space projects would unleash the same sort of energy on a global scale, ushering in a new period of growth and optimism that would benefit everyone, but especially the poorer countries that suffer most from any worldwide economic downturn. And it might be that the challenge and excitement of expanding into outer space would divert energy and attention away from warlike activity by providing a peaceful outlet for feelings of national pride and the need to overcome obstacles.

Physicist Freeman Dyson has argued along these lines in his book *Weapons and Hope.* In looking for ways to overcome the seemingly intractable problems posed by nuclear weapons and superpower conflict, he notes that President Kennedy pursued the moon program with the specific intent of providing an outlet for the frustrations created by the conflict with the Soviet Union:

Apollo was to be what William James had called for long ago, a moral equivalent of war. The idea was to escape from the stuckness of Soviet-American political quarrels by beating the Russians in a bloodless technological competition instead of by beating them in battle. The idea was a good one, and up to a point it worked. It stopped working when the symbolic battle of Apollo was displaced from the focus of public attention by the real battle of Vietnam. Unfortunately, nobody since 1961 has repeated Kennedy's tactic of deliberately committing a country to a daring nonmilitary enterprise as a substitute for the excitements of war. It is a tactic which we could profitably use again. . . .

[F. Dyson, Weapons and Hope 219 (1984).] It certainly seems worth trying. Outer space is not cheap, but compared to what the world spends on defense it is practically free. Those who are willing to spend hundreds of billions of dollars on tanks, guns, and missiles in the hope that they will deter a nuclear war ought to be willing to spend tens of billions on outer space in the hope that it will prevent the superpowers from reaching the point where deterrence takes on immediate significance.

Of course, for expansion into space to have these sorts of effects it must be carried out on a global scale. If it remains the enterprise of only a few nations, then it may not be seen as a project of humanity as a whole. During the pioneering stage this has not been true: the Outer Space Treaty describes astronauts as "envoys of mankind," and that is for the most part the way they have been perceived. As Apollo 11 astronaut Michael Collins recounts in his excellent history of the space program,

> Travelling around the world several months after the flight, I was continually impressed by the fact that no matter where we were, the reaction was the same and, to me, unexpected. Never did I hear, "Well, you Americans finally did it." Always it was "we," we human beings drawn together for one fleeting moment watching two of us walk that alien surface.

M. Collins, Liftoff 161 (1988). Settlers are different from explorers, though, and they will be perceived differently. If the nations of the world are to continue to see space as a domain for humanity and not an enclave of a favored few, some way of broadening participation will have to be found. It may be that the spread of technology to the third world will be enough; certainly that spread has occurred far faster than anyone (especially third world economists) thought possible, and already third world opinion leaders like China, India and Brazil have credible space programs. If such is not enough, then some other way of promoting meaningful participation (which means more than a simple rake-off of any profits that happen to emerge) must be found. For more on this see Reynolds & Merges, The Role of Commercial Development in Preventing War in Outer Space, 25 Jurimetrics: Journal of Law, Science & Technology 130 (1985). Whatever is done, space lawyers will play a crucial role, whether as advocates for clients or as policymakers, a role almost as common to those in the legal profession.

In general, though, the kinds of considerations discussed above will not directly affect space lawyers, although they may very well shape the environment in which they operate. They do, however, explain in part why considerations of space law will have greater importance than just that inhering in the particular issues they involve at any given time. As they deal with particular issues involving, say, rights in space resources or regulation of commercial space launch companies, space lawyers should bear in mind that bad law in those areas can create considerable obstacles to the overall goal of humanity's expansion into space, while good law could do much to promote that goal. As Chapter 1 describes, for example, the British Explosives Act effectively blocked any British work on rocketry in the 1930s, a time when Americans, Germans and Russians were making great strides; by contrast, new legal structures in the United States in the 1980s appear (at this writing, at least) to be creating an explosion of innovation and entrepreneurial activity. In a different way, a confiscatory regime relating to the development of space resources might drastically scale back the scope of space efforts for decades, while an intelligent one mixing incentives for developers with meaningful channels for less developed country participation might stimulate considerable effort and simultaneously help lift many of the world's poorer nations out of poverty.

In short, good law can make a great difference. The development of specialized law relating to maritime affairs is generally regarded as having encouraged a flourishing shipping industry and promoted widespread global commerce in a way that, more often than not, reduces global tensions rather than increasing them. This development was not accidental, but the result of deliberate government and industry efforts. *See* Black, Admiralty Jurisdiction, Critique and Suggestions, 50 Columbia Law Review 260 (1950); G. Gilmore & C. Black, The Law of Admiralty 958 *et seq.* (2d ed. 1975). *See also* Landes, European Expansion: The History of Innovation and Performance, in The Global Economy: Divergent Perspectives on Economic Change 25 (E. Gondolf, I. Marcus & J. Dougherty eds. 1986) (describing growth of global trading system). The challenge for policymakers and lawyers alike in the space arena will be to duplicate this task. Lawyers who understand this challenge, and try to meet it, will be doing a favor not only to the world at large, but also to their clients as they will, for the most part, then be swimming with the tide instead of against it.

It is our hope that this all too brief volume makes some contribution to that endeavor. Space law, like space flight itself, is a relatively new thing, and just as today's Young Astronaut Corps members are tomorrow's astronauts and engineers, so are today's law students tomorrow's lawyers and policymakers. It will be their task to deal with the challenges posed by the next century in ways that will make our world, and the new worlds yet unconquered, a better place for all humanity.

Credits

The excerpts in this book are taken from the following sources. Permissions to reprint are gratefully acknowledged.

Chapter 1

Walter A. McDougall, . . . *The Heavens and the Earth: A Political History of the Space Age* 43, 185 (New York: Basic Books, 1985). Copyright © by Basic Books, Inc. Reprinted by permission of the publisher.

Radford Byerly, Jr., "The Commercial/Industrial Uses of Space," in *Beyond Spaceship Earth: Environmental Ethics and the Solar System,* edited by Eugene C. Hargrove (San Francisco: Sierra Club Books, 1986). Copyright © 1986 by Eugene C. Hargrove. Reprinted with permission of Sierra Club Books.

"Power Stations in the Sky," in *The Illustrated Encyclopedia of Space Technology* 226, Kenneth Gatland, ed. (London: Salamander Books, 1984). Copyright © 1984 by Salamander Books, Ltd.; reprinted with permission.

Chapter 2

Hamilton DeSaussure, "Maritime and Space Law, Comparisons and Contrasts (An Oceanic View of Space Transport)," 9 *Journal of Space Law* 93 (1981). Copyright © by Hamilton DeSaussure; reprinted with permission.

White, *Decision-Making for Space: Law and Politics in Air, Sea and Outer Space* 179 (West Lafayette, Ind.: Purdue Research Foundation, 1971). Copyright © 1971 by Purdue Research Foundation; reprinted with permission.

Nicholas Matte, ed., *Space Activities and Emerging International Law* 161 (Montreal: Institute and Centre of Air and Space Law, McGill University, Montreal, Canada, 1984). Copyright © 1984 by Nicholas Matte; reprinted by permission.

Myres McDougal and Leon Lipson, "Perspective for a Law of Outer Space," 52 *American Journal of International Law* 407 (1958). Copyright © 1985 by American Society of International Law; reprinted with permission of the Society and of the authors.

Chapter 3

Philip Jessup and Howard Taubenfeld, "The United Nations *Ad Hoc* Committee on the Peaceful Uses of Outer Space," 53 *American Journal of International Law* 877 (1959). Copyright © 1959 by American Society of International Law; reprinted with permission.

Nicholas Matte, "The Treaty Banning Nuclear Weapons Tests in the Atmosphere, in Outer Space and Under Water (10 October 1963) and the Peaceful Uses of Outer Space," 9 *Annals of Air and Space Law* 391 (1984). Copyright © 1984 by Institute and Centre of Air and Space Law; reprinted with permission.

Paul G. Dembling and Daniel M. Arons, "The Evolution of the Outer Space Treaty," 33 *Journal of Air Law and Commerce* 419 (1967). Copyright © 1967 by Paul G. Dembling, Daniel M. Arons, and *Journal of Air Law and Commerce;* reprinted with permission.

Carl Q. Christol, "Article 2 of 1967 Principles Treaty Revisited," 9 *Annals of Air and Space Law* 217 (1984). Copyright © 1984 by the Institute and Centre of Air and Space Law; reprinted with permission.

John Orr, "The Treaty on Outer Space: An Evolution of the Arms Control Provisions," 7 *Columbia Journal of Transnational Law* 259 (1968). Copyright © 1968, Columbia Journal of Transnational Law Association, Inc.; reprinted with permission.

Stephen Gorove, "Arms Control Provisions in the Outer Space Treaty: A Scrutinizing Reappraisal," 3 *Georgia Journal of International and Comparative Law* 114 (1973). Copyright © 1973 by *Georgia Journal of International and Comparative Law;* reprinted with permission.

Chapter 4

Marion Nash, "Contemporary Practice of the United States Relating to International Law [Section on Moon Treaty]," 74 *American Journal of International Law* 421 (1980). Copyright © 1980 by American Society of International Law; reprinted with permission.

Stephen A. Spitz, "Space Law—Agreement Governing the Activities of States on the Moon and Other Celestial Bodies," 21 *Harvard International Law Journal* 579 (1980). Copyright © 1980 by *Harvard International Law Journal;* reprinted with permission.

Eilene Galloway, "Issues in Implementing the Agreement Governing the Activities of States on the Moon and Other Celestial Bodies," *Proceedings of the Twenty-Third Colloquium on the Law of Outer Space* 19 (Washington, D.C.: American Institute of Aeronautics and Astronautics, 1980). Copyright © 1980 by Eilene Galloway; reprinted with permission of the author and the Institute.

Walsh, "Controversial Issues Under Article XI of the Moon Treaty," 5 *Annals of Air and Space Law* 489, 1981. Copyright © 1981 by the Institute and Centre of Air and Space Law; reprinted with permission.

Carl Q. Christol, "Alternative Models for a Future International Space Organization," *Proceedings of the Twenty-Fourth Colloquium on the Law of Outer Space* 173 (1981). Copyright © 1981 by Carl Q. Christol, Professor of International Law and Political Science, University of Southern California; reprinted with permission.

Goedhuis, "Some Recent Trends in the Interpretation and the Implementation of the Rules of International Space Law," 19 *Columbia Journal of Transnational Law* 213 (1981). Copyright © 1981 by Columbia Journal of Transnational Law Association, Inc.; reprinted with permission.

Rene-Jean Dupuy, "The Notion of the Common Heritage of Mankind Applied to the Seabed," 8 *Annals of Air and Space Law* 347 (1983). Copyright © 1982 by the Institute and Centre of Air and Space Law; reprinted with permission.

D. Brian Hufford, "Ideological Rigidity vs. Political Reality: A Critique of Reagan's Policy on the Law of the Sea," 2 *Yale Law and Policy Review* 127 (1983). Copyright © 1983 by D. Brian Hufford; reprinted with permission.

Edward R. Finch, Jr., and A. L. Moore, "The 1979 Moon Treaty Encourages Space Development," *Proceedings of the Twenty-Third Colloquium on the Law of Outer Space* 13 (1980). Copyright © 1980 by Edward R. Finch, Jr., and A. L. Moore; reprinted with permission.

Arthur Dula, "Free Enterprise and the Proposed Moon Treaty," 2 *Houston Journal of International Law* 3 (1979). Copyright © 1979 by *Houston Journal of International Law;* reprinted with permission.

Webber, "Extraterrestrial Law on the Final Frontier: A Regime to Govern the Development of Celestial Body Resources," 71 *Georgetown Law Journal* 1426 (1983). Copyright © 1983 by *Georgetown Law Journal;* reprinted with permission.

K. Narayana Rao, "Common Heritage of Mankind and the Moon Treaty," 21 *Indian Journal of International Law* 275 (1981). Copyright © 1981 by Indian Society of International Law; reprinted with permission.

Wihlborg and Wijkman, "Outer Space Resources in Efficient and Equitable Use: New Frontiers for Old Principles," 24 *Journal of Law and Economics* 23 (1981). Copyright © 1981 by University of Chicago Press; reprinted with permission.

Chapter 5

Alexander Cohen, "Cosmos 954 and the International Law of Satellite Accidents," 10 *Yale Journal of International Law* 78 (1984). Copyright © 1984 by *Yale Journal of International Law;* reprinted with permission.

John Logsdon and Tracie Monk, "Remote Sensing from Space: A Continuing Legal and Policy Issue," 8 *Annals of Air and Space Law* 409 (1983). Copyright © by the Institute and Centre of Air and Space Law; reprinted by permission.

Hamilton DeSaussure, "Remote Sensing: The Interaction of Domestic and International Law," Paper presented at the 38th Congress of the International Astronautical Federation (1987). Reprinted by permission.

Chapter 6

Office of Commercial Space Policy, U.S. Department of Commerce, *Space Commerce: An Industry Assessment* (Washington, D.C.: Government Printing Office, 1980).

Chapter 7

W. Clark McFadden II, Jeffrey Snyder, and James A. Schoettler, Jr., "The Structure of Export Licensing," in *The Commerce Department Speaks,* D. Riggs, ed. (Washington, D.C.: Government Printing Office, 1987). Copyright © 1987 by W. Clark McFadden II, Jeffrey Snyder, and James A. Schoettler, Jr.; reprinted with permission.

Chapter 8

Glenn H. Reynolds, Book Review, 27 *Jurimetrics: Journal of Law, Science, and Technology* 431 (1987), Copyright © 1987 by Glenn H. Reynolds; reprinted by permission.

Robert P. Merges and Glenn H. Reynolds, "News Media Satellites and the First Amendment," 3 *Berkeley High Technology Law Journal* 1 (1988). Copyright © 1989 by Robert P. Merges and Glenn H. Reynolds; reprinted by permission.

Chapter 9

William J. Brennan, Jr., "Space Settlements and the Law," Address to the American Law Institute (May 21, 1987). Copyright © 1987 by Justice William J. Brennan, Jr.; reprinted with permission.

John Ragosta and Glenn H. Reynolds, "In Search of Governing Principles," 28 *Jurimetrics: Journal of Law, Science, and Technology* 473 (1988). Copyright © 1988 by the authors; reprinted with permission.

Chapter 10

Index

ABM. *See* Anti-Ballistic Missile (ABM) Treaty

ABM Treaty. *See* Anti-Ballistic Missile (ABM) Treaty

Abnormally dangerous activities. *See* Ultrahazardous activities

Abrahamson, General James A., 100

Absolute liability, 167, 175–177, 260–267

Adams, R., 266

Addis, Adeno, 226

Administrative law relating to space, 290–305. *See also* Office of Commercial Space Transportation, U.S. Department of Transportation

Admiralty jurisdiction, 250

A-4. *See* V-2 missile

Agreement Governing the Activities of States on the Moon and Other Celestial Bodies. *See* Moon Treaty

Agreement on the Rescue and Return of Astronauts, 194–195

Ahearn, Dennis, xiii, 274

Air/space delimitation, 5–7, 11–12, 59, 86–88

Aleinikoff, T. Alexander, 312

American Broadcasting and the First Amendment (L. Powe), 227

American Law Institute, 307, 308
conference on space legal issues, 308

American Rocket Society, 2

Anarchy, State and Utopia (Robert Nozick), 321

Antarctic Treaty of 1959, 41

Anti-Ballistic Missile (ABM) Treaty, xvi, 9, 22, 27, 96–102
reinterpretation, 98–102
text (excerpt), 97–98
See also Abrahamson, General James A.; Garthoff, Raymond L.; Sofaer,

Abraham D.; Strategic Defense Initiative

Antidumping law (U.S.), 231, 232

Antisatellite (ASAT) systems, 22–23

Appropriation of space resources. *See* Space resources

Arabsat (Arab satellite system), 225. *See also* INTELSAT Agreement; Separate international satellite systems

Ariane (launch vehicle). *See* Arianespace

Arianespace, 29, 229, 231, 233

ASAT. *See* Antisatellite systems

Assumption of risk, 261

Astronauts, Rescue and Return Agreement, 194–195

Asylum, political, and Rescue and Return Agreement, 194

Auction of development rights (proposed), 158

Augustine, Rene, xiii–xiv

Axelrod, Robert, 26

Ballistic missile defense (BMD) systems, 22. *See also* Anti-Ballistic Missile (ABM) Treaty

Barry, D., 265

Bedjaoui, M., 154, 155–156

Benko, M., 154

Bilateral agreement on remote sensing, 180

Black, Charles Lund, Jr., 43, 314, 329

BMD. *See* Ballistic missile defense systems

Bockstiegel, Karl-Heinz, 266

Boczek, B., 257

Bogota Declaration (geosynchronous orbit sovereignty). *See* Geosynchronous (Clarke) Orbit

Boyd v. White (case), 265

Boyne, Walter, xiii
Brennan, Justice William J., 307
    address (excerpt), 307–308
    remarks (excerpt), 314–315
British East India Company, 308
British Interplanetary Society, 2, 72
Brooks v. United States (case), 266
Brown, Bruce A., 263
Brumley, Robert, xiii
Brussels Salvage Convention of 1910
    (as analogy for space salvage), 35
Bueckling, Adrian, 138
Burke, W., 255
Burrows, W., 177, 178

Cabranes, Judge Jose, 312
Calabresi, Guido, 175
Califano, Joseph A., xiii
Canada, and crash of Soviet Cosmos
    954 satellite, 168–177
Cancellation of launch services
    contracts, 277. *See also* Contracts,
    space-related
Cargo damage, liability for, 270–272
Carnus, Richard, 156
Carriage of goods. *See* Common
    carrier, commercial launch
    provider as; Private carrier,
    commercial launch provider as
Carter, President Jimmy, 169, 174
CCIR. *See Comite Consultatif
    International des
    Radiocommunications*
Central planning, and space resource
    development, 143
Centre National d'Etudes Spatiale
    (CNES), 233–234, 235
Challenger disaster, 272. *See also*
    National Aeronautics and Space
    Administration
Chayes, Abram, 101
Chicago Convention of 1944 (air law),
    5, 28
Chisum, Donald, 287, 288
Choice of law provisions, 257. *See also*
    NATO Status of Forces Agreement;
    see under Contracts, space-related
Christian, J., 321
Christol, Carl, 78, 116, 120, 176
Church, Senator Frank, 110, 111
Clarke, Arthur C., 2, 4, 10, 199, 326

Cleator, Phil, 2
Cleveland Rocket Society, 2
CNES. *See* Centre National d'Etudes
    Spatiale
Coase, Ronald, 158, 159, 166
COCOM. *See* Coordinating Committee
    on Export Controls
Cohen, Alexander F., 168–175
Collins, Michael, 328
Colonialism in space, 146. *See also*
    Space resources
Columbus, Christopher, 326–327
*Comite Consultatif International des
    Radiocommunications* (CCIR) 200,
    202
Commercial Space Launch Act of 1984,
    229, 245, 252, 290–294
    amendments of 1988, 294
    excerpt, 290–293
    insurance requirement, 293:
    proposals for change, 294
Committee on the Peaceful Uses of
    Outer Space (COPUOS). *See under*
    United Nations
Common carrier, commercial launch
    provider as, 271–272
Common heritage of mankind. *See*
    Common heritage principle
Common heritage principle, 95, 106,
    112, 113–115, 118, 121–122
    criticism of, 140–142
    and Moon Treaty, 110–158
    origins of, 95, 131–134
    and Outer Space Treaty, 128
Commons, exploitation of, 165. *See
    also* Hardin, R.; *Tragedy of the
    Commons, The*
Communications Act of 1934, 204, 210,
    211, 212, 216, 217. *See also*
    Communications Satellite Act of
    1962
Communications Satellite Act of 1962,
    204–205, 207, 212, 214, 223. *See
    also* Communications Act of 1934
Communications Satellite Corporation
    (COMSAT), 18, 202–203, 204, 206,
    209, 216. *See also* INTELSAT
    Agreement
Computer II decision (FCC), 222
COMSAT. *See* Communications
    Satellite Corporation

Consequential damages, under the Liability Convention, 176
Contamination, 304–305
from space, 196
See also Quarantine, from risk of space-based microorganisms
Continuous Flow Electrophoresis (McDonnell Douglas experiment), 14
Contract carrier. *See* Private carrier, commercial launch provider as
Contracts, space-related, 273–282
choice of law provisions, 257, 262–264: sample, 279
as contracts of adhesion, 277
indemnification clauses, 267–270, 272
insurance requirements in, 269, 279–289
launch services, 273–282
performance guarantees in, 279–281
reflight clauses, example, 276
sample launch services contracts, 274–280
status of commercial launch providers as common carriers, 271
typical provisions in, 273
waivers of liability, 262–268: sample clause, 280
Contributory negligence, 261. *See also* Fault-based liability
Convention on Registration. *See* Registration Convention
Convention on the High Seas of 1958 (sea law), 28, 253
Cooper, John Cobb, 5
Coordinating Committee on Export Controls (COCOM), 243
COPUOS. *See* United Nations, Committee on the Peaceful Uses of Outer Space
Cosmos 954 (satellite crash and the Liability Convention), 32, 168–175
Cost of Accidents, The (Guido Calabresi), 175
Countervailing duty law (U.S.), 231, 232
Credits, 331–334
Criminal jurisdiction (inclusion of outer space within), 250
Cronkite, Walter, 308
Csabafi, I., 255

Cultural sovereignty concerns, 226–227. *See also* Direct Satellite Broadcasting; New International Information Order
Cunard S.S. v. Mellon (case), 249
Cunningham, B., 282

DalBello, Richard, xiii
Dasgupta, Pratha, 157
Data obtained via space remote sensing. *See* Space remote sensing
DBS. *See* Direct Satellite Broadcasting
de Graaff, W., 154
Dembling, Paul, 68
DeSaussure, Hamilton, 185–191, 259
Deudney, Daniel, 268
DeVany, A.S., 166
Developing nations. *See* Third World
Direct Broadcast Satellites (DBS). *See* Direct Satellite Broadcasting
Direct Satellite Broadcasting, 226–228. *See also* New International Information Order
Dispute resolution
in disputes over space remote sensing policies, 189, 194
in space tort actions, 261–264
Domestic Satellite (Domsat) Policy (U.S.), 205–206
Domsat. *See* Domestic Satellite Policy
Dornberger, Walter, 3
Dougherty, J., 329
Dula, Arthur, xiii, 96, 135, 139, 266
"Dumping" of launch services, 230, 231–232, 237–238
Dupuy, Rene-Jean, 95, 132–133
Dyson, Freeman, 21, 327

EAR. *See* Export Administration Regulations
Easterbrook, Gregg, 317
Ebel, Heidi, xiii
Economics, 149
and distributional concerns in Moon Treaty, 154
and frequency band allocation for satellites, 159–166
and INTELSAT pricing and competition, 203–204, 207–211
and orbital position allocation, 159–166

and public goods, 156
of space industries, 230–231
of technology-generating research and
  development, 154–155
  See also Property rights
Edgar, Harold, xiii
Efficiency in allocating space resources,
  165. *See also* Equitable sharing of
  space resources; Property rights
Eisenhower, Dwight, 70
Electromagnetic Pulse (EMP), 60, 89
EMP. *See* Electromagnetic Pulse
Environmental considerations, 148,
  195–198
  and crash of Soviet Cosmos 954
    satellite, 168–177
  space debris, 177, 197
"Envoys of Mankind" (astronauts), 64,
  194
EOSAT, 229
Equitable sharing of space resources,
  163, 165. *See also* Moon Treaty
ESA. *See* European Space Agency
European Space Agency (ESA), 232–
  236
EUTELSAT (European Satellite
  system), 225. *See also*
  International Telecommunications
  Satellite Organization; Separate
  international satellite systems
Execunet decisions (FCC), 217
Exploitation of space resources. *See*
  Space resources
Explosive Act of 1875 (Britain), 2, 328
Export Administration Regulations
  (EAR), 240–256
Export Controls, 184, 238–246
  special nuclear delivery system rules,
    241, 245–246
  technical data rules, 242, 244–245
  "validated license" defined, 243, 245
"Export" defined, 242, 244
  in connection with space launches,
    245
Externalities, in economic analysis of
  space development, 156. *See also*
  Public goods; Property rights
Extraterrestrial contact, 317–323
Extraterrestrial contamination. *See*
  Contamination

Fasan, E., 317
Fault-based liability, 167, 176, 260–267
Fawcett, James, 120
Federal Communications Commission
  (U.S.), 199, 204–206, 208, 211, 213,
  217–218, 219, 222–224, 298. *See
  also* Communications Act of 1934;
  Communications Satellite Act of
  1962; Domestic Satellite (Domsat)
  Policy; Separate international
  satellite systems; Transborder
  Satellite Policy
Federal Employee Claims Act, 272
Fellow servant rule (applied to
  astronauts and space station crew),
  261
Feres v. United States (case), 272
Fifth Legal Subcommittee, 68, 69
Finch, Edward R., Jr., 96, 135, 136–
  139
Finney, B.R., 310
First Amendment, as basis for critique
  of government licensing regime for
  news media satellites, 303–304
First Principles for the Governance of
  Outer Space Societies, 310–311
"Fishbowl" high altitude nuclear tests,
  196
Flag of convenience, 254, 257
Flag registry, 37–38, 45–46, 249, 253–
  257
"Floating island" theory of jurisdiction,
  249
Foss, P., 266
Foster v. Neilson (case), 257
France, Spot Image remote sensing
  venture, 185, 190. *See also*
  Arianespace
Free market, 143–144. *See also*
  Property rights; Space resources
Frequency bands, as scarce resources,
  159, 200

Gaia hypothesis, 325
Galloway, Eilene, 95, 117
Garret v. Moore McCormack (case),
  251
Garthoff, Raymond L., 100
Garver, Lori, xiii
GATT. *See* General Agreement on
  Tariffs and Trade

General Agreement on Tariffs and Trade (GATT), 231, 232, 236
General license (U.S. export controls), 243
GEO. *See* Geosynchronous (Clarke) Orbit
Geosynchronous (Clarke) Orbit (GEO)
access, 159–166, 214–215, 218
explained, 15
Gilmore, Grant, 43, 329
Gilpin, Robert, 238
Glaser, Peter, 20
Glazer, J. Henry, 256
Goddard, Robert, 2
Goldberg, Arthur J., 71
Golden Rule, applied to contact with extraterrestrials, 319
Goldman, Nathan, xiii, 131, 195
Gondolf, E., 329
Gore, Sen. Albert (Sr.), 85
Gorove, Stephen, 89, 196
Governance of space societies, 307–317
Government subsidies for space launch insurance, 270
Grotius, Hugo, 5

Haanappel, P.P.C., 259, 264
Hackworth, R., 257
Hague Convention on the Law Applicable to Products Liability, 264
Hague Convention on the Law Applicable to the Sale of Corporeal Movable Objects, 264
Hale, Edward Everett, 2
Haley, Andrew, xiii, 7, 264, 307
Halprin, Albert, xiii
Hardin, R., 157
Hargrove, Eugene, 310
Hazards to public of space launches, 269
Heal, G., 157
Henkin, Louis, 257
Herndon v. Piper Aircraft Corp. (case), 265
Hesse, Cheryl, xiv
High Technology Policies: A Five Nation Comparison (R. Nelson), 156, 238
Hofgard, Jefferson, xiii
Hohmann, Walter, 2

Hohmann transfer orbit, 2
Hord, R.M., 178
Hosenball, Neil, xiii, 140
Howard, A.E. Dick, 308
Hufford, D. Brian, 133–135
Hylton, Maria, xiii

Incentives to develop space resources, 145, 157–158, 159–166. *See also* Property rights; Space resources
IFRB. *See* International Frequency Registration Board
IGY. *See* International Geophysical Year
Indemnification, in space contracts, 267–270, 272
Individual liability. *See* Torts
Industrial Radio Service Regulations (FCC), 223–224. *See also* Federal Communications Commission; International Telecommunications Satellite Organization; Separate international satellite systems
INF. *See* Intermediate Nuclear Forces Treaty
INMARSAT. *See* International Maritime Satellite Organization
In personam actions, 251
In re Air Crash Disaster Near Chicago, Ill. (case), 266
In rem actions, 251
Insular Cases, 312
and applicability to outer space, 312–313
Insurance
estimated costs, 294
proposals for change, 294
provisions in launch services contract pertaining to, 280–282
requirement under Commercial Space Launch Act, 293
risk analysis in determining coverage for space launches, 269
for space accidents, 267–272
Intellectual property, 282–289
Intelligence information. *See* Satellite surveillance
INTELSAT. *See* International Telecommunications Satellite Organization

INTELSAT Agreement, 114, 123, 124–
127, 149, 157, 202, 205, 210, 212–
213, 217, 219–224
as model for space development
organization, 124–127, 146–147,
149–150
Intermediate Nuclear Forces (INF)
Treaty, 101
International Frequency Registration
Board (IFRB), 199, 200, 202. *See
also* International
Telecommunications Union; Master
International Frequency Register
International Geophysical Year (IGY),
5, 45
International liability. *See* Liability
Convention
International Maritime Satellite
Organization (INMARSAT), 123,
125
International Record Carriers (IRCs),
208, 216
International Satellite, Inc. (license
application), 219
International Telecommunications
Satellite Organization
(INTELSAT), 10, 114, 123, 124–
127, 149, 157, 199, 202–204
globally averaged pricing, 203–204,
209
as model for space development
organization. *See under*
INTELSAT Agreement
price decline, 209
and separate systems, 205–206, 206–
226
U.S. policy toward, 210–211, 216–217
International Telecommunications
Union (ITU), 50, 125–126, 199–
202
International Traffic in Arms
Regulations (ITAR), 204, 241,
244–245
INTERSPUTNIK (Soviet satellite
system), 123, 214, 225. *See also*
International Telecommunications
Satellite Organization; Separate
international satellite systems
Investment in space resource
development. *See* Common

heritage principle; Property rights;
Space resources
IRCs. *See* International Record
Carriers
ITAR. *See* International Traffic in
Arms Regulations
ITU. *See* International
Telecommunications Union

Jasentuliyana, Nasindiri, 150
Javits, Sen. Jacob K., 110, 111
Johnson, President Lyndon, 70, 71, 83
Joint and several liability, in Liability
Convention, 167, 177
and compensation norm, 174–175,
177
See also Contracts, space-related
Joint registration. *See* Registration
Convention
Jones, E.M., 310
Josephson, Diana, xiii
Jurisdiction, 248–258
over foreign nation's space stations,
251
non-exclusive causes of action under
Liability Convention,   261
over private commercial space
activities, 248–258
of proposed space tribunal, 125–126
by virtue of registry, 249
See also Criminal jurisdiction

Kennedy, President John F., 327
Kiefan, R., 178
Kitch, Edmund, 155
Krist, Ronald D., 272
Kronman, Anthony, 26
Krugman, Paul, 238

L5 Society, 10, 15, 22. *See also*
National Space Society and
involvement with Moon Treaty
ratification, 115
Lagrange, Pierre, 15. *See also*
Lagrangian points
Lagrangian points, 15, 21, 22. *See also*
Lagrange, Pierre
Land Remote Sensing
Commercialization Act of 1984,
185, 189–191, 299–304
regulations under, 301–304

Landes, David, 329
LANDSAT System, 179
Lasswell, Harold, xiii, 307
Launch service contracts. *See*
    Contracts, space-related
Law of the Sea Treaty, 123, 131–135
    as source of principles for space
    development, 114
Lay, S. Houston, 249
LDCs. *See* Less Developed Countries
Leff, Arthur A., 312
LEO. *See* Low Earth Orbit
Less Developed Countries (LDCs). *See*
    Third World
Lex fari, 262
Lex loci delecti, 261
Ley, Willy, 3
Liability Convention, 62, 167–177, 258
    choice-of-law rules, 177
    differing national conceptions of
    duties under, 170–172
    moral damages under, 176
    punitive damages under, 176
Liability for cargo damage. *See* Cargo
    damage, liability for
Liability for satellites that fall to earth,
    167–177
Liability limitation in space accident
    law. *See* Price-Anderson Act of
    1957
Liability rules, in allocating satellite
    orbits, 161–163
Libertarian view of space development,
    145
License requirement, Commercial
    Space Launch Act of 1984, 291–
    292
Licensing system for space
    development, 148, 159–166. *See
    also* Property rights; Space
    resources
Lillesand, T., 178
Limited Test Ban Treaty, 16, 49, 52–
    62, 83
Lipson, Leon, 43
Logsdon, John, xiii
Low Earth Orbit (LEO), 15
Lunar Receiving Laboratory. *See*
    Quarantine, from risk of space-
    based microorganisms

McAuliffe, Christa, personal injury
    claims, 272
McConnell, M., 272
*McCulloch v. Sociedad Nacional de
    Marineros de Honduras* (case), 249
McDougal, Myres, xiii, 7, 12, 43, 121,
    255, 307
McDougall, Walter, 3–4, 5–8, 315, 325
McFadden, Clark, xiii, 241
McIntyre, J., 195
McNamara, Robert, 59
McWhinney, E., 153
*Man Hing Ivory & Imports v.
    Deukmejian* (case), 257
Marcus, I., 329
Maritime law, as space analogy, 28–43,
    329
Market failure and government policies,
    155. *See also* Public goods
Market-share rule for liability, 177
Marshall, Chief Justice John, 248
Master International Frequency
    Register (ITU), 202. *See also*
    International Frequency
    Registration Board; Space WARC
"Maximum amount commercially
    available" (insurance coverage),
    269
Mayflower Compact, 308
Meckling, William, 166
Mediasat regulations, 301–304
    critique of, 303–304
Mediasats (privately operated media
    satellites), 185
Mendell, W.W., 309
Merges, Robert P., 185, 268, 303, 328
Metalaw. *See* Golden Rule, applied to
    contact with extraterrestrials
Meyers, H., 255
Mezzetti, Gueta, xiii
Minasian, Jora, 166
Mining in space. *See* Space resources
"Missiles capable of delivering nuclear
    weapons" defined (U.S. export
    controls), 245–246
Moon Treaty, 9, 10, 22, 77, 79, 81, 83,
    95, 96, 102–166
    interpretation generally, 154
    political compromise reflected in,
    128–129

proposed unilateral U.S.
  interpretation of, 136–138
signatories, 95
text, 102–110
Moore, Amanda Lee, 96, 135, 136–139
Moral damages. *See* Liability
  Convention
Morison, Samuel Eliot, 326
Munitions List (U.S.), 240

NASA. *See* National Aeronautics and
  Space Administration
National Aeronautics and Space
  Administration (NASA)
  Joint Endeavor Agreements, 282
  launch services agreements, 278–280
  launch vehicle commercialization
    agreements, 282
  NASA Act, 267
  site-use contracts, 282
Nationality principle of jurisdiction,
  248
National security
  and conflict with commercial goals,
    182–184, 301–304. *See also* Export
    Controls; Satellite surveillance
  as rationale for government licensing
    of satellites, 185, 301–304
National Space Society, 10, 15, 22. *See
  also* L5 Society
National technical means of
  verification, in Anti-Ballistic
  Missile (ABM) Treaty, 97–98
National tort laws. *See* Torts
NATO Status of Forces Agreements,
  264
Natural monopoly, in market for
  communications satellite orbits and
  frequencies, 149, 157
Natural resources. *See* Space resources
Negligence. *See* Fault-based liability
Nelson, R., 156, 238
Nesselrode v. Executive Beechcraft, Inc.
  (case), 265
New International Economic Order, 96,
  117, 142, 152–155
New International Information Order,
  226. *See also* Direct Satellite
  Broadcasting; New International
  Economic Order
Newton's Third Law, 16

Nichols, Nina, xiv
Nixon, President Richard, 178
Non-discrimination, in space remote
  sensing, 189, 193, 299
Norman, Colin, 102
Norms, international, 172–175
Nozick, Robert, 321
Nuclear Weapons (in space), 52–62, 64,
  71–72, 84, 88–90

Oberth, Hermann, 2
Office of Commercial Space
  Transportation, U.S. Department
  of Transportation, 268, 294–299
  regulations, excerpt, 295–299: launch
    licensing provisions, 296–299
Office of Technology Assessment. *See*
  U.S. Congress, Office of
  Technology Assessment
O'Neill, Gerard K., 21
Open Skies Principle, 98, 180, 183,
  186, 303. *See also* National
  technical means of verification;
  Satellite surveillance
"Operation Morning Light," 169
ORB-88 (World Administrative Radio
  Conference), 218. *See also* Space
  WARC
Orbital debris, 197
Orbital positions, as resource to be
  allocated, 159, 214–216, 218
Organizational structure for space
  development, 121–127, 163–166
  INTELSAT as model for, 124–127
Orion Satellite Corporation, 219
ORION spacecraft propulsion, 16–17,
  61–62, 88–89
  international legal status, 61–62, 88–
    89
OTA. *See* U.S. Congress, Office of
  Technology Assessment
Outer Space Treaty of 1967, xiii, xvi,
  8, 9, 22, 25, 31, 33, 36, 49, 62–93
  free use of space, 64, 79–80
  jurisdiction and control over space
    objects, 65–66, 76, 253–258
  national responsibility and liability,
    65, 74–75
  "no sovereignty" provisions, 64, 70,
    78–82

and Rawlsian "veil of ignorance,"
126
rescue and assistance to astronauts,
64–65, 73–74
text, 63–68
Overflight by spacecraft, 5–7, 38–39

Palapa (Indonesian satellite system),
225. *See also* International
Telecommunications Satellite
Organization; Separate
international satellite systems
Papp, D., 195
Passive personality principle of
jurisdiction, 249
Patent law, 155
application to space activities, 286
Patents. *See* Intellectual property
Patents in Space Bill, 286. *See also*
Intellectual property
Pauling, Linus, 49
Peaceful use of space, 129–130. *See
also* United Nations, Committee
on the Peaceful Uses of Outer
Space
Performance guarantees, in launch
services contracts, 279–281
Personal injury actions, 260–267, 268–
270, 272
Petree, Ambassador Richard W., 111,
112
Piercing the corporate veil, in space
liability suits, 266
Pigou, Arthur (British economist), 162
Plenipotentiary Conference (ITU), 201
Plessala, Laura, xiv
Polar orbit, 15
*Political Economy of International
Relations, The* (Robert Gilpin),
238
Postal, Telephone and Telegraph
authorities (PTTs), 225–226
Powe, L., 227
Power, in international relations, 153
Preemption of state law by federal law,
in space, 252
Prentiss v. National Air Lines, Inc.
(case), 265
Price-Anderson Act of 1957, 266
Priest, George, 265

Principles for governance of outer
space societies, 310–311
Private carrier, commercial launch
provider as, 271–272
Private commercial space activities,
247–305. *See also* Contracts,
space-related; Intellectual property;
Jurisdiction; Torts
Private radio regulations (FCC), 223–
224. *See also* International
Telecommunications Satellite
Organization; INTELSAT
Agreement
Problem of Social Cost, The (Ronald
Coase), 158
Property rights
data about a nation's natural
resources, 188
and economic rents, 164
under Law of the Sea Treaty, 134
and radio frequencies, 164
over space resources, 130, 136–139,
147–149, 155–158, 159–166
See also Moon Treaty; Space
resources; Third World
Protective principle of jurisdiction, 248
Public goods, 164
and property rights, 156
Public international telecommunications
services, 221–222. *See also*
International Telecommunications
Satellite Organization; INTELSAT
Agreement
Public telecommunications services,
220–223
compared to "common carrier
telecommunications services," 220–
221
as related to "public
correspondence," 221–222
Punitive damages. *See under* Liability
Convention

Quarantine, from risk of space-based
microorganisms, 196–197
as illustrated in movie *E.T.*, 322

Radiation
from Soviet nuclear-powered satellite,
169
See also Van Allen Belts

Radio Regulations (ITU), 202, 221–222
Ragosta, John, xiii, 309, 313, 314
RAND Corporation, 4
Rawls, John, 126
Reagan, President Ronald, 98, 133. *See also* Reagan Administration
Reagan Administration, 98, 99, 133–135
Reconnaissance Satellites, 8–9, 22–23, 85–86, 92, 93. *See also* Remote sensing regulations; Satellite surveillance; Space remote sensing
Redistribution of wealth. *See* New International Economic Order; Property rights
Reflight clauses, in launch services contracts, 276
Regional (non-INTELSAT) satellite systems, 220, 225. *See also* Arabsat; EUTELSAT; INTERSPUTNIK; Palapa
Registration Convention, 195
   exclusion of joint registration by more than one nation, 253
   space station, effects on, 253
   waiver of jurisdiction by agreement, 254
Reijnen, G., 154
Reimbursement of insurance costs, 267
Reisman, W. Michael, xiii, 26, 27, 121
Remote sensing. *See* Space remote sensing
Remote sensing regulations, 301–304. *See also* Land Remote Sensing Commercialization Act of 1984
Res communis character of outer space, 7, 78–80, 249. *See also* Moon Treaty; Outer Space Treaty of 1967
Rescue and Return Agreement, 62, 194–195
Rescue and Return of Astronauts. *See* Rescue and Return Agreement
Restatement of Torts, Sections 520 and 520A, 265
Reynolds, Dr. Charles, xiv
Reynolds, Glenn H., 23, 185, 195, 197, 268, 289, 299, 303, 309, 313, 314, 316, 326, 328
Risk allocation, in space insurance setting, 271
Risk analysis. *See under* Insurance

Rivard v. United States (case), 256
Robinson, George, xiii, 256, 308
Rocha v. United States (case), 256
Rosberg, Gerald, xiii
Rose, Carol, 157
Rostow, Walt W., 153
Rousseau, Jean-Jacques, 126

Sagan, Carl, 196
SALT. *See* Strategic Arms Limitation Talks; SALT I Treaty
SALT I Treaty, 9
Saltman, Jamie, xiv
Salvage, 34–35
Sandler, Todd, 156
Satellite remote sensing. *See* Space remote sensing
Satellite Solar Power Stations (SSPS), 20
Satellite surveillance, 8–9, 85–86, 92, 93, 98
   and crash of Soviet Cosmos 954 satellite, 168–177
   See also Space remote sensing
Saving clause, in Liability Convention, 261
Scale economies
   in launch services, etc., 230, 231, 237
   in space communications, 157, 203
Schachter, Oscar, 6
Scherer, F.M., 155
Schoettler, James, xiii, 241
Schooner Exchange v. McFadden (case), 248
Schwetje, Kenneth, 42
Seaworthiness requirement in Admiralty Law, and application in space, 33–34, 260–261
Section 301 actions (U.S. trade law), 231–232, 232–236
Security interests in satellites, 282
Sedou, L.I., 169
Senior Interagency Group on International Communication and Information Policy, 206
Separate international satellite systems, 205, 206–226
Settlement in *Challenger* disaster, 272
Sindell v. Abbott Laboratories (case), 177

Sofaer, Abraham D., 99, 101
Soviet Union
and crash of Cosmos 954 satellite, 168–177
and Moon Treaty, 111, 116, 117
and Outer Space Treaty, 71–77, 84, 85
Soyuz Karta (Soviet remote sensing venture), 185
Space colonization, 307–317
first principles for governance of, 310–311
Space Court proposal, 126
Space debris, 177, 197. *See also* Environmental considerations; *Sindell v. Abbott Laboratories*
Space object registry, 195. *See also* Registration Convention
Space remote sensing, 178–194
and natural resource inventorying, 180–194
and rights of a state, 179–182, 186–194
U.N. Remote Sensing Principles, 191–194
Space resources, 95, 106, 112, 113–166
development of, 95, 121–127, 139–145, 159–166
inventory of, 95
moratorium on development of, 110, 114, 120, 128, 140–145, 150
ownership of, 119–120, 121, 128, 159–166
and public goods analysis, 155–158
and squatters' rights, 163
Third World view of, 135, 150–152, 154
as threat to current earth-bound producers, 147, 150
Space rockets. *See* Common carrier, commercial launch provider as; National Aeronautics and Space Administration; Technology
Space Shuttle Commander's authority, 34, 316
Space station
and jurisdiction issues, 248–258
and tort law, 259–264
Space WARC, 165, 201–202, 215, 218. *See also* Geosynchronous (Clarke) Orbit, access; International

Telecommunications Union; ORB-88
Spaceworthiness, in space accident law, 33–34, 260–261
Specialized telecommunications services, 224. *See also* International Telecommunications Satellite Organization; INTELSAT Agreement
Spot Image, 229
"Spreading" of costs of satellite crash, 175
Sputnik, 4, 5, 10, 56, 190. *See also* Soviet Union
Squatters' rights regime for space resources, 163
SSPS. *See* Satellite Solar Power Stations
Stadd, Courtney, xiii
Standard of care
for common vs. private carriers, 271
See also Absolute liability; Fault-based liability
Stares, Paul, 178
"Star Wars." *See* Strategic Defense Initiative
State interest, as basis of jurisdiction for space-related actions, 262
Stein, Josephine, xiii
Steptoe, Jason, xiii
Stipulations, in contracts
choice of law, 262–264
See also Contracts, space-related
Stone, Senator Richard, 113
Strategic Arms Limitation Talks (SALT I), 9, 97, 98, 100
Strategic Defense Initiative, 98
Strategic Trade Policy and the New International Economics (Paul Krugman), 238
Strict liability. *See* Absolute liability
Sun Synchronous Orbit, 15

Taubenfeld, Howard J., 249
Taxes to finance space resource development, 148
Technology
as example of resource subject to common heritage principle, 153–155
and space flight, 14–18

Termination of launch services contract, sample provision, 277
Territorial principle of jurisdiction, 248
Theory of Justice, A (John Rawls), 126
Third-party insurance, 263–270
  as requirement in NASA launch services contract, 279–280
Third World
  resources as examples of public goods, 156
  views on space resource development, 135–136, 141, 143, 150–152
  See also New International Economic Order
Torts, 258–267. *See also* Absolute liability; *Challenger* disaster; Fault-based liability; Liability Convention; "Spreading" of costs of satellite crash
Trade secrets, 289–290. *See also* Intellectual property
Tragedy of the Commons, The, 157
Transaction costs, in negotiations and disputes over space resources, 158, 162
Transborder Satellite Policy (U.S.) 205–206, 209, 225
Transpace Section 301 Petition, 231–237
Treaty interpretation, 154. *See also* Moon Treaty
Treaty on Principles Governing the Activities of States in the Exploration and Use of Outer Space, including the Moon and Other Celestial Bodies. *See* Outer Space Treaty of 1967
Trudeau, Prime Minister Pierre, 169
Tsiolkovsky, Konstantin, 1, 21
Turnbull, Colin, 321
Turner, Frederick Jackson, 326

Ultrahazardous activities, 260–261, 264–267. *See also* Torts
Uniform Aeronautics Act, 265
United Nations, 103, 105, 106, 127, 131, 132, 135, 146, 153, 154, 185–191

Charter Article 73, Trust Territories, and application to space governance, 313, 318
Committee on the Peaceful Uses of Outer Space (COPUOS), 7, 8, 29, 47, 50–52, 69, 79, 117–118, 122, 174, 178, 226
Remote Sensing Principles, 185–194
role in space object registration, 195
Unispace Conference of 1982, 179
See also Law of the Sea Treaty
United States
  and Anti-Ballistic Missile (ABM) Treaty, 97
  Constitution, applicable to space, 312–314
  and crash of Soviet Cosmos 954 satellite, 168–177
  and Law of the Sea Treaty, 131–135
  and Moon Treaty, 110–115, 131
  and remote sensing policy, 178–191, 301–304
  waivers of liability in space-related contracts involving, 267–268, 272: sample clause, 279–280
  See also Federal Communications Commission; Office of Commercial Space Transportation, U.S. Department of Transportation; U.S. Congress, Office of Technology Assessment
United States v. Cordova (case), 250
Universality principle of jurisdiction, 248–249
U.S. Congress, Office of Technology Assessment (OTA), 195, 248, 258
U.S.S.R. *See* Soviet Union

Validated license (U.S. export controls), 243, 245
Van Allen Belts, 12
Vance, Cyrus R., 110, 111
  position on Moon Treaty, 111
Veil of ignorance (John Rawls), 126
Vlasic, Ivan, xiii, 307
Von Braun, Werner, 3–4, 10, 56
Voting in organization for space resource development, 124–125, 147
V-2 missile, 3–4, 56

Waivers of liability, 262–268
    sample clause, 280
Warranties. *See* Performance guarantees
Warsaw Convention (air law), 264, 270
Webber, Alan Duane, 96, 145
White, Harold, Jr., 256, 308

Whiteman, M., 256
Wihlborg, Clas G., 157, 159
Wijkman, Der Magnus, 157, 159
World Court, 125

Yale Rocket Club, 2